FURTHER PRAISE FOR *THE RECKONING*

"A dark and macabre story. . . . Mackey brilliantly packages the complicated details." —*Los Angeles Times*

"A savage indictment of Euro-American exploitation of the Middle East . . . [this] book is indispensable reading for anyone with an opinion on world affairs." —*Washington Post Book World*

"Sounds an important cautionary note." —*Publishers Weekly*

"This highly readable, jargon-free, and evenhanded book goes a long way in providing a comprehensive account of Iraq's recent political history to Western readers." —*Library Journal*

"*The Reckoning* is a gift to those who don't want slogans as they try to understand a hot spot getting hotter every day." —*San Francisco Chronicle*

"An extremely thorough appraisal." —*Booklist*

ALSO BY SANDRA MACKEY

The Saudis: Inside the Desert Kingdom

Lebanon: Death of a Nation

Passion and Politics: The Turbulent World of the Arabs

The Iranians: Persia, Islam and the Soul of a Nation

THE RECKONING

Iraq

and the Legacy of

Saddam Hussein

SANDRA MACKEY

W. W. NORTON & COMPANY

New York   London

For information about permission to reproduce selections from this book, write to
Permissions, W. W. Norton & Company, Inc., 500 Fifth Avenue, New York, NY 10110

The text of this book is composed in ITC Century Book with the display set in Futura
Composition by Tom Ernst
Manufacturing by The Haddon Craftsmen, Inc.
Book design by Joan Greenfield
Production manager: Andrew Marasia

Library of Congress Cataloging-in-Publication Data

Mackey, Sandra, 1937–
    The Reckoning : Iraq and the legacy of Saddam Hussein / Sandra Mackey.
        p. cm.
    Includes bibliographical references and index.
    ISBN 0-393-05141-2
    1. Iraq —Politics and government—1958– 2. Hussein, Saddam, 1937– I. Title.

DS79.65 .M24 2002
956.7044—dc21   2002016611

ISBN 0-393-32428-1 pbk.

W. W. Norton & Company, Inc., 500 Fifth Avenue, New York, N.Y. 10110
www.wwnorton.com

W. W. Norton & Company Ltd., Castle House, 75/76 Wells Street, London W1T 3QT

2 3 4 5 6 7 8 9 0

TO MY MOTHER,

who contained the furies of her anxieties to let me go where I chose

CONTENTS

PREFACE

I have been on a journey through the Persian Gulf since the late 1970s. It began in Riyadh, Saudi Arabia, where I arrived in 1978 at the height of the oil boom and lived until the mid-1980s. As a freelance journalist, I wrote about the effects of the money let loose by the explosion of oil prices in 1973, pouring blessings and curses on the countries of the Gulf. Iraq was one of them.

At the time, the influence of Saddam Hussein in his own country and the region was present but not omnipresent. He was a shadow in the background of Iraq, which moved to a quicker rhythm than the oil-rich monarchies of the Arabian Peninsula. In contrast to Riyadh, where the boom times strained against the strictures of Islam's most rigid sect, Baghdad throbbed with the beat of secularism and license. By the standards of Beirut in the days before civil war consumed Lebanon, the gaudy nightclubs of Baghdad were perhaps even louder and more raucous. The art scene was livelier as visual artists pushed the limits of the human figure in an Islamic society. Seduction was, in fact, everywhere. A government intent on buying the loyalty of its citizens dipped money out of its petroleum coffers and poured it into the hands of almost every Iraqi. As a result, optimism born of a prosperity never even imagined traveled down the socioeconomic scale and back up again. The vibrancy created by mass participation in a boom economy promised to seal the deep fissures in a society that had always challenged the integrity of the Iraqi state. But the cracks never closed. Although I wrote that Iraq's southern neighbors on the Arabian Peninsula shivered in what they regarded to be an ominous shadow cast by Baghdad, I joined other Western writers who perceived, but never fully comprehended, the depth of evil in the man who lurked just off stage.

By 1984, as my residency in the Persian Gulf region was ending,

Saddam Hussein already had held the president's chair for five years, oil prices had dropped below $30 a barrel, and Iraq was bogged down in the fourth year of the bloodbath known as the Iran-Iraq War. Although Baghdad outwardly looked much the same, the spirit of earlier years was gone. Copious amounts of money still flowed out of the national treasury but it largely went to the war effort, not to the citizenry. And the hobnailed boot of Hussein pressed ever harder on the neck of the Iraqis. When I left the Arab side of the Persian Gulf, Iraq was living amid the broken promises of the oil boom.

For the next several years, I worked away from the Gulf. I wrote about the war in Lebanon, the Palestinians, and the Arab world as a whole. When I returned to the Persian Gulf in 1992, it was to the eastern side, to the Islamic Republic of Iran. Over the next three years, my writing concentrated on Persian culture, Shia Islam, and the fierce tug of war for control of the Islamic revolution between the disciples of Ayatollah Khomeini and the growing number of moderates. It was not until I began to research this book that I returned to the Arab side of the Gulf.

I stepped into Iraq in 1998 to find the country a ghost of the Iraq of the late 1970s. The Iraqis had been devastated by two wars—the eight-year-long death struggle with Iran and the months-long conflict with the United States and the coalition that waged the Persian Gulf War. Seven years of sanctions had reduced members of the vaunted middle class created by the oil boom to paupers whose only guaranteed food supplies came from rations distributed under rules imposed by the United Nations. In comparison to the late 1970s, the streets were deserted. Most of Baghdad's flashy nightclubs were dark and silent. The showy hotels, where once guests pressed lavish bribes on the clerks at the front desk to obtain a room, stood nearly empty. The rooms that were occupied contained dingy, threadbare towels, perhaps the last survivors of the oil boom. Across the city, the shelves of stores that had once bulged with imported goods from the United States, Europe, and Asia were almost empty. The educational system that had promised to educate every child and to train the finest doctors, engineers, and scholars was in shambles. The hospitals that once served as the flagships of Middle East medicine were stripped of almost everything including sheets. But more than anything, Iraq had become a prison in which everyone lived in fear of its warden—Saddam Hussein.

I returned to Iraq again after oil prices began to escalate. The infusion of new money had brought marginal improvement on the physical side. I saw more medicine, more consumer goods, more infrastructure improvements, all made possible by the combination of increased oil revenues and a loosening of the sanctions. Still, the towering walls and miserable conditions of Hussein's prison remained the same.

For an American, a trip into Iraq requires enormous effort, a wide network of contacts, plenty of cash, and a strong heart. Until recently, the easiest way to reach Baghdad was over land via Amman, Jordan, an eight- to ten-hour trek across the desert. Once there, foreigners, particularly writers, are usually required to stay at the al-Rashid Hotel. The marble building and fenced grounds literally crawl with secret police. Everyone—gardeners, bellboys, clerks on the desk, switchboard operators, maids, waiters, the smartly uniformed attendants in the business center, the manager—is tied into the Mukhabarat, the Arabic name for the honeycomb of security services that constitute the backbone of Hussein's police state. Surveillance is so obvious that when I tried to switch on a bedside light, I found a microphone in place of the lightbulb. When I finally succeeded in convincing the Foreign Ministry to allow me to vacate the al-Rashid, I found my room at the new hotel facing a three-story building belonging to a branch of the Mukhabarat. Every time I peered out the window, men armed with automatic rifles circling the roof peered back.

To venture beyond Baghdad requires an official government escort. Labeled a "minder" by those put in his charge, he determines where and when you go. En route he drops questions and elicits answers, all of which he dutifully records in a daily report that goes into your personal file at the security services. Although it is possible to move around alone on the streets of Baghdad, the exercise can be perilous. Late one evening when I moved in too close on a birthday celebration for Hussein, I was apprehended by a gun-toting guard who summoned the security services. Although I managed to talk my way out of the clutches of four fearsome men in olive-green berets, the episode confirmed what I already knew—traveling in Iraq is a high-risk undertaking.

For Iraqis trapped in the fear and brutality of Hussein's despotism, ordinary life is a deadly serious game. Spies lurk everywhere,

ready to turn the most casual comment into grounds for imprisonment or execution. Engulfed in this cocoon of fear, people keep to
themselves. This isolation of Iraqis from foreigners and from each
other has totally changed the atmosphere of Iraq since I first arrived
in the Gulf. Arab society is notoriously hospitable. Entrance to an
office always means tea. A question asked to a total stranger can produce an invitation home. There among the family, the visitor experiences the Arabs' great art form—conversation. But in Iraq, all of that
has been crushed over the years since Hussein became the sole
leader of his tortured country. Now a current of tension runs through
every encounter with an Iraqi. There is no conversation, only an
exchange of banalities, which themselves are guarded and carefully
weighed. The occasional and dangerous furtive comment quickly
whispered is the only glimpse into the mind and soul of an Iraqi in
this third decade under the rule of the tyrant of Baghdad. How it all
happened lies in the nature and experience of Iraq before and after
the founding of the Iraqi state. The purpose of this book is to explain
what it all will mean to Iraq, the Persian Gulf, and the United States
after the political or physical demise of Saddam Hussein.

ACKNOWLEDGMENTS

No author ever writes in isolation. The difficult process of book writing requires the help and support of a wide circle of people. For this book, I owe an enormous debt of gratitude to Phebe Marr, who led me through so many of the intricacies of Iraqi culture; to Andrew Parasiliti, who not only graciously shared his expertise on Iraq but also read the manuscript; to William Quandt, whose wisdom on the Middle East is always so enlightening; to Ambassador W. Nathaniel Howell, who shared his many experiences of the Iraqi occupation of Kuwait; to Ambassador Morton Abramowitz for his efforts to gain me access to northern Iraq; and to Adam Stulberg for helping a novice understand the various levels of military threat posed by Iraq. Lastly, I must thank my dear friend and mentor, R. K. Ramazani, whose wisdom and understanding of the Persian Gulf always makes such an invaluable contribution to any work on the region. I also want to thank Nesta Ramazani, whose interest and hospitality mean so much to me.

I appreciate the dedication of my research assistant, Cynthia Ray. Her diligence and sense of humor helped enormously in the research phase of this project. I would also like to thank James Martone and Rural Amin of the CNN bureau in Baghdad, who gave me access to both their insights and the archives of their stories. I especially appreciate the time and effort James devoted to leading me through the mud and dark of the Protestant cemetery of Baghdad to visit the grave of Gertrude Bell.

I am grateful to the many Iraqis in London, Amman, Baghdad, Washington, New York, and a dozen other places who took the time to share with me their histories, their experiences, and their dreams for a better day in their country.

There is a special person to whom I owe a profound debt of gratitude. Because of the extraordinary circumstances that now exist in

Iraq, I must keep the name confidential. But he, or she, knows to whom I refer. To you, I say "thank you" with all my heart.

My thanks also goes to my agent, Gail Ross, and to my editor, Starling Lawrence. Their guidance made this book happen.

Finally, my appreciation goes to my friends and family. To my friends, I want you to know how much it meant to me for you to listen to my frustrations and to care about my safety as I wandered around the Iraq of Saddam Hussein. And to my family, as always, a deep felt thank you. Dan, you kept me trudging along the path to completion. And Colin and Patty, you never allowed me to take life's frustrations too seriously.

To all of these people, I am extremely grateful.

THE RECKONING

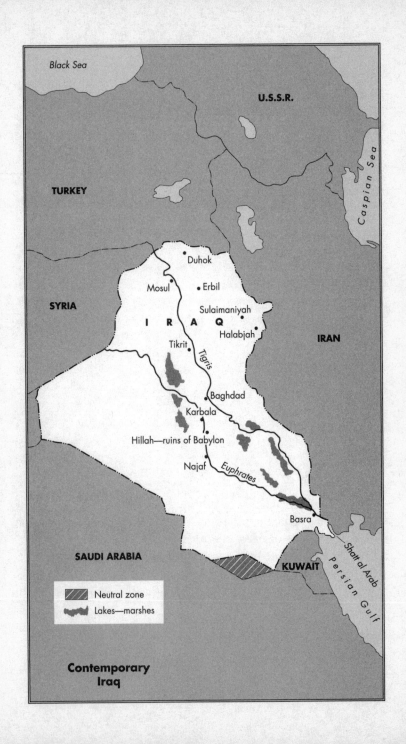

Contemporary
Iraq

INTRODUCTION

On the clear, bright morning of September 11, 2001, huge balls of orange flame and billowing clouds of black smoke engulfed New York's World Trade Center. In Washington, D.C., one side of the Pentagon collapsed under the assault of a hijacked civilian airliner. In sixty-eight minutes, the most potent symbols of American economic and military might had been hit by Islamic militants bent on humbling the superpower of the West.

Expressions of shock, horror, and sorrow reached the United States from all over the globe. But on the eastern edge of the Arab world, the Republic of Iraq, from its capital of Baghdad, heaped bitter words on wounded America: "It is a black day in the history of America, which is tasting the bitter defeat of its crimes. . . ."[1]

Suspicions of responsibility for the stunning acts of terrorism immediately fell on Osama bin Laden, the reclusive leader of al-Qaeda, the center of a web of Islamic militants who had been conducting their own private war against the United States for almost a decade. But within days, rumors began to circulate claiming an alliance of convenience between Osama bin Laden and Saddam Hussein, joined against their mutual enemy. As the United States deployed additional military forces in the Persian Gulf in anticipation of operations against bin Laden's bases in Afghanistan, voices inside and outside the Bush administration began to call for military action against Iraq as well. To those advocating an attack against Baghdad, it was immaterial whether or not Hussein was directly involved in the death and destruction of September 11. The United States had embarked on a new war—the war against terrorism—and Hussein was seen as a legitimate target. Yet many counseled caution,

---

[1] Republic of Iraq television, September 11, 2001, Foreign Broadcast Information Service translation from Arabic.

pointing out that the United States needed to stay focused on eliminating international terrorist networks before considering military moves against specific regimes.

Thus, ten years after the end of the Gulf War, Iraq and Hussein once again moved into the forefront of American foreign policy. The debate this time recalled 1991, when the United States ended the Gulf War short of Baghdad. One side argued the obvious benefits of wiping out Hussein and his suspected weapons of mass destruction, and the other side engaged in verbal gymnastics to avoid revealing to the American public the grave risks to U.S. interests that lurk in the internal dynamics of Iraq.

In truth, the 1991 Gulf War never ended. Every morning in the hot, heavy air of the Persian Gulf, a wasp-shaped F/A-18 fitted with six tubular missiles idles in waves of vaporous fumes produced by its high-octane fuel. When the on-deck "shooter" gives the signal, the high-riding craft screams down the deck of the Nimitz-class aircraft carrier, lifts into the air, and turns westward on yet another of the thousands of patrols that have flown over the flat landscape of southern Iraq since August of 1992. Over seven hundred miles to the north, in the cool mountain air of Turkey, another $20 million American fighter jet leaves the airbase at Incirlik to join in yet another exercise in Operation Northern Watch, the protective cover erected over the Kurds of northern Iraq more than a decade ago. Like its partner in flight in the south, the high-performance aircraft follows directions from the lumbering AWACS, a modified Boeing 707/320 with a thirty-foot-wide radar dish mounted on top that collects and feeds information into computers recording and processing the movements of every donkey, camel, truck, or tank on the Iraqi landscape. This seemingly endless task of containing the more aggressive ambitions of Saddam Hussein has consumed a decade of American effort, drained the U.S. Air Force of career pilots who take a million dollars' worth of training with them, and burned at least a billion dollars a year.[2] Still, Hussein, the man who ordered the invasion of Kuwait, defied a thirty-nation coalition organized against him, and suffered one of the most humiliating defeats in the history of modern warfare, never really lost the "Mother of all Battles."

---

[2] Budget figure is from the Congressional Record, March 29, 2000, p. H-1551, available at www.access.gpo.gov.

Saddam Hussein has literally risen out of the ashes of the Gulf War to stand in contemptuous defiance of the United States and its European and Arab allies in that war. At the same time, he boldly claims leadership over the Arabs' confrontation with Israel. Only days after the street power of the Palestinians collided with the armed might of Israel in late September 2000, Hussein began hurling words instead of stones at the Zionist state. At his instructions, official rhetoric from the Iraqi media proclaimed that Israel "is a midget entity, a usurper and a claw of colonialism . . . . Iraq does not, and will not, recognize this usurper entity."[3] Challenging other Arab leaders to join him in the fight against the Israeli state, "the Great Leader" himself declared, "There will be no security, safety, or stability for the Arabs if this entire Zionist entity is not removed."[4] Through passion or coercion, a half million Iraqis led by the president's son, Uday, volunteered to fight in Palestine. Military units, including the fifteen-thousand-strong Hammurabi unit of the elite Republican Guards moved toward Iraq's western border as forty convoys of trucks loaded with food and medicine—gathered out of the meager stores of sanctions-starved Iraq—rolled toward Amman for shipment to the Palestinians on the West Bank. Over the ensuing days, the number of volunteers escalated, reaching a claimed 6.6 million, 2 million of whom were women. More was to come.

On the eve of the new year 2001, the largest military parade since the Gulf War strutted through Baghdad's Grand Festivities Square to demonstrate Iraq's support for the Palestinian uprising against Israel. For four hours, uniformed units of the infantry, the navy, and paramilitary commandos escorted more than a thousand tanks, a mass of artillery pieces, and a line of trucks bearing a new generation of short-range missiles. Overhead jet fighters and helicopter gunships flew in concert. Presiding over it all was a somber Saddam Hussein, who stood on the reviewing stand firing a rifle into the air.

No longer solely the "God Supported Leader of Iraq," Hussein presents himself as the unbowed warrior ready to lead the masses of an Arab world increasingly disillusioned with their own political leadership, filled with loathing for Israel, and bitterly resentful of the United States.

---

[3] Republic of Iraq television, October 2, 2000, Foreign Broadcast Information Service translation from Arabic.

[4] Republic of Iraq radio, November 17, 2000, Foreign Broadcast Information Service translation from Arabic.

Aside from firing Scud missiles on Israel during the Gulf War, Iraq has largely stayed a step removed from direct confrontation with Israel. But with Egypt and Jordan wrapped up in treaties with Israel, Saudi Arabia and the Gulf states seeking accommodation with the Jewish state, and Syria with neither the money, the military, nor the seasoned leadership to back the Palestinians, Hussein has grabbed his chance to use the Palestinian *intifadah* to mobilize the Arab street. At the Arab summit in March 2001, in an attempt to humiliate more cautious Arab leaders, he thundered, "By God we will bring them with an army whose end will be in Baghdad and its forefront will make the criminal Zionist invaders' and occupiers' blood run cold."[5]

The Iraqi despot who promises to rid the Arabs of the hated presence of Israel and the perceived domination of the United States is riding the high tide of oil prices. With a hundred billion barrels of oil reserves, second only to those of Saudi Arabia among the Persian Gulf petroleum producers, Iraq is always a major player in the international oil market, but never so much as in a market driven by excessive demand. In a situation of tight supplies, Iraq's oil has become so important that the United States is importing some 700,000 barrels of Iraqi oil a day—nearly twice as much as before the invasion of Kuwait. This means that within the intricacies of the international oil markets, Americans depend to a certain extent on Saddam Hussein to heat their homes, run their utilities, and fuel their cars. Even the very ships and planes that enforce the sanctions against the bully of Baghdad are fueled in part with Iraqi oil. This is legal oil, approved for sale by the United Nations to buy food and medicine for the Iraqi population. There is also illegal oil: smuggling nets Hussein something between $1 and $2 billion a year. Much of this goes into rebuilding his stockpile of weapons of mass destruction depleted by war and arms inspections.

Even the United States concedes that in all probability Saddam Hussein possesses a collection of chemical and biological agents as well as the nuclear potential to intimidate, terrify, and kill his neighbors. Some of these weapons of terror are the remnants of 1991, hidden during eight years of defiant confrontation with UNSCOM, the United Nations Special Commission on Iraq. The rest are new acqui-

---

[5] Quoted in *New York Times*, March 28, 2001.

sitions, gathered since December 1998 when Hussein rid himself of UNSCOM's presence by refusing to continue even the most grudging cooperation with arms inspection mandated by the United Nations in 1991. The "son of UNSCOM," the softened, more politicized version of arms inspection known as the United Nations Monitoring, Verification and Inspections Commission, or UNMOVIC, assembled in March 2000, has yet to gain access to Iraq. In the absence of arms inspectors, Hussein no longer even attempts to conceal his intention to join the nuclear club. A new headquarters for his nuclear research program now stands on al-Jadriya street in Baghdad. This is simply a building. What is important is what is inside. According to one of Iraq's former nuclear scientists, only thirty-five pounds or so of uranium, obtainable at some point out of the black markets of the former Soviet Union, separate Hussein from his own atomic bomb.

Elsewhere, factories that purportedly make castor oil for brake fluid and pesticides for agriculture are only a step away from producing a deadly biological toxin called ricin and lethal chemical compounds such as VX, a nerve gas that blocks transmission of impulses along the central nervous system, causing convulsions, respiratory paralysis, and death. The system to deliver them is the al-Samoud, the liquid-fueled ballistic missile that rolled through Baghdad during the New Year's Day parade of 2001.

Hussein proved in the Iran-Iraq War, when he gassed the Iranians and his own Kurdish population, that he has the guts to use chemical weapons. Richard Butler, the former head of UNSCOM, warns, "This man has a track record. We do not want to wait until this stuff turns up in Trafalgar Square or Times Square and say we did not see it coming."[6] Perhaps Hussein has already struck against his enemies: there has been speculation about Iraqi ties to the bombings of American embassies in Kenya and Tanzania in 1998 and in the October 2000 attack on the USS *Cole* in Aden, Yemen. Although the embassy bombings and the hit against the *Cole* carry the signature of Osama bin Laden's network of Islamic militants, these are also targets in which Hussein shares an interest, for these are the buildings and weaponry of Hussein's greatest enemy—the United States.

Despite all the ominous signs that Saddam Hussein has established himself once more as a menace in the crucial Persian Gulf, the

---

[6] Quoted in *Guardian*, May 24, 2000.

cage of sanctions constructed around him in 1991 is breaking apart under the forces of moral disquiet and greed. For more than a decade, Hussein has allowed his own people to suffer malnutrition, disease, and economic deprivation in a savage propaganda war waged against the sanctions. Even with relief provided by the United Nations through the so-called oil-for-food program, babies are mal-nourished, toddlers drink contaminated water, children lack basic medicine, and families live in run-down hovels. The imagery and the reality of suffering innocents are powerful.

By holding the sanctions responsible for the deaths of thousands of innocent children, Saddam Hussein has consistently evoked cries of inhumanity. After ten years, the same charge is coming from nations everywhere and from voices of conscience such as the American Friends Service Committee and Voices in the Wilderness, who in turn feed the moral disquiet of the American public. They have been joined by the governments of three of the five permanent members of the Security Council under whose auspices the sanctions are imposed and administered—Russia, China, and France. Even Britain, in Margaret Thatcher's famous phrase, is "going wobbly." As a result, the wall of sanctions erected at the end of the Gulf War has become a sieve.

Along with smuggled goods, scores of businesspeople, diplomats, and entertainers flow into Iraq, hoping to capitalize on the opportunities that will surface in a postsanctions state. This tension between engagement and containment creates a surreal scene. In the air above Iraq, American jets enforcing the no-fly zones pass civilian jets on their way to Baghdad carrying sanctions-breaking goods and foreign emissaries. Unwilling to shoot down civilians, the United States, the self-appointed watchdog of the Persian Gulf, can do nothing but watch.

Both the Clinton and the George W. Bush administrations have attempted to grapple with Hussein's refusal to comply with arms inspections, at times using military strikes. Nothing has seemed to work. Like Gulliver tangled in the strings of the Lilliputians, the United States is immobilized by difficult dilemmas surrounding Hussein and post-Saddam Iraq for which there are no good policy options.

When Hussein sent Iraqi forces into the tiny, oil-rich shiekhdom of Kuwait on August 2, 1990, the issue thrown at the United States was simple—blatant aggression at the core of American vital interests. For reasons embedded in the long struggle between the Palestinians and Israel, the complexity for the administration of George H. W. Bush was to devise a mechanism by which the United States could, with the overt support of his Arab neighbors, deny Hussein possession of Kuwait. The president laid out the strategy— build a multinational force under the flag of the United Nations. Then he picked up the telephone and dispatched his emissaries to recruit thirty nations, including most of the Arab states, into a massive international force underwritten by American military might. Its mission: expel Iraq from Kuwait.

From the beginning of the crisis, General Colin Powell, the chairman of the Joint Chiefs of Staff, carried into the White House all the American military's anxieties implanted by the United States' long, torturous war in Vietnam. In reluctantly signing onto the president's grand scheme, Powell, among others, insisted on a sharply defined military mission executed with overwhelming force and a clear exit strategy. Thus, it was to avoid possible entrapment in the horror chamber of another Vietnam that the United States sent 600,000 men and women to the battlefield armed with the most technologically sophisticated arsenal in modern warfare for the sole purpose of liberating 6,532 square miles of Kuwait. It took forty-two days of punishing air assaults and a hundred hours of land combat to accomplish total victory.

As the flawless land assault rolled toward Kuwait, the defeated army of Saddam Hussein trudged northward through the suffocating smoke and stench pouring out of six hundred burning oil wells. By the time the troops of Saudi Arabia led the coalition forces into Kuwait City, the Iraqis were gone. With military evacuation satisfying the precisely stated goal of the Gulf War, the coalition that won the victory declared a cessation of hostilities and stepped back to wait collection of its political reward—the fall of Hussein's regime. History and reason argued that no political leader so widely detested among his own people could survive such a crushing defeat. Two weeks earlier, President Bush, whether by design or misstatement, had summoned the Iraqi military and the Iraqi people to "take matters into their own hands" and rid themselves of the most hated man in the history of modern Iraq.[7] On the last day of February, elements

---

[7] *New York Times*, February 16, 1991.

within the Iraqi population responded, threatening to destroy not only the regime but Iraq itself.

Iraq is a young fragile country patched together by the European powers that won World War I. Within its artificial boundaries, the Iraqis have lived for eight decades as a collection of competing families, tribes, regions, tongues, and faiths. This complex, multilayered mosaic of Arabs and non-Arabs, Muslims and Christians, is trisected by Iraq's three major population groups, each in possession of a distinct identity. The first two of these groups are Arab, divided between the minority orthodox Sunni Muslims and the majority Shia who follow Islam's largest dissenting sect. Juxtaposed against both are the Kurds who claim their own ethnicity and language. Each group dominates a region of Iraq—the Sunnis the center, the Shia the south, the Kurds the north. In the immediate aftermath of the Gulf War when the Iraqi military streamed in full-scale retreat toward Baghdad, Shia and Kurdish anger, amplified by decades of political and economic subordination to the Sunnis, exploded against the symbol and substance of their oppression—the regime of Saddam Hussein. In the unfolding savagery of Iraqi against Iraqi, the United States peered into a pool of chaos that once more tripped all images of American entrapment in Vietnam.

The fury began early in the morning of February 28, 1991, the day the cease-fire stilled the Gulf War. The lead tank in a jagged column fleeing Kuwait rolled into Saad square in Basra at the junction of the Tigris and the Euphrates. It stopped, aimed its long-nosed gun, and blasted to shreds a billboard-size portrait of Saddam Hussein. As if on signal, newly born rebels surged through the streets. Operating more as a mob than an organized force, they vented their hatred against the symbols of Baghdad. Fed by Shia soldiers deserting units under Sunni command, the rebellion swept north and west. The swelling waves of insurgents rushed from one government installation to the next to pass armaments from the warehouses and storerooms of the military and security services into the hands of wrathful men. In city after city wrested from the grip of Hussein, the rebels utilized their guns and numbers to seize the civilian operatives of the Baath government while former Shia conscripts turned on officers of the army. They hung their captives from the rafters of an Islamic school, shot them in the head before walls turned into execution chambers, or simply slit their throats at the point of capture. The abandoned bodies collected in the streets where enraged Shia spit their venom on the lifeless figures.

In Iraq's heartland, the stunned Sunnis began to gather behind their discredited leader for one reason. Over the short span of Iraq's national history, the Sunni minority has exercised an overwhelming dominance over the politics and economy of the Iraqi state. Now all those prerogatives plus the grim threat to physical survival rode on the wind of the Shia revolt. Suddenly Saddam Hussein no longer appeared as much despot as savior. As the Sunni ranks closed behind him, the embattled Iraqi president issued orders that quickly crafted an army from Sunni loyalists within his shattered forces. They were attached to units of his highly paid, well-equipped, and overwhelmingly Sunni Republican Guards, most of whom had escaped almost intact from the Gulf War. Less than a week after the Shia uprising began, the counterattack came at Basra, where the rebellion started. Backed up to the Persian Gulf, sealed in on the east by the swampy Shatt al Arab, and facing five hundred miles of open plains on the north, the rebels of Basra quickly fell before the flanking forces of Baghdad.

The assault on the rebels grew more fierce as it moved onto the mid-Euphrates plain. There the menacing machines of Saddam Hussein's defenders circled behind Karbala, site of one of Shiism's holiest shrines. In the uneven battle for the city, Hussein's loyalists under the protective cover of hovering helicopter gunships did to the Shia what the Shia had done to them. They hanged rebels from electrical poles, tied their bodies behind tanks to be dragged through the street, and as an anticlimax, shot one old man dead in the souk for denouncing Hussein. Within sight of the American military occupying a slice of southern Iraq, the Shia rebellion died.

Only days after the Arab Shia had risen up in the south, the non-Arab Kurds in the north hurled their own grievances against Baghdad, the guardian of Iraq's Arab identity. Trained and hardened by decades of revolt against the Iraqi state, Kurdish guerrillas garbed in their traditional baggy pants and checkered turbans swept down out of the mountains and onto the plains. With the Republican Guards tied down by the Shia rebellion in the south, the *pesh mergas*, the fabled Kurdish guerrillas, joined by army deserters and ordinary Kurds, seized town after town. On March 20, two-plus weeks after the rebellion began, Kirkuk, a city of one million people at the heart of Iraq's richest oil fields, fell to the Kurds. Over the next hours, no one bothered to count how many servants of Baghdad were shot, beheaded, or cut to shreds with the traditional dagger stuck in the cummerbund of every Kurdish man. By the time Kurdish rage had exhausted itself, piles of corpses lay in the street awaiting removal by bulldozers.

The capture of Kirkuk by the Kurds galvanized Iraq's Sunnis much as the fear for their survival had energized them against the Shia. Although most Sunnis might hate Saddam Hussein, they hated even more ceding control of Kirkuk's black gold to the Kurds. Thus, with the Sunnis holding the center of the country, Baghdad pulled more than 100,000 soldiers with their supporting arsenal out of the subdued south and swung them toward the north. Their battle orders were simple—conquest and vengeance.

Units of the Iraqi army hit Kirkuk with ground-to-ground missiles, helicopter gunships, Katyusha rockets, tanks, heavy artillery, and napalm. The *pesh mergas* fought back with everything they had—anti-aircraft guns, rockets, mortars, machine guns, and small arms. But none of it dampened the overwhelming firepower of Baghdad. Infused with the memory of poison gas dropped on the Kurds by Baghdad in the late 1980s, the guerrillas gathered their women and children to flee to the high mountains with the rest of the panicked population. By April 5, as many as two million people were on the move across northern Iraq.

By the beginning of the second week of April, roughly 650,000 Iraqi Kurds clung to the steep mountainsides along the Iraq-Turkey border. At seven thousand feet above sea level, they huddled in ad hoc camps under the shelter of tents, tarpaulins, sheets of plastic, and lean-tos constructed from pine branches stripped from the surrounding trees. In the raw spring of the mountains, there was no heat, no sanitation, and no food. When a grinding, wheezing relief truck out of Turkey managed to reach desperately hungry people, soldiers untrained for a humanitarian mission beat back surging crowds grabbing for loaves of bread, bags of potatoes and flour, packages of noodles, and sacks of apples. It was survival of the fittest in the dark reality that too few vehicles could navigate the steep mountain terrain to sustain life for so many. In the escalating desperation, a tall, eagle-faced man with pots, kettles, basins, chicken coops, and fourteen members of his family strapped onto a huge

John Deere tractor grabbed an American journalist and cried, "Why? Why do you Americans allow this to happen? . . . Why doesn't Bush do something? . . . Why?"[8] It was a question that has haunted American foreign policy ever since.

During that March and April of 1991, the United States and its partners from the Gulf War held back the massive military machine assembled against Saddam Hussein while the great villain of wartime rhetoric crushed the communal forces within Iraq committed to his destruction. When the United Nations formally declared the Gulf War ended, the overwhelmingly American force of occupation in southern Iraq began a rapid withdrawal. In this final act of the great victory of 1991, the allies left behind an Iraq defeated in war, splintered by rebellion, hammered back together by pitiless forces, and bathed in human suffering. In the end, the coalition that had so brilliantly fought the Gulf War had failed to achieve real victory in either a political or a humanitarian sense. Instead, they accepted the reality that massive military power could force Saddam Hussein out of Kuwait but it could not resolve the internal conflicts of the Iraqi state. The Butcher of Baghdad was allowed to survive because every partner in the coalition—the United States, the Europeans, Turkey, and Iraq's Arab neighbors—shared to some extent the Vietnam syndrome. A second, equally paralyzing fear—the territorial fragmentation of Iraq—hung on the first. Thus, behind lofty language that condemned Hussein's tyranny over his own people and the warnings of the threat he posed to his neighbors, the individual members of the wartime coalition as well as Iran concluded that the Baath regime served their own particular interests more than did a dismembered Iraqi state. So they moved on to the next step—containment of Saddam Hussein's weapons of mass destruction.

At the time, the strategy for emasculating Hussein's regime while keeping Iraq territorially intact seemed so logical. Iraq's military had already suffered a disastrous defeat on the battlefield. What followed was a widely supported international edict ordering the destruction of Iraq's nonconventional weapons coupled with enforcement of a total trade embargo until United Nations arms inspectors certified that chemical, biological, and potential nuclear weapons as well as the means of delivery were cleansed from Iraq. Like the strategy to

---

[8] Quoted in *Time*, April 15, 1991, p. 20.

liberate Kuwait, it was clear, precise, and neat. But Hussein, by defying unconditional arms inspections for a decade at the expense of dreadful suffering among his own people, has destroyed the whole scenario so carefully written in 1991. The question now is how to rid the world not only of Saddam Hussein's weapons but also of his ruthless regime that violates all the standards of civil society. The current situation deposits the United States back into its old anxieties fostered by Vietnam—entrapment in a long, costly civil conflict with no guaranteed outcome. But Hussein is only the first problem of American foreign policy in the Persian Gulf. Iraq is the second.

The United States fell into the quicksand of Vietnam by failing to understand the enemy. The Vietnamese possessed an intense sense of themselves and their history that rejected any foreign presence on their territory. In this context, Marxism, the dreaded word of Cold War politics, was first and foremost an ideology under which Ho Chi Minh waged a war of nationalism. In retrospect, it seems probable that the Vietnamese communists, while eagerly receiving tons of weapons from Beijing and Moscow, would have resisted incorporation into a Communist Chinese empire or the Marxist Soviet Union with the same determination that they fought first the French and then the Americans. Consequently, much of America's tragedy in Vietnam came out of the basic failure to comprehend the Vietnamese culture, history, and values that created the intensity of their nationalism.

In contrast to Vietnam, Iraq and its people pose a whole different framework for the United States. Here the central challenge is not intense nationalism but a feeble sense of nation. The Iraqis are fenced in by the boundaries of an artificial state, torn by sectarian and ethnic differences, and lacking any real sense of common identity. Over the last two decades, their already fragile society has lived under pervasive, politically motivated brutality that has further damaged any sense of commonality and drained the Iraqis of much of their humanity.

At some point, Saddam Hussein will fall from the oppressive weight of his own regime, rumored health problems, spontaneous rebellion, or American action precipitated by the war on terrorism. When that happens, the United States must be prepared for what will follow. Immediately after the boot is lifted from the neck of the Iraqis, a bloodbath is likely to ensue as each group pours out its

anger at decades of despotism, enormous suffering under the sanctions, and real and perceived injustices of one group against the
other. Even without blood, there will be chaos within the ruins of a
police state that never gave the Iraqis any opportunity to participate
in governing. The Iraqis will not be able to restore order alone. And
order cannot be maintained without an enormous, and perhaps
unsuccessful, effort at nation building. Failing that, Iraq will likely
fragment. Regardless of whether the Iraqis slaughter each other, go
their separate ways, or somehow hold themselves together, the
United States will be drawn into Iraq in a role it might not choose
but cannot avoid. Caught in the swift currents of geography, history,
ethnic identity, sectarianism, and tribalism, Iraq will become its own
imperative to American interests.

Iraq is the bridge between the Islamic Republic of Iran and the
heart of the Fertile Crescent. It possesses vast oil resources critically
needed by the American and world economy. It is surrounded by
neighbors, most of whom are American allies, who are terrified that
the country will fragment, creating another whole set of problems
for the internal order in each of these states. As a boiling cauldron of
bitter resentment against the United States for its enforcement of the
sanctions, Iraq is a place where ambitious China can flex its muscle
on the international stage and a hungry Russia can attempt to
reclaim its influence in the Middle East. For all of these reasons, the
United States, whether it wants to or not, is going to be ensnarled in
post-Hussein Iraq. To avoid the deceptive simplicity that the fall of
Saddam Hussein by itself will bring security and stability to the
Persian Gulf, both the U. S. government and the American people
must face with brutal honesty the realities of the country of Iraq.

Iraq is a state, not a nation. Over the eighty years of their common history, the Iraqis have engaged in a conflicted, and at times
convoluted, search for a common identity. At different times, different groups have sought this identity in the symbols of ancient
Mesopotamia, pan-Arabism, a nebulous Iraqi nationalism, and the
socialist agenda of Saddam Hussein. But Iraqis as a whole have never
reached consensus within either a real or a manufactured singularity.
Instead, they remain trapped in the mythology of Mesopotamia, the
great seventh-century schism of Islam, neglect under the Ottoman
Empire, misguided British colonialism, a failed monarchy, savage
domestic politics waged under military regimes, and the most brutal

of police states run by Saddam Hussein. Each of these elements in
its own particular way has contributed to what Iraq is today. This is
the Iraq with which American foreign policy must deal. The failure to
understand the complications of Iraqi political culture, with or without Hussein, threatens to spring the same trap of misperceptions that
ensnared the United States in Vietnam. But unlike the jungles of
Southeast Asia that only shaded the strategic interests of the Cold
War, Iraq sits on the Persian Gulf. What happens to the stability of
the Gulf directly relates to the economic well-being of every
American. A warning of the looming peril posed by chaos in Iraq
sounded before the first bomb fell in the Gulf War. Boutros
Boutros-Ghali, the Egyptian diplomat who later became secretary
general of the United Nations, voiced the troubling truth: "The real
problem for the Middle East is not the Gulf crisis per se, but the problems we will face after the crisis is 'resolved.' "[9] It is time to realize
why. The hour is late.

---

[9] Quoted in *Newsweek*, January 7, 1991, p. 22.

1

THE LAND BETWEEN
TWO RIVERS

ixty miles south of Baghdad, a nondescript road branches off the main highway at the exit for al-Hillah. Narrow and pockmarked by deep holes in broken asphalt, it winds eastward across flat sandy soil broken into small fields delineated by banks of irrigation ditches. It ends abruptly in a forlorn gravel parking lot in front of fabled Babylon. Part authentic historic restoration and part a Disneyesque rendition of Iraq's ancient past, contemporary Babylon's entrance is heralded by a half-size replication of the renowned Ishtar Gate. Constructed of vivid blue tiles inset with muscular stylized bulls and slender long-tailed dragons, it leads to the great ceremonial way that in ancient times ended at the soaring ziggurat dedicated to the god Marduk. Today the twenty-yard-wide processional avenue, paved with some of the original stones, runs no farther than the crenellated walls of the once massive palace of the legendary Nebuchadnezzar. Behind it, a berm formed from the rubble of the mud walls that once stood sentry for the city gives way to an open expanse of land. There on a stone pedestal stands the time-worn basalt statue of the Lion of Babylon. Symbolizing the king's protection over the people, the heavily maned lion sets its square paws around a supine man, pressing him against its belly. It is a simple yet powerful symbol of Mesopotamian civilization that in the fifth century B.C. underwrote the splendor of Babylon. Then the city fell. Inundated by salty groundwater and pillaged for building bricks by generations of nearby villagers, Babylon remained largely a jumbled ruin—that is, until the 1970s when Saddam Hussein ordered the restoration of Iraq's Mesopotamian past in an attempt to fortify the unity of the Iraqi state through the symbols and imagery of the Sumerians, Assyrians, and Babylonians, the lords of ancient Mesopotamia between the Tigris and Euphrates Rivers.

But Iraq possesses another past, more real and more immediate than the distant, misty centuries in which Mesopotamia cradled civilization. Ever since the seventh century A.D. when Islam rode into Mesopotamia on the hooves of Arab horses, the land along the Tigris and Euphrates has been enfolded in Arabic culture and language. Yet Arab culture and identity in Iraq dwell at the eastern edge of the Arab world. Bordering Persian Iran, Iraq is a crossroads where Arab culture has always been infused with influences of the east. These attitudes, perceptions, and values coming out of the east have shaped a people of whom large numbers have never accepted incorporation into the Arab world to the west. They are joined by the non-Arab Kurds and other minorities attached to Arab Mesopotamia after World War I. As a result, Iraqis have always struggled with the essential question of whether the Iraqi state is part of the Arab world or is a unique entity demanding its own particular definition. For the Iraqis as well as the whole region of the Persian Gulf, this question of identity is real, not existential. Within it lies the ultimate survival of Iraq, which depends in large part on the Iraqis' ability to reach consensus on an identity that draws all the Iraqi state's disparate communities into a nation.

In the perpetual search for definition, every leader of Iraq, including Saddam Hussein, has sought identity for the Iraqis in either Arabism or a contrived Iraqi nationalism constructed from the history and symbols of ancient Mesopotamia. Neither approach has succeeded because Mesopotamia means little to Iraqis, and Arabism, hung on the framework of the orthodox Sunni Muslims, is rejected by non-Arabs and most of the Arab Shia. Deprived by a ruthless regime of thirty years in which to develop an innovative alternative, these remain the only existing touchstones on which even democratic successors to Hussein must attempt to build a nation.

IN FEBRUARY 1991, when the phalanx of American tanks rolled into southern Iraq during the ground phase of the Gulf War, few of those manning the machines realized that they were sweeping across the soil of ancient Mesopotamia. Here on the flatlands of southern Iraq in what was the cradle of Western as well as Middle Eastern civilization, the Americans and Saddam Hussein perhaps shared their only commonality in the face-off in the Persian Gulf.

Mesopotamia, ancient history to most of the world and contem-

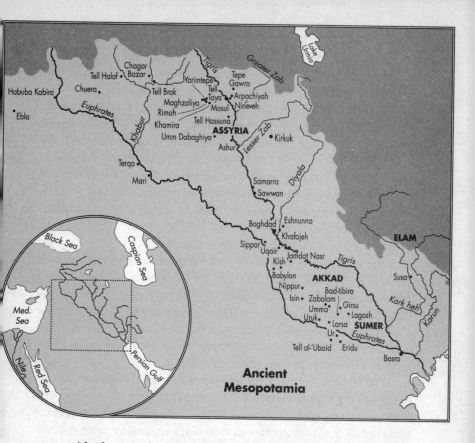

Ancient
Mesopotamia

porary ideology to the Iraqi regime, is, in perception and reality, a messy jumble of city-states that collected, expanded, contracted, and disappeared over a period of 4,500 years in what is now roughly the territory of Iraq. Blessed or cursed by whims of nature, the quality of leadership, and the power of rival forces, what is a chaotic succession of ministates and empires refuses to conform to constant boundaries or a neat story line. Instead, it draws a rough pattern— the triumph of cultural achievement juxtaposed against power and carnage.

It all began between the Tigris and Euphrates Rivers in what is now thousands of square miles of dried mudflats and reed-filled swamps: the wasteland of southern Iraq. In the long summer encompassing March through October, furnace-hot winds and fiery temperatures that stay locked between 100 and 120 degrees create a hell. Yet six thousand years before Christ, this harsh land between the great rivers hosted a veritable garden.

In the light of early morning, clouds of fowl took flight from the marshes, clusters of wild animals grazed on tender greens, and recently settled hunter-gatherers harvested the long, tough, abundant *qasab* reeds with which they built their U-shaped houses, a design that still dots the marshes. When climatic changes reduced rainfall, men who had farmed the wetlands learned to irrigate. And then they learned to write when the Sumerians, the founding fathers of Mesopotamian culture, began to press the wedges of reeds into wet clay tablets to create cuneiform.[1] Before the dawn of the second millennium B.C., clay tablets inscribed with the Sumerians' accumulated myths, history, and knowledge of subjects from agriculture to astronomy were stacked high in their libraries.

Fusing with a Semite tribe that swarmed out of the Arabian Peninsula sometime before 2500 B.C., the Sumerians and the invading Akkadians founded Ur.[2] In a phase of history written more by culture than politics, Ur gathered the cultural harvest of the previous 1,800 years to a create a golden age that has influenced sculpture, painting, and jewelry design ever since. Then Ur surrendered stewardship of Mesopotamian culture to Babylon.

King Hammurabi, with his arsenal of horses and spoked wheels, delivered to the city-state of Babylon the whole of southern Mesopotamia sometime around 1780 B.C.. Pressed to control rumbling unrest in his empire that grew out of a repressive military class and its accompanying bureaucracy, Hammurabi devised a stated set of rules for governing. Proclaiming equitable laws and decreeing barbarous punishments based on the simple philosophy of "an eye for an eye, a tooth for a tooth," Hammurabi added his code to the developing Mesopotamian concept of law that now underlies the whole Western legal system. Cutting his rules in stone, the Babylonian king erected stele throughout his domain that declared to all his ethos as a ruler: "In my bosom I carried the people of the land of Sumer and Akkad . . . in my wisdom I restrained them, that the strong might not oppress the weak, and that they should give justice to the orphan and the widow. . . . In the days that are yet to come, for all future time, may the king who is in the land observe the words of righteousness

---

[1] The term *cuneiform* is derived from the Latin word meaning "wedge."

[2] In Genesis, the city is called Ur of the Chaldaes. This is where scholars believe Abraham, the father of Judaism, Christianity, and Islam, lived until around 1850 B.C., when he left to travel west to the land of Canaan.

which I have written upon my monument."[3] This was the climax of
the early Mesopotamian civilization that had originally taken root
between the Tigris and Euphrates Rivers. Composed of Sumerian
learning and preserved in the Semitic language of the Akkadians,
custodianship of Mesopotamian art and learning would be seized in
the ninth century B.C. by raw power from the north.

For uncounted years, southern Mesopotamia had lived under the
protection of a stretch of largely uninhabited territory along its
northern perimeter. To the north lay high plains where rain fell in sufficient quantities to support winter crops and a scattering of small
city-states, including Ashur, Erbil, Nimrud, and Nineveh. Collectively
known as Assyria, the people of this territory outside the political
and cultural influence of Mesopotamia ruled by the Babylonians
came to possess a powerful military tradition born and suckled on
the necessity of constant warfare against mountain tribes to both the
east and the west. Joining military prowess with a burning ambition
for profit, a sense of divine protection from the sun god Ashur, and
fierce loyalty to their king, the Assyrians would become the new
masters of Mesopotamia and the heirs of the culture of the
Sumerians and the Akkadians. Around 900 B.C., they burst forth as
the Assyrian king led the attack on his southern neighbors "like a
wolf on the fold" followed by "his cohorts . . . gleaming in purple and
gold."[4] They brought with them an arsenal of chariots capable of
mowing down enemy soldiers, battering rams forceful enough to
break down the walls of resistant cities, and movable towers from
which armored warriors unleashed hails of spears and arrows on
their foes within a vast territory, from present-day Iraq to the western
Mediterranean. More than anything, the Assyrians brought to the battlefield a passion for war and a zeal for terror. Swooping down on a
targeted city, the highly disciplined Assyrian army overwhelmed its
defenses, looted its treasures, tortured its leaders, and butchered its
citizens. Piling the skulls of the hundreds of dead on the roadways
to give passing travelers food for thought, the Assyrians put the torch
to the vanquished city's gates, palaces, temples, and simple houses.
In testimony to brutality born of joy, King Tiglath-pileser III (745–727

---

[3] Quoted in Richard M. Powers, *The Land between Two Rivers* (New York: World
Publishing, 1962), pp. 89–90.

[4] Lord George Gordon Byron, "The Destruction of Sennacherib," composed
February 17, 1815.

B.C.) inscribed the pride of victory in stone: "In my fierce valour I marched against the people of Qummuh, conquered their cities, carried off their booty, their goods and their property without reckoning, and burned their cities with fire—destroyed and devastated them. . . . The people of Adansh left their mountains and embraced my feet. I imposed taxes upon them."[5]

At the center of the Assyrian empire reigned the all powerful king, "the great king, the legitimate king . . . king of all the four rims of the earth, king of kings, prince without rival, who rules from the Upper Sea to the Lower Sea."[6] Benefiting from a succession of exceptionally effective rulers, Assyria reached its zenith under Sargon II when "the mud culture of the south was joined to the rock culture of the north."[7]

Adding the wealth gained from the conquest of southern Mesopotamia, Sargon built the city of Khorsabad, to the north and east of the upper reaches of the Tigris.[8] There he gathered the artistic tradition of the Sumerians that had been nurtured by the Babylonians and added to it the force and power of the Assyrians. The walls were over seventy-five feet thick. Huge ornamental gateways dominated by winged lions framed the expansive quadrangle where the king's massive palace surmounted a vast artificial mound. In room after room, corridor after corridor, the sculptured bas-reliefs lining the walls depicted the king in battle, besieging cities, hunting game, and engaging in elaborate religious ceremonies. They were all executed in a style inherited from the Sumerians—human figures in profile, eyes and shoulders squared to the front, and feet again in profile.

The enduring splendor of Assyrian art is accomplished in part by the sheer scale of its statuary and friezes. Equally important is the exquisite detail that produces a mesmerizing beauty in an art form whose central theme is raw power. In repeating imagery, the king races into war in a mighty chariot or sits on a throne while tribute bearers humbly present to him the riches of the realm. Whole walls create battle scenes depicting enemy men and beasts run through

---

[5] Chester G. Starr, *A History of the Ancient World* (New York: Oxford University Press, 1991), p. 91.

[6] Ibid., p. 132.

[7] Muhammad Makiya, interview with author, London, October 7, 1999.

[8] Sargon originally named the city Dur-Sharrukin, "Sargon's Fortress."

with spears or cut into pieces; ominously deserted cities where lines of fearful women and children advance to meet the conqueror; corpses of men and horses floating on a river; and manacled prisoners impaled on eight-foot spikes. Assyrian art remains above all else the image of winning through intimidation.

Yet despite their excessive brutality, the Assyrian kings promoted and preserved much of the culture that began in Sumer. The first of Assyria's significant kings, Tiglath-pileser III, took the title "king of Sumer-Akkad" and the last notable ruler, Ashurbanipal, gathered into his vast library at Nineveh the works of Babylonian literature, religion, and law. Between the two, the Assyrian kings consolidated and spread the intellectual legacy of sixty generations of Sumerian, Akkadian, and Babylonian scholars. Nonetheless, the kings of Assyria never accepted the reality that empires, like modern states, survive only through a measure of consent by the governed. Like a series of ancient Saddam Husseins, each failed to lay the basis of a durable state. So it was that Ashurbanipal uttered the lament that would one day be shared by many leaders of twentieth-century Iraq: "I cannot do away with the strife in my country and dissentions in my family; . . . with cries of woe I bring my days to an end."[9] Once Ashurbanipal died, the mighty Assyrian empire also began to die. When the end came, it came swiftly.

Although subjugated to the Assyrian empire, Babylon had never totally surrendered to Assyrian rule. Beaten, burned, and banished for insurrection, the defiant Babylonians had risen time after time against their northern masters. In 626 B.C., a new king of Babylon mounted the throne both determined and able to break the chains of the Assyrians. Mobilizing the hatred subjects felt toward their Assyrian rulers, Nabopolassar called upon the occupied cities to end their enslavement. With the powerful Medes of northwest Iran in attendance, the Babylonian king attacked the Assyrian cities of the north one by one. By 612 B.C., his army stood at the gates of once mighty Nineveh. Motivated by vengeance as much as strategy, Nabopolassar set the Assyrian capital afire. In the final conflagration, the huge cedar columns of palaces and temples disappeared in flame, painted ceilings crashed, walls of magnificent reliefs cracked, ivory

---

[9] Quoted in Geoff Simons, *Iraq: From Sumer to Saddam* (London: Macmillian Press, 1994), p. 93.

inlays baked off furniture, and heavy silks melted. In far-off Judah, the Hebrew prophet Nahum exulted at the news of the Assyrians' demise: "Nineveh's laid waste: Who will bemoan her!"[10]

In the south where Mesopotamian culture had been born, Babylon became ascendant once more. Under King Nebuchadnezzar, the Babylonians took possession of southern Mesopotamia, ripped Syria away from Egypt, and marched westward across the desert trade routes to seize Palestine. Visiting his wrath on resistant Jerusalem in 586 B.C., Nebuchadnezzar razed the Temple of Solomon and marched the Jews off into captivity in Babylon. In the following years, his army roamed the Middle East collecting tribute through intimidation. Even so, the Babylonian king never created a real empire. Failing to stabilize his territories either geographically or politically, Nebuchadnezzar proclaimed the greatness of his realm in the grandeur of Babylon.

Splendid bridges spanning the Euphrates connected the city to the roads running north, south, east, and west that carried the lucrative trade underlying Babylon's boisterous economy. As the keepers of the Sumerian tradition, Babylon's temple priests repeated rituals almost three millennia old; judges tried cases under precedents set down by Hammurabi; businessmen figured their accounts on clay tablets much like the Sumerians; scribes wrote letters in an alphabet evolved from their early ancestors; musicians plucked stringed instruments in existence since Ur; and craftsmen sustained the Mesopotamian artistic tradition in what was the greatest metropolis of the ancient world. In the fifth century B.C., Babylon covered nearly fourteen square miles held within two walls, one inside the other, that measured fifty-six miles in length. The massive outer wall, eighty feet thick, was broad enough to accommodate two four-horse chariots abreast. Near the center of the city lay the sacred precinct of the god Baal. At its core, a solid masonry ziggurat ascending to an approximate height of 245 feet was perhaps the Tower of Babel. The great temple of Marduk stood to its south as did Nebuchadnezzar's grand palace with its columned halls and bronze doors that faced the broad "sacred way." At the head of this processional avenue was the resplendent Ishtar Gate, double portals flanked by two towers and adorned with glazed bricks and the figures of seventy-five bulls and

---

[10] Nahum 3:17.

dragons created from enamel tiles of yellow and white. Somewhere within the splendor, the fabled "hanging gardens" grew on a series of terraces, supported by a series of arches that soared some four hundred feet above the level of the plain.

Even though clay tablets embedded in the city's walls carried the cuneiform inscription "Nebuchadnezzar, King of Babylon, from far sea to far sea," the absolute monarch allowed dissolution and decay to eat away at the foundations of Babylon's magnificent facade. Consequently, seventy years after the destruction of the Assyrian capital of Nineveh, Babylon stood at the edge of its own abyss. The reigning king, Nabonidus, no longer seriously celebrated the New Year festival that, through the long history of Mesopotamia, had engaged the gods on the side of man in the coming year. Nor did he respect the legacy of equitable rule practiced by Hammurabi, the great law giver. In the east across the Tigris River and the Zagros Mountains, the principle of just rule resided with a new vibrant leader named Cyrus who was pulling together the Medes and the Persians. When he and his disciplined army arrived outside the walls of Babylon in 538 B.C., the Babylonian people chose to open their gates. Representing himself more as a liberator than a conqueror, Cyrus embraced the Babylonian god Marduk, spared the lives of the Babylonian leadership, and sent the Jews back to Jerusalem to rebuild their temple. For the next two centuries, Babylon lived as part of the Persian Empire. In 331 B.C., it fell to Alexander of Macedonia in his march eastward to conquer Persia. Alexander returned in 323 B.C. only to die following a banquet in the decaying palace of Nebuchadnezzar. In the third century B.C., Babylon functioned as nothing more than a commercial center for Alexander's heirs. Then the great metropolis, along with Mesopotamia's other cities, disappeared.

Today, a people known as the Marsh Arabs who live in a watery world of vast marshes in southern Iraq are perhaps the most direct, unsullied descendants of the Mesopotamians. Tormented by heat, cold, mosquitoes, malaria, dysentery, and bilharzia, they cling to their ancient way of life despite assaults by the forces of politics and modernization.

Recently, in air made stifling by heat, humidity, and enclosure, a sun-scorched man in a simple long shirt and tattered head cloth folded into a triangle dipped a wooden paddle into the shallow still water. It propelled a narrow canoe-like boat between stands of *qasab* that can reach twenty-five feet in height. In the quiet that has engulfed these marshes for five thousand years, the little boat glided past islands the size and composition of giant nests. Around them, big black buffalo snorted and wallowed in thick mud while men up to their waists in water cut reeds among the flotsam of dung and decaying vegetation. Slowly the passageway became so narrow that the boatman pulled his oar from the water, allowing the craft to drift the last few-dozen yards into a lagoon. In the little village clustered on its edge, it is easy to accept the theory that these people hidden away in the reeds are the descendants of the Babylonians whom the Assyrian king Sargon drove into the marshes in 720 B.C. Among the men squatted around a fire made from cow dung, the evidence of intermarriage with fugitives, migrants, and invaders is obvious. There is the fine long face of a desert tribesmen and the high cheekbones of the Mongol. But most of all there is the round face of the Mesopotamian depicted in the art of ancient Sumeria. The houses around which women with similar features tend simmering pots are constructed of thick pillars made from bundles of reeds covered with woven matting; their beached canoes, the *mushhufs*, are identical to those depicted on cylinder seals from Ur. They all create the sense that here the life of ancient Mesopotamia hangs on. But it is the code of the desert Arab that the Marsh Arabs now live by. For like most Iraqis, they claim another, far more powerful cultural legacy than Mesopotamia—that of the Arabic language and Islam.

THE FRAGMENTARY EMPIRE of the Seleucids, the generals who claimed Alexander the Great's conquests after his death, collapsed in the east by 163 B.C. In the aftermath, Mesopotamia lay like a carpet between the Fertile Crescent and the Iranian plateau. For almost two hundred years, land-hungry Roman emperors sporadically sent their armies eastward against the coveted territory of Persia. They were met by the Parthians, a tribe of leather-helmeted Aryans astride powerful, armor-clad horses from which the deadly accurate bowmen fired arrows capable of piercing Roman breastplates.[11] Unable to hold costly won territory, the emperor Trajan in A.D. 114 finally sur-

---

[11] In 36 B.C., Mark Antony lost 35,000 men out of a force of approximately 100,000 before retreating from the Parthian onslaught of men and animals.

rendered all Rome's aspirations to permanently expand its empire eastward beyond Syria. A little over two hundred years later, the Parthians at last gave way to the Sassanians, a tribal monarchy gathered around the former capital of Cyrus the Great in Persia. For the next four hundred years (A.D. 224–637), the Sassanians reigned over a revitalized Persian empire that tended the flame of ancient Persian culture.

A crucial part of the Sassanian empire that would stretch from the Indus River to the eastern border of Syria was Mesopotamia. Financially dependent on the agricultural produce of the Sawad, the irrigated area of southern Iraq, the Sassanians set their capital at Ctesiphon on the Tigris, about forty miles from what had been ancient Babylon. From there, they governed a Mesopotamian population that resembled a patchwork quilt. Most of the agricultural population that tended Sassanian fields were Aramaeans, the Aramaic-speaking descendants of the Sumerians, Akkadians, and Babylonians. They lived beside Greeks from the age of the Seleucids, Syrians captured in war, Persians from the Iranian plateau, Turkish-speaking mercenaries from Central Asia, and Arabs who had drifted north from the Arabian Peninsula. Although Aramaic constituted a loose but practical lingua franca, Persian, Greek, Arabic, and a smattering of other languages sounded from village to village.

Religion duplicated language. Mesopotamia played host to pagans, Christians, Jews, Buddhists, and a whole range of sects and cults tossed in a sea of religious uncertainty churned by centuries of political turmoil. With the imposition of Sassanian rule, Mesopotamians fell under the official and ancient faith of Zoroastrianism. But an official religion failed to give the Mesopotamians spiritual commonality. Instead, dissent fed by the increasingly corrupt priesthood that underwrote the authority of the Sassanian king only increased the numbers adopting a variety of faiths, especially Christianity. At the end of the sixth century, Christians may have comprised the largest single religious group in Iraq. But rather than surrendering to Christianity as the Roman Empire had, the Sassanian Empire fell to Islam.

SOUTH OF Sassanian Mesopotamia, in the great wastelands of the Arabian Peninsula, nomads dependent for survival on sheep and goats had followed the seasons across the baked barren landscape for hundreds of years. Known as Arabs, these desert dwellers had incorporated the domesticated camel into their primitive economic system sometime around the beginning of the Christian era.[12] Functioning as four-legged ships of the desert, the camel became not only a new dynamic in the scanty desert economy but also a major social force. Able to endure long distances without food and water, camels bestowed on their herders far greater mobility than did plodding sheep and goats that required pastures and oases. Free to wander the desert with animals that provided milk, meat, and transportation, small groups of nomads cut their bonds to settled communities to become the legendary Bedouin.

Independent and arrogant, the Bedouin came to define Arab society. Whether nomads, farmers cultivating the widely scattered oases, or residents of the few scattered towns, all people of Arabia held the Bedouin values of freedom, kinship, courage, loyalty, generosity, and veracity as their own. Every year on a high plateau east of Mecca, the Arabs met at Ukaz to trade and to celebrate their culture.

The oasis families arrived first with their trudging donkeys loaded with the annual production of grain, dates, baskets, palm-wood bowls, homespun cloth, and woven rugs. The nomads followed. Amidst the dust raised by nervously milling animals and the noise of grumbling camels, traders from the oases and the desert practiced the time-honored rituals of bargaining. By the time the sun set, it was finished. In the slowly descending darkness, the women and children retreated to their tents while the men gathered on blankets before a fire to talk of animals and trade, weather and politics, land and hunting. Gradually conversation gave way to the poets. Weaving verbal spells from the highly stylized patterns of word and meter that had mysteriously sprouted from the roots of earliest Bedouin life, one revered poet after another executed the great art form of Arab culture by wrapping magical words around the Bedouin way of life.

Yet at the beginning of the seventh century, these cherished Bedouin values suffocated under a stampede for wealth generated by trade routes that crisscrossed the Arabian Peninsula. Mecca, a town of mud and stone structures huddled against the low, black-rock mountains of northwest Arabia, was an important stop on the north-south caravan route that had long carried frankincense from Yemen to ports on the Mediterranean. Near the end of the sixth century, additional

---

[12] The earliest reference to Arabs is in Assyrian records dating to 854 B.C..

trade routes that bypassed the river pirates on the Tigris and Euphrates
increased the volume of goods moving from the markets of the
Sassanian Empire in the east to the Byzantine Empire in the west.
Stepping forward to seize control of the commerce of the whole of
western Arabia was the Quraysh of Mecca, a merchant group that operated through an assembly of clan leaders. In their rampant greed, they
began to undercut the basic values of Bedouin society. It was into this
changing social order that the prophet Muhammad was born.

Abu al-Qasim Muhammad ibn Abdullah ibn Abd al-Muttalib ibn
Hashim was the scion of the Banu Hashim, a poor clan of the
Quraysh. Orphaned at the age of six, the child passed into the care of
his grandfather and then his uncle, the custodian of the Kabah, the
windowless stone structure that housed the pagan idols believed to
provide protection against evil spirits. As a young adult, the progeny
of respectable bloodlines with little money or power seemed to have
met his fate when he secured a position as a camel driver in a caravan belonging to a wealthy widow. But at the age of twenty-five, the
handsome young man with wavy hair, dark eyes, thick lashes, and a
radiant smile married the widow, fifteen years his senior.

Freed from daily toil, Muhammad became increasingly interested
in the teachings of Judaism and the ministry of Jesus. Brooding on
the sins of society, he frequently withdrew into the desolate mountains outside Mecca to meditate. According to the classic biographies
of the Prophet, the year Muhammad turned forty the angel Gabriel
descended from heaven to convey a message to the man sleeping
alone on Mount Hira. It consisted of only one word—"recite."
Frightened and resistant, Muhammad hesitantly opened his mouth.
Out poured ominous words conveying the anger of an omnipotent
God resolved to punish mankind for the paganism of Arabia.
Descending from the mountain and inflamed with the passion of his
revelations, Muhammad admonished the people of Mecca to aban-
don their idolatrous practices and accept the one, universal God—
Allah, the all-powerful, the creator of the universe, the everlasting.
Thus was born the third great monotheistic religion—Islam, an
Arabic word meaning submission to the will of God.

Muhammad, a product of the city, preached to the city. But his
message spoke to the simplicity of Bedouin life. There is paradise
and there is hell. Splendid rewards come to those who obey Allah's
commands and terrible vengeance awaits those who disobey. Giving

voice and form to the restiveness of his time, his message of equality for all men attracted the desperate poor and gathered the restive young who had been shut out of the councils of power. For the Bedouin, he restored the ethics of the tribe through the words, "Look to those moral practices you had in the *jihiliyya* and apply them to Islam: give security to your guest, be generous toward the orphan and treat the stranger who is under your protection with kindness."[13]

Muhammad flung his challenge at the reigning power structure in the most propitious of locations. Tribal forms of Arab life tolerated neither kings nor municipal government. Hence, there existed no effective authority capable of imprisoning a man preaching the destruction of the existing order. Instead, the defenders of the status quo battled Muhammad and his growing number of followers with the only weapons at hand—clan solidarity, economic coercion, personal insults, and poetic barbs. These proved formidable tools for the already powerful Quraysh. In 622, Muhammad and his converts to Islam fled Mecca. Finding refuge in Medina, 225 miles to the north, the Prophet was transformed from a private person preaching a new faith to a sovereign ruler wielding political and military authority over a tight-knit community of Muslims, or those who submit to the will of God under the precepts of Islam.

Over a span of eight years, Islam grew into an irresistible force on the high desert of northern Arabia. In January 630, Muhammad, accompanied by thousands of followers, returned triumphantly to Mecca. Realizing the futility of any further opposition, the Quraysh stood aside as the once humble camel driver entered the Kabah, the religious shrine of pagan Mecca. In the name of Allah, he struck to the ground the 360 idols housed within its stone walls. In purging the Kabah of idolatry, Muhammad also restored to Mecca the supremacy of Bedouin culture. For within Islam, many of the values of the desert Bedouin found vindication, laying on future generations of Muslims much that is essentially Arab.

Even though Islam incorporated the ethos of Bedouin life, it rejected the Bedouin's fierce tribalism. Replacing fragmentation of family, clan, and tribe with the unity of religious belief, Muhammad instilled within his followers the idea of the *ummah*, the nation of believers. According to the Prophet, Islam encompassed more than

---

[13] Sura 4:36. *Jihiliyya* translates as the pre-Islamic period, the "time of ignorance."

the obedience of an individual to God. Acceptance of the faith carried with it acceptance of a compact of the faithful in which all Muslims are one. As the Arab poet spoke of his tribe, the Koran spoke of religious kinship: "Hearken, O ye men, unto my words and take ye them to heart. Know ye that every Muslim is a brother unto every other Muslim, and that ye are one brotherhood."[14]

Following Mecca's surrender to the message of Muhammad, representatives of tribes from all over the Hejaz, the western coastal area of the Arabian Peninsula, and the Nejd, the vast central desert, arrived at Islam's capital of Medina to seek accommodation with the new power. By the time the Prophet approached his sixtieth year and his own death, he presided over a monotheistic religion defined by precise ethical doctrines contained within an organized and armed state. When Muhammad died on June 8, 632, one of his earliest converts answered the question of the future of the faith in the stillness of the death chamber: "O men, if you worship Muhammad, Muhammad is dead; if you worship God, God is alive."[15]

In the interest of perpetuating the faith and the Islamic state, Muhammad's most trusted companions decided that Islam required a single leader to whom all Muslims would pledge their loyalty. Following the tribal custom of choosing the most respected man among them as the leader, the associates of Muhammad wrapped the mantle of the Prophet around Abu Bakr, one of Muhammad's initial converts. He became the caliph, the successor to Muhammad's temporal authority over the Muslim community. Never endowed with the Prophet's spiritual authority, Abu Bakr, more than anything, assumed responsibility for defense of the faith. Sounding the Koranic injunction, "Fight those who believe not in God and the Last Day," the new caliph ordered his Muslim army to reduce to obedience recalcitrant Muslim tribes that had been incited to rebellion by the Prophet's death. Forcing them back into the fold, the soldiers of Islam moved on to surrounding tribes who had yet to be converted. Consequently in less than two years after the Prophet's death, the Muslim community claimed more converts and more territory than it had during

---

[14] Sura 49:10. The Koran is the Holy Book of Islam, a transcript of God's word as revealed in Arabic to Muhammad. Recorded by the Prophet's followers, it came into existence in the earliest years of the faith.

[15] Quoted in Albert Hourani, *A History of the Arab Peoples* (Cambridge, Mass.: Belknap Press of Harvard University Press, 1991), p. 22.

Muhammad's lifetime. With the Arabian Peninsula secured for the faith, Islam's soldiers prepared to ride north out of the wastelands of Arabia bearing the green banner of Islam.

EVEN BEFORE the campaign to subdue the Bedouin of Arabia was complete, Arab Muslim warriors had been roaming north to raid the exhausted, spiritually defunct empires of the Christian Byzantines and the Zoroastrian Sassanians. Aware that rich booty lay ahead, the chronically poor soldiers of Islam's ragtag army exploded out of the Arabian Peninsula in 634 in the name of religion. One arm swung west toward Syria, Palestine, and Egypt, the heartland of the Fertile Crescent that arcs from the Nile to the Euphrates. The other raced east toward Mesopotamia. In 636, the Sassanians, who only a few years earlier had repelled the best Byzantium could throw against their territories, prepared to face an enemy of fewer numbers from a civilization as rudimentary as theirs was elaborate. Already alarmed by Arab success in Syria, the Sassanians drew the defensive line of their western frontier at Qadisiyah, a small town guarding the west side of the Euphrates. Ignoring the well-trod trade route that would take them up the river, the Arabs rode the short, brutal line across a pitiless desert. Within five days, perhaps ten thousand Arabs in sandals and frayed head cloths, carrying nothing more than ox-hide shields and crude swords sheathed in rags, gazed on an estimated eighty thousand well-armed Persians. But the Sassanian army, like Sassanian society, had grown ponderous. On a June day in 637, the Persian Cavalry, immobilized by its heavy armor and supporting elephants, flailed at the swarm of wasps that were Arabs mounted on swift horses. The victorious Arabs stripped their countless fallen foes of their golden, jewel-studded belts and silk brocade robes. Construed as a divine sign of their own superiority, the victory at Qadisiyah was elevated into Arab mythology as the cosmic contest between Arabs and Persians. It is a mythology that has never died. During the long Iran-Iraq War of the 1980s, Saddam Hussein enshrined the bloody encounter between Arab Iraq and Persian Iran as a contemporary replay of Qadisiyah.

After their victory on the banks of the Euphrates, the Arabs pursued Persian fugitives to their death in thickets, fields, and villages. Others pressed on to the vaulted palace at Ctesiphon, the physical embodiment of late Sassanian art and knowledge. Hundreds of fabulous objects of art passed from the cultured hands of the Sassanians into the rough callused hands of Arab warriors. The fabulous jewel-studded carpet, "Spring of Khosrow," went to Mecca where Islam's religious leaders, disdainful of all material possessions, cut it into pieces. And the massive libraries so carefully collected by the Sassanian kings were scattered according to the Arab edict:

> If the books herein are in accord with Islam,
> then we don't need them.
> If the books herein are not in accord with Islam,
> then they are *kafîr* (of the infidel).[16]

As the Arabs raced farther east, raids for booty changed into a full-scale campaign of conquest against the Sassanian Empire. By 651, essentially all of Mesopotamia as well as Iran and parts of Central Asia belonged to the Arab Muslims. With the Arab conquest in the east finally breaking against the mountains of what is now southern Turkey, the population of Sassanian Mesopotamia began to come to terms with the Arab occupation.

DESPITE THE religious fanaticism that had ignited the explosion out of Arabia, the Arab lords of the Islamic Empire proved more concerned with occupying territory than winning converts. So long as their subjects paid the poll tax, they need not fear the sword. Rather than a lack of religious fervor on the part of the zealots, this guarantee of life and property to non-Muslims simply confirmed that the conquerors believed Islam to be primarily, if not exclusively, reserved for Arabs. Thus, while there existed a strong sense among Islam's leaders that every Arab on the Arabian Peninsula should be Muslim, the purpose of religion in the occupied territories was to provide the foundation and framework of a political system under the exclusive control of Arabs. Consequently, under the new Islamic government of Mesopotamia and elsewhere, only Arabs, as a prerogative of their tribal genealogies, qualified as "privileged," or exempt from the poll tax. Everyone else fell together under the rubric of *dhimmi*, recipients of Muslim protection in return for submission to Arab Muslim rule. For the next 160 years, Mesopotamia lived as a province of an Arab empire ruled by an Islamic government belonging almost exclu-

---

[16] Richard N. Frye, *The Heritage of Iran* (London: Cambridge University Press, 1975), p. 214.

sively to Arabs. Although the people of Mesopotamia quietly surren-dered to this new order by quickly adopting the Arabic language and much of Arab culture, society remained bifurcated between Arabs and non-Arabs.

Arab natives of Mesopotamia, ethnically ordained to convert to Islam, climbed onto the lower rungs of the power structure. But the largest ethnic group in Mesopotamia, the Aramaeans, the heirs of ancient Mesopotamian culture and the beneficiaries of high Sassanian civilization, largely remained excluded. So did the Persians, particularly those who had once sat in the upper echelons of Sassanian government and society. As early as 670, Isaac of Nineveh wrote the epitaph for the Persian aristocracy in Mesopotamia: "They have entered it as an inn for a night and left it as travelers on a journey over the whole earth, without thinking of return. Some of them kings, some governors, some wise, some hon-ored. Some of them scribes, some orators, some judges, some com-manders of armies. Some of them possessors of riches, some lords of goods. And now . . . there is neither the order of their degrees, nor the crowns of the government, nor their dreadful thrones, nor their lordly pleasures nor the praise of those who honored them."[17] Accepting their reduced status, some members of the Sassanian landed aristocracy joined the lower grades of the old Sassanian soci-ety staying on in Mesopotamia. Together they formed a distinct com-munity maintaining their own cultural heritage. Yet like everyone else during these early days of Islamic Mesopotamia, they remained the subjects of an ever increasing Arab population.

With Arab possession of the land between the two rivers secured, a wholesale migration of tribes from all parts of Arabia poured into southern Mesopotamia to graze their herds on mounds that covered the forgotten palaces of ancient kings. Others fed into the new gar-rison towns built in the image of tribal Arabia where they lived as a separate conquering class. Kufa, just south and west of the ruins of Babylon, is still there. Founded in 638 by thirty thousand veterans of the Battle of Qadisiyah, it is a depressing collection of stucco and concrete-block buildings huddled on a gray stretch of desert. Much of the time the wind swirls in little eddies, catching the head cloths

---

[17] Michael G. Morony, *Iraq after the Muslim Conquest* (Princeton: Princeton University Press, 1984), p. 207.

of men whose dress is not too different from those who arrived here immediately after the Islamic conquest.

In the seventh century, Kufa centered around the main mosque that dominated an open square. Around it, the town's inhabitants lived in distinct areas drawn and ordered by tribal designations. Members of the all-important Quraysh of Mecca gathered along streets near the middle of the town while the minor clan of the Bani Amr clustered in a narrow alley on a distant edge. As a result, Kufa quickly evolved into an uneven parquet of separate tribal districts, each possessing its own mosque, its own cemetery, and its own gates. The city so copied Arabia in the physical sense that the doors of many of the new houses had traveled northward from the old houses in Medina. Most important of all, Kufa culturally moved to the rhythm of the classical Arabic poetry that sounded the cadence of tribal pride.

The Islamic state reinforced these tribal identities by creating a postconquest elite composed of Islam's original soldiers and their descendants, who lived on stipends paid from Medina. Even more, the Koran's emphasis on a tribal ethos, built on solidarity, joint responsibility, and defense against outsiders, guaranteed, in the short term, the survival of tribal society as it had existed on the leached arid deserts of Arabia. Consequently in the new garrison towns, it meant more socially, politically, and economically to be an Arab than a Muslim. In those early years even conversion to Islam remained the prerogative of Arabs. A non-Arab could become a Muslim with full rights within the Islamic state only by associating himself as a client of a Muslim Arab tribe. Still these *mawali*, or non-Arab Muslims, remained socially inferior to the pure Arab members of Islam's tribe. Yet the Arabs soon found it impossible to restrict religious conversions. Nor could they forever man the line between Arab and non-Arab in an empire built on Islam that preached the equality of all believers.

When the third caliph, Uthman, was murdered in 661 by Muslims shut out of the old order of Arab society that had reasserted itself since the death of the Muhammad, the heirs of the Prophet sitting in the capital of Medina faced the daunting challenge of holding the newly won empire together.[18] Despite the large numbers of

---

[18] See chapter 2.

non-Arabs now within the borders of the Islamic Empire, the men of Medina held firm to the principle of upholding Arab superiority over the increasing numbers of non-Arab converts. Attempting to balance the theological call to brotherhood with the political mandate for Arab dominance, the caliphate, the real and symbolic center of the *ummah*, the community of the faithful, passed into the hands of Ali, Muhammad's son-in-law and the favorite of many dissidents. After a turbulent era in which competing claims to the caliphate did battle, the house of Umayyad, a family within the Quraysh, firmly grasped the reins of the Islamic state.[19] The capital of Islam shifted from Medina north to Damascus, once at the heart of the Christian Byzantine Empire. In the move, Arabia lost its political primacy in the Islamic nation, although Mecca and Medina would forever retain their sacred rank for all Muslims. For twenty years, Muawiyah, the Umayyad caliph, ruled over the tribe of Islam in a style reminiscent of an Arab sheikh.

But as the empire continued to expand into non-Arab lands, the Umayyad caliphs that followed Muawiyah left behind the model of the sheikh legitimized by the respect of his peers. Becoming more like autocratic kings, the Umayyads began designating the caliph through heredity, ending forever any formal intervention on the part of the Arab notables of Medina. As these successors to Muhammad's secular authority grew ever more intoxicated by power unknown in Arabia at the time of the Prophet, the Umayyads feasted on the fruits of the empire. In lavish palaces scattered on the desert south of Damascus, they savored the pleasures of the flesh in rooms decorated with the figures of dancing girls and watched their bodyguards sport by hacking to death captives of the Muslim conquest. Even more significant to their future as the rulers of Islam, the Umayyads steadfastly refused to integrate and assimilate non-Arab Muslims into the power structure of the Islamic Empire. In the heartland of the Fertile Crescent, defended geographically against the cultural currents east of the Tigris, Arab dominance remained largely unchallenged. But in Mesopotamia by the middle of the eighth century, an Islamic society, as opposed to a purely Arab society, had begun to emerge. Even the garrison city of Kufa no longer tended the fantasy that it was, or ever had been, purely Arab.

---

[19] See chapter 2 for the schism in Islam that occurred in 680.

At the city's founding, four thousand Persian survivors of Qadisiyah, along with captive Persian women and children, had streamed into Kufa with the Arab manpower of Islam's army. Almost immediately, Arab soldiers deprived of sufficient numbers of Arab women broke the sacred boundaries of tribe to marry Jews and Christians of the Sawad. Those unwilling to soil their tribal genealogies with alien blood simply settled for non-Arab concubines. Later Shuways ibn Jabbash, a veteran of the conquest of the region around Maysan, candidly admitted the sexual liaison between Arab men and non-Arab women: "I took a slave-girl captive and had intercourse with her for a while until we received the letter of [the caliph] Umar, 'consider the captives of Maysan which you have and release them.' So I sent [her] back pregnant or not. Indeed, I fear that there are men and women in Maysan descended from me."[20]

By the second generation after the conquest, many of those within Kufa's population actually flaunted their mixed parentage by speaking the language of their mothers as well as the Arabic of their fathers. Although the pure Arabs indigenous to the peninsula struggled to preserve the patrilineal genealogies that constituted the framework of Bedouin society, tribal identities nonetheless faded when the stipends distributed to the heirs of Islam's original Arab army ended. By then, non-Arabs had settled in Kufa in such numbers that it had come to resemble an ordinary city where the children of the conquered knelt in communal prayer beside the children of the conquerors. Outside the garrison towns, nomadic Arabs that had come north after the conquest embraced the fertile land bequeathed by the Tigris and the Euphrates. Surrendering their nomadic ways, they settled among the Aramaean peasants.

In time, all Arabs learned to live a little less like Bedouin and a bit more like Mesopotamians and Persians. Numbers of Arabs whose grandfathers had ridden into Mesopotamia on the backs of camels had grown rich on the commerce of empire. As a symbol of status, members of this new merchant class assumed the trappings of the fallen Persian aristocracy. The prosperous merchant maintained a great household run by slaves and servants. He employed men to clear the way before him when he rode on horseback and assigned a retinue of women of lower status to escort his wives and daughters

---

[20] Morony, *Iraq after the Muslim Conquest*, pp. 237–238.

through the streets. He adopted Persian dining customs and ate the elegant dishes of Persian cuisine. Far removed from the simple robe and *gutra*, the ageless head cloth in which the Arabs had arrived in Mesopotamia, he wore perfumed linen and silk Persian robes inset with long wide sleeves, all crowned with a tall pointed hat.

Here was evidence enough that the Bedouin traditions imposed on Mesopotamia at the time of the Islamic invasion simply could not endure against the traditions of ancient civilizations embedded along the Tigris and Euphrates. At the same time, the almost universal adoption of Arab culture and religion encased in the Arabic language had altered Mesopotamia forever. Thus, rather than simply holding onto their own values and way of life, the Arabs and non-Arabs, the conqueror and the conquered of Mesopotamia, created a complex culture that transformed the people into a rich, multiethnic mix that spoke Arabic and predominantly accepted Islam while still tending many traditions as ancient as civilized man himself. As Muslims, they began to expect Islam to reflect a culture composed of law, learning, etiquette, and public order based on the eclecticism of the empire rather than the narrow perspective and traditions of the Arabian Peninsula.

Those who ascribed to Islam rather than Arabism grew ever more restive under the Umayyads and their Arab rule centered in Damascus. When Mesopotamia rumbled with revolt in 694, the caliph sent al-Hajjaj bin Yusuf to restore order. On arrival in Kufa, the notoriously ruthless al-Hajjaj ripped a page from the book of the Assyrians. Summoning the population, he warned, "O people of Iraq, O people of discord and hypocrisy. You have been swift to sedition; you have lain in the lairs of error and have made a rule of transgression. By God, I shall strip you like bark, I shall truss you like a bundle of twigs; I shall beat you like stray camels. By God, what I promise, I fulfill; what I purpose, I accomplish; what I measure, I cut off."[21] Although the brutal al-Hajjaj succeeded in imposing order on Mesopotamia, he failed to achieve peace. The Muslims between the two rivers joined Muslims elsewhere in the Islamic Empire in support of new leadership. They found it in the Prophet's cousin Abd-Allah ibn Abbas.

---

[21] Quoted in Judith Miller and Laurie Mylroie, *Saddam Hussein and the Crisis in the Gulf* (New York: Times Books, 1990), pp. 62–63.

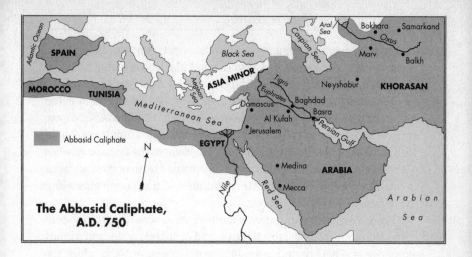

The Abbasid Caliphate,
A.D. 750

Although the Abbas branch of Muhammad's family and its supporters gathered in Kufa to challenge for the caliphate, the festering dissent against the Umayyads exploded in Khorasan in what is now eastern Iran. All across the Islamic Empire, the black banner of the Abbasids rose against the white banner of the Umayyads. In January 750, on a tributary of the Tigris, the supporters of the Abbasids destroyed twelve thousand Umayyad troops. The fourteenth Umayyad caliph, Marwan II, fled into Egypt. Caught hiding in a Christian church, he was decapitated. His severed head was passed to Kufa, where the Abbasids proclaimed themselves the new leaders of the Islamic Empire. In their victory, they not only overthrew a dynasty wedded to Arabism but also set the stage for a truly Islamic civilization. It played out in ethnically and religiously diverse Mesopotamia, at the crossroad where Semitic culture mingled with the intellectual legacy of Persia.

The Abbasids, anchored in the eastern Islamic Empire, took on the trappings of the Sassanians. Even a location for the new capital of Islam was sought near the site of the Sassanian capital of Ctesiphon. Thus, it was in 750 that Jafar al-Mansur, the caliph affirmed by the Abbasids, stood on a spot overlooking the legendary Tigris where so many empires had been born and died. Imagining the new capital as an elaborately walled fortress in the form of a perfect circle, he ordered hundreds of laborers to dig a shallow trench along the proposed circumference and to fill it with a mixture of oil and cotton seeds. At his signal, a torch touched the trench. In the ensuing blaze that satisfied the caliph's vision, al-Mansur ordered the construction of Baghdad to begin. It rose not as a reborn Ctesiphon but like a resurrected Babylon. The enormous palace of the caliph occupied the geographic center of the new city. From there, mosques, markets, and dwellings radiated outward to meet four grand gates opening onto broad roads that ran across the Islamic Empire. Over them, caravans of camels combined with flotillas of boats on the Tigris carried trade to the farthest reaches of the Muslim state. Back along the same routes from northwest India to the Atlantic coast of North Africa, tribute and taxation fed back into the treasure houses of Baghdad.

The urban environment of Islam's capital encased a magnificent court characterized by its rich robes, elaborate etiquette, and a court executioner. This bore no resemblance to the simplicity in which the first caliph had governed from the austerity of Medina. Although they still bowed to their role as heirs of Muhammad by wrapping themselves on appropriate occasions in a simple wool cloak allegedly worn by the Prophet, the Abbasid caliphs owed nothing to Arabia except religion and language. Nor did they feel bound to make any effective distinction between the old Arab families of Kufa and the new Muslims, the *mawali*, who belonged to the conquered population. Instead, the Abbasids presided over a glittering society that embraced the *ulama*, the custodians of Islamic law and tradition; Arab tribesmen; Persian landlords; the descendants of the Sumerians, Assyrians, and Babylonians; the heirs of Hellenism; and the captives of the Sassanians. Although wealth in the name of religious devotion had turned a barren spot on the Tigris into a magnificent collage of mosques, palaces, pavilions, and gardens, Baghdad's real glory radiated from the intellectual vigor that blended the learning of the Persians, Greeks, Romans, and Byzantines into the language of the Arabs. This was the Islamic Empire at its zenith. By wresting Islam from the austere and ardent Arab warriors and wedding it to the rich culture of Persia, the Abbasids from their magnificent capital of Baghdad once more bestowed on Mesopotamia a brilliant civilization.

THE LONG, often splendid span of history reaching from the Sumerians through the Abbasids seems to contain all the elements necessary to implant in contemporary Iraqis a deep sense of themselves as heirs of two great civilizations—one Mesopotamian, one

Islamic. But neither Mesopotamia nor Islam provides a common identity on which the Iraqis have been able to build a nation. Rather Mesopotamia's ancient past tends to serve in varying ways the interests of groups rather than the strength of the Iraqi state.

Inside Iraq, the regime of Saddam Hussein manufactures plastic images of Sumer, Assyria, and Babylon to promote its own political repression. Elsewhere the flame of Mesopotamia is tended by those who have migrated or fled Iraq. At the sad little Kufa gallery on Westbourne Grove in London, just around the corner from the Bayswater tube stop, Iraqi expatriates, mostly from the south, gather on Wednesday evenings to hear such programs as "Tales from Ancient Sumer" or wander in and out during weekdays to view rotating art exhibits. In May 1999, the Kufa mounted a one-man show by the noted Iraqi artist Faisel Laibi Sahi entitled, "O' My Country, O' Mesopotamia." Several months later, I sat in the nearly empty exhibition room talking to the artist, a man of striking good looks with a mane of silver-gray hair. I asked him to explain the title of the show. He pondered a moment before he responded: "It was to draw people into thinking about Iraq in its true light. To explain the suffering of the Iraqi people that began with Gilgamesh."[22]

The only thing this group of displaced Iraqis shares with Saddam Hussein's regime is the ghost of Mesopotamia. It is a unique bond, for outside the scattered dreamers and official discourse mouthed from Baghdad, the glory that was Mesopotamia hovers on the outer fringes of identity for most Iraqis. This irony—the absence of consciousness about a past that is so profoundly important to many of the world's civilizations—is due in part to how little was known about Mesopotamia until the late nineteenth century, when European scholars and adventurers began to unearth the ruins of Ur, Babylon, and Nineveh. Little physical evidence of the ancient Mesopotamian past remains within Iraq's borders. In contrast to the dramatic stone ruins of the Persian Empire's capital of Persepolis in Iran or the mammoth monuments of ancient Egypt, the towering ziggurats raised by the Sumerians, Akkadians, and Babylonians were constructed of mud bricks dried in the hot sun. Over the centuries, almost all have crumbled to dust. The stone edifices of Nineveh and Nimrud, capitals of Assyria, were dismantled for building material by the locals and

---

[22] Interview with author, London, October 9, 1999.

stripped of their magnificent sculptures by Europeans. Babylon, the most intact site of Mesopotamia, is a re-created stage set. But it is not this physical void that makes the essential statement about the Iraqi nation. It is its replication in the Iraqi psyche.

Mesopotamia simply does not vibrate in the soul of Iraqis the way the ancient past resonates within the heirs of the other great ancient civilizations to the west and east. Through Egypt's long history that encompasses everything from the reign of Ramses II to the Arab nationalism of Gamal Abdul Nasser, the Egyptians along the Nile have never lost sight of their ancient past. As a result, they see themselves as uniquely Egyptian, as much a part of the Mediterranean as the Arab world. To the east of Iraq, the Iranians, who claim a continuous history of 2,500 years, so closely identify with their Persian past that some of the causes of the 1979 revolution took root in the expectation of leadership established by Cyrus the Great in the fourth century B.C. Despite turbulent political histories in both of these societies, the Egyptians and the Iranians know who they are. And it is this clear and almost universal sense of identity that undergirds the deep and emotional nationalism that characterizes both countries.

The Iraqis are different. According to Dr. Sami Zubaida of London's Birbeck College, "Visions of Mesopotamia are not important to Iraqis. It is nothing but official discourse. For the people, Mesopotamia is a dead issue."[23] This leaves hanging the question of why the Iraqis share so little genuine sense of an ancient past, of continuity, of common identity. The answer is that few Iraqis see themselves as descendants of the Mesopotamians for the most basic and simple of reasons—their ancestors never lived in the land between the rivers. They are the people of the high mountains of the north. They are groups from Central Asia who came through immigration and persecution. Most of all, they are the products of the Islamic conquest and the tribal migrations out of the Arabian Peninsula that laid the Arabic language and culture on what had once been Mesopotamia. Nevertheless, Iraqis find no commonality in their cultural legacy that came out of the Islamic Empire.

The overwhelming majority of the population of Iraq defines itself as Arab through the Arabic language. And almost all of these Arabs

[23] Interview with author, London, October 5, 1999.

are Muslims. But they adhere to two forms of Islam—orthodox Sunni Islam and dissenting Shia Islam, each of which claims its own distinct identity. As a result, the Arabs, inextricably bound together by language, are segregated theologically, socially, and politically. Other fissures opened when imperial Britain created the state of Iraq by welding the non-Arab Kurds to the Arab population of Mesopotamia. Today Arabs and non-Arabs, Sunni and Shia, circle each other as separate and distinct planets within a galaxy known as Iraq.

2

THE HUMAN MOSAIC
OF IRAQ

The Petra is a small, unimposing hotel located on Baghdad's Sadoun street just beyond the shadow of the stone spire of an Armenian Orthodox Church. In the tired lobby with a decor dating to the 1970s, a small, middle-aged Assyrian Christian manned the worn reception desk. His younger assistant who pulled room keys for guests, the fair-haired woman operating an antiquated switchboard, the men waiting tables in the unadorned restaurant, and the cook grilling kabobs over an open fire were all Assyrians. The clientele that drifted in during one afternoon when I sat in a sagging chair near the front door represented Iraq's multifaceted society.

The nook at the far end of the small lobby was occupied by two wide-girthed men in nondescript Western suits with almost identical molded plastic briefcases between their feet. By their dress and demeanor, they were Baghdadis out of the Arab Sunni establishment, engaged in the Arab art form of bargaining. They had yet to seal the deal when a stately sheikh draped in a snow-white *gutra* and dark-brown *bisht*, or cloak, swept through the outside door. His retinue followed, clothed in a hodgepodge of worn suit jackets and mismatched pants. Each man took his seat at a low table while the sheikh instructed the groveling waiter to bring tea and pastries. Then he took his place, which by his very presence became the head of what was a round table. To the left, a young man, wearing the ubiquitous rubber-thong sandals of the lower-class urban Shia, moved his mop back and forth over the marble floor. He was small and thin, the lower-class product of the slums. Just as he raised his foot to push his bucket forward, I became aware that someone was watching me with the same level of interest that I was watching everyone else. To my right, a weather-beaten Kurd garbed in traditional baggy pants lounged on a broken-down brown vinyl sofa. Seeming to have nothing to do and nowhere to go, he lay on his right side with his legs curled up under him, smoking the stub of a cigarette. In that hotel lobby, the staff, the businessmen, the sheikh, the laborer, and the tribal Kurd created the collage of Iraq where religious, tribal, ethnic, regional, and class identification compete against the very concept of the state.

Every society in the Middle East is fragmented by family, tribe, region, and religion. Even so, each somehow radiates its own particular character. The Saudis proudly bear their Bedouin heritage. The Egyptians carry a sense of themselves as descendants of the pharoahs under a comfortable coat woven of Islam. Jordan's majority Palestinian population largely accepts the reality that they are also Jordanians who hold a stake in the future of the country. Syrians, particularly bedeviled by fragmentation, somehow hold a level of commonality that comes through an appreciation of Damascus as one of the historical pivots of the Arab world. Iraq is different in the degree to which the state has been able to surmount, contain, or repress the diversity of cultures and ethnicities that have so complicated the Iraqis' quest for a national identity. Sunni and Shia Arabs, Kurds, Turkish-speaking Turkomans, Persians, indigenous and immigrant Assyrians, Chaldean Christians claiming to be the descendants of the ancient Mesopotamians, Armenians from west of the Caspian Sea, and a truncated throng of other ethnicities and faiths all express their own separate identity while subscribing, in differing degrees, to an identity acknowledged as distinctly Iraqi.

Despite the number of pieces in the human mosaic of Iraq, the population is overwhelmingly Arab by language and culture. On one level, Arab society expresses the strong tradition of urbanization between the Tigris and Euphrates since the time of Ur and re-enforced by hundreds of years of rule by the Islamic and Ottoman Empires. On another level, it replays the tribalism of the Arabian Peninsula that arrived with the Islamic conquest. On still another level, Arab society breaks along a line drawn by Islam's great schism of the late seventh century that severed the dissenting Shia from the orthodox Sunnis. Weighed against both are the Kurds who possess their own language, culture, and identity. But they are no more a monolith than the Arabs. Divided by dialect, they are the sons and daughters of the high mountains of the north organized around a tribal leader. And they are the children of the cities committed to their own leaders chosen by political ideology or personal charisma. Together Arabs and Kurds claim over 95 percent of Iraq's population.

Jammed into the boundaries of a state smaller than Texas, this mix of ethnicities, languages, tribes, two strands of Islam, multiple sects of Christianity, and a collection of religions singular to themselves could be the description of a rich multicultural society. But over Iraq's eight decades as a state, the population has developed only the most vague sense of national identity. Instead, this collection of distinct communities simply competes from one generation to the next for the right to define a state that lives in the milieu, if not the soul, of Arab culture.

PERHAPS 3 PERCENT of the population of Muslim Iraq is Christian. Some are leftovers from the age of the Byzantine Empire when Christianity dominated Mesopotamia. Others have been swept down the historic routes of migration west of the Caspian Sea. Whatever their origins, the often highly educated Christians are an inescapable presence on the Iraqi landscape. The fortress-like walls of St. Behnam's monastery have stood on a hill outside Mosul since the thirteenth century, when a group of Assyrian Orthodox moved into Iraq from northern Syria. The steeple of the Church of the Virgin Mary that rises above eastern Baghdad serves the descendants of the Armenians who in 1915 escaped massacre at the hands of the Turks. The Church of Mary Mother of Sorrows near Baghdad's Wathbah square has housed the Chaldeans since 1898. Once Eastern Orthodox, the Chaldeans returned to the Roman Church in 1552. Today they are the largest Christian group in the country. The National Protestant Evangelical Church, a product of the missionary zeal of the American Presbyterian Church in the late nineteenth century, is probably the smallest. Every Friday evening, its sole congregation in Baghdad rises before an electronic keyboard set at maximum volume to belt out the old American hymn "There is power, power, wonder working power in the precious blood of the Lamb."

Still other religious as well as ethnic minorities dot the demographic landscape. A tiny remnant of Jews left over from Iraq's large vibrant Jewish community that was destroyed in the aftermath of the 1948 war for Palestine hangs on in Baghdad. The Yazidi, the "devil worshippers," live in exclusive close-knit communities around Jebel

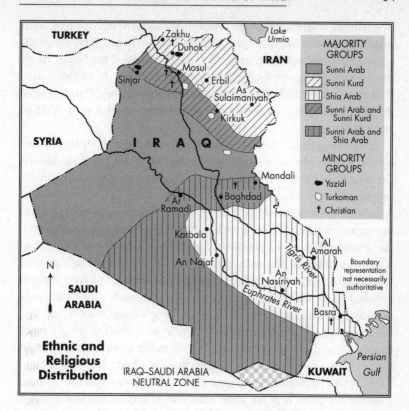

Ethnic and Religious Distribution

Sinjar.[1] Those remaining of the Persians who once dominated the religious schools and commerce of Najaf and Karbala still live in the south. The Turkomans, Turkish-speaking people exhibiting pronounced Mongolian features, are a significant presence in the oil-rich region of Kirkuk. And then there are the Kurds, roughly 20 percent of Iraq's population.

A LITTLE MORE than a hundred and fifty miles north of Baghdad the dusty, scrub-dotted plain gradually gives way to rolling rocky hills dabbed with green. At Kirkuk, the road that leads eastward climbs steadily through small fields marked off by stone fences and past an

---

[1] The Yazidi follow a synchronistic faith incorporating elements of Zoroastrianism, Judaism, Christianity, and Islam. They are inappropriately called devil worshippers because they include Satan in their pantheon of spiritual beings.

occasional settlement of flat-roofed houses. Worn women, their heads covered in brightly hued scarves hung with tiny jangling coins, tend cook fires and wash tubs. At Sulaimaniyah, all the major roads dwindle into the majestic Zagros Mountains. From the protection of those rugged peaks and deep gorges, oak forests, and fern thickets, the Kurds trumpet their distinctive nationalism and defiantly demand their autonomy.

Posed against the mountains clothed in their traditional garments, the Kurds are a stunning people. Although small in stature, the Kurdish male becomes a giant in his tasseled turban called a *mishki*; his *sharwal*, baggy trousers constructed of narrow strips of hand woven wool sewn together; and *mrakhani*, a short jacket under which is worn a cummerbund of every color and pattern. Into the cummerbund is invariably stuck the dagger that proclaims Kurdish manhood. These tough, hardy warriors who fought against Baghdad through most of the twentieth century, are often draped in crossed bandoleers heavy with cartridges. Kurdish women are only slightly less dramatic. As a hostess serving a guest thickly sugared tea from a brass samovar, a Kurdish woman will often wear a long, loose-fitting dress of purple, pink, yellow, or a combination of all three colors, over which is hung intricately worked silver jewelry and a shawl woven in some bold pattern. The Kurds are said to feel such passion for color that a bandit who was asked for his last request before execution replied, "I should like to be hanged with a red-and-green rope."[2]

There is a mystique about the Kurds that comes in part from the puzzle surrounding their origins. Claiming no ancient religious texts and possessing only scraps of written history, they have been left to search out their roots in mythology. One such myth traces Kurdish descent from four hundred virgins raped by devils on their way to King Solomon's court. Another weaves an elaborate tale around a giant mythological tyrant named Zohhak who usurped the fictitious throne of ancient Persia. A terrifying creature with snakes growing out of his shoulders, he demanded from his subjects a daily meal of brains taken from young humans. Day by day, the number of adolescents among his vassals dropped, threatening the eventual annihilation of a whole people. On a particular day when the king sat at his

---

[2] LeRoy Woodson, "We Who Face Death," *National Geographic* 147 (March 1975): 375.

table, ingenious servants substituted calves brains for those of their children. When the sated unsuspecting king fell into a deep sleep, they gathered the few surviving boys and girls and smuggled them into the mountains. There they begat the children who became the Kurds.

Far less dramatic but infinitely more plausible is the opinion that the Kurds are probably descended from the ancient Medes, an Indo-European tribe that found its way into the mountains of northwestern Iran at an undetermined date. Around the second millennium B.C., what has become Kurdish society began to organize itself in the pockets of the high ranges. Although migrations over many centuries have planted Kurds from the Caucasus to Syria, they remain concentrated in what the Kurds themselves call "Kurdistan." This geographic region that begins in northwestern Iran, arcs across northern Iraq, and reaches into southern Turkey encompasses a people defined more in terms of cultural identity than ethnicity, for the Kurds carry the genes of multiple ethnic groups. Rather than blood, a powerful cultural tradition honed over the centuries gives a Kurd what is a near spiritual identity in which he suffers no existential doubts. I have met with Kurds who have spent thirty years in the mountains as guerrillas fighting for the elusive Kurdistan, and talked with others who have devoted the same amount of time in good jobs in the West, producing money to finance the idealized homeland in which most Kurds invest their faith and honor.

This rabid singularity the Kurds feel as a people comes from the mountains they inhabit. Peaks that reach twelve thousand feet above sea level have always stood as a formidable physical and cultural barrier between the Kurds and the inhabitants of the lowlands. The mountains have also dictated the Kurds' meager, largely self-sufficient economy and their traditional society organized around the village. In villages typically built along a cold rushing stream surrounded by fields, orchards, and a cemetery, the Kurds live in a tight-knit, semifeudal social structure.

Originally Zoroastrians, the Kurds converted to Islam during and after the Islamic conquest. Today some are Sunni, some are Shia, and still others follow a variety of mystical orders within these sects. Although various religious leaders have crossed over to serve as political leaders, religion has never tormented Kurdish unity to the extent that language has.

Across Kurdistan, Kurds speak different dialects of an

Indo-European language related to Persian. At least two of these dialects are heard in Iraqi Kurdistan—Kurmanji, belonging to the tribes of the deep mountains, and Sorani, spoken by the more urbanized Kurds who live in the eastern and southern reaches of the Kurdish arc. Each carries its own social connotation. To the Kurmanji speaker, he is the true Kurd, the unsullied son of the mountains. With equal arrogance, a Sorani speaker believes with every fiber of his being that he is more educated and certainly more cultured than the largely tribal Kurmanji speakers. Each is quick to characterize the other as "the effete of the city" or "the primitive tribesmen who live by the gun." Thus, dialect draws the major battle line through what has been a savage arena of inter-Kurdish politics.

Organized along tribal lines that follow geographic area more than relationship to a common ancestor, the Kurds lived for centuries under their *agha*, the authority figure chosen by heredity or election from a major landowning family. As many Kurds have drifted out of the mountains over the last decades to settle in the cities, tribe often has become a political group led by a charismatic ideologue who voices the issues and grievances of followers unrelated by either blood or locality. In spite of the pressures of modernization that have eroded the position of the *aghas* and increased the power of political and ideological leaders, Kurdish society remains intensely tribal, pitting the highlanders against the lowlanders, both of whom in turn wage their own internal wars. As a constant in Kurdish life, this tribalism engenders bitter rivalries that fracture Kurdish society and bleed Kurdish political power. In this century, including the years following the Gulf War, a Kurdish leader has risen from time to time to claim autonomy for the Kurds. And time after time, competing leaders from rival groups play the spoiler by making deals in exchange for cash, trade concessions, or local influence with the very government against which the Kurds, as a people, are rebelling. As a result, the Kurds have consistently proved strong enough to challenge central authority but too weak to sustain autonomy or to win their own homeland. Instead, the Kurds wail the old lament about their lot: "a thousand sighs, a thousand tears, a thousand revolts, a thousand hopes."

The irony of the Kurds in Iraq is that despite a series of rolling revolts against Baghdad, they have never been totally alienated from the Iraqi state. Many Kurds, in fact, have played significant roles in government and society. But the relationship has never been easy for either the Kurds or the other Iraqis because the Kurds trust no one. And almost all subscribe to the Kurdish saying, "Level the mountains, and in a day the Kurds would be no more." Like most widely accepted maxims, it bears an element of truth. Kurds who have settled in the cities to the south of the high peaks usually have found their Kurdish identity muted. Nonetheless, all Kurds to one degree or another emotionally cling to the mountains and the Kurdish adage, "To a Kurd the mountain is no less than the embodiment of the deity; mountain is his mother, his refuge, his protector, his home, his farm, his market, his mate . . . and his only friend."[3] Consequently, the mountains, the womb, cradle, and home of a passionate and powerful cultural nationalism, have made the Kurds, of all the groups in Iraq, the most difficult to assimilate into what is an overwhelmingly Arab society.

AT THE DAWN of history, the almost empty region between the Persian Gulf and the Red Sea functioned as a vast junction where migrating people coming out of Africa and other pockets of human development mingled and merged into a people known as Semites. By 3000 B.C., waves of these Semites had settled in the flat fertile lands between the Tigris and Euphrates Rivers. Others found their way to the Nile, where they merged into the great Egyptian civilization of the pharaohs. The Semitic Canaanites, Phoenicians, Nabataeans, Amorites, and Hebrews followed later, making their way into the Levant, the coastal area along the eastern end of the Mediterranean. But most stayed behind on the wide barren peninsula to become Arabs imbued with the values of the Bedouin.

The next great migration out of the Arabian Peninsula came in the seventh century A.D. when Arabs aflame with the new faith of Islam conquered an empire. Over time, the conquerors and the conquered melded inside the boundaries of the Arabic language that above ethnicity or religion determines Arab identity. Within that identity, not only have Bedouin values survived but also the Bedouin himself, that arrogant son of the desert, still reigns in the Arab mind as the legendary knight of Arab culture. Even today when old men sit around a campfire and young men gather over coffee to tell legendary tales

---

[3] Michael M. Gunter, *The Kurds of Iraq: Tragedy and Hope* (New York: St. Martin's Press, 1992), p. 35.

of courage and generosity, "it [is] never of the two-horned Alexander the Great that they [speak] of, nor of the Caliph who . . . ruled in splendor in Baghdad, but of tattered herdsmen in the deserts of Arabia."[4]

Nowhere beyond the Arabian Peninsula has the Bedouin mystique played more into the character of a state than Iraq. The reason springs from the final phase of large-scale migrations out of Arabia between the seventeenth and the late nineteenth centuries that poured Arab tribes into the Tigris-Euphrates valley.[5] Because they came as pure Bedouin, bearing their genealogies and their way of life, they have fed much of the political disorder that has been a hallmark of the Iraqi state.

The Arab tribesman unsoiled by urban life is still part of the Iraqi landscape. On the desert north and west of Samarra in the last month of the twentieth century, I encountered a tall proud man with skin the hue and texture of leather. He stood outside his home—a cement-block room with an attached lean-to fashioned from a scrap of tent woven of black goat hair. Wrapped against the winter cold, he wore heavy socks on his sandaled feet and a stretched and faded sweat suit, over which was draped the heavy sheep-lined brown cloak that has warmed the Bedouin forever. He was surrounded by his flock of barefoot children who seemed oblivious to the temperature. Behind him, his wife hung in the doorway of the one-room house. Her head was covered with a once white scarf that accentuated the blue tattoos around her mouth, which by their pattern designated her tribe. Except for the small television set operating on stolen electrical power and the absence of the long, open-fronted communal tent, the scene was not much different from those I had experienced among the Bedouin on the deserts of the Arabian Peninsula. This man's pride of genealogy and his sense of who he is reflect an age-old identification with tribe.

Tribalism on the Arabian Peninsula resulted from an environment capable of providing nothing beyond bare subsistence. On the harsh baked desert of early Arabia, the absence of surplus food to feed a leader and a handful of men capable of enforcing his rule doomed the development of even the most rudimentary form of gov-

---

[4] Wilfred Thesiger, *The Marsh Arabs* (London: Longmans Press, 1964), p. 93.
[5] See chapter 3.

ernment. With no government, no force existed to police cooperation among the Bedouin and no ruler acted as arbitrator of competing claims on sparse, life-giving water and pasture. Therefore,
survival for anyone depended on membership in a tight cohesive unit
bound by ties of blood.

From the dawn of their society, the Bedouin organized around
the patrilineal family defined by a common male ancestor. Locked
together in steadfast fidelity and sacred obligation, the family, like
a fort, gathered its members within walls laid along exact bloodlines. Together, father and son, brother and brother, cousin and
cousin wandered in search of pasture, camped as a coterie, practiced group marriage, and perpetuated the bonds of kinship. Within
this tightly knit group, each member internalized, as the supreme
and unquestioned value of life, a commitment to group integrity
and the assumption of mutual responsibility. In small social units
in which every person knew every other person, in which all were
related by blood, or at least by a fiction of common descent, the
imperative of family assumed the aura of the sacred. Pressures to
conform, to uphold the collective good, and to live by the unwritten
but universally recognized moral code of the group bound every
member. Cohesion held because every individual recognized that
without the support and protection of the kin group, he would be
lost. Little has changed. The family remains "the alpha and omega
of the whole system; . . . the indissoluble atom of society which
assigns and assures to each of its members his place, his function,
his very reason for existence and, to a certain degree, his existence
itself."[6]

In early Arabia, families bought additional protection by joining
together in clans that grafted themselves onto tribes formed through
links of common blood.[7] Although important in expanding the pool
of marriage partners, the ultimate function of the tribe was the same
as that of the family—to supply the crucial protection that members
needed to survive. Without any political structure capable of enforcing equitable distribution of the desert's meager and finite vegetation, water, and livestock, a tribe claimed for itself exclusive right to

[6] Pierre Bourdieu, quoted in David Pryce-Jones, *The Closed Circle: An
Interpretation of the Arabs* (New York: Harper Perennial, 1991), p. 27.
[7] An entire tribe, even if numbering thousands, considered itself the offspring of one
single mythical ancestor.

the grazing lands and wells within an area it could defend. Faced with starvation, rival tribes swept down on the controlling tribe to free a water hole or drive off random livestock. In this game of life and death, the only way to survive "was by letting others know that if they violated you in any way, you would make them pay and pay dearly . . . in a manner that signaled to all other families, clans, or tribes around that this is what happens if anyone tampers with me . . . 'I am my own defense and I am good.' "[8]

In the ebb and flow of dominance, any group's security depended on numbers. Marriage between cousins was prized because it kept the offspring of such a union within the kinship group, and divorce ranked as a communal concern because it destroyed alliances within and between families seeking marginal advantage in the struggle to survive. With numbers so crucial, the death of one man at the hands of a rival tribe required killing a member of the offending group to once more even out the relative numbers. Thus developed the vengeful cry of "blood demands blood." They were words that called every male member of the victim's kin group, the *khamsa*, to wreak revenge in the name of the whole. Ignoring the wear of time, the demand for vengeance passed from year to year, generation to generation.

In return for this corporate protection, members of the tribe surrendered their allegiance to a leader charged with defending the whole against threats from outside the walls of the tribe. He was the *sheikh*, the community's term for whoever currently fulfilled the traditional responsibilities of leadership, including mediation of disputes within the tribe. Often the title was contested, "for the question of who was sheikh was tied to the issue of which descent group was equal to another, where the cleavages between groups should be and what their proper ranking was, as well as the personal history and reputation of a man who would be sheikh."[9] Since the title of sheikh was bestowed by consensus within the group, not wrested from it by overwhelming power or simple heredity, the traditional sheikh held his position only through a deep understanding of tribal mores combined with infinite tact and judgment. Instantly identifiable by the *bisht*,

---

[8] Thomas L. Friedman, *From Beirut to Jerusalem* (New York: Farrar, Straus and Giroux, 1989), p. 88.

[9] Robert A. Fernea, "State and Tribe in Southern Iraq: The Struggle for Hegemony before the 1958 Revolution." In *The Iraq Revolution of 1958: The Old Social Classes Revisited*, ed. Robert A. Fernea and William Roger Louis (London: I.B. Tauris, 1991), p. 145.

the cloak, the sheikh remains the authority figure around whom tribal life functions. In a selection process contaminated for decades by politics and economics, a sheikh can be ignorant and venal, self-serving and corrupt. But if he is a true sheikh by the traditional code of the desert, he is the first among equals, a man of respect more than power. On her first meeting with a well-known sheikh, Elizabeth Warnock Fernea, an American who lived among the tribes of southern Iraq during the late 1950s, had this reaction: "I cannot say exactly what I had expected this man to be like, whose lineage was one of the oldest and purest in southern Arabia and whose position had become synonymous in my world with romance, wanderlust, and mystery. But I didn't expect him to be quite so solid and digni-fied, exuding an air of middle-aged respectability and authority."[10]

Now, as in the past, this whole set of attitudes about family and tribe is sewn into the fabric of Arab societies across the Middle East. The result is that nationalism, whether seen as good or bad, simply does not exist in the sense that an individual feels a strong primary loyalty to his country. Nor do political organizations within a country cross the family or tribal lines on which real power rests to embrace a broad political philosophy or pursue the national interest. As a con-sequence, the great weakness of all Arab states is that the particular interests of family and tribe override any sense of the common good. Iraq is different only in the strength and complexity of tribal affilia-tions. This complexity begins with the fact that tribes are not absolute institutions. Rather they are social amoeba that expand and contract, move up and down in the rankings that separate the superior from the inferior, according to numbers and influence. Who belongs to a tribe and who does not is a state of mind as much as the mythol-ogy of blood or the reality of geography. A man or woman hemmed into the boundaries of a city can be as much a tribesman as some-one at home in the heart of the desert. Once bloodlines are mutually accepted, an individual's embrace of tribe is a matter of self-identity.

Although tribalism as planted in Iraq by the Islamic conquest was originally weakened through its entanglement with the strong urban tradition bequeathed by Mesopotamia and nurtured by the Sassanians, it nevertheless shaped much of the character of the Iraqi

---

[10] Elizabeth Warnock Fernea, *Guests of the Sheikh: An Ethnography of an Iraqi Village* (Garden City, N. Y.: Anchor Books, 1969), p. 99.

state. Courted, resisted, and quelled by every occupying force and every domestic government, tribalism was revived by Saddam Hussein, the coarse son of rural peasants with Bedouin origins, to save his regime after the Gulf War. More than the president of a country, he functions as the leader of an extended tribe that includes his family, his genealogical tribe, his regime, and his political party, all locked together in the interest of status, advantage, and survival. In a sense, Iraq has always been a confederation of great tribes of Muslims and non-Muslims, Arabs and non-Arabs who then segment into subtribes. Within the tribe of the Arabs, the great watershed is religious sect. In their common house of Islam, 60 percent of Iraq's population crowds into the chamber of the Shia and 20 percent gathers in the room of the Sunnis.

ON ANY FRIDAY MORNING, large numbers of people from the mostly Sunni population of Haditha, a town in western Iraq, crowd into the narrow passageways of the souks. Women clutching the hands of their children while managing large striped shopping bags woven from synthetic fiber jostle for position in front of straw baskets displaying an array of pungent spices. Pointing to cardamom and tamarind, they begin the verbal sparring with the vendor that will set the ultimate price. Farther into the maze of commerce, men dexterously fingering amber prayer beads contemplate sandals piled on a rickety stand and shiny velvet prayer rugs stacked on the ground. Some are lookers, others buyers. When the call for noon prayer sounds, everyone exits the souk past a plain, squat, flat-roofed mosque constructed of cement block covered in dust-stained stucco. It could be a scene from almost any Arab country in the Middle East.

The Sunni Arabs are perhaps the least distinct and the least cohesive group in Iraq. In the "Sunni triangle" of central Iraq that begins at the border of Iran northeast of Baghdad and fans out westward to the border of Syria, there are tribal Sunnis who live on the broad expanse of desert flowing into the eastern border of Syria and peasant Sunnis who farm the river valleys north, south, and west of Baghdad. But until the regime of Saddam Hussein, Sunni power resided within the urban classes that concentrated in the capital. In contrast to the tribesmen who lay claim to precise genealogies that supposedly certify pure Arab blood, the lineage of the urban and many of the rural Sunnis winds its way through the mix of the ethnic groups who lived in the Tigris-Euphrates valley when Islam arrived. Other branches of that lineage come out of the genetic brew created by urban elements of both the Islamic Empire and the later Ottoman Empire of the Turks.

If the Sunnis have a distinguishing mark, it is the business suit. They always have been the power brokers of politics, the elite within the bureaucratic structure of the state, the international traders, and the professional class. Kurds, Shia Arabs, and Christians have been there also. But it is the Sunnis, through prerogatives bestowed on them by every governing authority since the Islamic invasion, who have operated almost by birthright the levers of power in Iraq. Who actually comprises this elite depends on the timeline drawn by Saddam Hussein. The pre-Hussein elite were urbane people, many of whom now live in exile. I found them in Amman, London, New York, and dozens of other places where they follow events in Iraq with the same regrets and hopes that characterize all exiles. Others from the lower levels of the old establishment are trapped in Iraq, huddled in a decimated middle class laid to waste by war and sanctions. The current elite is composed of the rough country cousins of Hussein attended by members of the urban class who have signed on to his regime. Since the Sunnis—urban and rural, the elite and the masses—have always reigned as the dominant political group, they have never suffered significant group repression or experienced the real fear of annihilation that welds individuals together in the dense solidarity necessary for group survival. Nevertheless, the Iraqi Sunnis see themselves as a distinct community. The comparative weakness of Sunni coherence to that of other groups in Iraq results in part from the fact that within the orthodox tradition of Islam there are no absolute authority figures around whom tight communities form.

After the death of Muhammad, the leaders of Islam preserved and propagated the faith by memorizing and reciting the Koran more like popular preachers than absolute authority figures. Even the first four caliphs, esteemed as the "rightly guided," claimed their position through their relationship with the Prophet. As a whole, they led like tribal sheikhs, the first among equals in the tribe of Islam. The dynasties of the Umayyads and Abbasids began with the caliph reigning much like a king and ended with a series of diminished figures who sat in the ruins of authority. When the last Abbasid caliph died at the hands of the Mongols in the thirteenth century, the Sunni community lost even a figurehead of authority. Instead, preeminence in Islam rested with the *ulama*, the religious scholars who as individuals won their position through their ability to interpret the collected body of traditional religious writings. Although the *ulama* exercised, and continue to exercise, great influence within orthodox society, the Sunnis have never bestowed strong religious authority on these scholars and judges who act as their spiritual guides. It is to the Sharia, the law itself, that individuals within the Sunni community owe their devotion. According to the most basic tenet of the sect, no person stands between the believer and God. Thus, when Sunnis gather in the mosque for communal prayer, one man after another lines up row by row behind the most respected among them. Yet this leader of the prayers is superior to the other worshippers only by the measures of age or esteem. In Iraq, the real authority figures for the Sunnis come from outside the formal clergy. For those in the countryside, it is the sheikh of the tribe exercising tribal authority to whom they pledge allegiance. For the urban Sunni, it is often the political leader who attempts to exercise authority over a group of followers attracted sometimes by military power, sometimes by kinship, sometimes by ideology, but always by common interest. Therefore, in the question of faith and the state, the Sunnis of Iraq have been largely secularists. Within this secularism, there is a certain spirituality found in the ideology of Arab nationalism.

Emerging in the dying days of the Ottoman Empire, the concept of Arab nationalism proposes that all Arabs are part of a mythological nation whose boundaries are drawn by Arabic language and culture.[11] As a result, Iraq's Sunni Arabs, particularly those of the cities, have tended to look for definition beyond their own borders. On the grander horizon of the Arab world, they find political concepts, goals, and loyalties to which they, as Arabs, can subscribe. Through the recurring theme of Arab unity, these are often given voice by the charismatic leader of the moment. At the same time, this mythology of Arab unity does battle with the particular interests and sovereignty of each nation. In Iraq more than all other Arab countries, the central question within the body politic has always been and still is, where does Iraq's identity as a state lie—with the idealized Arab nation or with a specific national entity called Iraq? Within this ques-

---

[11] See chapter 3.

tion of identity resides the character and political construct of the Iraqi state. As Arabs who have largely rejected Persian influences from the east, the Sunnis are pulled to the Arab world to the west, where they seek weight for their numbers against Iraq's Shia majority. This majority among the Arabs and within the country stands apart from the Sunnis on everything from doctrine to the source of religious and secular authority, to the nature of government, and to the cultural context within which each community lives.

On the west bank of the Tigris in north central Baghdad, a section of the city called Kadhimiya surrounds the imposing shrine of Kadhimain. Constructed in 1515, the shrine is a massive collection of gold domes, ornamented minarets, and masonry walls inset with thousands upon thousands of blue and turquoise tiles. In its shadow, people stroll along narrow streets, stopping to look in shop windows filled with gaudy necklaces worked in thin 21-karat gold and heavy bangle bracelets crafted of the lesser 18-karat metal. On the other side of the slim storefronts, women draped in the black chador, a bell-shaped garment that falls from the head to encompass the entire female figure, stand before glass-top counters. Depending on the family's current economic situation, they buy or sell jewelry. When they leave, those who have sold likely go toward the shrine. There they rub a hand and place a kiss on the heavy wooden gates set in thick walls before going into a courtyard dotted with the robed officials of Shia Islam.

The Shia are the product of the late-seventh-century clash in Islam that erupted over the issue of who should lead the faith. When Muhammad died in 632 without designating a successor, a group of his contemporaries and early converts took it upon themselves to choose the next leader of the Islamic community. The men of Medina, the products of the tribal culture of the Arabian desert, knew only two models to follow. The first was bloodlines, and the second, tribal consensus. Since the Prophet left no direct male heir, bloodlines proved murky. Muhammad's only living child was Fatima, the wife of the Prophet's cousin and first convert, Ali. Claiming both religious credentials and family ties, Ali seemed the logical choice to don the mantle of the Prophet. Instead, Abu Bakr, Muhammad's closest confident, was named caliph. To prevent a similar dispute on his own death, he designated as his successor, Umar, a member of the Quraysh, the old aristocratic clan of Mecca. Once again Ali was passed over. Refusing to fill any office in the Islamic state, the short,

bald, white-bearded Ali devoted himself to teaching a growing number of disciples. So it was that during the ten-year reign of Umar
(634–644), Ali remained noticeably absent from the great wars of
conquest that the caliph waged in the name of Islam. Nonetheless,
Ali's following continued to grow for reasons beyond political power
and military exploits. His image as a champion of egalitarianism
within the pristine Islam of the Prophet amplified the deep emotional
appeal of his personal attributes—modesty, self-sacrifice, knowledge
of the sacred texts of Islam, and a passion for justice. Yet when a
Persian slave murdered Umar in 644, Uthman, another of
Muhammad's early converts and a member of the Umayyad clan
within the Quraysh, became the third caliph.

The choice of Uthman over Ali agitated the waves of discontent
already rolling within the Muslim community. Dismantling the model
constructed by Muhammad, Islam's leadership had begun to live like
an idle aristocracy on the booty of war flowing in from the Islamic
Empire. In the territories, a second generation of Bedouin warriors
was coming to full manhood as an Arab elite corrupted by the raucous life of the new camp cities. As Uthman took his place at the helm
of Islam, scattered groups of Muslims within the empire protested by
designating themselves as Shia Ali, supporters of Ali. Rejecting the
existing system of choosing the caliph by consensus among the leadership in Medina, they insisted that the leader of Islam must come out
of Muhammad's house, from among his descendants who alone possessed the knowledge and wisdom of the Prophet. In contradiction,
those in the elite of Arabia insisted that any man within the aristocracy of Medina could assume the position of caliph through the
process of consensus among Muhammad's early converts.
Consequently, a little more than a decade after the Prophet's death,
the pieces that would determine the future direction of Islam and create the torment of contemporary Iraq fell into place.

From 644 to 656, Uthman, a handsome man of feeble character,
presided over a foul regime polluted by the economic rewards of the
Islamic conquest. While the reigning lords of Islam amassed wealth,
Ali continued to live in the simple manner in which the Prophet had
lived. Outside the boundaries of political power, he taught his followers that all believers are created equal, that only through virtue is
one Muslim more dear to God than another. Thus, visibly and theologically, Ali counterpoised Muhammad's teachings of equality and

piety against the growing wealth and elitism of Islam's establishment. This strengthening perception of Ali as the upholder of personal and moral virtue against the corrupt and unjust Muslim state began to widen the cleavages within the Islamic community, particularly in Kufa in Mesopotamia. When the dissidents murdered the despised Uthman, Ali, at last, emerged as caliph.

Doom seemed to hang over Ali's caliphate from the beginning. Rejected by the Umayyads and resented by tribal Arabs who detested his widespread following among non-Arabs, Ali, by his very nature, proved incapable of playing the game of power politics. As he labored to establish his authority as caliph, Muawiyah, Ali's Umayyad rival, continued to press to unseat him. Shut out of Medina and Damascus, Ali installed his capital in Kufa. But he never succeeded in establishing himself as the head of the Islamic state. In 661, five years after his troubled caliphate began, Ali exited a Kufa mosque following prayers. In the falling darkness, a waiting assassin struck the unsuspecting caliph across the head with the broad side of a sword. (Ali was killed by a Kharijite, one of a group of tribal Arabs who held that any male believer, regardless of blood, tribe, or class, possessed the right to assume leadership of the Muslim community.) According to religious tradition, the dying Ali asked in a whispered voice to be placed on a camel and laid to rest wherever it knelt. Najaf, now in southern Iraq, became his burial place.

Although followers of Ali persisted in their claim that the caliphate belonged to the House of the Prophet, the Umayyads seized the title and deposited it in their own house. Refusing to relinquish the claim of Muhammad's descendants, Hussein, the grandson of the Prophet, and the second son of Ali, challenged Umayyad power. When warned that his small numbers and simple weapons could not win against the Umayyad's well-manned and well-armed forces, Hussein echoed Ali's dedication to social justice for all Muslims: "O people, the Apostle of God said during his life, 'He who sees an oppressive ruler violating the sanctions of God . . . and does not show zeal against him in word or deed, God would surely cause him to enter his abode in the fire.'"[12]

The Umayyads, now led by Yazid, son of Muawiyah, answered.

---

[12] Quoted in Manocher Dorraj, *From Zarathustra to Khomeini: Populism and Dissent in Iran* (Boulder, Colo.: Lynne Rienner Publishers, 1990), p. 50.

On the second day of October in 680, they met Hussein, his family, and his followers at Karbala on the flat salty plains south of the future site of Baghdad. Hussein's force numbered a meager seventy-two, including women and children. The Umayyad army, employing the famed training and tactics of both the Byzantines and the Sassanians, counted four thousand. Engaging the battle on what is now known as the "Plain of Sorrow and Misfortune," the Umayyads butchered Hussein along with the rest of his companions. His severed head went to Damascus, where Yazid slashed it across the mouth with his cane. In the appalled silence that followed, an old man raised his voice, "Alas that I should have lived to see this day, I who saw those lips kissed by the Prophet of God."[13]

As news of Hussein's death spread, waves of anguish and anger flowed with the blood of the Prophet's grandson. Islam ruptured into its two great branches—the orthodox Sunnis and the breakaway Shia, the followers of Ali and Hussein. While most Muslims stayed within the fold of orthodoxy, communities of Shia put down roots in Mesopotamia.

Shia Iraq begins at the Persian Gulf, follows the Shatt al Arab north to Basra, broadens out over the Tigris-Euphrates valley, and flows north to Baghdad before fading into Samarra. Within this vast area of marsh, desert, town, and city, the Iraqi Shia assume two unequal configurations—the shrunken populations of the shrine cities of Najaf and Karbala who once traced their ancestry to Persian Iran, and the tribes, the linguistic and cultural brothers of the Sunni tribesmen. I once caught the two faces of Shia Islam in Iraq in a rare photograph snapped outside Ali's shrine of Najaf. A cleric swathed in a black turban and black robes so common in Iran stands in studied conversation with a tribal sheikh wearing the traditional *gutra* and *bisht*. One represents the authority of religion; the other, the numbers and power of the Shia tribes.

Over several centuries, the historic conditions and geographic locations in which the Shia sect of Islam developed bred a culture distinctly different from that of the Sunnis. Shia Islam, in everything from theology to architecture to authority, is as complex as Sunnism is simple. In Iraq, these differences have mattered and continue to matter to the most fundamental issue facing the country—who gov-

---

[13] Quoted in Thesiger, *The Marsh Arabs*, p. 43.

erns Iraq under what kind of government? The answer to that question ultimately rests with numbers translated into political power. Although now outnumbering the Sunnis at least three to one, the Shia have not always been the majority.

During the early centuries following Islam's great schism, the Shia remained what they originally were—a small, dissenting sect bobbing on the ocean of orthodox Islam. Until Iran adopted Shiism as the state religion in the sixteenth century, most Shia resided in the Arab world, principally grouping in and around the great Shia shrines at Najaf and Karbala in what is now Iraq. Persecuted by the orthodox Sunni leadership of the Islamic Empire, Shia theologians secreted themselves away in these centers of learning to develop their own particular view of Islamic law and to cultivate the sect's own forms of piety. In this unfolding Shia theology, the Sunni doctrine that the community of believers as a whole is charged with upholding the collection of teachings and interpretations that make up Islamic law was not enough. Rather, the faith, as in the time of Muhammad, required the presence of an authoritative figure possessing the wisdom and knowledge to interpret divine will to the faithful.

In Shiism, the whole question of religious leadership has always been significantly more important than it is in Sunnism. The scholar, the master of Islamic law, is charged with interpreting all moral questions—social, political, and religious—until the return of the Mahdi, the Shia savior figure. Over the centuries, these men of great learning have developed "a profile of a just Shiite figure of authority, however temporary and fallible, who could . . . follow the Quranic mandate of creating a public order that would 'enjoin the good and forbid the evil'."[14]

These clerics, the moral guides of the Shia, are instantly identifiable by a cloak draped over an ankle-length robe, a turban (black for those descended from the Prophet, white for the rest) and an unmistakable air of authority. This is the aristocracy of Shiism, the elite to whom commoners pay obedience. Yet this is the great paradox of Shiism. As part of Islam in which the equality of all believers is so

---

[14] Abdulaziz Abdulhussein Sachedina, "Activist Shi'ism in Iran, Iraq, and Lebanon." In *Fundamentalisms Observed*, ed. Martin E. Marty and R. Scott Appleby (Chicago: University of Chicago Press, 1991), p. 425.

firmly rooted, the Shia follow authoritarian lines that divide those who interpret religious law from those who are qualified only to obey the law. Tradition stretching back to Ali, the fourth heir to the Prophet, determines who in the faith leads and who follows. In what might be called the "church" in Shia Islam, the leaders are a brotherhood of the learned, trained in an ascending order. On the first level, a young man begins the rigorous, "chest to chest" study of Islamic law and Aristotelian logic with one or more teachers, who through their own scholarship have earned their reputations and positions as Islamic scholars. The gifted among these students spend years working their way through the tortuous curriculum that gives a cleric the right to claim the title of *mujtahid*, or "jurist."

The *mujtahid* is not simply a cleric tending a flock of the faithful. He is a potent combination of theologian and judge who, through the process of his own learning, has acquired the ability to interpret all religious, social, and political issues to the Shia community. The *mujtahids* literally man the front lines of issues facing the Shia community.[15] Because the upper levels of the clergy hold their position only with the acclamation of their followers, the hierarchical structure of Shiism is certified by no one. Position and authority depend on a constituency, a group of followers who look to a particular cleric as a model of emulation. Rather than commanding a following, a cleric must attract disciples to him. The greater the number of lower-level clerics and ordinary people who pray behind any given *mujtahid*, the greater his standing and power. But just as every *mujtahid* can issue his own opinion on questions of faith, every believer can select which *mujtahid* he or she accepts as a spiritual guide to whom religious obedience and financial support are owed.

The early clerics of Shiism, acting as theologians of an ever evolving doctrine rather than functioning as lawyers interpreting a static Sharia, kept the sect's basic tenets fresh for an expanding number of converts. When Shia Islam became the state religion of Iran in

---

[15] *Mujtahid* is both a specific and a general term. Specifically it means an Islamic jurist on the lower rungs of the clerical hierarchy. Generally it encompasses the whole hierarchy, including the titles of the esteemed *hojjat ol-eslam*, the "proof of Islam," and the revered *ayatollah*, the "miraculous sign of God." The latter is a title reserved for a small cadre of clerics who are the most admired and respected for their learning and personal integrity. Rarely, a cleric becomes a *marja-e taqlid*, "source of emulation," the most authoritative religious title in Shiism.

the sixteenth century, the Shia schools in Najaf and Karbala fed highly trained teachers and students into the Persian clerical establishment to the east. In return, Iran provided the holy cities with pilgrims, many of whom stayed on to profit in the lucrative commercial trade that flowed back and forth across the Iranian border. They, along with a large percentage of the clerical establishment, would form the Persian component of Iraq's population. Once significant, this component has now been largely cleansed from the country by successive Sunni governments. But the Persian influence planted through commerce and more so through religion remains ingrained in Iraq.

The shrine cities, now the domain of Arab religious custodians rather than Persian clerics, have never lost their sacred aura. Whatever the fortunes of the institutions of the sect, they remain the sites on which Shiism's most revered figures—Ali, the fourth caliph, and his grandson Hussein—died. Within the walls of the magnificent shrine in which each is buried, centuries of pilgrims have sought shelter from the heat and cold and rain and wind of the desert. Tradition has moved this sense of sanctuary one step further. The faithful believe that rewards accrue to those buried in what are now vast cemeteries surrounding the holy cities. To observe the death ritual of the Shia is to experience something found nowhere else in the Arab world.

In Najaf toward the end of 1999, the day was uncommonly gray and overcast. The golden splendor of the dome of Ali's shrine set on a forlorn spot a hundred-plus miles south of Baghdad was rich but dull. It was the third day of Ramadan, the Muslim month of fasting, and the noon prayers had just begun. The whole *haram*, or walled courtyard of the shrine, was packed with black-clad women and men in long, loose dress-like *disdashas*, many of whom held their hands aloft in subjugation to Allah and praise of Ali. Suddenly, a band of people burst through a far gate in the wall of the *haram*. They bore a rough hewn casket draped with the Shia flag of mourning. Instantly, the crowd peeled back to allow the little procession to pass. Reaching the broad golden front of the shrine, the pallbearers turned right, raised the box of the dead over their heads, and plunged inside. Followed by wailing mourners, they circumambulated the silver grille enclosing the tomb of Ali and exited along the same route by which they had entered. Back on the street, they strapped the casket on the top of a waiting taxi. With the mourners trailing behind in a procession of battered taxis, the deceased moved toward the enormous cemetery to join thousands of other Shia buried in hallowed ground.

The Shia never even approached a majority of the population of what is now Iraq before the nineteenth or perhaps the early twentieth century. In the eighteenth century, Shiism that was concentrated almost exclusively within the Persianized region around the shrine cities of the south received a heavy infusion of Arabism. It was at that point that Shiism in Iraq formed two informal yet distinct branches, one preserving the Persian model and one reflecting the tribalism of the Arabian Peninsula.

Ever since the Islamic invasion of the seventh century, knots of black-veiled Bedouin women urging on heavily laden donkeys had followed their men and livestock across the upper reaches of the Arabian Peninsula toward the fertile lands of the Tigris-Euphrates valley. In the last decades of the nineteenth century, this trickle of Arabs into Mesopotamia turned into a flood unleashed by religious and political warfare on the deserts of Arabia.[16] Their black, goat-hair tents scattered across the grazing grounds west of the Euphrates and hung along the edges of the marshes of southern Iraq. Like the Bedouin who had arrived with the Islamic invasion, these men and women hardened by the ceaseless tribal wars of the desert gave obedience to nothing but tribal law dispensed from the tents of their own sheikhs. Wielding primitive yet potent military power, the tribes quickly cowed the disorganized Iraqi peasantry already present on the land, who, much as they had in the seventh century, subjugated themselves to whatever tribe dominated the area. At the same time, the Shia of the shrine cities sought to enlist the immigrant tribes to serve their own interests.

Early in this latest phase of Arab immigration and domination, the Shia clerics of the shrine cities recognized in the newly arrived tribes a source of protection against marauders and a font of revenue for the shrines. In hot pursuit of converts, the Persian religious authorities dispatched sayyids, descendants of the Prophet, to the

---

[16] See chapter 3.

tribal tents and villages of southern Iraq.[17] Dressed in black and wearing small, tightly wound turbans, they delivered the rituals of Shiism
to audiences who found in them components of their own culture.
Obsessed with lineage, tribal Arabs emotionally bonded with Ali, the
blood kin of the Prophet. No less important, the recently arrived
tribal Arabs also found psychological and practical benefits in
Shiism. The transition from nomadism to settled agriculture cut
beneath the tribal order that descended from the sheikh. Organized
around the need for defense, the tribes and the sheikhs who led them
watched as much of their relevance drained away in surroundings
where there were no more wells to protect or herds to guard. In what
amounted to escalating social chaos, tribesmen and sheikhs
searched for any elements in their new environment that promised
some kind of stability and order. They found them in the motifs of
resistance to oppression and the intolerance of organized government embedded in Shia Islam.

Acting as a faith, a tool of social stability, and a doorway into the
economic system entrenched in the shrine cities, Shia Islam pulled
the Arab tribesmen of southern Iraq into a new society. Yet while
Shiism gave the tribesmen a sense of acceptance and a measure of
power, the tribesmen gave Shiism little of themselves. Shia by con-
fession, they remained Bedouin by birth. Refusing to surrender the
traditions of the tribe to the dictates of religion, Arab families and
clans continued to resolve their conflicts through blood money, not
the courts of Shia judges. And declining to explore the real meaning
within the tenets of Shiism, the tribesmen remained little more than
the followers of the religious sect dictated by their sheikh. Accepting
these realities, Shia missionaries who were more interested in conversions than theological purity adjusted their religious teachings to
the Arab value system. Ignoring the theme of suffering by the weak
that has such resonance for Persians, the sayyids exalted the ideal of
Arab manhood. Thus, Ali in his courage, honesty, and concern for justice became a heroic example of the Arab tribal values of masculin-
ity—honor, pride, and chivalry. Similarly Hussein, who to the Persians
died a martyr to injustice at Karbala, was transformed into a glorious

---

[17] The sayyids were a mixed lot. The official emissaries came out of the shrine cities,
carrying credentials bestowed by family and education. Others were simply wandering
holy men, diviners, or soothsayers with little or no connection to the organized faith.

victor in defense of Muhammad's lineage. Writing in commemoration of his death, poets portrayed the Prophet's grandson as the avatar of virtue, the sheikh who gives to his followers strength against their enemies, bounty of their crops, and fertility for their women.[18]

Similarly, Abbas, Hussein's half-brother who valiantly died fetching water from the Euphrates for the parched rebels at Karbala, took his place in Bedouin-inspired theology. Essentially absent in Persian accounts, Abbas for the Arabic-speaking Shia was endowed with all the ideal Bedouin attributes. He became the fearless lion protecting his brother, his family, and his faith. At a time when the sheikhs' political power and moral authority lay in doubt, Abbas became for the tribesmen a new father figure capable of exercising command over their life in Mesopotamia.

Even the *hausa*, the most timeless and dramatic of Bedouin rituals, moved into Shiism in Iraq. Still seen on the occasion of weddings, circumcisions, holidays, deaths, and celebrations, the *hausa* is performed around a pile of wood engulfed in lapping flames. In Sunni tribes, men wearing the simple traditional robe of the desert move in a circle, left to right, stamping out a slow measured rhythm in which they chant the past glories of their kin. Among Shia Arabs, the only difference is that the repetitious sound often comes in praise of Ali. In celebrating Ali with the most Bedouin of rituals, the tribesmen confirm that they are both Arab and Shia.

In spite of all the factors feeding the rapid conversion of Iraq's tribes, Shiism never encompassed the whole. Outside the newly settled tribes of the south, Shiism generally failed to establish itself across the region. As a consequence, the Arab tribes in the deserts north and west of Baghdad remained almost exclusively Sunni. And many of the confederations and tribes that did convert still retained segments that remained orthodox Sunnis. Even so, by the early twentieth century, Shia Islam, layered on top of a strong Arab tribal system, claimed the majority of the Arab tribal population. Led more by sheikhs than *mujtahids*, they still constitute the largest segment of Iraq's Arab population.

---

[18] The Arab Shia, reflecting the Arab concern with bloodlines, concentrated their veneration on Ali's tomb at Najaf. Reflecting their cultural concern about justice, Persians focus their devotion on Hussein's shrine at Karbala.

THE HUMAN MOSAIC OF IRAQ 83

GRAND EVENTS coupled with accidents and manipulations of history have jammed a collection of people with competing identities rooted in ethnicity, language, religion, sect, tribe, family, and region into a political shell called a state. One of the ironies of that state is that regardless of the clear demarcations between groups, individuals and sometimes communal segments have always moved economically, politically, and sometimes socially back and forth across communal lines. A single tribe can claim both Sunnis and Shia. Muslims and Christians meet on occasion at the old Armenian church in Baghdad, which both regard as a historic treasure. Kurds, Persians, Arabs, and almost every other language and confessional group intermarry. The Shia, consistently repressed by the Sunnis, at times have dominated the commercial sector of the economy, raising some of their number into the ranks of the richest people in Iraq. Kurds have often served in government in numbers disproportionate to their share of the population. And Christians have always operated the machinery of the bureaucracy far in excess of their numbers within the population. Nonetheless, these groups remain a collection of separate identities that has always challenged the integrity of the Iraqi state. However much Sunni and Shia, Arab and Kurd, Muslim and Christian have met in the marketplace and sat in the councils of government, they have most often placed their interests as individuals within families and communal groups above the interests of the state. Like so many other postcolonial countries, Iraq, in the pursuit of a national identity, has been required to constantly struggle against the complications of its own internal divisions.

Nothing speaks to national dysfunction better than the words of the Iraqis themselves. Across the country, an Iraqi occupying one square in the patchwork of the state discerns an Iraqi occupying another square through the lens of his own communal group. Perceptions often ignore reality. Or perhaps more accurately, how one Iraqi regards another confirms the reality of fragmented Iraq. A Shia archeologist inspecting an old drawing of the shrine of Karbala told me in the most matter-of-fact way, "You know, of course, that the culture of the Shia is far superior to the culture of the Sunnis." An urbane Sunni ensconced in his office in the heart of Baghdad swept his hand toward a window overlooking the skyline and declared, "This is Iraq. Not those bigoted religious cities and miserable villages of the south inhabited by nothing but sheikhs and their primitive tribesmen." An ethnic Persian sitting on the sidewalk out-side his small shop in Karbala expressed a different view: "Iraqis are unique in the Arab-speaking world because most are not Arabs." A Marsh Arab gazing across the southern swamps near Amarah quietly ruminated, "The Kurds are too far from the purity of the south." As if in reply, a Kurd, a young female architect, confessed, "We don't dif-ferentiate between Arab Sunnis and Shia because we hate all Arabs." A priest sitting in a small dark church in Mosul voiced his own opin-ion of the Arabs, this time the Arab Muslims: "Sunnis think the Shia are dirty and anti-Arab. The Shia don't like the Sunnis. And both would rejoice in seeing the Christians disappear." A young man of advanced education bent over a map of Iraq spoke a simple truth: "The Sunnis deeply fear the Shia majority."

Having experienced centuries of human interchange, Iraq is so plu-ralistic and idiosyncratic that even spoken Arabic, incorporating a mul-titude of loan words from Persian, Turkish, and Kurdish, far exceeds the linguistic variants found in other Arab states. Perhaps if left alone, the people between the Tigris and Euphrates would have gradually integrated all these influences into their own unique society upon which a common nationalism might have come. But they were not left alone. Instead, the land between the rivers fell victim to invasion, occu-pation, and foreign imperialism. When statehood came for the people called Iraqis, it came at the hands of outsiders who drew boundaries serving their own imperial needs and incorporating into them the nationalism of the Kurds. Over eight decades of turbulent, often ruth-less politics from a monarchy to the totalitarianism of Saddam Hussein, the Iraqis have struggled to define themselves and their state.

3

THE IMPROBABLE
COUNTRY

The *shanashils*, shuttered wooden balconies that once secluded veiled women, clung to brick buildings constructed before Iraq became a state. In line, form, and feel, each edifice on the rutted street kept alive the traditional architecture once prized by the upper class of Baghdad. That is why it was surprising to find inside a well-stocked antique shop near the center of the block, an inventory containing so little that might be construed as indigenous to Iraq. The dark, heavily embellished furniture crowding the floor space mocked the elegance and simplicity of Mesopotamian art. Instead, the carved blossoms and elaborate florid whorls flaunted the taste of Istanbul, which, as the capital of the Ottoman Empire, ruled Mesopotamia for four hundred years. The tables wedged between sofas and chairs held oil lamps of red, blue, and delicate pink glass imprinted with the portraits of the Qajars of Persia who had cast their shadow over Ottoman Mesopotamia during the nineteenth century. Around the walls, photographs in dusty frames hung above boxes of cracked-leather riding crops and tarnished military insignia, a legacy of the British who arrived at the end of World War I. The moustached proprietor lounged in the corner of a particularly ugly settee studded in mother-of-pearl. I paused in my browsing to ask where I might find articles tied to the customs and tastes of Iraqis. He waved an arm at his merchandise: "These are the relics of Iraq's history. This is the bric-a-brac of those who created us."

THE HISTORY of Mesopotamia is, in important respects, a chronicle of conquest. It was as conquerors that the Arabs wrapped Mesopotamia in the Arabic language and Arab culture. The Abbasid Dynasty, ruling the Islamic Empire from Baghdad, remained the master of its own destiny for only two centuries before a powerful wind from the east blew a series of new invaders through Mesopotamia—the Buyids, the Seljuk Turks, and the Mongols.[1] Whereas the Buyids and Seljuks treaded lightly on the land between the rivers, the Mongols laid it waste.

In 1258 the Mongol hordes behind Hülegü stormed into Baghdad, dragged the caliph into the street, rolled him into a carpet, and trampled him to death under the hooves of stout Mongol ponies. But the Mongols killed more than the last symbol of the Islamic Empire. For no other reason than efficiency in drowning Baghdad's panic-stricken inhabitants, the leather-helmeted men of the steppes ruptured the dikes of the laboriously built irrigation system that had supported settled agriculture since the time of the Sumerians. The swords and arrows of nomadic tribesmen slaughtered 800,000 people, most of them clerics, teachers, merchants, and skilled farmers. Gathering up the treasure of the Islamic Empire's golden age, men who knew little beyond warfare mounted their ponies and galloped away. In the late fourteenth century, the Mongols returned under the banner of Timur the Lame.[2] At the small town of Tikrit on the Tigris River, they erected a gruesome pyramid constructed from the skulls of their slaughtered victims before once more disappearing into the east. At the beginning of the fifteenth century, the distant descendants of Genghis Khan again rode through Baghdad to murder another 20,000 people. Finally, the Mongols were gone forever. The only thing they left behind was their ruinous legacy.

For thousands of years, Mesopotamia had been a settled land of towns and farms. From time to time, one group or another sacked cities and massacred inhabitants. But until the Mongols came, the Mesopotamians revived and grew, incorporating into their own civilization that which they had learned from the invaders. Most important, they diligently repaired the irrigation canals through which the life blood of society flowed. But after the Mongols, the broken spirited survivors of the nightmare never began this rebuilding process. Perhaps they found it impossible to summon the energy necessary to laboriously dredge the canals, strengthen and restore their banks, and rebuild the barrages that controlled the floods. So instead of

---

[1] The Abbasid caliphs began to lose control of their own house when Turkish and Circassian slaves were incorporated into their court as mercenaries. Under their protection, the caliphs ruled from Samarra from 836 to 892. Yet it was the former slaves, known as Mamluks, who came to function as the de facto rulers of the Abbasids' Islamic Empire.

[2] Also known as Tamerlane.

rebirth, the lush productive fields along the great rivers reverted to desert, as the precious water flowing down from the faraway mountains drained into the great swamps of the south. Baghdad, the jewel of the Abbasids, lay hopelessly wasted, its exhausted population reduced to a mere 150,000. Mesopotamia's other cities degenerated into squalid villages characterized by poverty and intellectual stagnation. Around them, the nomads, whose pastoral economy and tribal social structure better fit the existing realities, roamed the vacant countryside. In what had once been rich and fertile land, "there [was] no life for miles around. No river glades in grandeur at the base of [Mesopotamian] mounds, no green dates flourish[ed] near its rivers. . . . A blade of grass or insect" found no existence there.[3] Only aged broken bricks testified to the forgotten greatness of Mesopotamia.

FAR TO THE NORTH and east of decayed and impoverished Mesopotamia, a new empire had crested the horizon. It originated with the Oguz, a Turkish-speaking tribe that grazed its livestock across the vast treeless plains north of the Aral Sea. In the fourteenth century while Timur the Lame was butchering and burning, the Oguz pushed their territory outward under the leadership of their tribal chief, Osman.[4] Radiating a magnetic charisma that came from personality and religious devotion to Sunni Islam, Osman pulled followers from among adjacent Turkish-speaking tribes who shared his faith. Together they moved westward along the shifting frontier of the moribund Byzantine Empire, seizing territory in bits and pieces all the way from western Asia to the Balkans. In the early fifteenth century, the Ottomans stopped, paralyzed by their own internal struggles. It was in 1451 that an extraordinary leader rose out of this internecine conflict to fulfill the dynasty's great ambition—the conquest of Constantinople, the last surviving piece of Byzantium.

While the Christian bishops inside the thick stone walls of Constantinople debated whether angels are male or female, Mehmed II constructed a fortress on the European shore of the Bosporus. Around it, he gathered an army of eighty thousand men, more than

---

[3] William Kennet Loftus, quoted in Brian M. Fagan, *Return to Babylon: Travelers, Archaeologists, and Monuments in Mesopotamia* (Boston: Little, Brown, 1979), p. 3.

[4] It is Osman who gave the Ottomans their name. With no ethnic significance, *Ottoman* is simply a dynastic term.

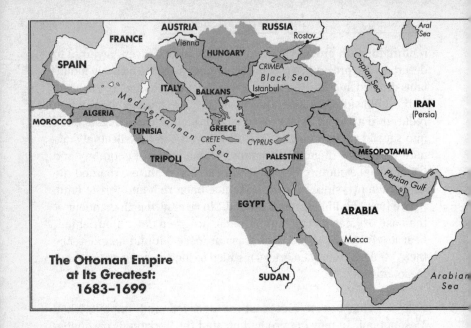

The Ottoman Empire at Its Greatest: 1683–1699

seventy ships, and a cannon capable of firing iron balls weighing twelve hundred pounds. In March 1453, he threw it all against the ramparts of Constantinople, the beleaguered Christians' only defense. After three months of siege, a point in the massive fortification gave way. Following his troops through the hole, Mehmed stepped into the city and made his way to the Hagia Sophia, the heart of Byzantium. This was literally and symbolically the end of the debilitated Christian empire of the east. Constantinople would become Istanbul, the capital of Islam's new imperial age.

Mehmed II ordered Istanbul's walls repaired and new public buildings constructed. He commanded that the depleted population be increased by adding Muslims, Jews, and Christians collected from all parts of his realm. When he died, he left to his successors a proud imperial metropolis reflecting the complex character of an Ottoman Empire that had yet to be completed.

In 1515 and 1516, Selim I gathered into the Ottomans' imperial fold Mesopotamia, Syria, Egypt, Palestine, and Islam's two sacred cities—Mecca and Medina. Beginning in 1520, Suleiman the Magnificent took the Ottoman Empire to its zenith. For forty-six years, he reigned over a brilliant civilization encompassing Anatolia, the Balkans, the Fertile Crescent, and the coasts of the Arabian Peninsula and North Africa as far west as Algeria. Within these borders resided a population of 20 to 30 million people and a staggering array of cultures and languages. Over the next four hundred years, the Ottoman Empire in both greatness and decline would be ruled from Tokapi Palace in Istanbul.

The sultan, a title meaning "he with authority," secured his throne by military might and maintained it through a highly organized administration expanding out in concentric circles from his person. The first circle was composed of Janizaries, tribute children from Christian areas of the Caucasus who were converted to Islam and educated in the palace. They shared power derived from proximity to the throne with the harem. Dominated by the sultan's mother, the harem housed the mothers of his children, other assorted favorites, and female slaves, all trained in domestic arts and feminine sensuality. From this inner core around the person of the sultan, the administration headed by the grand vizier descended in levels from Istanbul to the provinces to the localities. The symbols of legitimacy of the elaborate system resided in four domed rooms in Tokapi Palace. Known as the "apartment of the blessed robes," the rooms housed two coats hanging on headless forms that purportedly belonged to Muhammad. A sword, bow, and seal that carried the same claim of ownership by the Prophet lay before them. These were the foundation of the Ottoman Empire that replicated the orthodox Sunni Muslim civilization of the vanished Islamic Empire. From the great centers of Islamic culture now within the bounds of their empire, the Ottoman rulers drew men from Damascus, Cairo, and Baghdad to install at the center of their empire the traditional principles and practice of Islamic law, administration, and finance. Yet while the Ottoman Empire revived the Islamic state, the sultans of Istanbul made no attempt to restore the primacy of Arab culture. Although he included caliph among his titles, the Ottoman sultan never laid the same claim to religious legitimacy as did his Arab predecessors. He did not pretend to be a descendant of the Prophet nor did he trace his origins to Mecca. He was not even an Arab. Roughly the equivalent of the king of the Turkish people who possessed their own language and culture, the sultan stood at the head of a military/political caste ruling over a miscellany of subject peoples, of whom the Arabs were only one. At the same time, the sultan was a Sunni—an orthodox Muslim who, like the Arab caliphs before him, ruled a vast state in the name of orthodox Islam. To the east of

Istanbul, another ruling house also drew its legitimacy from Islam — the Safavids of Shia Persia.

SHIISM IN PERSIA came out of a mystical sect within Islam known as the Sufis. The ascetics of the faith, they were born in protest against the Umayyads following Islam's Great Schism of 680.[5] During the torment of the Mongol invasions, Sufism gained strength particularly in Persia, where the Mongol hordes inflicted even greater suffering than in Mesopotamia. In the chaos of the late thirteenth century, an order of Sufis was established in a wild remote place called Ardabil, roughly halfway between the present Iranian city of Tabriz and the eastern shore of the Caspian Sea. Led by Sheikh Safi al-Din Abdul Fath Ishaq Ardabili, the order prospered due to the sheikh's reputed wisdom and saintly way of life. Gradually his followers assigned to him heroic qualities that were passed on to a line of his descendants, who also were regarded as radiating special spirituality.

After two centuries, what had become known as the Safavid order entered a new phase. No longer satisfied with a solely religious role, the Safavids reached for political power. It was achieved in the early sixteenth century under a charismatic twelve-year-old who had been educated by a Shia tutor. Proclaiming his divinity, Ismail enveloped nearby Turkoman tribes in his aura. Wrapping his devotees in scarlet turbans, he sent them into battle carrying the words and images of Shia Islam:

We are Hussein's men, and this is our epoch,
In devotion we are the slave of the Imam;
Our name is "zealot" and our title is "martyr."[6]

Man by man, tribe by tribe, Ismail separated most of the Turkomans living at the foot of the Zagros Mountains from the Sunni Ottoman Empire.

Following the magnetic Ismail, the Turkomans and the Sufis, now turned into Shia zealots, plunged south to take parts of Persia. Assuming the title of shah, or king, in 1501, Ismail declared Shiism

---

[5] In the West, the Sufis are best known as the fabled long-haired "whirling dervishes" who rapidly spin around and around until they achieve a near-hypnotic state in which they find union with God. They are only one sect within Sufism.

[6] Quoted in Roy Mottahedeh, *The Mantle of the Prophet: Religion and Politics in Iran* (New York: Pantheon Books, 1985), p. 171.

the official faith of his new Safavid kingdom. From his throne, he sent forth an edict denouncing Islam's first three caliphs with the following instructions: "Men should loosen their tongues in the street and square for the profanation and cursing of Abu Bakr, Omar and Uthman," and that they should chop off the heads of any that stood in the way of this.[7] Continuing to gobble up territory, Ismail freed the city of Khorasan from Sunni control by personally killing the Uzbek king, the ruler of what is now Uzbekistan. Severing the head from the neck, he ordered the skull set in gold to create a drinking cup, which he sent to the sultan of the Ottoman Empire as a hideous statement of rising Safavid power. When Ismail's army finally completed its sweep of Persia less than a decade later, the Safavids stood within the rough borders of Sassanian Persia won under the banner of Shia Islam.

In Istanbul, the Ottomans shuddered. Here was Shia Islam challenging not only Ottoman control over much of Asia Minor but also the very foundation of their legitimacy—Sunni Islam. So began a long struggle for power between the Ottomans and Persia, first under the Safavids and then their successors, the Qajars. Wedged between the two was Mesopotamia. For three hundred years, it periodically served as a battlefield of culture and sect —Turks versus Persians, Sunnis versus Shias.

The Safavids won the first skirmish when they seized parts of Mesopotamia in 1508. Attempting to override orthodox Islam in the very heartland of the old Abbasid caliphate, they desecrated Sunni religious sites and persecuted teachers of orthodox religion. Although the repression bore all the marks of ethnicity and sect, it also included its economic dimension. With control over both Persia and Mesopotamia, the Safavids straddled the Ottoman trade route between Asia and Europe. To reopen this door to their trade, Suleiman the Magnificent, at the crest of his powers, rode toward Baghdad in 1534. The city's Sunni religious leaders called on their people to massacre most of the Shia soldiers and Shia clerics who had been oppressing them. After making his grand entry into Baghdad, Suleiman spent the winter restoring the orthodox institutions that had

---

[7] Hasan Rumlu quoted in I. P. Petrushevsky, *Islam in Iran* (Albany: State University of New York Press, 1985), p. 321.

been emasculated by the Safavids and installing the characteristic Ottoman administrative system in his reclaimed territory.

The Safavids returned to Baghdad in 1623 under the mighty Shah Abbas. As soon as they secured the city, the Shia conquerors set about slaughtering the Sunni inhabitants. In 1638, the Ottomans retook Baghdad before sending troops to the south to murder 1,700 Persians, most of whom lived in the Shia shrine cities of Najaf and Karbala. Peace prevailed under Ottoman dominance until January 1733. It was then that the Persians under the Qajar successors to the Safavids once more invaded Iraq, lay siege to Baghdad, and starved to death 100,000 people, most of whom were Sunni. Less than a century later, the Ottomans wreaked their revenge when they massacred perhaps many as 30,000 Persian Shia in Karbala in 1843. The cycle of violence finally ended in the mid-nineteenth century. Even though Mesopotamia stayed within the Ottoman Empire until the end of World War I, the land between the rivers remained the field on which the cultural-religious-political competition between the Sunni Ottoman Empire and Shia Persia played itself out. Ever present in the minds of the Ottomans was the fear that the Shia of Mesopotamia lurked as a fifth column for despised Persia. It was a fear that would surface again in 1980 when Iraq went to war with Iran.

In the seventeenth century, the more tangible threat to the Ottomans were the Arab tribes. No effective administration had ever been established over the tribal lands in southern Mesopotamia, and the situation only worsened during the increased migrations from the Arabian Peninsula. The Kab tribe lay claim to much of the Shatt al Arab; the Bani Lam moved into the lower Tigris; and the powerful al-Muntafiq confederation took shape east of the marshes. Meanwhile, the mighty Shammar moved northward into the Syrian Desert where they clashed with the Anayzh, disrupting the east-west trade routes across Mesopotamia. In the nineteenth century, a larger wave of tribes came out of Arabia, pushed by the fanatical Wahhabis.

The Wahhabis came out of the religious reform movement of Muhammad ibn Abdul al-Wahhab. In crude sandals and a tattered robe that failed to reach his ankles, al-Wahhab traveled the camps and oases of the central Arabian Peninsula, preaching the need for Muslims to return to the teachings of Muhammad unsullied by elements of mysticism injected by the Sufis and the Shia. Striking his camel whip against any shrine or tomb declared holy by superstition, he railed against those he charged with deviating from the path of truth. "Mud cannot save you. Pray to God and God alone."[8] Religion made alliance with politics around 1744 when al-Wahhab joined the court of Muhammad ibn Saud, the ruler of the small market town of Diriyah outside of Riyadh, the present capital of Saudi Arabia.[9] Together they created a rustic state founded upon their pristine interpretation of Islam. Lighting the desert with the flame of jihad, or holy war, Wahhabism's warriors butchered resisting tribes en route to conquest of the holy cities of Mecca and Medina. In 1801, the Wahhabis charged into Mesopotamia to sack Karbala and twice lay siege to Najaf. The terrified Shia clerical establishment of the shrine cities sent out emissaries to the Arab tribes who were fleeing the zealous Wahhabis. Converting them to Shiism, the clerics succeeded in defending not only Shiism's holy sites but also the Shia Persian *ulama* within Arab Sunni Mesopotamia. They also created a source of perpetual resistance to Ottoman rule. Embracing Shia theology in which protest against government injustice forms a central tenet, these Arab Shia tribes rejected Sunni authority. Thus, the fear of Persia on their eastern border and the dread of the Shia tribesmen in their own countryside led Istanbul to structure its rule in Mesopotamia on the one element in society it trusted—the Sunnis of the city.

The Sunni Ottomans came to rely on the cities, particularly Baghdad, to hold the desert Arabs in check. These urban populations were largely a mix of Sunni Arabs, Jews, and Christians. Although intertwined socially and economically, each community lived in its own district, distinct and separate from the city's other communities. This demographic patchwork testified to the power of communalism but it also reflected how the Ottomans structured their empire. In such a large, far-flung dominion containing so many component parts, the Ottoman order could survive only with a level of cooperation from its subject people. Rather than building allegiance between the individual citizen of the empire and the sultan in Istanbul, the Ottoman administrative system constructed alliances with groups of subjects. Each was represented by an intermediary, usually a person

---

[8] Quoted in Robert Lacey, *The Kingdom* (New York: Harcourt, Brace, Jovanovich, 1981), p. 56.

[9] Muhammad ibn Saud's descendants are now the rulers of the Kingdom of Saudi Arabia.

exercising moral authority or possessing some other form of legitimacy within his own community. His role was to voice the grievances of his group to Ottoman officials and to win compliance of the group to government directives. Within the Ottoman system, these collections of individuals could be geographic units (a village, a tribe, or a quarter of a city) or economic units (trades or crafts). In regions of mixed faiths like Mesopotamia, the Ottoman system segmented subjects by *millet*, a community of people adhering to a particular religion. Istanbul bestowed on each of these *millets* the right to speak its own language; possess its own religious, cultural, and educational institutions; and maintain its own courts. But one *millet* was not necessarily equal to another. In Mesopotamia, the Arab Sunni community ranked at the top of the social and political order for a significant reason—to act as the defender of the Ottomans' Islamic state against Persia and the Shia. As a result, members of old notable Sunni families held almost all the key posts in the administrative apparatus. Members of these same families staffed the bureaucracy while the clerics among them constituted the Sunni *ulama*. In this closed world, there were few places for either Persians or Arab Shia citizens of Mesopotamia.

Although Christians and Jews were recognized as distinct *millets* entitled to their own courts, the Ottomans denied the Shia clerics the right to render judgments under their own schools of Islamic law. Shia laymen were largely excluded from administrative positions, from the military, and even from what little secular education existed. Working their own side of what was a two-way street, the Shia themselves fed this process of exclusion. Since only Sunni judges were appointed in the courts, the Shia declined to take their cases before them. And since none but Sunnis were recognized as teachers in Ottoman schools, the Shia refused to attend. Similarly, they declined to study the Turkish language, thereby closing any chance of entree into the bureaucracy. Living away from urban areas and therefore cut off from the few currents of progress and reform that flowed in Sunni Arab cities, the rural Shia as a whole drifted in ignorance and isolation. This made it easy for the Sunni political elite concerned with protecting their own vested interests to brush the Shia off as unprepared for inclusion in the official life of Ottoman Mesopotamia. Consequently, generation by generation, the cycle was repeated. Excluded from government, the Shia refused to participate, prompting even more alienation, resentment, and defiance. Acknowledging the Ottomans' control of the urban areas, the Shia held sway in the rural south.

As the nineteenth century ticked away, the Ottomans gathered their resources to enforce their will on the Shia of Mesopotamia. They began with the Persians of the shrine cities. Istanbul had grudgingly accorded the Persian community in Mesopotamia privileged status in the shrine cities of Najaf and Karbala for one reason—to avoid renewed conflict with the Qajars who continued to claim the right to protect Persian nationals in Iraq. But what had been a gain for Ottoman administration was also a loss. In granting special status with its accompanying economic benefits, the Ottomans had essentially relinquished Istanbul's authority over two of the three cities south of Baghdad. Only Basra was left to unimpeded Ottoman control. Therefore, when Russia made military advances into Persia's northern territories in the mid-nineteenth century, the Ottomans seized the moment to pull the rug out from under the economies of the shrine cities. Trade with Persia became restricted, barriers at the border of Mesopotamia stopped Shia pilgrims on the way to Karbala, and taxes descended on every salted and dried corpse arriving from beyond the borders of Mesopotamia for burial around the shrine cities. Even with smuggling of everything including bodies, the incomes of Najaf and Karbala sank lower and lower.[10] Finally, the Ottomans succeeded in clamping their hand firmly on the cities of Ali and Hussein.

Next, Istanbul moved on the Shia Arab tribes. The strategy centered on a land policy intended to supplant the traditional practice under which tribes held land in common. The Ottoman Land Law of 1858 bestowed on individual farmers the rights of tenure through a deed or TAPU, the acronym for the department of issue. The theory behind this distribution of land to those who worked it reasoned that a peasant owner would no longer need to look to the surrounding tribes for rights of cultivation and the tribesmen, as individual landowners, would be lured into settling down into the Ottoman order. The grand scheme failed. The *fellahin*, the peasants, refused to appear at a government office to collect their deeds for fear of

---

[10] To avoid both taxes and freight, one astute Persian divided his grandfather's skeleton among several parcels and mailed it to Karbala.

being drafted into the Ottoman army. The tribesmen saw landown-ership as nothing but a prelude to taxation. With those in the lower echelons of the social order refusing the offer, urban speculators, many of them Sunnis, bought up the land of the peasants while cer-tain sheikhs registered the lands of their tribes in their own names. As a result, the speculators as absentee owners held the *fellahin* in their grasp, and the colluding sheikhs no longer sat as the first among equals but reigned as the economic masters of their tribesmen. Although land distribution ceased in 1881 due to a lack of effective machinery to enforce the tax laws, the program did succeed in paci-fying the countryside by corralling the forces of tribal power that had characterized Mesopotamia for centuries. According to Muhammed Salam Hasan, an Arab scholar, "Nomads who were no longer in a position to rely on camels or plunder for their livelihood . . . were still subject to the discipline of tribal organizations regarding the relations between the followers and their leaders. [They] had no alternative but to follow their sheikhs into settlement on the land."[11] There was a second result, disastrous for Mesopotamia's long-term political interests. As major landowners, a segment of the Shia sheikhs joined the economically powerful Sunni urban elite. Together the urban Sunni landlords and the Arab Shia sheikhs would ensure that the economic and social status quo continued, blocking the evolution of a more inclusive political system even after Ottoman rule over Mesopotamia ended.

BY THE TWENTIETH CENTURY, twilight had descended on the Ottoman Empire. Tokapi Palace had become riddled with corruption, trapped in the machinations of the harem, and captive to the ever escalating demands of the military. Mesopotamia, always a wild frontier, had started to function as a virtually autonomous province within the crumbling empire. Ignored and debilitated, it seemed a target for any disaster. In the spring of 1831, bubonic plague struck Baghdad. Two to three thousand people died each day while the spring floods mocked the sick by sending water over the banks of the Tigris to surge into hundreds of buildings. Constructed of mud brick, the structures simply dissolved, reducing mosques, public buildings, and

---

[11] Quoted in W. Thom Workman, *The Social Origins of the Iran-Iraq War* (Boulder, Colo.: Lynne Rienner Publishers, 1994), p. 62.

ordinary dwellings to sticky brown heaps. Across the land, the Ottoman administration struggled to reform itself enough to contain if not rule its all but ungovernable province. At midcentury, administrative reorganization strengthened the hand of Baghdad, and educational reform established secular schools outside the orbit of the religious schools, or *madresehs*. The imperfect TAPU scheme was initiated in 1858. The arrival of the telegraph and a commercial steamer line on the Tigris, as well as increased trade from India, Persia, Alleppo, and Damascus and the opening of the Suez Canal in 1869, began to change the economic stagnation that had existed for centuries between the Tigris and Euphrates. But it all came too late for the enfeebled Ottomans to hold Mesopotamia in check. In March 1891, the French consul described Baghdad: "Disorder has reached a new height: robberies are continuing and in the course of the last eight months, at least 200 murders have been committed in the city; not one effective sentence has been passed; the magistrates sell indemnities to the criminals and cases are reported of assassins who commit their crime in broad daylight only to be freed on the pretext that there were no witnesses; . . . from the governor down to the lowest gendarme everyone steals and anarchy would be preferable to the regime now experienced."[12] To the southeast where Western archeologists were digging at Nippur in 1894, the local Arabs killed seventy-one Turkish authorities in some now-misty dispute. These same archeologists sometimes saw their workmen suddenly drop their tools, seize their weapons, release a loud war cry, and rush off to battle. By the turn of the twentieth century, a tribe on the Euphrates chanted at the Ottoman government in Baghdad, "[You are] a flabby serpent which has no venom; we have come and have seen it. It is only in times past that it kept us in awe."[13]

Long regarded as the "sick man of Europe," the Ottoman Empire at the turn of the twentieth century was bleeding from wounds inflicted by uprisings among its subjects and capitulations to the imperial lusts of the major European powers. In 1908, the Ottomans were stabbed in Istanbul itself. The Young Turks, a clique of Turkish

---

[12] Quoted in David Pryce-Jones, *The Closed Circle: An Interpretation of the Arabs*, (New York: Harper Perennial, 1991), p. 95.

[13] Hanna Batatu quoted in Andrew Cockburn and Patrick Cockburn, *Out of the Ashes: The Resurrection of Saddam Hussein* (New York: HarperCollins, 1999), p. 63.

nationalists including Mustafa Kemal, seized control of parliament.[14] Rejecting the Ottoman dynasty's pan-Islamic ideology that had always undergirded the rule of the sultans, the Young Turks raised the flag of a secular nation-state of Turkey promoting Turkish interests and Turkish culture. The glue that had held the Ottoman Empire together for centuries dissolved. Calling all Ottoman subjects to patriotism and loyalty to a new concept of government, the Young Turks held elections for a new parliament in which the Ottomans' subject people would participate. The three Mesopotamian *vilayets*, or provinces, of Baghdad, Basra, and Mosul elected seventeen delegates, all from old, well-established Sunni families. When they arrived in Istanbul, they discovered a commonality not with the new rulers of Istanbul but with the Arabs from other Ottoman provinces. Instead of embracing the Turkish state, they came home infused with the idea of Arab nationalism. Not a new concept, it came out of a movement of early-nineteenth-century Arab intellectuals centered in Beirut and Damascus.

Arab nationalism had germinated in the intellectual stagnation that had paralyzed the Arab spirit since the end of their classical age. In the long dark period following the decline of the Abbasid civilization that had underlay the golden age of the Islamic Empire, the Arabs had lost touch with the creative and liberal values of their own tradition. The Arab malaise continued in an empire that drained all energy and resources toward Istanbul. In the early nineteenth century, contact with the West and the resulting spread of education among the Arabs of the Levant sparked the "Arab Awakening." In Damascus and Beirut, the Arab Sunni and Christian intelligentsia began to perceive the solution to the debilitation of Arab society in *nahda*, the revival of Arab culture.

The Arabs had every right to sing the litany of abuse under the Ottomans—poor administration, a deplorable lack of education, essentially no health care, and repressive despotism under local governors. Out of the maltreatment and neglect, a vague sense of Arab patriotism developed around the image of *watan*, or homeland. It was verbalized by the writer al-Kawakibi, who sounded the cry of native speakers of Arabic against their Ottoman masters: "You there! Leave us to manage our own affairs, to communicate among our-

---

[14] The Young Turks were also known as the Committee of Union and Progress.

selves in eloquent Arabic and to show respect and understanding for each other as brothers. . . . Leave us to rally around the same message. Long live the nation! Long live the homeland!"[15] Growing numbers of nascent Arab nationalists within the small intellectual class began to define the steps toward their vision: throw off the traces of colonialism, release the flow of intellectual discourse in the Arabic language, bring all Arabic-speaking people together in one nation under Arab culture.

For educated Arabs in the backwater of Ottoman Mesopotamia, the idea of Arab nationalism seemed revolutionary. As a consequence, secret societies, including the predominant al-Ahd, sprang up in the central and northern towns of Mesopotamia. But just beyond the cities, the ideology fell on ground rendered infertile by a population still rooted in tribe, clan, family, and religion. Fragile Arab nationalism, not only in Mesopotamia but also across the Fertile Crescent, proved unready to challenge the Ottoman Empire still claiming the legitimacy of orthodox Islam and standing as a bulwark against the increasing encroachment of Christian Europe. When the gauntlet of Arab nationalism was thrown down, it was by Hussein ibn Ali, the Sharif of Mecca, a man claiming impeccable Islamic credentials and commanding an army that carried the guns of Britain.

FOLLOWING THE CRUSADES, the great cataclysmic battle between Christendom and Islam that consumed the twelfth and thirteen centuries, only a few Europeans found their way into the Middle East. But in 1798 Napoleon Bonaparte and the army of France landed at Alexandria in Egypt, signaling the start of move and countermove in Europe's new conquest. By the mid-nineteenth century, Britain was the country showing the most interest in Middle East territory. At the time, the British were warily watching Russia bite off chunks of Persia in what London perceived as a march toward the warm-water ports of the Persian Gulf. Even so, it was the 1857 Sepoy mutiny in India that threatened British control of the vast subcontinent which led to English engagement in Mesopotamia. Sounding the call to defend India against all comers, Lord Curzon, the future viceroy, declared that the first duty of British foreign policy "is to render any hostile intentions futile, to see that our own position is secure and

---

[15] Quoted in A. A. Duri, *The Historical Formation of the Arab Nation: A Study in Identity and Consciousness* (London: Croom Helm, 1987), p. 193.

our frontier impregnable, and so to guard what is without doubt the noblest trophy of British genius, and the most splendid appendage of the Imperial Crown." [16] In pursuit of that goal, Britain in 1879 secured a major share in the Suez Canal, the western end of the sea routes to India. In 1903, the gateway to India was again threatened when German financiers secured from the Ottoman government the final concession to build the Berlin-to-Baghdad Railway. From Baghdad, imperial Germany could lay tracks south to Basra at the head of the Shatt al Arab, which flows into the Persian Gulf. Once in the Gulf, Germany stood before an open door to the Indian Ocean. With Russia already looking toward the Gulf from its position in Persia and France casting an eye on Mosul on the upper Tigris, Europe's imperial giants faced off in a determined game for Mesopotamia.

For Britain, Mesopotamia held the prize of petroleum. In 1908 when the massive Masjid-i-Suleiman (Temple of Solomon) well in Persia began to flow, Britain staked its claim to what would become the most coveted resource in the world. With oil on one side of the Gulf, London questioned not whether but how much lay on the other. After all, the people of Ur had decorated their ziggurats with bitumen, and boatmen on the Tigris had always sealed the bottoms of their flat barges with the black pitch that bubbled out of the ground of southern Mesopotamia. Interested in neither art nor river commerce, the British coveted petroleum for a new generation of battleships fueled by oil rather than coal. The presence of any rival south of Baghdad menaced the dominance of British naval power by threatening to lay claim to the potential oil resources of Mesopotamia and the wells and refineries of the Anglo-Persian Oil Company in southern Persia.

Thus, the British imperatives of geography and resources in the Persian Gulf fed into the storm clouds gathering over Western Europe, Eastern Europe, and the Ottoman Empire since the mid-nineteenth century. In the summer of 1914, all the forces of nationalism, militarism, and imperialism met to thrust the world into war. The Triple Entente of Britain, France, and Russia squared off against the Triple Alliance of Germany and the empires of the

---

[16] Quoted in Kenneth Rose, *Superior Person: A Portrait of Curzon and His Circle of Late Victorian England* (New York: Weybright and Talley, 1969), p. 215.

Hapsburgs and the Ottomans. Determined to secure Mesopotamia to serve its strategic interests, Britain landed the Indian Expeditionary Force "D" at Fao on the Shatt al Arab in November 1914 and moved rapidly toward Basra. With the far south secured by the fall of 1915, the advance toward Baghdad began. Slowed to a wretched pace, soldiers inched their way through desert alive with flies and swamps infested with mosquitoes. At Ctesiphon, the old Sassanian capital twenty-five miles southeast of Baghdad, the re-enforced Turkish army pushed the British back over a hundred miserable miles to Kut al-Amarah, a village set in a loop of the Tigris. For 140 days, the British endured the pounding of Turkish artillery until thirteen thousand starving, diseased, and demoralized men surrendered on April 26, 1916.

Fresh troops under the command of Major General Sir Stanley Maude arrived in December 1916 to resume the advance toward Baghdad. Encouraged by a rebellion at Najaf that had expelled the Turks, the British sent out agents to contact Shia tribal leaders in an attempt to gather allies. The strategy was simple—draw support from the traditional leadership without disturbing the status quo in the countryside. Its failure reflected how little the British understood Mesopotamia. Few tribal Arabs proved willing to give their horses, their guns, or themselves to any alien force. The Ottomans fared no better. The Marsh Arabs from the shelter of their swamps murdered and ravaged both sides indiscriminately, while the tribes of the flatlands hung around any military camp like jackals, looting stores and passing the weapons into their own arsenals. Fending off tribal raids and the Turkish army, the British crept northward. On March 10, 1917, His Majesty's troops marched past dingy tents of the Turkish army pitched around the ruined wall of the tomb of Zobeida, the favorite wife of Harun al-Rashid, and on through the dilapidated gates of Baghdad. In the glow of triumph, General Maude proclaimed that Britain intended to deliver to the people of Mesopotamia some control over their own affairs, thus paving the way for the final end to alien rule they had endured since the latter days of the Abbasid caliphate. Then he died of cholera. He left to Mesopotamia as well as the rest of the Ottomans' Arab provinces the great struggle between European colonial interests and Arab aspirations.

Two and a half years earlier, when the Ottoman sultan exercised his role as caliph to declare jihad against the Triple Alliance, Britain began the search for its own ideological weapon to throw back at the Turks. They found it in amorphic Arab nationalism. The grand nebulous idea that the Young Turks had unintentionally ignited in the Ottoman territories had found a voice in Hussein ibn Ali. The imperious sharif, a direct descendant of the Prophet through the House of Hashim, had an unmistakable aura of authority and piercing black eyes that could paralyze those who came within his gaze. Although born in Mecca, Hussein had been raised in the urbane and cultivated atmosphere of Istanbul. For fifteen years, he lived as a well-kept hostage of the caliph Abdul Hamid II, who correctly distrusted Hussein as a schemer committed to his own ambitions. Finally the schemer succeeded. On November 1, 1908, Hussein at the age of fifty-five secured the coveted title of Sharif of Mecca, the caliph's representative as protector of the two holiest cities of Islam. In possession of an appointment that was spiritual in nature, Hussein turned it into a base of political power. Winning the allegiance of the Bedouin tribes, he soon forced the Turkish governor of the Hejaz to humble himself in public by kissing the hem of the sharif's robe.

As the thunder preceding World War I rumbled in early 1914, Hussein dispatched his second son, Abdullah, to Cairo to hint vaguely to the British resident minister, Lord Kitchener, that the sharif, with British support, might mount an Arab rebellion against the Turks. Although discreet in nature, the message implied that Hussein wanted the same deal the British maintained with the Arab sheikhs strung along the eastern coast of the Arabian Peninsula. In each of these petty principalities, a British resident minister doled out gold sovereigns or Maria Theresa silver dollars while he stood ready at the first sign of encroachment by a hostile power to summon the British fleet anchored over the horizon.

When World War I broke in August 1914, Kitchener recalled his conversation with Emir Abdullah. By October 5, the general had dispatched an emissary code-named "Messenger X" from Suez to Jeddah. Finally arriving in Mecca astride a donkey, Kitchener's envoy found that "every man he met, even if he possessed an insufficiency of clothes, was armed to the teeth and bristling with weapons."[17] Anxious to disrupt the Ottoman Empire's front on the Red Sea,

---

[17] Randall Baker, *King Husain and the Kingdom of the Hejaz* (New York: Oleander Press, 1979), p. 51.

Britain decided to commit to some form of Arab independence as long as the Arabs, under Sharif Hussein, effectively helped the British war effort. So began the celebrated correspondence between Sir Henry McMahon, British high commissioner for Egypt and Sudan, and Hussein, keeper of the Holy Places, prince of Mecca. McMahon began: "To the excellent and well-born Sayyid, the descendant of the Sharifs, the Crown of the Proud, Scion of Muhammed's Tree and Branch of the Quraishite trunk, him of the Exalted Presence and of the Lofty Rank . . . the lodestar of the Faithful and cynosure of all devout Believers . . . may his Blessing descend upon the people in their multitudes."[18] To Hussein and those who supported his cause, this exchange of letters constituted a solemn British promise of an independent Arab state following the defeat of the Ottoman Empire. The state Hussein envisioned and believed Britain had promised would include the entire Arabian Peninsula, north to Alexandretta in Syria, eastward to the Iranian frontier, and south to the Persian Gulf. Excepted from its boundaries were the British port at Aden and the districts of Syria west of Damascus—Homs, Hama, and Aleppo.

Yet while McMahon and Hussein exchanged their letters, Britain and its wartime allies negotiated secret agreements among themselves that divided the territories of the Ottoman Empire. In February 1916, the infamous Sykes-Picot Agreement between Britain and France ignored the Arabs, giving Palestine to Britain and Syria and Lebanon to France. A new kingdom of Transjordan, now simply Jordan, passed under British control along with tutelage over Egypt and possession of the oil-rich sheikdoms of the Persian Gulf. France took the city of Mosul in Mesopotamia, while Britain separated Kuwait from the province of Basra to ensure access to the sheikhdom's developing oil resources. It would not be until after the Bolsheviks released the documents during the Russian Revolution that the Arabs would know the full extent of British perfidy.

Confident that he had the promise of an Arab state, Hussein himself lowered a rifle on the Turkish barracks at Mecca to fire the first shot in the Arab Revolt against Ottoman rule. The secularism and zealous nationalism advanced by the Young Turks, combined with the seduction of Britain and France and the spirit of Arab nationalism, had broken the Arabs' emotional ties with universal Islam,

---

[18] Quoted in Peter Mansfield, *The Arabs* (New York: Penguin Books, 1985), p. 165.

enabling them to rebel against the Ottoman Empire in support of a Western alliance.

What the Arab Revolt was or was not lay in the eye of the beholder. To the sharif, it was a war to win an independent Arab nation ruled by himself and his sons. Despite his rhetoric, the imperious Hussein had never been an Arab nationalist ideologue, only an ambitious man carrying religious credentials. Still, he understood the psychology necessary to draw to his cause the Arabs from outside his own political alliances. Speaking to all Arabs, he declared, "We are Arabs before being Muslim, and Muhammed is an Arab before being a prophet. There is neither minority nor majority among us, nothing to divide us. We are one body. . . ."[19]

Despite the lofty rhetoric, the Arab Revolt never meant very much to anyone other than the sharif's own followers. The better measure of Arab sentiment was found in the 1915 Damascus Protocol, which defined the conditions under which Arab leaders were prepared to support rebellion against the Ottomans. The protocol, which came out of a broad conclave of Arab leaders, called for complete Arab independence from any foreign power. It drew the boundaries of an Arab state to encompass the Arabian Peninsula, Palestine, and what is now Syria, Lebanon, and Iraq. Finally, it declared that this Arab state would commit to a defensive alliance with Britain and would grant the British Empire economic preference within its borders. The whole concept of a commonwealth arrangement with a Western imperial power confirmed just how unsure the Arabs were about what Arab nationalism meant. In many ways, those at Damascus engaged in an ideological search for something to replace "Ottomanism." So long accustomed to membership in the universal Islamic state, the Arabs could not reasonably be expected to develop a clear sense of national identity overnight. Nor were they willing to accept Sharif Hussein as the Arab caliph. Nowhere was this more true than Mesopotamia where Arabs divided between Sunnis and Shia.

For all of these reasons, the Arab Revolt that unfolded was a British-Hashemite adventure in which the British paid and the Hashemites led. It took form on November 2, 1916, when Sharif Hussein stood in the Great Mosque at Mecca to proclaim himself

[19] Quoted in Milton Viorst, "The House of Hashem," *The New Yorker*, January 7, 1991, p. 46.

King of the Arab Lands. The Turks responded by threatening to march on Islam's holiest city to hang the "Old gray devil." Instead the desert turned into a battlefield on which Arabs attacked Turks. Hussein's largely Bedouin army, possessing only light arms and numbering somewhere between ten thousand and forty thousand men, depending on the day and place of battle, proved no match for Turkish artillery. Engaging in combat with the wisdom of the Bedouin, Hussein's forces chose to fight only when victory was certain and to withdraw to make coffee when it was not. The British command in Cairo, desperate to bring some order and direction to this chaotic Arab effort, sent several British officers to make contact with Hussein's forces. One was T. E. Lawrence, the legendary Lawrence of Arabia.

In the autumn of 1916, Lawrence, a young British eccentric educated at Oxford, arrived at Arab headquarters in Hama in Syria. There he encountered the dashing, white-robed Faisal, the third son of the Sharif of Mecca, framed in the uprights of a garden door. According to Lawrence, "I felt at first glance that this was the man I had come to Arabia to seek—the leader who would bring the Arab Revolt to full glory."[20] Lawrence proved right. Faisal, the tall dark scion of Islam's most distinguished family, wooed the Bedouin tribes of Arabia into revolt against the Ottomans, while Lawrence, the small blond Englishman, hit Turkish rail lines and garrisons in lightning raids that would immortalize the guerrilla fighter. What was in essence a Bedouin army immobilized thirty thousand Turkish troops strung out along the railway from Amman to Medina; prevented Turkish forces from linking up with the Turkish garrison in Yemen; and interfered with the Turks in Arabia from linking up with the Germans in East Africa to shut off the Red Sea to allied shipping. The Arab Revolt had earned its prize.

With the Ottoman Empire collapsing and the British under General Sir Edmund Allenby advancing north and east out of Palestine, Lawrence raced his Bedouins toward Damascus to lay claim to the capital of the Umayyads for Emir Faisal and the Arabs. Arriving first, the Arab army in their dirty stained *thobes* overlaid with belts of ammunition nosed their horses through the narrow

[20] T. E. Lawrence, *Seven Pillars of Wisdom: A Triumph* (New York: Anchor Books, 1991), p. 64.

streets.[21] Before them, the men of the city laid down carpets over which the Bedouin warriors walked, while veiled women hidden in the overhanging balconies poured dippers of rose water on the liberators. Over and over, the people of Damascus chanted, "Faisal, Faisal, Faisal." Acting as the emir's deputy, Lawrence announced Faisal's government, later saying, "Our aim was an Arab government, with foundations large and native enough to employ the enthusiasm and self-sacrifice of the rebellion translated into terms of peace."[22] Unknown to the jubilant Lawrence and Faisal, the fate of the Arabs that had already been decided in the Sykes-Picot Agreement would be sealed in the smoke-filled rooms of Paris.

When the Paris Peace Conference convened on January 18, 1919, Faisal, accompanied by Lawrence, joined the politicians and diplomats, bankers and oilmen, bondholders and missionaries who gathered to push their respective interests in the peace accord that would mark the end of the Great War. The idealistic American president, Woodrow Wilson, was perhaps the only honest broker present. While the other victors schemed for territory, Wilson argued for peace based on his lofty Fourteen Points, which the Allies had embraced in the heat of war. But with peace, Lloyd George, the British prime minister, abandoned the troublesome idealism of Wilson's visionary plan to pursue aggressively territory for the British Empire. After four years of bestial warfare that had threatened to drain from Britain a whole generation, George lay claim to Egypt, Arabia, Palestine, and Mesopotamia as legitimate rewards for national sacrifice. In essence, the entire Middle East, with the exception of Syria and the Christian areas north of Beirut, became for Britain the realization of a predominately British Middle East. The French premier, Georges Clemenceau, proved less ravenous. Yet he insisted that France hold Syria and southern Anatolia and envisioned placing a French adviser at the elbow of the sultan of shrunken Turkey. Amid receptions, dinner dances, and weekends at rented châteaux within easy motoring distance of Paris, the future of the Middle East was decided.

Although the conference opened at the Palace of Versailles in mid-January, it was not until March 6 that Faisal was reluctantly

---

[21] The *thobe* of Arab men of the Arabian Peninsula is the same thing as the *disdasha* of the Iraqi Arabs. Both terms have cultured implications and therefore are not interchangeable.

[22] Lawrence, *Seven Pillars of Wisdom*, p. 649.

allowed to speak—for twenty minutes. With Lawrence at his elbow, Faisal, dressed in the flowing robes of Arabia, sat before George, Clemenceau, and Italian Premier Vitorio Emanuel. Speaking in classical Arabic, he explained to the Western-dominated conference that his father was asking for the right of self-determination for the Arabs and recognition of an Arab state as an independent geographic entity.

While the conference participants publicly listened to petitions from those who populated the lands of the former Ottoman Empire, British and French mapmakers huddled behind closed doors to draw the boundaries of what would become the Arab states of Lebanon, Syria, and Transjordan.[23] In every instance, boundaries met the needs of European colonialism. When Mesopotamia's turn came, the British once more rolled out the map. Skipping over Mosul with its large Kurdish population and historic tie to Syria, the mapmakers quickly drew a line around the Ottoman *vilayets* of Basra and Baghdad, the core of British interests. A wooden ruler laid down across the northern Arabian Peninsula set the southern boundary, bisecting a region in which large and powerful tribes had historically moved unchallenged by any authority except submission of the weaker tribe to the stronger. Thus, Mesopotamia re-entered history as a creature of its fragmented past. It was a contrived political entity with no natural center of gravity. Baghdad looked west as much as east, the Shia holy cities of Karbala and Najaf retained their centuries-old connections to Persia, while Basra in the south looked toward the Persian Gulf and India. Within each region, the population divided into a series of tribal federations and near autonomous cities. Within these cities, divisions following the lines of class, religion, and tribe separated group from group. The incongruous whole passed to the new and unproved League of Nations, the shell of respectability under which the victors of the war attempted to hide their avarice. Along with a host of other territories, Mesopotamia was to become a mandate under the supervision of a League member. To no one's surprise, newly configured Mesopotamia went to Britain. And it would be left to Britain to devise the means and the mode by which its people would achieve independence.

---

[23] The British and French also tinkered with other boundaries—Egypt, Palestine, Kuwait, and the other sheikhdoms of the Persian Gulf. Only the near empty center of the Arabian Peninsula escaped European cartography. Ironically Mark Sykes, one of the authors of the Sykes-Picot Agreement, died in Paris on February 2, 1919, a victim of the flu.

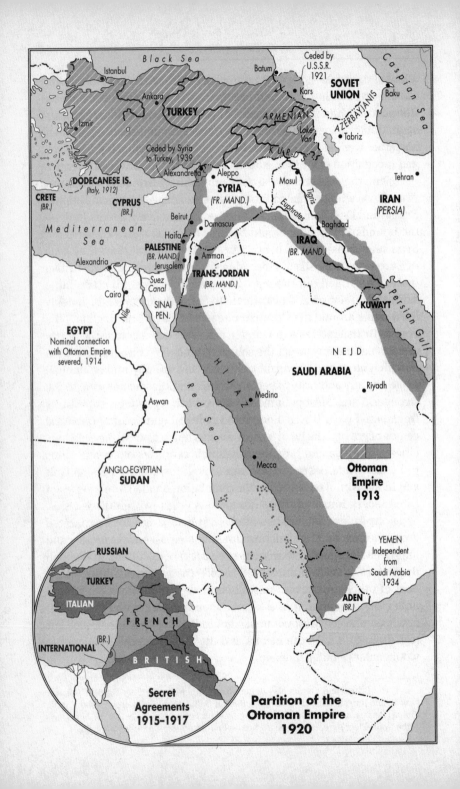

Partition of the
Ottoman Empire
1920

Secret
Agreements
1915–1917

WHEN THE MANDATE'S administrators sent from London arrived in Mesopotamia, they quickly dismantled Ottoman administration and replaced it with the same imperial structure that ruled British India. A staff from the Indian subcontinent supervised a new civil and criminal code modeled on Anglo-Indian law and organized the army and police force around skeletal units brought from India. Even the postage stamps confiscated from the Ottoman administration were overlaid with a new price denominated in Indian rupees. Although modifications to the Indian model came quickly, the British already had offended almost every sector of Mesopotamian society. In the cities, former officials and military officers of the Ottoman regime bitterly resented their abrupt loss of position and salary. The tribes railed because the British were proving more diligent in collecting taxes than the Turks. The Shia clergy detested the new authorities as Christians as much as anything else. And Arab nationalists, mostly Sunnis, chafed under yet another occupier. Jamiyat an Nahda al Islamiya, or the League of Islamic Awakening, an organization of Shia religious leaders, tribal sheikhs, journalists, and landlords, took form in Najaf. In Baghdad, a coalition of Sunni teachers, civil servants and former military officers, Shia merchants, and members of the Sunni and Shia *ulamas* formed the Haras al Istiqlal, the Guardians of Independence. When news reached Iraq that the San Remo Conference sponsored by the League of Nations in April 1920 had officially conferred the British mandate, Sunni-Shia cooperation solidified. Part of this power surge came from the *mujtahids*, the clerics of Shia Islam, who emerged from their shrines and *madresehs* to engage in politics.

Despite fundamentally different aspirations that posed a theocracy against secular government, prominent Shia *mujtahids* and Sunni nationalists in support of the Sharif of Mecca agreed to work together under a vague formula that called for an Arab-Islamic state ruled by an Arab emir whose power would be limited by a legislative assembly. But each side interpreted the ultimate aim of the declaration according to its own vision. The *mujtahids* saw it as enabling the Shia clerics to oversee the legislative process and the affairs of Iraq once the British mandate ended with independence. The Sunni nationalists behind Sharif Hussein considered it the formula for their own rule of Iraq through the nomination of one of the sharif's sons as king. At the moment, neither side explored these differing visions, for all attention focused on objection to British rule.

While the Arab nationalists in Baghdad fanned the flames of anti-British resentment and the Shia religious leaders in the holy cities called for *jihad*, the tribes revolted on June 2, 1920.[24] Arab Sunnis and Shia gathered in the mosques to denounce the British mandate as a disgrace to Arab honor. Raising the ideal of Arab unity and burying the reality of sectarianism, Sunnis and Shia decided that no matter how much they despised each other, at this moment they hated the British more. For both the Sunni and the Shia, the poet Muhammad Habib al-Ubaydi wove the words of rebellion:

> O you the people of Iraq, you are not slaves
> to adorn your necks with collars
> O you people of Iraq, you are not prisoners
> to submit your shoulders to the chains. . .[25]

Violence consumed the countryside as tribesmen wielding rifles and wide curved knives overran military posts, cut roads, severed lines of communication, and savagely murdered British soldiers and civil servants. In the cities, the souks shut up like oysters as merchants and customers took to the streets to denounce the mandate. By mid-August, the rebels had declared a provisional Arab government, prompting the British to send in fresh Indian troops to restore order. The towns quickly yielded to superior force but the countryside continued to burn out of control. Determined to impose order on its mandate, the British sent their air power into the skies to drop bombs on marauding tribesmen and their ground forces armed with artillery into the field to level whole villages before lining the insurgents up before firing squads. By late March 1921, the British had dismantled the provisional Arab government. But the cost had been high—2,269 British dead and wounded and £40 million.[26] In quelling the 1920 revolt, Britain had expended more than three times the amount required to finance the entire Arab Revolt against the Ottomans.

Shaken by the rebellion, Winston Churchill, secretary of state for the colonies, summoned Britain's experts on the Middle East to the

---

[24] The immediate cause of the tribal revolt was the imprisonment of a sheikh who refused to pay an agricultural debt.

[25] Muhammad Habib al-Ubaydi, "Ibrahim al-Wa'ili," *Thawrat al-ishrin fi al-shi'r al-'Iraqi*, Baghdad, 1968, p. 37, quoted in Yitzhak Naksah, *The Shi'is of Iraq* (Princeton: Princeton University Press, 1994), p. 69.

[26] An estimated ten thousand Arabs were killed in the revolt.

Semiramis Hotel in Cairo. Their mandate was, among other things, to draft a solution to London's Mesopotamia problem. Dubbed the "Forty Thieves," they constituted a remarkable cast of characters, particularly those who knew Iraq best. There was "Lawrence of Arabia," now an international celebrity created by a popular biography written by the American journalist Lowell Thomas. There was Sir Percy Cox, the British high commissioner for Iraq. Knighted for his long and fruitful diplomatic record, Cox, a tall, distinguished man, was universally respected for his knowledge, wisdom, and administrative skills, and through the multitude of caged birds and the pet bear that inhabited his home, was endowed with the eccentricities of the British upper class. Finally there was Gertrude Bell, one of the most extraordinary women of the early twentieth century. A student at Oxford at a time when few women were allowed to pursue higher education, she had trekked across the vast expanses of southern Iran, Syria, Saudi Arabia, and Mesopotamia with no companions other than a retinue of servants. But it was her mind more than her courage that won her a place at Cairo. Certainly more than Lawrence, perhaps more than Cox, she was the great political strategist. Under hats adorned with feathers, flowers, and artificial fruit, she blended the needs of Britain with an understanding of the Arab hunger for sovereignty. Each of those gathered around the table in Cairo held a personal stake in the future of Mesopotamia, where British interests and Arab aspirations tangled in the bitter brew of imperialism and nationalism. But none among the British had more to lose in the region between the Tigris and Euphrates than Churchill, who openly admitted, "I feel some misgivings about the political consequences to myself of taking on my shoulders the burden and odium of the Mesopotamia entanglement."[27]

It was at Cairo that Mesopotamia was formally christened Iraq. Like so much else connected with the policies of the foreigner, the name lacked clear meaning. Undoubtedly ancient in origin, some believed it came out of a lost language in which the word meant "a sunny land" or "flat plains" or "coastline" or "the country of dark color," perhaps a reference to the fertility of Iraq's agricultural land.

---

[27] Spoken by Churchill at the time of the Cairo Conference; quoted in *Washington Post*, September 15, 1996.

Whatever its meaning, the name was assigned by the British, not cho-sen by the Mesopotamians.

The other clear conclusion to come out of the Cairo Conference was to install Faisal, son of the Sharif of Mecca, friend of Lawrence, on a contrived throne of Iraq. In 1920, Faisal had ignored the British pay-masters of the Arab Revolt by establishing himself in Damascus as the head of his self-declared Syrian Arab Kingdom. To the emir and his fol-lowers, it was payment for services rendered to Britain's war effort against the Ottoman Empire. But in the diplomatic intrigue surround-ing implementation of the Sykes-Picot Agreement, France, not Britain, sided with Syria. Refusing to recognize Faisal's Arab government, the French on July 14, 1920, sent General Henri Joseph Eugène Gouraud to Damascus, accompanied by French regulars and Senegalese re-enforcements, to tell Faisal that he had four days to vacate the city. When the British refused to intervene, the emir proceeded to London to deposit himself on the doorstep of an embarrassed British govern-ment. Faisal, promised an Arab nation during World War I, had no throne. Britain, awarded Iraq as a result of the same war, had no gov-ernment for its mandate. Suddenly, the needs of the Hashemites and the interests of Britain merged.

The British perceived Faisal not only as the symbol by which they could restore their tarnished image among the Arabs but, more impor-tant, as a malleable monarch through whom they could rule Iraq. According to a hastily drawn plan containing all the elements of strategic planning executed through drama, Faisal was dispatched to Mecca, the holiest site in Islam, to emphasize his religious credentials as a descendant of the Prophet. While there, a proclamation went out from London announcing that the field commander of the Arab Revolt had been invited by the mandatory power to take the newly created throne of Iraq. In Baghdad, a segment of the "Forty Thieves" from the Cairo Conference led by Sir Percy Cox and Gertrude Bell went into action to ready Iraq for its new king. According to their instructions, Faisal arrived in Basra on June 23, 1921, and went directly to Karbala and Najaf as a gesture to Iraq's Shia majority. This is where the can-didate for king came face to face with the reality that he was Britain's choice, not the Iraqis'. Instead of the warm welcome the British had led him to anticipate, Faisal met a wall of hostility built by objection to a Sunni king and the desire for autonomous Shia rule under their own *mujtahids*. Carrying the weight of his rejection, the royal nominee nonetheless boarded a train, which delivered him to Baghdad on the morning of June 29 according to the British schedule. Looking every inch the king that London intended to make him, Faisal, wearing white robes and draped in a white headcloth, stepped onto the platform festooned with flags, flowers, and bunting to review an honor guard assembled by the British legation.

The carefully mapped British plan moved to its next step. On July 11, 1921, the Iraqi Council of State, a body contrived by and beholden to the mandatory power, passed a unanimous resolution declaring the thirty-six-year-old Faisal king of Iraq. The date was set for a well-managed plebiscite in which the Iraqis would approve the choice. To guarantee its outcome, Mrs. Percy Cox invited the major opposition figure, Sayyid Talib al-Naqih, to tea. The guest of honor was allowed to drain his cup before being whisked away in an armored car for a long enforced stay in British Ceylon. When the results of the plebiscite were announced, 96 percent of the populace allegedly favored Faisal as their king.[28] The stage was now set for the final scene of Britain's grand drama of king making.

By six o'clock on the morning of August 23, 1921, which dawned hot and still, fifteen hundred dignitaries representing the multiple elements of the British mandate of Iraq had already gathered in the courtyard of the Serai, the 1861 Ottoman building in Baghdad that now served as the seat of government. Faisal, in a khaki uniform and spiked helmet, walked from his quarters along a path carpeted with Persian rugs, entered the courtyard, and mounted a dais holding some chairs and a hastily constructed throne. Supposedly a rough reproduction of the British throne in Westminster, it was nailed together from packing cases still carrying the imprint "Asahi Beer." Saluted by the Honor Guard of the First Battalion Royal Berkshire Regiment, flanked by Sir Percy Cox, the British high commissioner, General Sir Aylmer Haldane, the British military attaché, and the towering Kinahan Cornwallis, the king's British adviser, Faisal listened as Cox read the proclamation declaring him king. After a few carefully scripted words of his own, Faisal stood ramrod straight as the new national flag broke over the dais to the accompaniment of a twenty-one-gun salute and

---

[28] Many Iraqis had no idea what they were voting for. Some Shia never realized Faisal was a Sunni, whereas some of the tribes in the north interpreted the ballot as a requisition for sugar.

"God Save the King," played by a British military band deprived of the yet-to-be written Iraqi national anthem. When the sound died, His Majesty, followed by a small procession, returned to his quarters. In all, the ceremony took a total of thirty minutes.

No matter how they manipulated the imagery that Faisal's government constituted a real gesture to Arab independence, the British had put the Hashemite on the throne in order to secure their own influence over the former Ottoman *vilayets* of Baghdad, Basra, and a slice of Mosul. Faisal was nothing more than a convenient symbol chosen to pacify the Arabs in Britain's raucous territory. Yet when the state Faisal nominally headed became complete, it included a significant minority that neither was Arab nor shared with the Iraqi Arabs any sense of common identity.

No sooner had Britain occupied Mesopotamia in World War I than London's imperial vision for Iraq confronted two irreconcilable forces—oil and Kurds. Both resided in the former Ottoman *vilayet* of Mosul, whose oil fields, legend asserts, were Nebuchadnezzar's furnace. Britain lusted for Mosul's coveted oil resources but recoiled from taking on the Kurds, whom they judged as an untamable tribal people better left in the wilderness of the mountains. The Treaty of Sèvres of 1920 aimed to do just that. Negotiated between the victorious powers of World War I and the moribund Ottoman sultanate, the treaty created an autonomous Kurdish state encompassing most of the Kurds living on the bridge of mountains that begin in northern Iran and pass through northern Mesopotamia into southern Turkey. Confirming their intention to grant Kurdish independence, the powers at Sèvres stated that the new entity would be eligible for membership in the League of Nations in 1921. But the British reconsidered after the Kurds added their own energy to the revolt of 1920, and the Turkish nationalist Mustafa Kemal, the famed Atatürk, seized control over the Kurds of southeastern Turkey. Initial thinking focused on carving out a series of autonomous provinces in the Kurdish areas of the Mosul *vilayat* that would be loosely attached to the Arab administration of Baghdad. To that end, the British appointed Sheikh Mahmud al-Barzinjah, the venerated leader of the Qadiri dervish community and one of the largest Kurdish landowners, as governor of Sulaymaniyah. As soon as he took office, Sheikh Mahmud began to act as the sovereign of an independent state tol-

erant of violence against the policies and personnel of the mandatory power. Consequently, the British removed Mahmud in May 1920
and put him on trial for "Rising against Great Britain and spilling
much blood . . . [and] lowering the Flag of Great Britain and tearing
it up and replacing it with that of Kurdistan."[29] But when the sheikh's
brother began conspiring with Turkey in 1922, Britain called
Mahmud back from exile in India. Exceeding his instructions from
London, he declared himself Mahmud I, king of Kurdistan. Again,
exercising the prerogatives of sovereignty, he formed his own government, issued postage stamps, and published a newspaper called
Rhozh-i-Kurdistan, or the *Kurdish Sun,* which proclaimed "the
right to life of a great independent people with a country of its
own."[30] By February 1923, Sheikh Mahmud was gone again, the victim of both Britain and tribalism among his own Kurds. His departure again left to Britain the question of Mosul.

British colonial policy demanded retention of the oil-rich Mosul
province, which was deemed vital to the economic viability of the
rest of the Iraqi mandate. Thus, at Britain's urging, the League of
Nations convened the Lausanne Conference, which concluded by
invalidating the Treaty of Sèvres. The future state of Kurdistan, envisioned and confirmed at the end of World War I, ceased to exist. The
defiant Kurds shouted a popular refrain against all who would control them. It continues to reverberate today:

> If we had a king,
> Turk and Persian and Arab
> Would all be our slaves.

Faisal's clear indication that he held no objection to an
autonomous Kurdish government within the political and economic
boundaries of Iraq did nothing to quell the anger the Kurds hurled at
Baghdad. As with the uprising of the Shia tribes, the airplanes of the
mandatory power again took flight. This time they descended on
Kurdish villages. In the mountains, both the use and the threatened
use of poison gas held the rebelling tribes in check while a League
of Nations commission sent in between January and March of 1925

---

[29] Rafiq Hilmi, *Kurdistan at the Dawn of the Twentieth Century,* vol. 1 (Uppsala,
Sweden: Rabun Forlag, 1998), p. 135.

[30] Quoted in Jonathan C. Randal, *After Such Knowledge, What Forgiveness?*
(Boulder, Colo.: Westview Press, 1999), p. 122.

assessed Kurdish wishes for their future. With independence taken off the table as an option, the Kurds split between those favoring rule by Turkey and those favoring rule by Britain. Almost all rejected inclusion in the Arab state of Iraq. Yet in the eyes of London, the Kurds remained essential to the stability of the mandate. It was not simply that the economy required the oil pooled beneath Kurd-populated land. The Sunni Arab minority in whom Britain had entrusted power needed the Sunni Kurds to help balance the numbers against the Shia majority. As if the Kurds had never spoken, the commission in March 1925 recommended that the Mosul *vilayat* be attached to Iraq. That decision snapped another incompatible component into the Iraqi body politic. And so Iraq—drawn out of the wilderness of Mesopotamia and pasted together from three provinces of the Ottoman Empire—took its present form.

With King Faisal in place and the final borders set, Britain looked on a colonial prize of deserts and swamps riven with communalism, private blood feuds, and sullen resentment toward the occupying power. Britain attempted to build a political system based on the model of its own constitutional monarchy. The Organic Law, approved and signed on March 21, 1925, gave the king considerable power, including the right to convene and adjourn the parliament, appoint ministers as well as the prime minister, and designate members of the upper house of the legislative assembly. Only the election of a lower house was left to the people. But rather than the constitution of an independent state, the Organic Law contained all the constraints of the mandate as did the treaty that had been concluded between Britain and the monarchy in 1922. It allowed the mandatory power control over Iraq's foreign affairs and a military presence on Iraq's soil. It required that the king heed British advice on all matters affecting British interests, and obliged Iraq to appoint British officials to specified posts to act as advisors to their Iraqi counterparts. These Iraqi counterparts were almost exclusively Sunni Arabs.

When the British arrived in Mesopotamia, the Sunnis, the favored class of the Ottomans, were so burrowed into Iraq's administrative structure that to remove them meant precipitating profound economic, political, and social change. That smelled of instability, the last thing British colonial policy would permit. As a result, the Sunnis were left in place, maintaining political dominance, enjoying most of society's benefits, gaining greater social mobility, and acquiring a vested interest in the new, emerging Iraqi state. Fearing what would happen once the British were gone, Shia leaders from the shrine cities attempted from time to time to counter Sunni dominance by proposing some kind of permanent British presence in Iraq, which they saw as preferable to full Sunni hegemony. At one point, the urban Shia floated the idea of creating an independent Shia state or to create an autonomous Shia territory in southern Iraq administered and protected by Britain. These adherents to Islam's dissenting sect even went so far as to invite British officials to take up residence in the holy cities, the very heart of their communal and religious life. This preference of infidels over orthodox Muslims demonstrated more than anything else just how much apprehension the Shia felt about the Sunnis who held the levers of the state. But the British, secure in the existing power balance, rejected all the entreaties of the Shia in favor of perpetuating their existing relationship with the Sunnis.

As for the tribes, the bulk of the population, the British allowed traditional tribal organization, mores, and customs to continue among all tribal groups—Sunni, Shia, and Kurd. Ottoman tribal policy that had so fragmented the great tribal confederations and tamed the once feared paramount sheikhs was reversed. When the British took possession of Iraq, they chose to impose order and improve tax collections by reconstituting the power of tribal leaders through economic fat dispensed by Baghdad and arms supplied by the government. By bestowing upon the tribal population special privileges not enjoyed by those in the cities and by preserving tribal customs and practices that were incompatible with nation building, the British turned back the clock. The net result was that at the very dawn of the Iraqi state, Shia and Kurdish populations became stalled in their intensively tribal societies, tied ever more closely to their sheikhs created by tradition and economics, and resentful of any authority outside the kinship group. Therefore in the countryside, the individual, more than at any time over the last century, constructed his allegiance to his tribe, his village, his sheikh, his religion, and his sect. The same could be said in varying degrees for the rest of Iraqi society, for Britain had deliberately brought together competing sects and ethnicities into the boundaries of an artificial state "without providing a set of satisfactory mechanisms by which their various interests and demands could either be reconciled with one another or contained within some overall national framework of accepted political practice."[31] As a result, fixed, singular communal identities of most Iraqis formed the base of the political system, precluding all serious efforts to meld Sunni and Shia, Christian and Jew, Arab and Kurd into a viable nation. Thus, the tragedy that Iraq is still living began in the mandate in which British administration centered on one goal: maintaining enough internal control to secure British territorial interests as they related to the issues of India and oil.

Ironically, after securing these vital interests, Britain over the decade of the 1920s grew increasingly weary of administrating Iraq. The energy and expense of its self-imposed entanglement in a territory and society that possessed little cohesion seemed to offset the gains encased in the mandate. British rule remained precarious, dependent on a few old war planes, some armored cars, a Christian militia, and the Arab Sunnis of Baghdad. Year by year, the burden of Iraq recalled Winston Churchill's comment on the day of Faisal's coronation: "If there is one thing that [Britain] grudges in the present deplorable state of its finances, it is the expenditure of further large sums in the deserts of Mesopotamia."[32] When the great global depression hit in 1929, the British government found itself under escalating economic pressure and mounting domestic criticism regarding the cost-benefit ratio of staying in Iraq. Many of the old mandate responsibilities had already been jettisoned to stanch the flow of half a million pounds per year. The British lion was ready to retreat to London if British interests could be protected in what was still scarcely more than a geographic expression.

King Faisal, who had always told the British with complete frankness that he would fight the mandate to the death, sensed Iraq's long-awaited independence. With the Arab Sunnis, the most trusted of Iraq's communal groups, in positions of authority, the two countries agreed to the 1930 Anglo-Iraq Treaty designed to pave the way to Iraqi independence in two years. The treaty safeguarded British interests, partly by assigning to London sovereign rights over two military bases—Habbaniyah, fifty miles from Baghdad, and Shaiba near Basra—plus unrestricted use of Iraqi airfields, ports, railways,

---

[31] Roger Owen, "Class and Class Politics in Iraq before 1958: The 'Colonial and Post-Colonial State.'" In *The Iraqi Revolution of 1958: The Old Social Classes Revisited*, ed. Robert A. Fernea and William Roger Louis (London: I.B. Tauris, 1991), p. 157.
[32] Quoted in *The Times* (London), August 23, 1921.

and roads in time of war. In addition, Iraq committed itself to "full and frank consultations" in all matters of foreign policy, agreeing "not to adopt in foreign countries an attitude which is inconsistent with the alliance." Denounced by Arab nationalists who hated the remaining British presence, by Shia religious and tribal leaders who saw the treaty as nothing more than a British umbrella over Sunni power, and by Kurds whose aspirations for self-government were ignored, the Anglo-Iraqi Treaty of 1930 would prove a plague on the monarchy. In perception and reality, Iraq had swapped the formal mandate for indirect dependency on Britain. Still, Faisal had won a singular victory by making Iraq the first Arab state in the Middle East to exercise even token sovereignty.

As the occupying force departed, Baghdad was a far different place than the broken, poverty-ridden city that the Ottomans occupied in 1534. It was also a far different city than the destitute backwater that the British had entered in 1917. Here and there irrigation works had been slowly rebuilt for the first time since the Mongol invasion. Administration was better than under the Ottomans. Education had improved in the urban areas. Revenues from the fledgling oil industry had begun to dull some of the sharp edges of rural poverty. An uneasy peace prevailed between city and countryside, between Arab and Kurd, Shia and Sunni, and Muslim, Christian, and Jew. But all the deep fissures were still there. Aggravating them all was Sunni dominance of the political system. Begun by the Ottomans to undergird their legitimacy and to maintain a bulwark against Shia Iran, this privileged position of one element of Iraqi society was propagated by the British to shore up a monarchy with little authentic legitimacy. The difference between the rule of the Ottomans and the rule of the British was that the Ottomans tied the territory of Mesopotamia to Istanbul through Islam. The British gave Mesopotamia its own nation-state but bound it to a Western country toward which most Iraqis felt no cultural or political affinity. It was the monarchy so carefully constructed by the British that would pay the price. Token independence did nothing to close the chasm of sectarianism, tribalism, conflicting economic interests, and differing definitions of identity that divided the urban Sunnis and the rural Shia. Nor did it even begin to resolve the animosity that existed between Sunni and Shia, who as "peasant and townsman alike reciprocated the hatred of the 700,000

Kurds, half-Moslem, half-animist, who glowered down on them from the mountain fastness of the northeast."[33] After 1932, the central issue of the monarchy would become whether Iraq was part of the mythological Arab nation dominated by Sunni Arabs or a state in which Arab and Kurd, Sunni, Shia, Jew, and Christian could build a common identity within a unique territorial unit.

---

[33] Howard M. Sachar, *The Emergence of the Middle East 1914–24* (London: Allen Lane, 1970), p. 366.

4

THREE KINGS:
MONARCHICAL IRAQ

A square-shaped mausoleum with a dome overlaid in a mosaic of black, white, and rose marble stands on the east bank of the Tigris, far from central Baghdad. When the taxicab stopped in front of Iraq's royal cemetery, the sun was releasing its last rays. In the descending dusk and in the absence of any human activity, the place seemed haunted. I walked around the corroded iron fence surrounding a weedy garden and the mausoleum. Inside lay some of the central figures of Iraq's early history as a state. Here one feels their presence, but beyond this site, most are forgotten, their memories as much a victim of the 1958 revolution as the institution of the monarchy they served. The irony is that those who are buried here are central to what Iraq is today, for they presided over the early struggle between Sunni and Shia, the Arab nationalist and the Iraqi patriot, for the right to define the state. As the last thin light disappeared, a heavy question descended with the darkness: if the men lying in these coffins had been insulated from the destructive forces pressing against Iraq from the outside, if they had been wiser and more tolerant, where might Iraq be today?

The Iraqi monarchy to which Britain gave life endured for a little less than four decades. Over that time, a succession of kings and politicians faced the challenge of turning a contrived state into a nation. Typically, national identity grows out of a common ethnicity, a common past, and a common culture that together imbue a geographic area with a particular meaning. This collective consciousness in turn provides the social cohesion that creates a viable and stable political system. None of these prerequisites of nationhood existed in nascent Iraq where each segment of society possessed its own distinctive vision of the state's common future.

This challenge of nation building was handed to a monarchy that, like the state, was imposed from the outside. The Hashemite dynasty placed on the throne by Britain came out of the Arab Revolt and the mythological concept of the Arab nation. But only the Sunni minority had any emotional commitment to Arab unity, and so from birth the political system of Iraq was manipulated by the Sunnis to the detriment of the Kurds and the Shia majority. Essentially shutting both out of the councils of power, the monarchy and its allies turned the state into the private agency of the privileged community, which had the effect of dividing the various factions rather than uniting them. Compounding the difficulty was the parade of external pressures that came from the British, the 1948 war for Palestine, the pan-Arabism of Gamal Abdul Nasser, and the Cold War. The challenge of nationhood proved too much for the fragile monarchy, which had neither the vision nor the power to deliver the basic reforms that might have created a nation. As a result, the issues of identity, equity within the political system, and Iraq's position in the world beyond its geographic boundaries have never been resolved. Their destructive forces tear at Iraq today as much as they did when the mapmakers at Versailles carved a fledgling state out of Mesopotamia.

BORN OF impeccable stock, Faisal, third son of the Sharif of Mecca, claimed a place in the thirty-seventh generation directly descended from the prophet Muhammad. Sickly as a boy, he spent much of his childhood among the Bedouin of the Hejaz to be hardened by the demands of the merciless desert. He learned to shoot, to manage the cranky bellowing camel, and to ride the fine Arabian stallion. In the tents of the sheikhs, he listened to the cadence of classical Arabic poetry and learned the skills of tribal leadership. Strengthened and tuned, he went to Constantinople as a deputy to the Ottoman Parliament and fought for the Turks in Yemen. In 1917, he took his experiences and skills into the Arab Revolt. In the last days of World War I, he established in Damascus the Arab government obliquely promised by Britain in the Hussein-McMahon letters of 1915–16. Fine boned, with a long face set with large liquid eyes, Faisal looked every inch a great Arab sheikh.

During his two years in Damascus, Faisal filled his house with a throng of black Abyssinian eunuch slaves imported from Mecca and a select group of khaki-clad officers who had deserted the Ottoman army to join the Arab Revolt. Brimming with the passion of Arab nationalism, they had fought across the deserts from Mecca to Damascus. Now the group that would become known as the Sharifians gathered around Faisal to fulfill the dream of an Arab state. When Faisal lost his Arab government, they followed him to London and then to Baghdad, where they formed the core of the court and acted as the custodians of Sunni political influence.

When Faisal and the Sharifians arrived in Baghdad in 1921, Iraq bore the scars of Ottoman neglect. Mosul, across the Tigris from the ruins of ancient Nineveh, languished within decaying stone walls where Arabs and Kurds engaged in desultory trade. In once glorious Baghdad, the richly colored tiles decorating the mosques barely clung to structures seemingly untouched since the days of the Islamic Empire. Water still came to homes in leather skins filled from the Tigris and delivered on the backs of donkeys. The city on the east side of the river was tied to the city on the west side by swaying pontoon bridges that floated on the round reed boats that Herodotus had described two thousand years earlier. There were only three of these bridges, for superstition held that when Baghdad possessed five, as in the days of the caliphs, the city would fall.

Since Baghdad had not been a true capital for nearly seven centuries, no palaces or buildings possessed even a modicum of grandeur. So after his coronation, Faisal went to the Citadel by the North Gate, driven in a car provided by the British. It traveled by the only real street in the city, a rutted unpaved road named for General Maude that cut a straight line through a maze of covered bazaars seemingly untouched by time. The sparse and antiquated infrastructure of Baghdad was symbolic of the new state of Iraq. It literally sagged under the accumulated weight of poverty, ignorance, and isolation that had reduced the land between the rivers to little more than an outpost of civilization.

The day Faisal picked up the reins of government, a simple street scene drew a complex sociological picture of his realm. Sunni bureaucrats and merchants proudly garbed in the newly popular Western clothes gathered around small tables outside the coffee shops strung along the Tigris. From there, they watched Jews hurry toward their banks; Christians move their crafts to the souks, followed by Persian merchants toting fine carpets; Kurds in their baggy *sharwals* unload a barge of produce from the highlands; and Shia sheikhs in flowing robes pass by on their way back to their villages in the south. In real terms, the social structure mirrored Ottoman times. The monarchy, with British contrivance, soon superimposed on it the Sharifians, who from the court took all the key military and governmental positions. Products of Ottoman education, many were related by blood or marriage. Claiming neither a local following nor a power base within Iraq, they depended on the government for their position, and the government depended on them to be the loyal cadre of Hashemite rule. Below the Sharifians, grouped in an imprecise and often fluid order, were the old Sunni elite, the Baghdad Jews, the Persian clerics and merchants of the shrine cities, the Christian elite of Mosul, the Sunni and Shia tribal notables, and at the bottom, the peasants, most of whom were Shia. Finally, there were the Kurdish clan chiefs, added in 1925 by the incorporation of Mosul province into Iraq. But before Faisal could even approach this internal tangle, he first had to secure his borders against his neighbors—Turkey, Saudi Arabia, and Persia, all of them geographically larger than Iraq.

The British, protecting their own interests in the oil resources of the Mosul region, took care of Atatürk's threat from Turkey. But in the south, Abdul Aziz ibn Saud and his Wahhabi zealots posed a serious challenge to Faisal's claim to the tribes of southern Iraq.[1] Beginning in March 1922, the Ikhwan, the fanatical Muslim brotherhood within the Wahhabi sect that often defied the authority of Abdul Aziz, periodically rode into Iraq to raid for faith and booty. In 1927 when Ikhwan raiders mutilated tribesmen in southern Iraq, it was Britain as the mandatory power that went into action. In a spate of low-tech warfare, single-engine Royal Air Force planes swooped low to drop pint-sized bombs on the marauding tribes while Model T Fords mounted with machine guns chased the Ikhwan back into Arabia. By 1929, the immediate threat from the south was over.[2]

The threat from the east, from Persia, defied simple military tactics. The Persian government, claiming Najaf and Karbala as "holy places of Persia," refused to recognize the infant state of Iraq. But Persia, like Turkey and Abdul Aziz, was in no position to threaten the British mandate of Iraq. Not only did Britain control Iran's oil

---

[1] In the West, the legendary Abdul Aziz ibn Saud, the father of modern Saudi Arabia, is most often known as Ibn Saud, "the son of Saud." In the Arab world, he is more correctly known as Abdul Aziz.

[2] The border disputes between Iraq and Saudi Arabia have never totally ceased, playing a role in the 1991 Gulf War. See chapter 9.

resources, but the Qajar dynasty sat in the dying embers of its own regime. In 1925 when Reza Shah Pahlavi ascended the Peacock Throne, Iran and Iraq, prodded by Britain, negotiated a boundary agreement that held until the 1980 Iran-Iraq War.[3] Thus, with the borders calm on the east, south, and north and the British military umbrella spread over Iraq, Faisal turned his full attention to the challenge of consolidating his state.

FAISAL I was one of those men whom circumstance plucks from history to impose form and meaning on chaos. In Faisal's case, he stood over a cauldron filled with boiling issues that swirled around the definition of national identity, the ability of the Shia religious establishment to challenge the authority of the state, the constant threat of rebellion by the tribes, and the distribution of power within the political system. The king approached them all individually and collectively.

Although branded a British puppet, Faisal, from the day he sat down on the throne, clutched the promise of Arab independence and gripped the torch of Arab nationalism. This had been his strength in Damascus. But in Baghdad Arab nationalism created the central tension within the nascent state at the moment of birth—a tension that has never been resolved. For the king, the Sharifians of the court, and much of the Sunni elite, Arab nationalism constituted their passionate political ideology. Although citizens of a state labeled Iraq, the Arab nationalists emotionally embraced an identity rooted in the concept of an Arab nation that transcended artificial political borders to encompass all those who spoke Arabic and called themselves Arabs. This was the spiritual level. In practical terms, pan-Arabism bestowed on the Sunni minority the political legitimacy to rule over a Shia majority. This is precisely why the definition of Iraq's national identity in the first days of the monarchy ignited sectarianism in all its complexity. Defined by the Sunnis as the heretics of orthodox Islam, the Shia within an Arab state enveloped in an Arab nation would lose not only their majority status in Iraq but also all hope of achieving political and economic supremacy or even equality. There was more. Deeper and wider than the demand for equity, the issue of Arab nationalism among the Shia plowed to the very depth of cultural identity. Shia Islam that supported its own social structure

---

[3] It was Reza Shah Pahlavi who would change the name of Persia to Iran in 1935.

shaped the parameters of a cultural life different from that of the orthodox Sunnis. Feeling no less Arab in the ethnic and linguistic sense than the Sunnis, the Arabic-speaking Shia yearned for a national identity in which their own cultural and religious motifs, their own local traditions and mores, would be woven into the fabric of the nation. In defining their own identity, the Arabic-speaking Shia in contrast to the Arabic-speaking Sunnis regarded themselves first as Iraqis and second as Arabs. But there was another element among the Shia who were not Arab—the ethnic Persians who challenged both the Sunni Arabs of Baghdad and Arab nationalism by depositing their identity with the *mujtahids* of the shrine cities.

Sunni animosity to the Persian Shia of Iraq ran deep. Its source lay in the distant yet vivid memories of the territorial contest in Mesopotamia between the Ottomans and the Persians. This was a prominent point around which the Sunnis constructed their defense of hegemony of the minority. Pounding away at the idea that Iraq's national identity dwelled in pan-Arabism, the Sunnis around the throne questioned the ethnic origins of the Persian Shia and their loyalty to an Arab state. Resurrecting the noble image of the Arab Islamic Empire, the Sunni political elite characterized the Shia as devotees of a subversive heresy propagated by the ethnic Persians of Iraq who harbored a centuries-old hatred of the Arabs. A letter circulated through Arab nationalist circles in the late 1920's sounded the theme: "These wavering [*mujtahids*] played around and sought shelter in Arab Iraq. . . . Their intention was to undermine the blessed Arab movement. In doing so, they betrayed the country under the protection of which they have led a life of ease and comfort so as to serve a foreign people [the Persians] who were one of the major causes of the termination of the Arab Empire."[4]

Consolidating their Persian and Arab wings, the Shia answered by denouncing pan-Arabism as a political ploy of a Sunni urban minority intent on excluding Iraq's rural majority from the body politic. Targeting the Sharifians, the Shia of the Arab tribes argued that it was they, the "indigenous sons of the country," who for centuries had preserved the true spirit of Arabism. Angered when Baghdad's Sunni politicians refused to acknowledge a Shia role in the

---

[4] Quoted in Yitzhak Naksah, *The Shi'is of Iraq* (Princeton: Princeton University Press, 1994), p. 91.

Iraqi state, a Shia student asked: "[Have] the Shi'is sacrificed their men, orphaned their children and widowed their wives in order to set up governmental chairs for the Sunnis on the skulls of their martyrs."[5]

Wounded by these verbal arrows, the Sharifians of the court, like the Sunni Ottomans before them, bore in on the roughly eighty thousand ethnic Persians residing in and around the shrine cities. Faisal, already alarmed by the opposition he had encountered among the Shia *mujtahids* when he arrived in Iraq to claim his throne, recognized that in the authoritarian structure of Shia Islam, the Persian-dominated Shia religious establishment held in its hands the power to compete for public support with any government. They were the Trojan horse within the walls of the Arab state. Propelled into action, Faisal moved to eradicate the power of institutional Shiism largely ruled by the Persian *mujtahids*. Lining up behind him were many Arabic-speaking *mujtahids* who were descended from Arab tribes in Iraq. Motivated by their own ambitions to rise within Iraq's Shia hierarchy dominated by Persians, the Arab *mujtahids* tapped out their denigration of the Persians on the wires of their tribal connections. They echoed the charges of the government of Baghdad by accusing the Persian *mujtahids* of fattening themselves on the wealth of Iraq and hinted that they should return to Iran, leaving the guidance of the Arab Shia to them.

The Persian *mujtahids*, by way of theology and political blindness, played into the hands of their enemies. In 1923, *fatwas*, or religious rulings, forbade the followers of the issuing clerics to participate in the elections to Iraq's first parliament. Anxious that a secular legislative assembly would limit their power as clerics, the Persian *mujtahids* called the elections a "death penalty for the Islamic nation." Faisal countermoved, determined to break the power of the principle clerics by forcing them to leave the country. The British concurred. Henry Dobbs, the high commissioner, told the king, "Present is [a] unique opportunity through which the Shia holy cities can be purged of predominance of Persian influence which has been exercised . . . to [the] detriment of true Arab interests. . . . There might never be recurrence of so favorable an opportunity."[6] All that remained was

---

[5] Quoted in Liora Lukitz, *Iraq: The Search for National Identity* (London: Frank Cass, 1995), p. 62.

[6] Quoted in Naksah, *The Shi'is of Iraq*, p. 84.

an amendment to the existing Law of Immigration that permitted the deportation of foreigners found engaged in antigovernment activity.

The willing or forced departure of their leading religious figures to Iran resulted in far-reaching consequences for the Shia in Iraq at the very dawn of the Iraqi state. With so many *mujtahids* flushed out of the country, the Shia religious hierarchy in Iraq floated in a vacuum. As a consequence of that vacuum of leadership, successive Sunni governments succeeded in drawing the most distinct line between religion and state found anywhere in the Islamic world of the Near East. From Baghdad, the hand of the Sunni-dominated government reached out year by year to grasp control of Shia institutions, charities, and observances, denying to the Shia what are potent political instruments in other Shia societies. It was effective. Near the end of his reign, King Faisal I would confidentially write, "The Shia ulama have no connection with the government and are at present estranged from it, particularly inasmuch as they see the Sunni ulama in possession of funds and properties of which they are deprived. . . ."[7]

If the grand Persian *mujtahids* formed one component of the Shia power structure in monarchical Iraq, the sheikhs of the major tribes and confederations comprised the other. Here the problem for Baghdad was not only sectarian antagonism but the fragile state. The tribes over which both Shia and Sunni sheikhs exercised influence were perpetual troublemakers. According to Gertrude Bell's assessment, the tribes "rule this country with a rod of iron. Not a caravan that passes up and down from Tikrit to Mosul, but pays them tribute on every animal. . . ."[8] Aware of the latent strength particularly of the southern tribes, and realizing that they must be brought to heel if Iraq were ever to be a sovereign state, Faisal put an iron hand into a velvet glove. Having grown up with the Bedouin, the king understood the subtle balance between exhibiting power and winning allegiance. On his arrival in Iraq in 1921, Faisal had acknowledged tribal power by visiting some of the most prominent tribes of the south before

---

[7] Quoted in Hanna Batatu, "Shi'i Organizations in Iraq: al-Da'wah al-Islamiyah and al-Mujahidin." In *Shi'ism and Social Protest*, ed. Juan R. I. Cole and Nikki Keddie (New Haven: Yale University Press, 1986), p. 189.

[8] Quoted in Janet Wallach, *Desert Queen: The Extraordinary Life of Gertrude Bell: Adventurer, Adviser to Kings, Ally of Lawrence of Arabia* (New York: Anchor Books, 1999), p. 89.

proceeding to Baghdad to take the throne. Approaching their encampment, the motorcade carrying the candidate for king was sur- rounded by a mass of sun-baked desert men astride their best horses who shouted their ancient tribal greetings. Faisal, draped with a *bisht*, the traditional cloak that signifies authority, humbly received the hospitality of his hosts. But before he departed hours later, he announced firmly that there was a new paramount sheikh in south- ern Iraq: "From this day and this hour of the morning any tribesman who lifts his hand against [another] tribesman is responsible to me— I will judge between you, calling your sheikhs in council. I have my rights over you as your lord." [9]

Although intent on subordinating the sheikhs to his authority, Faisal had no intention of destroying them as a group. Like the British, the king also needed the sheikhs. Acutely aware that he lacked his own political base in the country, Faisal maneuvered to draw the sheikhs into the power structure in order to maintain and improve his own hold on Iraq. Thus, in 1923 while the Persian *muj- tahids* prepared for their departure from Iraq, the king toured the tribes to promise the sheikhs a larger personal stake in the economy and politics of Iraq. He delivered. In 1924 the Tribal Disputes Regulations gave the sheikhs almost despotic power over their tribesmen. And under the land policy of the monarchy, the tribal sheikhs became even larger landowners than they had been under the Ottomans. Despite the fact that the majority of the sheikhs were Shia, they were plugged into the same political and economic inter- ests as the Sunnis of Baghdad. Spending the greater part of the year in the capital as part of the elite, the sheikhs within their pretentious townhouses deserted the traditional mode of leadership. Turning their fellow tribesmen into peasant slaves, the major Shia sheikhs joined the Sunni landlords in a vigorous defense of an unbalanced social system based on outmoded patterns of land tenure. Still, the power in this Sunni-Shia alliance of common interests was unequal. The Sunni landlord, much better connected than the tribal sheikh and more familiar with the game of politics, held a greater advantage in an administrative apparatus whose echelons were manned by Sunni officials. The Shia masses who had been deprived of both their sheikhs and their religious leaders found themselves essentially

---

[9] Quoted in Philip Ireland, *Iraq* (London: Jonathan Cape, 1937), p. 466.

immobilized in the contest for control of the politics and culture of the Iraqi state.[10]

The manipulation of the tribes by the Baghdad politicians and Britain's support of the Sunni establishment in what was a colonial state ensured that the Sharifians and their allies continued to reign as the political elite of the country. As a result, political life in the organized sense soon became sterile. The political parties that were allowed to function were seldom more than temporary combinations between individuals who shared a common interest for the moment. Thus, for most of the life of the monarchy, a basic caucus of 166 men would follow each other in and out of power. Demonstrating the resiliency of the Ottoman tradition that excluded the Shia from government service, the civil service belonged almost exclusively to the Sunnis, as did the command positions in the army. Yet the very small number of Shia in government also reflected the reluctance within the Shia community to accept government positions. The faithful faced the same theological dilemma under the Iraqi state they had faced under the Ottoman Empire: whether or not it profaned a believer to accept a position in a government considered illegitimate in the absence of the Twelfth Imam. While some Shia sought government positions to gain social mobility and political influence in the new state, many more individuals refused to accept the handful of positions offered by the Baghdad elite for fear that the condemnation of his community would deprive him of his wife, prohibit him from entering the public bath, and ostracize him from Shia society. Confirming the warning from another perspective, those educated and ambitious Iraqi Shia who did risk ostracism by accepting a place in government usually found themselves isolated within the apparatus of the Sunni-dominated state.

INCREASINGLY SENSITIVE to the conflicting sectarian and linguistic identities that threatened to rip his country apart, Faisal came to realize the imperative of constructing a national identity apart from Arab nationalism. As the king, and as the sheikh, responsible for the country's divergent communities, Faisal quickly began to devote his energies and his prestige to the challenge of building an Iraqi identity that would hold together all the elements of his improbable state. He began with a national army.

---

[10] For the monarchy's relationship with the Kurds, see chapter 6.

Originally Faisal, along with the Sharifians, coveted an army as a symbol of national sovereignty and a bulwark of the king's authority. But early in his reign Faisal grasped the idea of an army as an instrument for inculcating an Iraqi patriotism among all the country's varied communities. The task of building a military organization from scratch went to Jafar al-Askari. Round and good-humored, al-Askari came out of a family of largely Kurdish descent from Mosul. Fluency in seven languages—English, French, German, Arabic, Turkish, Kurdish, and Persian—attested to his prodigious intelligence. Trained in the Military College in Istanbul before World War I, al-Askari fought with Faisal and Lawrence from Mecca to Aqaba, inflicting the Arabs' final blow on the Ottomans at Mann in southern Jordan. In Baghdad, he became Faisal's military advisor.

Al-Askari began the construction of the Iraqi army by placing a huge ledger on a table in a humble room designated the Ministry of Defense. Into it, he wrote a military vocabulary derived by assigning Arabic words to English military terms. They ranged from commands issued in battle to the names of utensils required in every field kitchen. Next, he moved to a blueprint for universal military conscription. During the parliamentary debate on the issue in 1927, al-Askari, following the mandate of Faisal, raised the national draft beyond the realm of defense: "We will . . . open the door of participation in the defense of the country before all classes of the nation. There is no doubt that an army in which all these classes participate will be more inclusive of the racial qualities and national virtues with which the Iraqi nation is graced than an army built on any other basis."[11] The Shia tribesmen shouted condemnation at conscription, viewing the draft as a means by which Baghdad would increase the central authority of the state. Across the south, the tribes circled their campfires in the dance of war and chanted their defiance of the government with the words, "Those who impose conscription, let them come."

If the Shia hoped to cause a political crisis over the conscription bill, they succeeded. Under intense pressure, the government withdrew the bill from parliament. If the Shia rejected the army as an

---

[11] Quoted in Reeva S. Simon, *Iraq between the Two World Wars: The Creation and Implementation of a Nationalist Ideology* (New York: Columbia University Press, 1986), p. 117.

implement of societal unification, however, they embraced another of Faisal's nation-building ideas—public education. But as the details of implementation unfolded, the whole issue of a national educational system proved more complex but no less contentious than conscription. And like conscription, it highlighted again the challenge of nation building in this multidimensional society.

The Shia and the Sunnis initially embraced public education for different reasons. For the rural Shia, education spelled literacy and the acquisition of technical skills, which they saw as opening the gateway to economic and political equity with the Sunnis. From their point of view, the urban Sunnis perceived a national educational system as a vehicle by which a politically and, more important, culturally focused Arabism would be delivered to all of Iraq's varied communities. The man responsible for conceptualizing this all-embracing, identity-forging educational policy was Sati al-Husri.

A Syrian by birth, al-Husri arrived in Iraq in 1921 carrying all the attitudes and passions of an Arab nationalist. To him, "school was to be not only a place for study but also the theater of a new life, the mechanism for social change," through the inculcation of Arab culture as defined by the nationalists.[12] A fervent believer that language equates with identity, al-Husri envisioned the creation of a unified society by implanting in all Arabic speakers—Sunni, Shia, and Christian—appreciation of the common language that binds all Arabs. Moving out from the Arab mass of the population, he argued that compulsory education constructed on the Arabic language would break down the walls of communal loyalties, thereby tying all Iraqis to the state. Thus, united by the commonality of language translated into a common culture, Iraq's raft of communities would become a nation. Seemingly simple in concept, al-Husri's grand scheme aimed to create an artificial cultural homogeneity intolerant of attitudes outside the bounds of Arab nationalism.

While the Kurds cried foul against education in Arabic, the majority Shia denounced al-Husri's plan on the grounds of theology and culture. The rigid curriculum was to be controlled by a highly centralized system catering to the interests of a Sunni urban population rather than the needs of the rural Shia. They repudiated an educational philosophy and the nationalist ideology of an outsider who

---

[12] Ibid., p. 77.

ignored the special attributes of Iraqi Shia society. And they condemned standardized Arabic mandated from Baghdad, considering themselves no less guardians of the Arab language than the Sunnis. Perhaps more than anything, the Shia resented the less than subtle stereotype projected by Sunni educators that derided Iraq's Shia population as "ignorant and fanatic."

Shia resistance to al-Husri's educational policies only grew with the realization that government education was designed to sacrifice Shia religious and cultural values on the altar of Arab nationalism. Even the resignation of al-Husri and the appointment of a series of Shia as the minister of education did little to still the community's suspicions. In the end, the Shia objection to national education centered neither on the standardization of Arabic as the language of instruction nor on the inculcation of Arab culture, for both language and culture formed primordial elements in the Arab Shia's own collective identity. Rather it was the Sunnis' interpretation of Arabic language and culture and the Sunnis' control over the educational system that the Shia rejected. Thus, education, like conscription, failed to lay the first stones of a national identity that would encompass at least the Arabs in Iraq's population. As the second decade of Iraq's life as a state opened, the Sunni-Shia differences had come to mean more than a doctrinal schism. The two communities were split along the lines of education, politics, and emotion.

It was a bitter reality for King Faisal, who was toiling away at the task of turning his state into a nation. In the process, he had grown in his role as king to become a far greater statesman than anyone had expected in 1921. Although still cherishing the ideals of Arab nationalism that he had carried since the days of the desert revolt, Faisal had come to see Iraq as a unique piece on the Arab landscape. More than his subjects and the Sharifians around his throne, he understood that his country was both Arab and non- Arab, containing powerful aspects of Arab history and identity but also heavily influenced by the non-Arab territories that lay to his country's east and north. If Iraq were ever to become a nation, Faisal realized that he must convince his people that before they defined themselves as Sunni or Shia or Kurd, they must see themselves first as Iraqi. Considering the tribal nature of his realm, this process of self-realization had to be accomplished tribe by tribe, clan by clan, family by family.

From early morning to late midday, the official chamberlain led

Faisal's subjects, one by one, into their monarch's palace. In the main salon where servants passed coffee, lime tea, and gilt-topped cigarettes, urban and rural notables were carefully shifted and maneuvered from place to place for hours and sometimes days to ensure that the most important reached the royal presence in the order dictated by the complex social hierarchy. Each came with a request that the king would grant or negotiate but seldom flatly refuse. Across the hall, the less important sheikhs and clan leaders of the nomadic tribes gathered around the coffee hearth of a king from Mecca who perfectly understood their Bedouin ways. Each of these visitors required a present—guns, money, clothes, supplies of food, or all four, depending on the power he wielded among the ever restless tribes. It was in this way that Faisal balanced one group against another as he went about the effort of building a nation for a thankless people who felt little love for their king. Even in delivering a measure of independence from Britain, Faisal had won little popularity. Failing to understand that their king had accepted the 1930 Anglo-Iraq Treaty as the price required for an end to the mandate and British protection against hostile neighbors, the Iraqis laid on Faisal their hostility toward their colonial masters. This was the sad fate of the man on the throne. In 1932, an American minister to Baghdad sympathetically noted, "I have seen [the king] pass along New Street time after time but the only people who seemed to pay attention to his passing were foreigners who . . . paused and lifted their hats."[13]

Compounding Faisal's problems was the political system imposed by the British , which the monarch dragged along like a ball and chain. In an act of enlightenment gone awry, Britain had given its mandate a limited democracy. But the Iraqis were not ready. Personal cliques of politicians fed constant intrigues that sabotaged one government after another, making and breaking fifteen prime ministers during Faisal's twelve-year reign. During the frequent election campaigns, all government business ceased while the civil service disappeared into the labyrinth of election rigging. Beyond elective politics, courts handed down judgments determined by political games or the desperate need of judges to supplement their meager salaries by selling out to the highest bidder. In 1933, in the most ominous portent of the future of Iraq, the army, Faisal's promised imple-

---

[13] Ibid., p. 60.

ment of national unity, wounded the state in a blatant act of communalism.

Despite deep Shia distrust of the army, it was the Assyrian Christians who became the military's first victim. Largely mountain villagers living in what is now southern Turkey, they had been imported into northern Mesopotamia by the British during World War I to fight against the Turks. Once the war ended, many stayed to serve the British as levies during the mandate. With Iraqi independence in 1932, the Mar Shamun, the Assyrians' spiritual-temporal leader, petitioned the League of Nations for Assyrian autonomy within Iraq. At the beginning of August 1933, escalating tension ignited a skirmish between Assyrian dissidents and the Iraqi army. At the sight of thirty-three dead Iraqi soldiers, Baghdad panicked. Fearing the Assyrians as a formidable fighting force capable of provoking a general uprising in the north, the Arab nationalist Ikha Party that headed the government at the time took advantage of Faisal's absence from the country to unleash Kurdish irregulars on two Assyrian villages. A hundred Assyrians died in what was the beginning of a bloodbath. On August 4, General Bakr Sidqi led a contingent of the regular army into the northern hills carrying one simple order—massacre. Storming through Assyrian settlements, green uniformed soldiers reached Duhok on August 13. Herding batches of eight or ten Assyrians into trucks, they drove a short distance from the village, ordered their captives out, and machine-gunned them to death. Then the army withdrew, leaving the Shammar tribe to loot what was left. In Baghdad, Iraqis representing most of the other communal groups poured into the streets to declare Sidqi a conquering hero. In a real sense, the Assyrian massacre constituted the final event of Faisal's difficult reign.

In a confidential memo, Faisal had earlier mourned,

> In Iraq, there are ideas and aspirations that are totally antagonistic. There are innovating youngsters, including government officials; the zealots; the Sunna; the Shia; the Kurds; the non-Muslim minorities; the bribes; the shaykhs, [and] the vast ignorant majority ready to adopt any harmful notion . . . Kurdish, Shia, and Sunni tribes who only want to shake off every form of [central] government. There is still—and I say this with a heart full of sorrow—no Iraqi people, but an

unimaginable mass of human beings devoid of any patriotic ideas, imbued with religious traditions and absurdities, connected by no common tie, giving ear to evil, prone to anarchy, and perpetually ready to rise against any government whatsoever. Out of these masses we want to fashion a people which we would train, educate, and refine. . . . The circumstances being what they are, the immenseness of the efforts needed for this [cannot be imagined]."[14]

At the time of the Assyrian incident, fifty-six-year-old Faisal was discouraged and ill. Forced to abandon his medical care in Switzerland in order to rush back to Iraq to try to repair the damage done to the Assyrians by the army, the king prepared to return to Europe in early September 1933. On the eve of his departure, he bid farewell to his people: "I hope that my absence will not last for more than six weeks. . . . Relying on the assistance of almighty God, I shall continue to do my best to serve my country and nation. . . ."[15] The next morning he stole out of Baghdad almost unnoticed. Five days later in a hotel on the shore of the lake at Interlaken, Switzerland, he died of coronary thrombosis.

HMS *Dispatch* bore Faisal's body to Haifa on the eastern shore of the Mediterranean, where a Royal Air Force plane picked it up and carried it on to Baghdad. The aircraft touched down on September 15 and taxied toward waiting officials. After opening the cargo hold, the British escort eased the coffin forward onto the shoulders of eight senior Iraqi military officers. No one had thought to warn them that the Swiss undertaker had sent their king home in a heavy copper casket. When the portly Arab generals sagged under the weight, British airmen raced forward. Lending their shoulders, the young men of the former mandatory power moved with the men now in command of independent Iraq toward the gun carriage that would bear the king's remains through the city. Crowds of wailing people lined the streets to mourn their king, loved only in death. When Faisal's grieving subjects surged into the street, the solemn procession lost all semblance of order. Most of the senior Iraqi officials and

---

[14] Quoted in Amatzia Baram, *Culture, History and Ideology in the Formation of Ba'thist Iraq 1968–89* (New York: St. Martin's Press, 1991), p. 129.

[15] Quoted in Majid Khadduri, *Independent Iraq 1932–1958: A Study in Iraqi Politics* (London: Oxford University Press, 1960), p. 43.

the British civil servants who had stood behind the king through his reign were separated from the funeral cortege by the crowd before Faisal was lowered into his grave at Adhamiyah on the outskirts of Baghdad.

Faisal I had nurtured the institutions of the state he was bequeathed. They included the army that was to preserve internal order and defend Iraq's territorial borders against its formidable neighbors; the bureaucracy that was proving to be reasonably successful in executing the various functions of government; and a legal system that despite serious faults at least held out some promise of the rule of law. The tribes had been corralled, if not tamed. Religious unrest fomented in the shrine cities had been suppressed through expulsion of the major *mujtahids*. Revolts among the Kurds had been contained, if not crushed. A political process had at least begun in which there was give, take, and chaos between the king, cabinet, parliament, army officers, tribal sheikhs, and the old and new elites of Baghdad. Faisal had achieved much, but his efforts at nation building were hampered by a Sunni minority that jealously guarded its advantages and the government of Britain that continued to demand from Baghdad the protection of its interests. All of Iraq's achievements and problems under Faisal now passed to the second Hashemite king, Ghazi.

GHAZI IBN FAISAL, "victorious son of Faisal," was only twenty-one when he succeeded to the throne of still-infant Iraq. Born in Mecca in 1912, he was raised in the harem under the adoring care of his mother, Princess Rafia, whom members of the court regarded as not quite stable. In 1924, the small shy Ghazi was summoned to Baghdad to begin his preparation for the throne. A barely literate adolescent, he spent less than a year with a tutor before he was sent to Harrow in England. The experience proved unpleasant for both Ghazi and his teachers. Frustrated by his studies and miserable in an alien environment, the Iraqi crown prince once screamed at his housemaster that he intended to summon the Iraqi army to burn down his residential hall. At night, he slept in a fur-lined aviator's cap to prevent the *jinn*, the evil spirits that had always terrorized the Bedouin, from entering his ears while he slept. Ghazi never finished Harrow. Instead, he came home to play his way through the Military Academy in Baghdad.

Temperament alone destined that Ghazi would never be the leader his father was. Nor were the times the same. When Faisal I arrived in Baghdad in 1921, public scribes squatted in rows outside government offices waiting to serve a population overwhelmingly illiterate. Now, under the much-maligned national education system, boys and even a few girls sat at desks in gaunt new buildings studiously pursuing a range of subjects deemed necessary for a modern country. The ramparts and gates of the old city had been pulled down, and the traditional Arab theaters had been replaced by cinemas and cabarets offering cultural imports from the West. The *effendi*, the new man of property and education, set the tone of an urban society imitating the manners, if not the values, of the West. Commenting on the new order, a schoolmaster at Baquba once told Freya Stark, "There is not an Arab who does not take refuge with Allah from the discomfort of your socks."[16]

Ghazi, a product of the younger generation that grew up expressing its animosity toward the British presence in Iraq, was far more popular than his father when he mounted the throne. But it was a popularity that reflected the baser instincts of Iraqi society. A few days before Faisal's death, the crown prince had personally decorated the "victorious" Bakr Sidqi, the army commander whose troops had massacred the Assyrians. Perhaps Ghazi best served Iraq by wearing the crown for only six years. Usually appearing in public in dark sunglasses with a revolver strapped to each hip, he lacked both the intellectual equipment and the interest in public affairs necessary for the tough job of being king of Iraq. More inclined to concentrate on pleasures than duties, tactless to the point of rudeness, he avoided the time-consuming ceremony and arduous dialogue that his father had so effectively used to keep the tribal leaders in check. Unreceptive to the rules and mentality of tribal life, he spent his time and attention pursuing his own pleasures in urban Baghdad.

The real power in Iraq was wielded by Nuri al-Said. Born in Baghdad in 1888, al-Said was slim, slightly built, and marred with large scars from "Baghdad boils."[17] He attended the Military College in Istanbul where he formed a strong bond with the future father of

---

[16] Freya Stark, *Baghdad Sketches* (Evanston, Ill.: Marlboro Press, 1996), p. 28.

[17] "Baghdad boils" are actually signs of cutaneous leishmaniasis, a parasitic infection that is endemic to the Middle East.

the Iraqi military, Jafar al-Askari.[18] Exhibiting a keen political mind, he served as Faisal's chief of staff when the Arab army fought its way northward out of Arabia. In Damascus, al-Said, always neatly dressed and usually fingering a chain of amber beads, filled the same role in Faisal's court. When the French dismissed Faisal and his government, al-Said followed the emir to Baghdad.

No one could match Nuri al-Said's intelligence, ability, self-assurance, and skill at political maneuvering. He was a man who would have made his mark in any country. In Iraq, he was a giant who participated in every major decision made over the entire life of the monarchy, whether he happened to be in office or out of it. Much of the reason for this extraordinary power is that al-Said's talents perfectly fit the Iraqi political environment. Politics was a ferris wheel on which eight ministers sat in eight seats. In the words of the scholar Majid Khadurri, "There were always some 15 or 20 ex-ministers waiting impatiently for [the wheel] to stop; and if it happened that the wheel did stop and the eight ministers left their seats then another eight of the waiting ex-ministers would at once hasten to jump on to the wheel and occupy the vacant seats. The wheel would then resume its cyclic movements, and the remaining ex-ministers including the eight ministers who had just left their seats, would all co-operate for their mutual end, namely, to stop the ferris wheel again in order that each might have another chance."[19] The ministers on board had no time for the work of government, only time to defend themselves from the unrelenting assault of ex-ministers waiting to grab their seats.

This debilitating charade that was Iraqi politics came out of the gut of society. On the plain of the state, community stood apart from community. Inside these communal groups, class stacked upon class. Cross-communal connections between Sunnis and Shia, Arabs and Kurds, were shifting the associations of Baghdad's elite Sunni politicians, Shia tribal sheikhs, and Kurdish aghas who never assumed a common goal or transcendent cause. At the same time, the *ulama* (the religious leaders among the Sunnis and Shia), the tribal leaders in the Kurdish areas, the patriarchs in the Christian communities, and the chief rabbi of the Jews functioned as more than religious fig-

---

[18] Nuri al-Said and Jafar al-Askari married sisters.
[19] Khadurri, *Independent Iraq 1932–1958*, p. 76.

ures. Each acted as the guardian of the cultural heritage and collective identity of his community. It was the religious leader who shaped the parameters of consciousness for his confessional, determined his community's political dimension by setting the level of its activity in the political process, and confronted the government in defense of the community's common interests and values. Because few, if any, politicians or religious leaders addressed the question of how to define the common good or the Iraqis' collective identity, Iraqi nationality simply could not surmount the traditional loyalties to faith, language, tribe, and town.

Through it all, al-Said, surrounded by his band of Sharifians and their allies within the court of Ghazi, kept power centralized in Baghdad. Without the reassuring presence of Faisal, the Shia more and more identified the Sunni-dominated government as a "government of occupation." Armed with the British census of late 1932, which confirmed them as the majority of Iraq, the Shia in the tribes, villages, and shrine cities murmured about rising up to wrest their rights from the Sunnis. The government countered by upping the bribes to the *hukuminun*, partisans of the government, who from their traditional positions of leadership were expected to keep their communities in line. Thus, ownership of even more land passed into the hands of the greedy sheikhs who collaborated with Baghdad politicians to ensure that the status quo prevailed.

In September 1934, Iraq's Arab population arranged itself in a triangle of power. One side was composed of Sunni politicians supported by the court; another, of the Sunnis' political allies among the Shia sheikhs; and the third side, of the educated Shia, lesser tribal sheikhs, and the Arab *mujtahids* who were opposed to the whole rotten order in Baghdad that imposed miserable economic conditions on them. With the tribesmen of the middle Euphrates beginning to take up arms, the king dismissed one group of politicians and summoned another. In the political melee, Sheikh Muhammad Kashif al-Ghita warned the rebellious Shia, "If [you are] united, any government will listen to you, but if [you are] divided, no benefit whatsoever will derive from it."[20] Taking heed, a group of Shia lawyers gathered in Baghdad to formulate a manifesto of Shia demands. Among other things, it called for Shia participation in government,

---

[20] Quoted in Lukitz, *Iraq*, p. 70.

parliament, and the civil service in proportion to the Shia's share of the population; the teaching of Shia jurisprudence in the law school; an inclusion of Shia members in all sections of the courts; distribution of government-collected *waqf*, or charity, revenues among all Islamic institutions; agricultural reforms; and government investment in education and infrastructure in Shia areas. Although failing to break the configuration of power in Baghdad, the Shia staked their claim to a place on the political map of the Iraqi state. But it was the old issue of conscription that finally forced the Shia to rebel.

Parliament had at last passed the National Defense Law in 1934, making conscription a reality. In 1935, partly in response to unrest in the south, the law was put into force. Threatened politically by the long-term implications of a Sunni-dominated army, angered by general maladministration of the south, and manipulated by opposing constellations of politicians in Baghdad, the Shia tribesmen rose up in arms. Fatla tribesmen cut roads and destroyed bridges; the Abu-Sukahr closed the main route between ad-Diwaniyah and Najaf; the Agra took control of al-Hillah just south of Baghdad. Contained momentarily by the army they opposed, the tribes rose up again in April 1936. This time the Sunni-led army imposed its will by burning crops, leveling entire villages, and executing tribesmen. No one in Baghdad stopped to remember the solemn words of King Faisal: "This government . . . rules a Shia plurality which belongs to the same ethnic group as the government. But as a result of the discriminations which the Shia incurred under Ottoman rule which did not allow them to participate in the affairs of government, a wide breach developed between these two sects. Unfortunately, all of this has led the Shia . . . to abandon a government which they consider very bad."[21]

The 1935–36 Shia revolts not only seriously damaged the already tenuous relationship between Arab Sunnis and Shia within the Iraqi nation but also wedged the army into the configuration of Iraqi politics.[22] Throughout the tumult Ghazi sat passively on the throne.[23] The semiliterate and emotionally immature king seemed to possess no

---

[21] Quoted in Edmund Ghareeb, *The Kurdish Question in Iraq* (Syracuse: Syracuse University Press, 1981), p. 1.

[22] See chapter 5.

[23] At the time, the monarchy was suffering its own crisis that erupted when Ghazi's sister, Azza, ran away with a servant from a hotel on the Island of Rhodes and allegedly converted to Christianity.

real sense that developing a nationalism specific to Iraq was crucial to the health of his country. Instead, he stepped forward as the most visible Iraqi spokesman for the ideology of Arab nationalism as defined by the Sunnis. Over his private radio station, Ghazi filled the airwaves with attacks on those who refused to hew a hard pan-Arab line. His targets included his uncle, King Abdullah of Transjordan.

Ghazi's stint as the voice of Arab nationalism might have proved more serious if he had been anything but a playboy king. His radio station, which in other hands might have become a vehicle of serious ideology, served principally as personal entertainment. It broadcast from Ghazi's palace, the Qasr al-Zuhur, which reflected nothing of Arab culture. Rather, it resembled a French villa, complete with pepper-pot turrets. Furnished by a London decorator, it suffocated under chintzes, tasseled flounces, and broad pink lamp shades. Dominating the center hall was a partially draped female figure carrying a torch. In this Disneyesque setting, Ghazi indulged himself in his favorite trick, attaching electric batteries to cigarette boxes, tissue holders, and drink trays to shock anyone who touched them.

Instead of growing in his role as Faisal had done, Ghazi increasingly diverted himself from the tedium of kingship with light aircraft, fast cars, and companions gathered off the lower rungs of the social ladder. On a spring night in 1939, the king had invited some of these friends to the palace for drinks and supper. Afterward he decided to entertain them with a film he had left on a table at al- Harthiya, a cottage built by his father on a backwater of the Tigris. Directing his chauffeur into the passenger seat, Ghazi leapt into his new Buick convertible, careened down the palace drive at great speed, and flew past the stables and onto a narrow road bordered by trees. At a humpbacked bridge, the front wheels of the speeding car left the ground. The automobile slammed into a telegraph pole, which cracked and fell forward, smashing the king's head. Panicked servants who had witnessed the crash carried their bleeding and unconscious sovereign back to the palace to the care of the royal physician. He could do nothing. At forty minutes past midnight on April 4, 1939, Ghazi ibn Faisal died at the age of twenty-seven.

Rumors racing through the country charged that the king had died as the result of a plot instigated by the British. At noon on the day of Ghazi's death, an irate mob attacked the British consulate in Mosul to burn the building and bury an ax in the brain of the consul,

George E. Monck-Mason. In Baghdad, throngs in the street screamed at the British embassy, "Thou shalt answer for the blood of Ghazi!" On al-Rashid street, the royal coffin strapped to a gun carriage moved through crowds wailing and beating their breasts in mourning for the young monarch whose resistance to British hegemony had elevated him to the status of hero. At the royal mausoleum, where his father had been buried six years earlier, Ghazi's body slid into its marble sarcophagus as buglers sounded the last post and a military honor guard fired a ninety-nine-gun salute. Far away in Tulsa, Oklahoma, a luxuriously appointed plane with furnishings of rich maroon leather inscribed in gold with the king's coat of arms sat on the runway of the Spartan Aircraft Company. All work was complete on Ghazi's new royal toy, except for the painting of his crown on the fins and wingtips.

In a real sense, the death of Ghazi doomed the monarchy. Many ordinary people held the belief that the British had murdered Ghazi to demonstrate that no Iraqi king could thwart their bidding. To the Arab nationalists particularly, the monarchy had become nothing but a screen behind which Britain foiled any Iraqi attempt to become a magnet for the political aspirations of the Arabs of the Middle East. Much of the popular blame for this real and perceived submission to Britain would fall on the court and Iraq's leading politician, Nuri al-Said. Eventually, the monarchy would be destroyed by collaboration with London.

THE COURT and the British, acting as the protector of the monarchy, faced the difficult question of who would rule for Ghazi's heir, his three-year-old son Faisal II. At the urging of al-Said, the cabinet invited Emir Abdul al-Ilah to become regent "in accordance with the wish expressed by King Ghazi as testified by the Queen in a statement to the Council of Ministers."[24]

Abdul al-Ilah, the tallest and fairest member of his family, was the son of Ali ibn Hussein, the last Hashemite ruler of Mecca, and the brother of Ghazi's widow, Aliyah. He shared with the Sharifians the lore of the Arab Revolt. On the night his grandfather, Hussein, the Sharif of Mecca, denounced Ottoman rule, he was one of the children rousted from bed, put on the back of a black slave, and carried

---

[24] Quoted in *New York Times*, April 5, 1939.

through the dark to safety in the high hills around Mecca. But as regent Abdul al-Ilah would prove to be more of an Anglophile than an Arab nationalist. Only twenty-seven years old when he became regent, the shy prince, along with the indefatigable Nuri al- Said, would dominate Iraqi politics and government until the last day of the monarchy. Together they would maneuver the alliance between the declining numbers of Sharifians and the tribal leadership to ensure control of the central apparatus of the state, even while the internal dynamics of the country changed radically. Within the major communal groups, the Sunnis, the privileged minority, began to split over the issue of Iraq's relationship with Britain, and the Shia, along with the Kurds and others who felt alienated from the economic and political hierarchy, drifted toward Communism. It all happened in the shadow of World War II.

During the 1930s, many Iraqis—both Sunnis and Shia, Arabs and Kurds—became captivated by Fascism. The appeal of Mussolini's Italy and, to a lesser extent, Hitler's Germany lay in the promise of escape from the strong hand of Britain, not in the ideology of Fascism itself. Ridding Iraq of British influence through Fascism was especially attractive to the officer core of the Iraqi army, most of whom were Sunnis. Thus, for the first time in Iraq's short history, the Sunni elite lined up on opposite sides of an issue central to the concept of Arab Iraq. On one side stood the palace, Nuri al-Said, and the Sharifians who were increasingly trading in their pan-Arab ideology for protection of their position by Britain. On the other side stood a nationalist faction of the army that saw in the tie between the monarchy and Britain the repudiation of Arab nationalism. Each backed by a corps of supporters epitomized the polarization of the old Arab Sunni bloc that had so well contained the Arab Shia in the contest for control of Iraq's identity. In 1936, Bakr Sidqi, the butcher of the Assyrians, led a coup d'etat against the pro-British government in power. In 1941, a second coup came, this one inspired by the reigning prime minister, Rashid Ali al-Gaylani.[25]

Rashid Ali al-Gaylani, a descendent of a twelfth-century Muslim mystic, had grown up poor as the consequence of his father's dismissal from the family fortune because he had married beneath his station. Trained as a lawyer, Ali entered politics and rose to a cabinet

---

[25] See chapter 5 for further discussion of the 1936 and 1941 coups.

position in 1935. "A hard worker, a persuasive speaker, a passionate nationalist, ambitious and reckless," he replaced Nuri al-Said as prime minister in 1940 through the help of four prominent Iraqi generals known as the "Golden Square."[26] Pushing aside the Sunni-Shia contest for the Iraqi state, Sunni went against Sunni in a fierce struggle between old and new forces contesting for control over Iraq's political destiny.

Appalled that the nationalist army officers resurrected "King Ghazi the Martyr" as the symbol of pan-Arabism, the regent, al-Said, and the British attempted to maneuver Rashid Ali out of office. With elements of the army at his side and with the clandestine help of Italy, Ali stayed. Next, the regent attempted to break the prime minister's power by ordering the generals of the Golden Square out of Baghdad. They ignored the command. Instead, on the night of April 1, 1941, the generals brought their troops into the capital to surround key points, including the palace. When the regent's cook handed him a sealed envelope that had been delivered to the kitchen door and contained a copy of his death certificate signed and dated for that night, Abdul al-Ilah fled to his aunt's house on the east bank of the Tigris. There he dressed in women's clothes, flagged a horse cab, and went to the American Legation. The American ambassador and his wife hid the regent beneath a blanket on the floor of their car and sped out of Baghdad to the British air base at Habbaniyah, where Abdul al-Ilah escaped on a British military plane. From the safety of Kuwait, the regent plotted his return while the child king, Faisal II, and his mother remained "under house arrest" in Kurdistan.

From a boat anchored at the mouth of the Shatt al Arab, Abdul al-Ilah attempted to raise the tribes in support of the crown. The nomads refused. It was the Arabian summer, and no Bedouin was willing to move in the heat. The riverain tribes also declined to fight but did agree to stay neutral in return for bundles of money dropped out of airplanes. The British, executing their rights under the hated 1930 Anglo-Iraq Treaty, replayed World War I by landing troops in Basra and proceeding to Baghdad. With Britain's second occupation of Iraq, the notables of Baghdad assembled on June 1, 1941 to welcome the regent back. He came under the protection of Britain that once more had demonstrated London's potent influence on the polit-

---

[26] Freya Stark quoted in *The Times* (London), June 28, 1941.

ical system of its former mandate. Although the British occupation ended with World War II, the close relationship between the regent, al-Said, and the British continued. It came at a price—a prolonged vendetta against the monarchy by the armed forces that became magnified by al-Said's order to publicly hang many of the leaders of the Rashid Ali coup.

In the spring of 1946, Iraq, in the deep economic trench dug by World War II, faced the ravaging forces of nature. Melting mountain snows followed by heavy rains forced the rivers and tributaries out of their banks. In Baghdad, colonnaded al-Rashid street was under eight feet of water. Upstream, nine-year-old King Faisal II encouraged a corps of men, stripped to their waists in raging water, to plug a break in the earthworks that threatened the whole western side of the city. The following year, the country suffered a disastrous harvest. Rural destitution pushed peasants toward Baghdad, where they settled in massive slums that were periodically swamped by the muddy overflow of the Tigris. Within them one observer noted, "There is much trachoma and dysentery, but no bilharzia or malaria, because the water is too polluted for snails and mosquitoes. The infant mortality is 250 per thousand. A woman has a 50:50 chance of raising a child to the age to ten. [And] there are no social services of any kind."[27]

All of Iraq's lower classes suffered in the economic malaise but few as acutely as the Shia. In their reed and mud shantytowns on the outskirts of the cities, the Shia laboring class composed of temporary construction workers, hawkers, porters, and watchmen harbored no illusions about where they fit in the political system—at the bottom. In rural areas, the Shia *fellahin*, the peasants, groaned under a land policy that allowed two-thirds of all cultivatable land to remain in the hands of perhaps 2,500 people. Whether the agricultural worker labored on large plantations owned by Sunni landlords or lived as a settled tribesman on land possessed by his sheikhs, the Shia peasant understood his landlord's dependence on a status quo that shut out all hope of reform.

The parliamentary elections in March 1947 had produced a

---

[27] Quoted in Geoff Simons, *Iraq: From Sumer to Saddam* (London: Macmillan Press, 1994), p. 210.

Chamber of Deputies composed of 68 Sunnis, 57 Shia, 6 Christians, 6 Jews, and 1 Yazidi that seemed more inclusive than previous elections. However, neither the increase in Shia representation nor a cabinet comprising 3 Sunnis, 3 Shia, and 2 Kurds meant a more equitable distribution of power. The Kurds had always claimed a presence in the councils of power. The Shia representatives in parliament were, as usual, landowning sheikhs whose numbers had increased in 1943 as a reward for their support of the crown against Rashid Ali. Protecting their self-interests, they showed no more inclination to serve as advocates of Shia needs or of the Shia community's particular values than they ever had. Nonetheless, the struggle for power between the Shia and the Sunnis intensified. As the result of dramatically increased numbers of young Shia coming out of the state education system, the Shia possessed a sizeable cadre of men capable of competing with Sunnis for positions in government and the civil service. For the first time in Iraq's brief history, Sunni politicians met rising Shia demands for a greater share in the state by gradually increasing their numbers at the table of power. But they did so by expanding the size of the bureaucracy to ensure continued Sunni control of the state machinery. Thus, whenever the need for a new official post arose, two were created, one for a Sunni and the other for a Shia. It amounted to nothing but a slight of hand meant to fool the *rafidi*, a derogatory term for Shia.

The Shia, however, would not be duped. Instead, the late 1940s brought into alignment all the communal stresses that had characterized political life since Iraq's birth. Faced with growing frustrations, the younger educated generation led by the Iraqi Shia marched toward Communism in protest against the entire order of Iraqi society and politics. Rejecting the elitism and Arab nationalism of the Sunnis, the majority of educated Shia embraced what they saw as Communism's promise to resolve the social, economic, and political disparities of Iraq.[28] Gathering under the hammer and sickle, urban intellectuals prepared themselves to attack the barriers between the Sunnis and Shia, the privileged and underprivileged. But before they could make their presence felt in the streets, they found themselves

---

[28] Communism also appealed to many urban Kurds, Christians, Jews, Armenians, and Assyrians for the same reasons.

deprived of the numbers necessary to force social and economic change. The masses of Shia, chained to their rural mentality, remained untouched by the flood of ideas that flowed among the small cadre of intellectuals within the cities. Debilitated by malaria and malnutrition, the rural peasants took no interest in topics not directly linked to their daily survival. And so the monarchy moved on, tied to its remaining Sunni supporters and its British protector.

An explosion of rage in January 1948 against the monarchy and London threw all the resentments against the British presence in Iraq at the feet of the throne. Al-Wathbah—"The Leap"—exceeded in numbers and intensity all previous revolts against British influence in Iraq. Although the underlying causes were just as they had been for so long—the privileged status of the Sharifians, Sunni domination of the bureaucracy, and the collaboration of sheikhs sitting on their large landholdings—the immediate eruption of violence came when the monarchy once more laid the detested Anglo-Iraq Treaty of 1930 on the table. The old treaty, the price Faisal I paid for token independence, in popular imagination had reduced Iraq to an appendage of the British empire. Now it required renewal by the monarchy whose control of the administration and politics of Iraq had come to require almost total subservience to Britain. Negotiations in London produced the Portsmouth Treaty, which essentially reconfirmed its 1930 predecessor. By mid-January, the tide of popular discontent prompted every opposition group to demand "the immediate absolution of the Treaty, the dissolution of parliament, a new, free election, and a prompt supply of bread."[29]

On January 26 hatred against the regime exposed itself in dreadful scenes between the Communists and the police that unfolded in the streets. As protestors stormed against authority, al-Said announced that the dignity of the government would be restored whatever the cost. The regent, who had at first backed off from the treaty, climbed on al-Said's wagon as did Salih Jabar, the Shia prime minister who had been set up to negotiate the explosive treaty. The Communists had already responded to the issue of law and order in a statement issued to anyone who would listen: "There is no danger of 'civil war' or of 'a

---

[29] Marion Farouk-Sluglett and Peter Sluglett, "The Social Classes and the Origins of the Revolution." In *The Iraqi Revolution of 1958: The Old Social Classes Revisited*, ed. Robert A. Fernea and William Roger Louis (London: I.B. Tauris, 1991), p. 127.

Communists revolution' or of other such prattle. . . . The real danger lies in foreign interference in the affairs of our country."[30]

By the morning of the twenty-seventh, Baghdad was more a battlefield than a city. Crowds of workers and students marched onto Mamun bridge, which led to al-Suwaidi square where other protesters waited. They were met by police who opened fire. Bodies of laborers and intellectuals lay entangled in the iron girders of the bridge. More dropped into the river below to be swept downstream in the current. When news of the slaughter reached Amin square, the demonstrators who congregated there let loose their anger. Again, the police unleashed their weapons. The only person left standing in the advancing column was a fifteen-year-old girl carrying a banner. How many died during those days of January will never be known. Some were buried with no record of their death. Others never surfaced from the river. That left somewhere between three and four hundred confirmed dead by most common estimates. Yet in death there was victory. Premier Salih Jabar fled for his life, first to the Euphrates and then to England. And the regent canceled the Portsmouth Treaty with Britain.

In 1952, young Faisal II stood at the threshold of his majority. Born in 1935, he had been sickly like his grandfather, Faisal I. Suffering from asthma brought on by trapped dust in horses' coats, he escaped a childhood with the Bedouin. Instead, the small delicate boy went to Harrow in England. There he specialized in history and proved an adequate if not brilliant student. Very different from his father, Ghazi, he developed a genuine attachment to his school and remained there until graduation. His subjects were left to watch their king grow up on succeeding issues of postage stamps. When he returned to Baghdad, his British advisors glowed with satisfaction. According to Gerald DeGaury, a British military officer assigned to Baghdad, "He was by training as nearly a British product as it is possible for a foreigner to be."[31] And it was as a British product that Faisal II took his long-delayed place on the throne of Iraq.

---

[30] Manifesto from the Central Committee of the Communist Party, January 22, 1948, quoted in Hanna Batatu, *The Old Social Classes and the Revolutionary Movements of Iraq: A Study of Iraq's Old Landed and Commercial Classes and of Its Communists, Ba'thists, and Free Officers* (Princeton: Princeton University Press, 1978), p. 554.

[31] Gerald De Gaury, *Three Kings in Baghdad: 1921–1958* (London: Hutchinson, 1961), p. 167.

On May 1, 1953, eighteen-year-old Faisal stood on the terrace of
the Qasr al-Melik gazing across the Tigris at the lights of Baghdad.
The monotonous rhythm of Arabic music drifting across the water
from cafes and the beat of Western songs blaring from the nightclubs
celebrated his coming coronation. The next morning at the stroke of
eight, the now-handsome young man, resplendent in a white military
uniform embellished with epaulets and heavy gold braid, took his
place before parliament to swear the oath that would put him on the
throne almost fifteen years after his father's death: "With God's will,
your cooperation, and that of my noble people, I shall be a constitutional monarch and safeguard democratic principles."[32] As the new
king accepted a gold, field marshal's baton inscribed with texts from
the Koran, a 101-gun salute roared from the banks of the Tigris.
Stepping outside the parliament building, the king and the former
regent donned plumed cocked hats and climbed into a landau bought
from Hooper's on St. James Street, London. Behind it, a mounted
escort arrayed in red uniforms with white helmets preceded a parade
of floats. Atop the float contributed by of the Department of
Archaeology, an Assyrian king proudly stood in a war chariot surrounded by his spearbearers. But Faisal II was no Assyrian king. Nor
was he a Hammurabi. Lacking the instincts of a natural leader, he
would not, like Faisal I, appear unannounced in the marketplaces,
ride with his army into the desert, or sit with the sheikhs as the first
among equals. Instead, he would leave the running of the country to
Abdul al-Ilah and Nuri al-Said.

The ascension of Faisal II marked the zenith of Iraq's monarchy. A
spontaneous artistic movement had spawned the most brilliant sculp-
tors, architects, and painters since the days of Mesopotamia. In the
highly charged intellectual atmosphere, the intelligentsia bragged
with a certain justice that "books are written in Cairo, printed in
Beirut, and read in Baghdad." Escalating oil revenues provided by the
world demand for petroleum were slowly lifting the living standards
of everyone, including the peasants. Whatever their shortcomings, the
palace and the power structure around Nuri al-Said acted as good
stewards of the new national wealth. A 1950 law set aside 70 percent
of the income from petroleum to be fed into development of an eco-

---

[32] Quoted in *The Times* (London), May 4, 1953. King Hussein of Jordan was crowned
the same day in Amman.

nomic infrastructure encompassing roads and power plants, schools and houses, flood and irrigation projects. A new, 1,500-foot-long bridge would span the Tigris at the site of Baghdad's old South Gate. When a planned second bridge was completed in the northern suburbs, the capital would have five crossings over the river. In days of so much promise, few cared to remember the superstition that when five bridges spanned the Tigris, Baghdad would fall.

Riding the wave of optimism within the court, Faisal II made a state visit to Britain in July 1956. At Buckingham Palace, al-Said told some old friends among the British officer corps, "The plan for developing the country is a good one. . . . By the time the oil dries up we will have our agriculture booming and our new industries in full production; and when we have that kind of prosperity we shall have internal security."[33] But inner peace never came to Iraq. A British intelligence report in 1945 had said it all: "There are few countries which at the best of times present more security problems than Iraq. It has tribal and minority problems. The maintenance of security with so many political causes would tax the ingenuity of a sophisticated country, how much more so of Iraq."[34]

The old communal divisions that blocked the development of a specific Iraqi identity had been joined by new divisions of economics and ideology. Three decades after Faisal I died trying to wrap all Iraq's competing factions into a nation, no group or leader had succeeded in dominating the state apparatus to the extent necessary to convince the majority of Iraqis that the nation-state was different from society, an abstract idea to which they owed their undivided loyalty and allegiance. Yet it was neither economics nor communalism that finally triggered the downfall of the monarchy. It was Arab nationalism and the monarchy's relationship with Britain.

A new wind had been blowing out of the western reaches of the Arab world ever since a group of army officers led by Gamal Abdul Nasser overthrew Egypt's King Farouk in 1952. Almost overnight, Nasser became for Arabs throughout the Middle East the new Salah al-Din, a warrior armed with words who would purge the imperialist West from their midst. The Iraqi monarchy, afraid to let loose its

[33] De Gaury, *Three Kings of Baghdad*, p. 172.
[34] Jonathan C. Randal, *After Such Knowledge, What Forgiveness?* (Boulder, Colo.: Westview Press, 1999), p. 122.

security blanket stitched with the flag of Britannia, stayed firmly attached to Britain. But to do so, the men in the palace were forced to sever the last strands of their historic ties to pan-Arabism.

The ideology of pan-Arabism had always presented the monarchy with the dilemma of maintaining a commitment to Arab nationalism while developing in Iraq a particular definition that would give competing communal groups some sense of common identity. Faisal I began the process of moving away from pan-Arabism. Ghazi moved back. The regent Abdul al-Ilah, following the lead of Nuri al-Said, talked about Arab nationalism but carefully avoided union with any Arab state. In the explosion of passionate Arab nationalism ignited by the 1948 war for Palestine and fed by Nasser, the monarchy tentatively reached toward a new identity for what the court had always considered Arab Iraq. The vague new definition of self left Iraq's Arabism untouched but layered on it elements unique to the land between the rivers. The concept was neither new nor revolutionary. Iraqi intellectuals had been borrowing from the cultures of ancient Mesopotamia since the 1940s. By the early 1950s, Mesopotamian motifs were frequently spoken in poetry and woven into the visual arts. Putting forth the same ideology that Saddam Hussein would one day use to promote an Iraqi-centered pan-Arabism, Dr. Fadil al-Jamali, the one time director general of education, postulated that Iraq "is the heir of the civilizations of . . . Sumer, Akkad, Babylon, Assyria, Chaldea . . . and the Arabs, who never left Iraq from the earliest history to our day."[35]

But other voices sounding other issues were stronger. The poet Bakr al-Ulum echoed the cry of people racked with poverty and disease, ruled by a small elite in collaboration with despised Britain:

How can the majority continue to see these comedies,
People toil without reward for a few individuals,
And millions of victims between peasant and worker,
Are still stricken by injustice calling:
"Where is my right?"[36]

---

[35] Quoted in Amatzia Baram, *Culture, History, and Ideology in the Formation of Ba'thist Iraq* (New York: St. Martin's Press, 1991), p. 114.

[36] Quoted in Abdul-Salaam Yousif, "The Struggle for Cultural Hegemony during the Iraqi Revolution." In *The Iraqi Revolution of 1958: The Old Social Classes Revisited*, ed. Robert A. Fernea and William Roger Louis (London: I.B. Tauris, 1991), p. 174.

The new poetry, whether written by romantics or Communists, was characterized by rebellion against authority, tradition, and the old order. To the Arab nationalists arrayed against the status quo, the new order lay in passionate Arab nationalism where the rejuvenated Arab nation would sweep away all traces of foreign control that sheltered princes, landlords, and corrupt politicians. In this brave new world, "there would be no more poverty and disease, no more opulent palaces, no more bribery and corruption."[37] This vision of an Arab world freed from the shackles of Britain drew the Sunni officers of the army as much as the discontented intellectuals.

As Nasser speeded up the cadence of anti-imperialism in the mid-1950s, regional, religious, tribal, ethnic, class, and political groups across Iraq united at different times and in varying degrees in opposition to Britain and to the Western-oriented Hashemite monarchy. Inside the Iraqi army, a clandestine group known as the Free Officers began to plan revolution. Except for two, the fourteen conspirators were all Sunni Arabs. Unaware of the plot within the military and denying the mounting pressures from elsewhere in society, Nuri al-Said continued to insist that "the house of the master is secure."[38] That was until Britain pushed Iraq into the freezer of the Cold War.

On February 24, 1955, Iraq, at the urging of Britain, reluctantly agreed to join in the Baghdad Pact, an alliance against the Soviet Union composed of Pakistan, Iraq's two long-time enemies, Turkey and Iran, plus Britain, its former colonial master. From Cairo, Nasser threw the spear of Arab nationalist ideology directly at the monarchy. The accusation of "lackey of Western imperialism" hit its mark. Trying to explain to his Arab Sunni constituency the monarchy's leap away from pan-Arabism, Nuri al-Said argued as an Iraqi, not an Arab, nationalist. The old warrior of Iraqi politics claimed that the security against external threats provided by the alliance would allow Iraq to develop economically, thereby leading to a society that was uniquely Iraqi. It would be Arab and Kurd, Christian and Muslim, Sunni and Shia. In his enthusiasm about the future, he resurrected the image of medieval splendor that had surrounded Baghdad in the days of

---

[37] Sir John Troutbeck, "The Revolution in Iraq," *Current History* 38 (February 1983): 83.
[38] Quoted in Hanna Batatu, "The Old Social Classes Revisited." In *The Iraqi Revolution of 1958: The Old Social Classes Revisited*, ed. Robert A. Fernea and William Roger Louis (London: I.B Tauris, 1991), p. 214.

Harun al-Rashid in the eighth century, when diverse cultures met and mingled at the crossroads of Mesopotamia. But what al-Said failed to admit was the price Iraq would be forced to pay for these promised benefits. In what amounted to a bargain with the devil, Iraq went under the protective umbrella of the Baghdad Pact in return for acting as the vanguard of Western interests in the Arab world.

In July 1958, as Nasser threatened to topple the pro-Western government sitting in Beirut, al-Said sent Iraqi troops into Jordan to stand ready to intervene on the side of Western powers, who were moving military forces into Lebanon.[39] Refusing to lead Iraqi troops against other Arabs, General Abd al-Karim Qasim turned on Baghdad. With this one act of defiance, all the elements of discontent in Iraq fused. For the Shia, those elements were elitism, poverty, and deplorable conditions in education and health. For the Kurds, it was the lack of autonomy. For the middle- and lower-class Sunnis, it was the apparent rejection of Arab nationalism. Thus, they all stood and watched while the army rid Iraq of the monarchy and the legacy of imperialism.

In the early morning hours of July 28, 1958, soldiers loyal to General Qasim moved into Baghdad's main intersections, the railroad station, the telegraph offices, and the radio station. At the palace, twenty-three-year-old King Faisal II, clad only in his underwear, stood before his shaving mirror. Without warning, gunfire announced the army's encirclement of the palace. With no hope of resistance, the king surrendered in return for a promise of safe conduct for himself and his family out of the country. Halfway across the front courtyard, the officer in command turned and opened fire with a machine gun, killing the king, Abdul al-Ilah, and fifteen to twenty others.

The king's body was wrapped in a carpet and whisked away for secret burial. Lacking any real political instincts, interested in skiing, modern art, and jazz, the king had never really ruled and the Iraqis knew it. Therefore, they vented their anger on the former regent. Abdul al-Ilah's body was tossed from a palace window into the angry crowd below where his hands and feet were cut off. Then, men screaming their pent-up rage stripped the clothing off the torso and dragged it through the street before stringing it up on the same spot where the

---

[39] Nasser had successfully joined Egypt and Syria in an Arab political union in February 1958. Nuri al-Said countered by announcing Iraq's federation with the Hashemite kingdom of Jordan. It amounted to nothing more than a desperate move in the name of two boy kings to defend their regimes against the fires of Arab nationalism.

bodies of the Golden Square of the Rashid Ali coup had been brutally exhibited in 1941. By the time the souvenir hunters had their way, all that remained was some flesh attached to a piece of backbone.

Elsewhere an angry crowd gathered around the statute of King Faisal I, toppled it, and cast it in the Tigris. Meanwhile, others engaged in the hunt for seventy-year-old Nuri al-Said. Still called "the fox," he had once boasted that "the man has not been born who can assassinate me."[40] But the next day, he was found on a street in a Baghdad suburb garbed and veiled as a woman. Peeled of his disguise and impaled alive, he was buried in a shallow grave beyond the North Gate. Revolutionaries, whose hatred of the ancient regime made Sunnis and Shia one, dug him up and dragged his body to the main road into central Baghdad. There cars ran back and forth over the mutilated corpse. What remained was left to rot in the sun.

The savagery of the revolution only demonstrated that the forty years between the withdrawal of Ottoman rule in 1918 and the revolution of 1958 had not provided enough time for three backward Ottoman *vilayets* of mixed ethnicity and religious allegiance, split between city and country, to coalesce into a nation. Furthermore, the dynamic force essential to the process of nation building had not been provided by a ruling regime imposed and defended by a bitterly resented foreign power. So it was that at the death of Iraq's last king, no weeping crowds clogged the streets, no gun carriage slowly rolled to the royal mausoleum. Instead, a small memorial service in London paid respects to the fallen Iraqi monarchy. Those in attendance recalled the ghosts of the past. There was the aged Colonel Pierce Joyce who had fought in the desert with Faisal I, T. E. Lawrence, Jafar al-Askari, and Nuri al-Said; Lady Cornwallis representing her aged and ailing husband, Kinahan Cornwallis, who had come to Iraq with Faisal I and stayed on through the coup of 1941; and the frail Lady Richmond, the sister of Gertrude Bell. In the stillness of the Queen's Chapel in the Savoy Hotel, they all had to wonder if another ruling family, a less intrusive British presence, or a government committed to building a nation rather than preserving a state could have done any better at ruling the tormented country of Iraq.

---

[40] Quoted in *Time*, July 28, 1958, p. 25.

5

IDENTITY IN A DECADE OF DISORDER

n the Iraq of Saddam Hussein, deep penetrating fear ingrained by over two decades of tyranny has effectively shut the doors of Iraqi homes to foreigners. Conversation with ordinary people is achieved only by prowling the streets in innocent activity. That is why on a hot, humid morning, I crossed to an island cut by rivers of asphalt to wander through the collection of alleyways fanning out from the sunken entrance of Baghdad's Mustansiriyah school. Anxious merchants in every doorway sounded the hustler's universal phrase, "Come in, come in, just look, I have the best." They thrust at me mass-produced statues of Assyrian warriors made of shiny metal, imitations of the long rectangular boxes with an attached ink pot in which Islamic scholars once stored their pens, and "Damascus silks" spun from polyester in China. No one was willing to venture beyond the tight parameters of commerce. I wandered on. At one door, a middle-aged proprietor standing at his door fingering a string of prayer beads caught my attention. Inside his small crowded shop, he turned out to be more talkative than he originally appeared. Between bursts of praise for the regime and grumbling through carefully coded messages about the current state of life in Iraq, he showed me a collection of tin boxes shaped like pumpkins in which women once carried their soaps and perfumes to the public baths. There were other objects that allowed me to open the less threatening topics of Iraqi history and culture. A glass-fronted china cabinet pushed hard against the wall held a Koran bound in a weathered-leather and wooden cover, a heavy silver belt that had once been part of the wedding jewelry of a Bedouin, and an octagonal bottle that once served up the black kohl used to outline the eyes of women. I looked at each slowly, attempting to drag out the conversation with the shopkeeper, who was now more eager to sell than to talk. Finally my eye reached the bottom shelf. There, behind some old locks and brass door knockers, was a silver-tipped wooden rod. Curiosity prompted me to ask to see it. It was roughly twenty inches long. One side of the elaborately worked silver cap bore a name inscribed in Arabic—"Muhammad al-Ubayid." I realized that what I held was a general's baton belonging to the generation preceding the 1958 revolution. The simplicity of the object contrasted with the complex and contradictory role that the army played in Iraq's struggle to define itself before and after the revolution of 1958.

For a decade—1958 to 1968—a succession of military governments was interrupted only by a seven-month stint of quasi-civilian rule. The origins of governance by men in uniform traced back to the creation of the ennobled national army conceived during the period of the British mandate. As envisioned by the British and the monarchy, the military was to be the protector of the nation and the guarantor of the authority of the central government. But rather than fulfilling its exalted role, the army, only four short years after independence, thrust itself into politics as the arbiter of the fledgling state's orientation and identity. Under the revolutionary government ruled by generals, the compromises between ethnicities, sects, regions, and classes by which the monarchy had held Iraq together for four decades shattered. In the resultant turmoil, civilian society, stripped of its unifying hostility toward British imperialism, bereft of any overriding ideology, and void of any sense of common destiny, proved unable to construct a new political paradigm. Instead, the army, the Iraqi Communist Party composed largely of Shia Arabs, the Arab nationalist Baath Party, ethnic groups, and a few genuine democrats warred against each other for the right to define the state. The essential question over which they fought has never been totally resolved: is Iraq a unique piece of geography within the Middle East, or is it an integral part of the mythical Arab nation?

FOR MOST IRAQIS, the revolution of 1958 promised to break the last chains of imperialism and right the inequities of society. At six o'clock on the morning of July 14 when Baghdad Radio trumpeted, "Citizens of Baghdad, the Monarchy is dead! The Republic is here!" crowds in the streets erupted in rejoicing at the fall of the Hashemites.[1]

---

[1] Quoted in *Time*, July 28, 1958, p. 25.

In Iraq where it is too hot in summer to stage a revolution, it had all happened with lightning speed. The reason was that not a single army unit had injected itself between the monarchy and the Free Officers.

Over the first few days of the new republic, only an early curfew that curtailed Baghdad's nightlife dampened the enthusiasm for the new order. The capital's buses plied their regular routes and men played backgammon at sidewalk tables while crowds of curiosity seekers pushed through Nuri al-Said's sacked house, where a broken vermouth bottle sat on the pasha's bar. The city fathers of al-Hillah near ancient Babylon changed without protest the names of the major streets. King Faisal I became Revolution Street; King Faisal II, Freedom Street; and Prince Abdul al-Ilah was converted to the poetic-sounding Street of Awakening.

In every city, the reassuring presence of the army broke up disorderly mobs, dispersed student demonstrators, and controlled visiting tribesmen, who in the euphoria took their pleasure in menacing the urban effete. In revolutionary poetry that circulated through the cafes, *al-jaysh*, the army, reigned as the new king of Iraq:

> The sun shines in my city
> The bells ring out for the heroes,
> Awake, my beloved,
> We are free![2]

In the rejoicing no one cared to consider the comment of the departing British ambassador: "Iraqis have always been known for their turbulence and their latest revolution is unlikely to herald an era of tranquility, foreign alike to their history and their temperament."[3] Since the founding of the state, much of that turbulence had been fomented by the very stars of the revolution—the army.

When Iraq claimed its token independence in 1932, strengthening the national army created in 1927 ranked among the imperatives of the new state. The army not only filled the state's need to secure its borders but also served the monarchy's need to defend the central government against the power of the tribes. The fragility of

---

[2] Abdul Wahhab al-Bayati quoted in Abdul-Salaam Yousif, "The Struggle for Cultural Hegemony during the Iraqi Revolution." In *Iraqi Revolution of 1958: The Old Social Classes Revisited*, ed. Robert A. Fernea and William Roger Louis (London: I.B. Tauris, 1991), p. 183.

[3] Sir John Troutbeck, "The Revolution in Iraq," *Current History* 38 (February 1983): 85.

Baghdad's hold on the countryside could be read in King Faisal's confidential memo of 1933, which stated that the restless mutinous tribes possessed more than 100,000 rifles compared to the army's scant 15,000. In the imbalance, the ultimate survival of central authority depended on the national army. But this promised font of stability and national unity broke in the boiling water of communalism when the army massacred the Assyrians.

The outpouring of popular support for the army in its macabre victory in the north suddenly seemed to promise the central government real security. This initial enthusiasm for the military only increased in 1935 when the army crushed twin rebellions by the largely Shia tribes of the central Euphrates in defiance of conscription and by the Kurds in defiance of Baghdad. But hidden beneath the image of effective military power lurked the reality that Iraq's infant army represented neither nationalism nor professionalism. Instead, officers and enlisted men wearing the uniform of the national army polarized into competing ideologies. The Sharifians who had conceived the army grudgingly recognized the need of Iraq to remain under Britain's protective umbrella. The remainder of the officer corps dedicated to ridding Iraq of the British comprised two pillars of national identity. One stood on the ground of a specific Iraqi nationalism encompassing all the characteristics and interests particular to Iraq. The other soared into the clouds of pan-Arabism where dwelled the dream of the great borderless Arab state. It was around these competing visions—Iraq as a unique and separate state and Iraq as an element in the Arab nation—that factions within the army would battle in recurring cycles from 1936 to 1968 for the right to define the Iraqi state. The first confrontation was led by Bakr Sidqi, commander of the pogrom against the Assyrians.

The chain-smoking, heavy-drinking Sidqi was once described by a British advisor to the Iraqi government as singularly unattractive with a flat head, thick neck, sensuous lips, and the vulgar brutal "face of a man born to be a criminal."[4] The scion of a Kurdish family, the determined and tenacious Sidqi had climbed over his Arab rivals to become perhaps the best commander among Iraq's first officer corps. Looking for the solution to Iraq's problems beyond its borders,

---

[4] Gerald de Gaury, *The Three Kings of Baghdad: 1921–1958* (London: Hutchison, 1961), p. 87.

Sidqi concluded that the military governments of Atatürk in Turkey and Reza Shah in Iran served as models for Iraq's own salvation from petty politics and foreign control. As the national hero of the Assyrian incident, he pointed his finger at Baghdad's quarreling, intriguing politicians and declared, "Just as the military regimes in Turkey and Persia [are] eliminating foreign control and carrying out reforms, so should the army officers in Iraq rule the country in order to eliminate the last vestiges of foreign control [and] to create a stable political machine."[5]

Gathering around him a cadre of officers sharing the same sentiments, Sidqi linked up with al-Ahali, a group of civilians genuinely committed to reform of the Iraqi social, economic, and political system. Together they vowed to rid Iraq of the corrupt and ineffectual cabinet headed by a revolving-door politician named Yasin al-Hashimi. Ignorant of the brewing plot, the army chief of staff departed for Turkey near the end of October 1936, leaving Sidqi as the acting commander of the annual military maneuvers. In that position, Sidqi rapidly dispatched the entire Iraqi Air Force to the Iranian frontier and split the bulk of the army's battalions along the Tigris in the north and the Euphrates in the south. In between, two divisions commanded by Sidqi's allies took their position at Qaraghan, just above defenseless Baghdad. At 11:30 A.M. on October 28, four single-engine planes droned over the capital. Each released its load. One bomb fell on the Parliament House, one on the Council of Ministers building, and a third on the post office. The fourth explosive device, presumably aimed at another structure of government, fell into the Tigris, destroying nothing but fish. In the panic and confusion, General Sidqi, "Chief of the National Reform Force," told the people of Iraq that the intolerable political situation had "compelled [the army] to take unavoidable measures which may cause some harm to those who do not answer our sincere appeal, materially and morally."[6] The cabinet promptly resigned, theoretically ending the crisis. But Sidqi and his clique of army officers refused to return to the barracks.

At the palace, Jafar al-Askari, the father of the Iraqi army, insisted on delivering to General Sidqi a personal letter from King Ghazi ask-

---

[5] Quoted in Majid Khadduri, *Independent Iraq 1932–1958: A Study in Iraqi Politics* (London: Oxford University Press, 1960), p. 78.
[6] Ibid.

ing for a cessation of military action. When word came that al-Askari was en route alone, Sidqi decided to rid himself of the popular defense minister. With all the drama of a classic tragedy, four officers of the army that al-Askari organized accosted him between Baghdad and Baquba. They marched him down a deserted road, shot him dead, and threw his body into a crude unmarked grave.[7] At five o'clock in the afternoon the same day, Sidqi and his Army of National Reform paraded through the heart of Baghdad to the cheers and applause of the crowds. Nuri al-Said and the Sharifians had lost control to the military they had created.

Hikmat Sulayman became the civilian prime minister backed by Sidqi, who wielded the power of the military. Although linked more by political expediency than mutual respect, the elder statesman and the renegade general shared an orientation that focused on Iraq as a specific collection of ethnic, linguistic, and religious groups rather than a monolithic element in the mythical Arab state. Nor did Sulayman and Sidqi make any secret of their "Iraq-first" creed. As the British ambassador reported, "At one of my early talks with the new Prime Minister, he said that he did not want to see Iraq busying herself with the interests of sister Arab states, she had too much to do at home."[8] The general echoed the sentiment: "I keenly sympathize with the Arab cause. I however feel compelled to first establish my own country on a firm footing."[9] In a more perfect world, perhaps Sulayman's commitment to internal reform and Sidqi's commitment to Iraqi particularism could have been the warp on which a specific Iraqi nationalism might have been woven. Instead, the challenge they threw at pan-Arabism, the core element in Iraq's identity, aroused a murderous hostility among Arab nationalists in the government and the army, forcing both Sulyaman and Sidqi to shift Iraq's orientation back toward Arab nationalism. Yet it was Sidqi's own ego more than anything else that shaped the character of government by military edict.

Cognizant of British power standing behind the throne, Sidqi never challenged the institution of the monarchy. Instead, he

---

[7] The perpetrators later divulged the location of Jafar al-Askari's body. It now rests in the royal cemetary in Baghdad.

[8] A. Clark Kerr quoted in Liora Lukitz, *Iraq: The Search for National Identity* (London: Frank Cass, 1995), p. 88.

[9] Quoted in *New York Times*, November 26, 1936.

deported leading figures in Iraqi politics including Nuri al-Said. Openly interfering in cabinet meetings and ignoring the objections of the prime minister, the general slotted his personal cronies into key political and military posts. Often drunk, always exhibiting behavior that offended polite society, the general's appointees crowned their arrogance with the wanton murder of a Baghdad notable while the general himself flaunted the standards of decorum by marrying a Viennese dancing girl. Through it all, Sidqi squeezed the life out of civilian reformers and exercised the muscle of a vengeful military dictator feared and hated by all.

On August 10, 1937, Sidqi, en route to Turkey to observe military maneuvers, spent the afternoon in the lounge of the Mosul airport leisurely chatting with his cohorts. Just as the sun began to fade, a young soldier dispatched by Sidqi's opposition within the military approached him, ripped a gun out of his jacket, and fired two shots at the general at point-blank range. Thus, ten months after his celebrated entry into Baghdad, Sidqi returned to the capital to be buried with full military honors. That night, at a usually dark and silent house on the outskirts of Baghdad, lights blazed and streams of people passed in and out amid the sounds of music and revelry. Madame Jafar had invited her family and friends to celebrate the death of her husband's murderer.

For a month Iraq teetered on the brink of civil war. Finally, the Arab nationalists in the army's officer corps coalesced to restore order. The exiled Nuri al-Said returned from Cairo about the same time the young solider who had killed General Sidqi took up his well-paid post as chief gardener of the few struggling zinnias planted around the Ministry of Defense. With all attempts at reform quickly pushed aside, the circle around the status quo appeared to close. But the coup of 1936 had brought profound changes to the power structure of the flimsy Iraqi state. In simply executing the coup and standing behind the civilian government, Bakr Sidqi announced that the army was now part of the political equation. In the absence of a political system that bound the people to the custodians of authority, the army became the guarantor of any government. And it was the army that judged who among competing political factions won the right to exercise authority. For the monarchy that continued its tenure on the throne of Iraq under the protection of Britain, the army became one of the essential elements holding the crown in place.

Even national education succumbed to the influence of the army. Paramilitary youth movements inspired by those in Fascist Germany and Italy organized students by military rank, as indicated by chevrons and badges sewn onto uniforms. In 1937, Dr. Sami Shawkat, director of education, gave voice to the concept of military power and the idea of armed strength. In a famous speech entitled "The Profession of Death," he thundered, "The nation [that] does not excel in the Profession of Death with iron and fire will be forced to die under the hooves of hordes and under the boots of a foreign soldiery."[10] "I hereafter shall permit no one to make any propaganda for peace. . . . It is our duty to perfect the Profession of Death, the profession of the army the sacred military profession."[11] Although criticized by the more moderate elements in the population, Shawkat's speech electrified the younger educated urban generation that had matured under British colonialism. As a consequence, a whole political culture began to develop in which the army served as a "national vanguard" ready to thwart the "corrupt interest" and "inclinations for compromise" that supposedly characterized the Sharifian generation then in power.

The army itself, the symbol of national bravado, was a cracked vessel. The officers clustered around the throne found little problem in trading a measure of sovereignty for a British guarantee against external threats. Others sought arrangements with the Fascist powers, which they saw as promising escape from Britain. As seen in the previous chapter, this contest within the military spawned the Rashid Ali coup of 1941 and Britain's second occupation of Iraq. Regarded almost solely as an anti-imperial drive against Britain, the Rashid Ali movement had surmounted momentarily the fragmentation of Iraqi society. It attracted, in varying concentrations, the Arab nationalists among the urban educated classes; the Communists largely representing the Shia and Kurds; a small Arab nationalist group called the Baath; some Shia *mujtahids*; and even a few scattered tribes. These remained in loose alliance through the British occupation. But as soon as London withdrew its troops at the end of World War II, the factional rancor, particularly within the Iraqi military, reasserted itself.

---

[10] Quoted in Ahmad Abdul Razzaq Shikara, *Iraqi Politics 1921–1941: The Interaction between Domestic Politics and Foreign Policy* (London: LAAM, 1987), p.121.

[11] "The Profession of Death" speech, quoted in Lukitz, *Iraq*, p. 120.

The commanding officers who held the top ranks of the Iraqi army were predominately Sunni Arab nationalists. Collectively they adhered to what amounted to an ethnic nationalism. Emphasizing the cultural homogeneity of the Arabs, they ignored the realities of Iraq in which ethnic and cultural diversity demanded a nationalism based on territory and rooted in the cultural traditions of the area defined by the borders of Iraq. By its very nature, ethnic nationalism shut out the non-Arab elements of the population—the Kurds, Yazidis, Turkomans, Armenians, and others. And the doctrine of pan-Arabism that endeavored to fold Iraq into an overwhelmingly Sunni Arab superstate posed enormous difficulties for the Shia. Thus, the ethnic, sectarian, and ideological divides in Iraq's population that had entangled the monarchy were reproduced in the military. These divides in the army, largely a split between the loyalists to the monarchy and the ideologically pure Arab nationalists, were less complex than in broader society but were no less fierce. The contest within the army for the right to define the state quickly evolved into an open discussion of the essence of Arabism, its ethnic dimensions, and its cultural and ideological implications. The debate intensified against a backdrop created by events unfolding in Palestine.

LYING ALONG the eastern coast of the Mediterranean at the Levantine crossroads of empires, Palestine for centuries served as a battleground for the competing powers of the ancient world. By 63 B.C., the Romans possessed the territory, imposing on it a stability unknown during many of its years of independent existence. But on the death of Herod in A.D. 4, Palestine once again plunged into disorder. The Jews hurled their challenge at foreign rule and Rome responded with a vengeance. In A.D. 70, torches lighted on the orders of Roman commanders destroyed the Second Temple, leaving only its western wall. In the wake of a second revolt in A.D. 135, the Jews scattered into their diaspora. Only a remnant remained behind to live side by side with the rest of Palestine's indigenous population.

Little in the relationship between Jew and non-Jew changed with the arrival of Islam. Most of Palestine's population was Christian when the Muslim armies rode into the Levant. But few remained so. Nonetheless, all in Palestine—Muslim, Christian, and Jew—claimed in Abraham a common ancestor, and all lived in harmony as monotheists recognizing the same God. And again, little altered under the Ottoman Empire, which governed Jerusalem directly from Constantinople and granted to Christians and Jews the same millet status that they enjoyed in Mesopotamia. Consequently, the Jews, clustered within close-knit communities in and around Jerusalem, adhered to their traditional way of life. They posed no threat to Palestine's Arab majority nor its Arab character, for culturally they also formed part of the Levantine collage. All that changed in 1877, the watershed year in Palestine.

It was then that European Jews out of the diaspora returned to the land of Palestine to establish the tiny colony of Petah Tikva near what is now Tel Aviv. In 1881, other Jews began to arrive. The first wave came out of Orthodox communities in eastern Europe. Like the Jews already living in Palestine, most were pious and apolitical, seeking only to live on the ground walked by Abraham. But in 1882, the next wave of Jews waded ashore carrying the flame of Zionist ideology that envisioned the establishment of a Jewish homeland on the ancient stones of Palestine. Coming principally out of Poland and Russia, the Zionists followed the example set by Petah Tikva. Establishing small agricultural communities, this influx of Jews scattered over the coastal plain, into the hills of Galilee, and over the western approaches to Jerusalem. Ignoring both the existing Jewish communities and the region's dominant Arab population, they remained separate, for these new immigrants were not in Palestine to assimilate but to reclaim Eretz Israel, the Hebrew term for "the land of Israel."

Strengthened by their organizations in Western Europe, the Zionists used the war years of 1914 to 1917 to put in place in Palestine the essential building blocks for the Jewish homeland. Capitalizing on the bloody stalemate on the Western Front that was draining away Britain's youth and its resources, the Zionists led the British government toward a public commitment to the Zionist vision for Palestine. In the offices and country homes of Britain's political elite, Zionists such as the imposing Lionel Walter Rothschild, the head of the British banking family, transmitted promises of international Jewish support for the British war effort in return for some commitment to a Jewish homeland. The wartime pressures of money, the alluring prospect of creating a fifth-column movement among Germany's Jews, and the tantalizing possibility of a Western-oriented Zionist state strategically placed near the all-important Suez

Canal seduced Britain into issuing the 1917 Balfour Declaration. Its key clause read, "His Majesty's government views with favor the establishment in Palestine of a national home for the Jewish people and will use their best endeavors to facilitate the achievement of this object. It being clearly understood that nothing shall be done which may prejudice the civil and religious rights of existing non-Jewish communities in Palestine."[12] With the flourish of a pen, Palestine became a thrice-promised land. Britain had already pledged Arab independence in the Hussein-McMahon documents. It then determined Palestine's future as a British colony in the secret Sykes-Picot Agreement. Now the British embraced the Zionist agenda.

When the guns of World War I fell silent, Zionist efforts to populate Palestine began in earnest. The Palestinians behind Haj Amin al-Husseini, the mufti of Jerusalem, fought back. After bloody encounters between Arabs and Jews in 1929 and 1936 tested the Zionist colonies, the contest for Palestine paused as Nazi Germany threatened to annihilate Europe's Jews. When World War II ended, the Zionists, empowered by the West's shame of the Holocaust, began the final push toward the Jewish homeland. With the unspeakable horror of genocide beginning to sink into the world's collective conscience in 1945, the Zionists declared war on the British presence in Palestine, defiantly shouting, "In blood and fire Judah fell; in blood and fire it will rise again."[13] Two years later the campaign against the British mandate reached its symbolic peak when Zionist bombs planted in the basement of the stately King David Hotel, the home of the British military command, reduced one wing to dust. After almost twenty years of standing between warring Arabs and Zionists, Britain, drained by a global war and verging on bankruptcy, saw Palestine as an intolerable burden. Powerless to stop the escalating violence, enfeebled Britain laid its mandate from the defunct League of Nations on the doorstep of the infant United Nations. When the United Nations recommended partition into Jewish and Arab sections in 1947, the Palestinians said no. The war for Palestine was on. While Palestinian guerrillas hit Jewish targets and a well-armed Zionist army cleaned out Arab villages across Galilee, British mili-

---

[12] Quoted in Ibrahim Abu-Lughod, ed., *The Transformation of Palestine: Essays on the Origin and Development of the Arab-Israeli Conflict* (Evanston, Ill.: Northwestern University Press, 1987), p. 46.

[13] Quoted in *Time*, July 8, 1946, p. 31.

tary forces remained in their barracks. And in the midst of a flood of fleeing Palestinian refugees, the British, as scheduled, hauled down their flag and sailed out of Jaffa on May 14, 1948. Just to the north, David Ben-Gurion in Tel Aviv proclaimed "the establishment of the Jewish state in Palestine, to be called Israel."

The following day, May 15, the war for Palestine became an Arab war. The Egyptians moved out of the Sinai, rolling along the coast toward Tel Aviv and through the Negev to Beersheba. A few thousand Syrians, followed by a small force of Lebanese, pushed down through Galilee. From the east, an Iraqi force of fifteen to twenty thousand soldiers crossed the Jordan River. To confirm Iraq's commitment to the Arab cause, the Regent Abdul al-Ilah and the ladies of his household took to the field alongside units of the Red Crescent, the Muslim equivalent of the Red Cross. Only Abdullah, the Hashemite King of Jordan, stayed out. But the Arab effort to defend Palestine failed. By December, Israel's army had shoved all the Arab forces back beyond Palestine's prewar boundaries. When armistice came in February 1949, the Arab armies, including Iraq's, went home.[14]

Across the Arab world, the loss of Palestine translated into a tormenting symbol of Arab humiliation at the hands of the West. It was an attitude that resulted from the Arabs' perception that Israel was a creature of the West, and it played forcefully to Arab nationalism. One of the central tenets was that ever since the European Crusaders came searching for the Holy Grail in the twelfth century, the Arabs had suffered invasion, war, economic servitude, colonialism, and cultural repression at the hands of European imperialism. Now the Zionist conquest of Palestine fused all the Arabs' emotional and psychological grievances against the West. Suckled on Western diplomatic and economic support, Israel loomed as the new citadel of Western arrogance. As a consequence, Arab resentment against Israel became the crucible of Arab unity. Over the last decades of the twentieth century, every reigning regime in the region, including Iraq, would face the test of its Arab credentials on the street and within the councils of power.

Despite its heterogeneous population, Iraq, as the first Arab territory to achieve its independence, had become a hotbed of Arab

---

[14] Iraq is the only Arab participant in the 1948 Arab-Israeli war that never signed a permanent armistice with Israel.

nationalism as the contest for Palestine amplified during the 1930s. Pan-Arab ideology drew not only Arab nationalists but also many Iraqi nationalists who were driven as much by resentment of the British as affection for the Arab cause. Most Sunnis marched to the cadence of Arab nationalism. Condemning the monarchy as an artificial creation designed to maintain Britain's imperialist interests in Mesopotamia, they demanded a united Arab state encompassing the still-Western-occupied territories of Palestine and Syria. Scores of Palestinian and Syrian teachers employed in government high schools and colleges sold this vision of the Arab state to Iraqi students sitting at their desks. In the military, the zeal for pan-Arabism all but emptied the military college of non-Arab Sunnis. In this accumulation of societal pressures, Arab Shias confronted an ongoing challenge to their feelings of *urubah*, or "Arabness." In October 1939, a new jolt of energy shot through Arab nationalism when Haj Amin al-Husseini, the mufti of Jerusalem, arrived in Baghdad.

As the celebrated face of the 1936 Arab revolt that shook the chains of British control of Palestine, the mufti was stripped of his position and deported by the colonial administration. Dumped into Damascus, he came to Baghdad at the invitation of the extreme pan-Arabs. Described by the British as possessing a "cunning expression" and "watery pale-blue eyes," he was a hypnotic presence. A dominating personality, and a direct descendant of the Prophet claiming not only religious credentials but pure Arab blood, he also demonstrated the courage to snap his whip at the British lion. Although his arrival in Baghdad embarrassed the reigning pro-British government of Nuri al-Said, the mufti nonetheless floated through state functions on the wave of Sunni adulation.

Gathering five to six thousand followers, the charismatic mufti gave form and direction to what had been a nebulous ideology of Arab nationalism in Iraq. Installing his own mini-government in Baghdad, he began to build bridges to the radical pan-Arabists in the Iraqi military. In 1941, al-Husseini lurked off-stage as Rashid Ali and the pan-Arab generals of the Golden Square drove the pro-British regent, Abdul al-Ilah, and Nuri al-Said into exile. When British military forces marched toward Baghdad, the mufti fled to Iran and then to Rome. Although he never returned to Iraq, he left behind a legacy of bitterness and resentment over the issue of Palestine.

The Palestinian conflict after World War II so enflamed the Arabs of Iraq that even the Shia Arabs could no longer avoid the issue of pan-Arabism. Yet those of Kadhimain, Nassariyah, and Basra, for all the reasons that had kept the Shia apart from the ideology of Arab unity, never responded with the same enthusiasm as the Sunnis to the idea of "shedding blood for the sake of Arabism." Nor were they interested in "combat for the land of Palestine." For the non-Arab Kurds, Palestine dwelled on the periphery of their own nationalist struggle. In the end, the Iraqi community most affected by the death struggle being waged in Palestine was that of the Jews.

The Jewish community in Iraq traced its ancestry back through the centuries to the Babylonian captivity. Even though they formed a distinct group with a sharply defined identity, the Jews, like the rest of Mesopotamia's population, submitted to the cultural forces that came with the Islamic invasion. Although refusing to desert the faith of Judaism for the theology of Islam, the Jews adopted the Arabic language and with it many elements of Arab culture. They ate Arabic food, repeated Arabic proverbs, and adhered to Arabic superstitions. By the twentieth century, the Jews of Iraq were so Arabized that even the Arab nationalists regarded them as an integral part of the Arab race built on language. In 1915, a manifesto issued by the Arab Revolutionary Committee included Jews when it called all Arabs to rise up against the Ottoman Empire: "Arabs of the Christian and Jewish faiths join ranks with your Moslem brethren. Do not listen to those who say that they prefer the Turks without religion to Arabs of different beliefs; they are ignorant people who have no under-standing of the vital interests of the race."[15]

Perhaps because they so closely identified with Arab society, most Iraqi Jews never took up the cause of Zionism. Yet pressures against Iraq's Jewish community began to build with the 1929 and 1936 Arab revolts in Palestine. When the British expelled Rashid Ali and with him the mufti of Jerusalem, Baghdad's Arabs declared war on the Jews. Over the first two days of June 1941, the *farhud*, the outbreak of rage against Zionism, killed 179 Jews and destroyed millions of dollars in Jewish property.[16] That it happened in Baghdad signified just how

---

[15] Quoted in Hanna Batatu, *The Old Social Classes and the Revolutionary Movements of Iraq's Old Landed and Commercial Classes and of Its Commumists, Ba'thists, and Free Officers* (Princeton: Princeton University Press, 1978), p. 258.

[16] The was also a powerful anti-British sentiment in the attacks on the Jews as well as the participation of individuals pushing political interests not associated with the issue of Palestine.

powerful the issue of Palestine had become for Arab nationalists.

Although Jewish communities were to be found in many of Iraq's cities, the Jews concentrated in Baghdad. Living in the quarters of Mahallah at-Tawrat, Taht-it-Takyah, Abu Saifain, and Souk Hannum, they constituted at least 15 percent of the city's population at the end of World War II. They were mostly peddlers, craftsmen, and shop-keepers, but a small minority of Jews sat at the pinnacle of Iraq's commerce. Ten out of the twenty-five first-class members of the Baghdad Chamber of Commerce were Jews. Thirty-five of the thirty-nine registered banks and money-lending establishments were owned by Jews. But wealth and status provided no protection as the passion of Arab nationalism targeted the Jews following the 1948 war for Palestine. Charges of Zionism or the lesser offense of Communism fueled a campaign of arrests and persecution of Jews who never considered themselves anything other than Iraqis belonging to a minority faith. In this climate of fear, Iraq's Jews packed their belongings, pulled their money out of the economy, and sold or aban-doned their property to relocate in Israel. To assist in the process, parliament in March 1950 passed a law permitting any Jew to leave the country with his assets in return for surrendering his Iraqi nation-ality. Caught up in the whirlwind, vibrant Jewish communities across Iraq vanished without a trace. With the exodus virtually eliminating Iraq's Jewish population, a 1952 revision to the electoral law of 1946 canceled the six seats in Parliament set aside for Jews. The six thou-sand or so Jews who remained in what they considered their home-land hunkered down as Gamal Abdul Nasser rose out of Egypt.

ON JULY 26, 1952, a group of young army officers in Cairo rid Egypt of its monarch and the last vestiges of British colonialism. Leading them was a handsome figure named Gamal Abdul Nasser, who soon vowed to lift the yoke of humiliation clamped on Egypt by the loss of Palestine in return for absolute power. Abolishing political parties, jailing opposition leaders, closing liberal newspapers, and emascu-lating trade unions and student groups, Nasser, by 1956, reigned as the undisputed leader, the caudillo of Egypt, promising to strip Western chains from Arab dignity and self-respect. Seen as the sym-bol of Arab redemption, he was worshiped by "heaps of humanity without a mind or thought of their own, without an independent voice emanating from their gatherings. They became a collection of waving arms and applauding hands, and cheering mouths. And the Chief in his dominating presence, towering over them from his podium, spoke alone for long hours, interrupted only by the hysterical cries: 'Nasser, Nasser, Nasser.' "[17]

Riding this wave of public adoration, Nasser struck against the West in March 1956 by nationalizing the Suez Canal. The following October 29, Britain and France, who had financed and built the canal, hit back. Israel, "the Zionist usurper," joined hands with the "Western imperialists" in a war designed to topple Nasser. Britain and France operating in concert and Israel acting outside the alliance rained destruction on Port Said, smashed Egypt's air force on the ground, and chewed up a quarter of Nasser's army while the Arab states, including Iraq, helplessly maneuvered a few divisions on the periphery of the conflict. However, the decisive battle of the 1956 Suez War was fought in the chambers of the United Nations. President Dwight Eisenhower, enraged by the actions of U.S. allies, which he saw as drawing the Soviet Union into the Middle East, threw American power behind a series of UN resolutions aimed at removing the British, French, and Israelis from Egypt. Consequently, on November 5, a gray and exhausted Anthony Eden led his French counterpart before the world press to announce a cease-fire. The old colonial powers of the Middle East in addition to Israel had won the battle of Suez but lost the war. Rather than toppling Nasser, the Suez War birthed "Nasserism," a blend of Arab nationalism, anti-imperialism, and cult of personality built around the Egyptian president. As foreign forces withdrew from Egypt, Nasser stood before Cairo's al-Azhar mosque to receive the adulation of hundreds of thousands of his frenzied followers. Beyond Cairo and Egypt, Arabs on the streets and within the chambers of power turned their eyes and their hearts to Nasser as the long-awaited leader capable of removing Western might and influence from the Arab world.

Nasser roused the passion of Arab nationalism as no other leader before or since, and he did it by commanding two potent weapons: an elaborate propaganda machine and an extensive intelligence network. One sought control of the Arab streets, the other control of the machinery of state in Arab countries. From Morocco to Iraq,

---

[17] Tawfik al-Hakim quoted in P. J. Vatikiotis, *The History of Egypt* (Baltimore: Johns Hopkins University Press, 1980), p. 291

from Lebanon to Yemen, Nasser's Voice of the Arabs delivered his words through cheap radios put into the hands of the masses by the technological revolution. Broadcasting on four wavelengths, the station poured out songs and rhetoric that reverberated with the passion of the Arab cause. Woven together, words and music aroused all the Arab resentments against the old colonial powers. Nasser preached subversion, rebellion, intransigence, and hatred of "imperialists." He promised that Arab honor—honor destroyed by the West and its Israeli ward—would be restored. Through Arab unity, the Arabs would once again take their exalted place within the world. "Follow me, follow me!" And follow they did. From the coastal villages of Kuwait to the camps of Palestinian refugees to the halls of the American University of Beirut, the image of the dashing Nasser plastered walls and bobbed on placards in street demonstrations.

In Iraq, the appeal of Nasser's anti-imperialism, if not his Arab nationalism, reached across the Arabs' religious divides to gather opposition to the monarchy. Whatever lingering pan-Arab sentiments that the monarchy brought with it to Baghdad died in the face of the Egyptian president's ceaseless assault on the Iraqi monarchy as "the lackey of the West." In the ensuing chess game for Iraq, Nuri al-Said and Gamal Abdul Nasser moved and countermoved. Al-Said embraced the 1955 Baghdad Pact and proposed union with Jordan. Nasser, on February 1, 1958, tied Egypt and Iraq's neighbor Syria together in the United Arab Republic. The following May, al-Said sent Iraqi troops to Lebanon to help shore up its pro-Western government while Arab nationalists within Iraq trekked back and forth to Cairo to sit at Nasser's feet. In July 1958, Nasser's vendetta against the pro-Western king of Iraq came to fruition. In the early hours of the fourteenth, two Iraqi army brigades swept into Baghdad and destroyed the monarchy in the name of anti-imperialism.

IN THE AFTERMATH of the revolution, the leaders of the Free Officers, General Abd al-Karim Qasim and Colonel Abd al-Salam Arif, appeared committed to political and social reform that would address the endemic problems of Iraqi politics and society. Civilian rule was invested in a three-man council composed of an Arab Sunni, an Arab Shia, and a Kurd. The council in turn formed a cabinet remarkable for its broad inclusion of respected leaders of opposition to the monarchy. It all lent legitimacy and respect to what was in reality a military

A section of the so-called standard of Ur, an elaborately inlaid work of art, found in a tomb at Ur. About 2600 B.C. (Courtesy of Emory University, Atlanta, Ga.)

Relief from the palace of Ashurbanipal at Nineveh. Seventh century B.C.
(Courtesy of Emory University, Atlanta, Ga.)

Sunni tribesman of
central Iraq.
 (Author's photograph)

Cleric and sheikh, the
authority figures of Shia
Islam in Iraq. Najaf.
(Author's photograph)

King Faisal I of Iraq, circa 1930.
(Courtesy of Hultonn-Deutsch
Collection/Corbis)

King Faisal II. The boy king on
the throne of Iraq. Photographed
by the famous photographer
Cecil Beaton. (Courtesy of
Hultonn-Deutsch Collection/Corbis)

Abd al-Rahman Arif with Mullah Mustafa Barzani. In
1966, Iraqi president Arif traveled to northern Iraq
to meet with Barzani in an appeal to the Kurds to
cooperate with Iraqi Arabs in the preservation of
the state of Iraq. (Bettman/Corbis)

Vice president Saddam Hussein with Algeria's president Houri Boumedienne and
Muhammad Reza Shah of Iran. It was at the Algiers conference that Hussein and
the shah struck the bargain that ended the Kurdish rebellion of 1970–75.
(Bettman/Corbis)

Babylon's Ishtar Gate, as restored by
Saddam Hussein. (Author's photograph)

The crossed swords of the monument to the Iran-Iraq War, Baghdad.
The model for the forearms may have been Saddam Hussein.
(Shepard Sherbell/Corbis)

Kurdish refugees in the mountains of northern Iraq. While the Shia rebellion of March 1991 unfolded out of sight of the international press, the Kurds benefited from full media coverage. (David and Peter Turnley/Corbis)

Saddam Hussein in a rare public appearance among the Shia, the majority of Iraq's population. (Courtesy of AFP/Corbis)

Female members of the Baath Party parade on April 28, 1999, celebrating Saddam Hussein's birthday in Tikrit in the Sunni triangle of Iraq. (Courtesy of AFP/Corbis)

The new tribal elite of Saddam Hussein's Iraq. (Author's photograph)

Public art in Iraq. Saddam Hussein as a tribal sheikh. (Author's photograph)

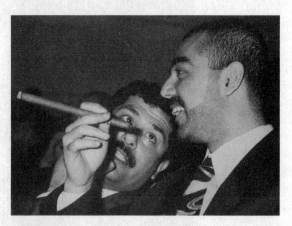

Saddam Hussein's two sons, Uday (right) and Qusay
(left). Qusay, more competent and stable than his
older brother, appears to be Hussein's choice as his
successor.
(Courtesy of AFP/Corbis)

regime driven by anti-imperialism. General Qasim summed up the attitude of those who made the revolution: "If you tour any part of this country, you will see how extensive misery, poverty, and deprivation are in the life of the people. You will see the cottages [of the villages] . . . moving skeletons. . . . The wealth of this country was robbed and wasted in the interest of imperialism and the foreigner."[18]

Over the next weeks, the revolutionary government closed British military bases, purged the government of its Western advisors and contractors, promised Kurds a level of autonomy, lifted the restraints on radical ideological groups representing workers, and announced land reform that intended to release the peasants from their serfdom to the tribal sheikhs. Still, the new political, social, and economic paradigm left unresolved the problem of communalism, which had tormented Iraq since its inception. The Sunnis, Shia, and Kurds would continue to pursue their contradictory visions of Iraq while tribes and families within each community fought their own battles of interest and honor. In the councils of power, the army, torn by the competing ideologies of pan-Arabism versus Iraqi particularism, would preside over a bloody struggle for power on the streets among the Nasserites, the Arab nationalists opposed to union with Egypt, the Communists, and the few genuine democrats. Iraq would enter a decade in which leaders exercised a total monopoly of state power and exhibited the characteristics once admired in tribal sheikhs: "fearlessness towards one's enemies, swift punishment to those judged wrong, and loyalty to kinsmen and supporters."[19]

To the Arab nationalists within the army, the revolution, by overthrowing the Western-tainted monarchy, had proved Iraq's Arabism. With the throne dismantled and the British military presence gone, Iraq could now meet Nasser on the high ground of pan-Arabism. In 1958 the dream of an Arab superstate from the Nile to the Euphrates seemed within reach. The three great centers of Arab power—Cairo, Damascus, and Baghdad—were seemingly under pan-Arab governments, making it difficult, if not impossible, for reluctant Jordan, Lebanon, and other lesser Arab countries to stay removed. But it was

---

[18] Quoted in Richard P. Hunt, "Clues to Iraq's Mystery Man," *New York Times Magazine*, June 28, 1959, p. 34

[19] Robert A. Fernea, "State and Tribe in Southern Iraq: The Stuggle for Hegemony before the 1958 Revolution." *In Iraq Revolution of 1958: The Old Social Classes Revisited*, ed. Robert A. Fernea and William Roger Louis (London: I.B. Tauris, 1991) p. 152.

not to be. General Qasim, the hero of the revolution, was the embodi-ment of his nation, sure in its opposition to the old regime, yet uncer-tain about the future course of the state as part of Nasser's Arab nation.

Qasim appeared to be the perfect Iraqi, the son of a Sunni Arab father and Kurdish mother and the grandson of a Shia. Slender, with magnetic eyes, a close-clipped moustache, and an uneasy smile, Qasim represented the lower-middle-class Iraqis without family name or fortune who during the 1930s found social mobility in the new national army. He also reflected the new generation of officers in the Iraqi army who, in contrast to the first generation, held a vari-ety of views about the identity of the Iraqi state. Qasim sided with that element focused on Iraq and the Persian Gulf, not pan-Arabism and especially not pan-Arabism under Nasser. The irrepressible Abd al-Salam Arif, conversely, gathered with those whose ardor for pan-Arabism included Iraq's union with Nasser's Egypt. On September 12, just less than two months after the revolution, Arif disappeared from the revolutionary leadership as a result of his basic ideological difference with Qasim over Iraq's identity.[20]

Surprisingly, the starkly unimaginative General Qasim turned to Baghdad's modern art movement to draw out the symbols of the new Iraq. Employing the work of a group of highly talented visual artists who had begun to revive Mesopotamian themes during the monar-chy, Qasim plugged Iraq's pre-Islamic heritage into the national con-sciousness. Postage stamps suddenly bloomed with Sumerian and Assyrian art. The Akkadian sun, an eight-point star with light waves connecting its points, and the hexagonal star of Ishtar took their place as the new emblems of Iraqi nationalism. In the dust storm that blanketed Baghdad on the first anniversary of the revolution, a parade of large floats would bear a stele inscribed with Hammurabi's laws; a model of the Ziggurat of Ur; and an oversized portrait of General Qasim flanked by the symbols of Tammuz-Dumuzi, the spring god of the ancient Iraqis. Even the revolution itself was stamped with the seal of Mesopotamia. Recognizing the Iraqi's keen appreciation of sculpture, the government commissioned Iraq's lead-ing sculptor, Jewad Salim, to create a monument to the 1958 revolu-tion. When it was dedicated, the Freedom Monument at Tahrir

---

[20] Arif was subsequently convicted of trying to assassinate Qasim. Sentenced to death, Arif was spared by his partner in the revolution.

square near the Jumhuriya bridge stood a full 30 feet high and 150 feet long. Inspired by the walls of ancient Assyria and Babylon, it was constructed from slabs of marble that formed the backdrop for a bas-relief of metal figures, many of which faced sideways in the typical style of ancient Mesopotamian art. Symbolizing Arabs and Kurds, two male peasants dressed as a Sumerian and an Assyrian gaze on two females representing the Tigris and Euphrates. They hold a single spade—the country of Iraq. The official publication issued at the dedication describes the monument as "purely Iraqi art, whereby the Iraqi epic theme . . . [is] expressed in an Iraqi style, a mixture of contemporary manner and age-old tradition." The artist himself believed his work of art would create a lasting symbol of the true Iraqi man.[21]

Through symbols and art, General Qasim hoped to lay the foundations of an identity unique to Iraq. In further attempts to diminish religion and communalism as polarizing forces in Iraqi society, the general appeared at the inauguration ceremony of the new Assyrian church to praise freedom of worship and denounced an attack on a Shia procession to the Haidar shrine as sectarian violence. But these efforts were strangled by the tensions between inwardly looking Iraq-firsters and the outwardly oriented pan-Arabists. The pan-Arabists, particularly those in the army, saw in Qasim's initial appeals to communal tolerance nothing more than the rejuvenation of the confessional character of monarchial Iraq. To them, the republic meant the total elimination of confessional boundaries in order to fuse all Iraqis into a modern revolutionary type of Arab society modeled on Nasser's Egypt. In order to expedite the process, the pan-Arabs of the army thrust Iraq toward the recently created United Arab Republic composed of Egypt and Syria. But for the Iraq-firsters, union with the United Arab Republic amounted to nothing less than Iraq's subjugation to the interests of Egypt. Qasim agreed: "We have just rid ourselves of the Hejazis who ruled us for the last thirty-seven years. Now why for God's sake should we turn around and deliver ourselves to foreign domination [again]?"[22] This was the essential question for postrevolutionary Iraq. Seeking the right to answer it, competing groups, both inside and outside the army, took to the streets to fight a war over Iraq's identity.

---

[21] Jewad Salim never lived to see his monumental work completed. He died of a heart attack during its installation.

[22] Quoted in Lukitz, *Iraq*, p. 141.

Qasim, who had frustrated Cairo's bid to become the capital of a unified Arab world, became the focal point of Nasserite rage. Threatened by the legions of Nasserites that included much of the officer corps of the Iraqi army, Qasim turned for protection to the Communists, Iraq's only deeply rooted political party. Trading on the social and economic inequalities in Iraqi society, the Iraqi Communist Party (ICP) had established by the late 1950s a massive presence on the streets of most Iraqi cities. Pictures of Marx, Lenin, Nikita Khrushchev, and Mao Tse-tung competed for space on the walls and fences of every city and town with those of Nasser. Bookshops and newsstands overflowed with Communist literature, which was snatched up and devoured by students and the literate within the lower classes. In one cafe after another, intellectuals wearing bushy moustaches that imitated Stalin met to discuss "the actualization of utopia, the embodiment of liberty, democracy, progress, and the elimination of all forms of discrimination."[23] The best organized of any political group in Iraq, the Communists collected petitions, convened rallies, and mobilized parades to protest any union between Iraq and the UAR or any other Arab political constellation. Whereas this opposition to Arab unity lay in the ideology of the international working class, it more strongly reflected the reality that most Communists in Iraq were Shia and Kurds. Together they held nearly 80 percent of the seats on the Central Committee of the ICP. Their interests in joining the party were as much communal as ideological. To Iraq's disenfranchised Shia and Kurds, the ICP stood as their best defense against a Baghdad-centered Sunni Arab government. In the wider context of Middle Eastern politics, the ICP represented an obstacle to Nasser's call to Iraq to join an Arab state overwhelmingly populated by Arab Sunni Muslims.

Adopting the Communists' social program, Qasim pushed social and economic reform while the Nasserites urged union with Egypt. With Nasser's Voice of the Arabs inciting Iraqis against Qasim and the Communists, street mobs of Nasserites attacked anyone wearing red. In retaliation, the Communists plastered public spaces with obscene pictures of Nasser, urged their children to chant that the ever smiling Egyptian president smoked hashish, and sent their ruffians to drive the Nasserites underground. With the leftists and the

[23] Yousif, "The Struggle for Hegemony," p. 192.

Communists occupying top positions in the ministries of economics, education, agriculture, and justice, the country marched toward the left despite the large numbers of anti-Communist pan-Arabs within the officer corps of the army.

In this growing polarization of Iraq's body politic, a group of pan-Arab army officers attempted a coup against General Qasim in Mosul in March 1959 on charges of betraying the July 14 revolution and the Free Officers. It began as a showdown between proponents of Nasser's Arab nationalism and Qasim's alliance of Communists and Iraq-firsters, but it let loose the fury of all the elements of communal hatred that had been fomenting in Iraq through the years. According to Hanna Batatu, "Kurds and Yazidis stood against Arabs, Assyrians and Aramean Christians against Arab Muslims, the Arab tribe of Albu Mutaiwit against the Arab tribe of Shammer, the Kurdish tribe of al-Gargariyyah against the Arab Albu Mutaiwit, the peasants of Mosul country (Christian and Arameans) against their landlords (Muslim Arabs), the soldiers of the Fifth Brigade (Kurds) against the officers (Arabs)."[24] Group preyed on group, employing every device of elimination from gunfire to dragging victims behind cars until they died. Each group was motivated by the fear that if it did not prevail, it would be destroyed at the hands of its adversaries. Shaken by violence that threatened to rip the country apart, Qasim initiated a crackdown on his leftist supporters in order to balance power between the competing forces. Ordering his faction of the army to round up Communists across the country, he put them into prison with the pan-Arabs he had put there earlier. The small but organized Baath Party that had survived the decimation of Mosul moved into the breach left by Qasim's repression of the ICP.

THE NASSERITES came out of one strain of Arab nationalism. The Baath Party came from another, initially dedicated to cutting Arab nationalism from the culture of Islam. Because Arab Christians have always felt isolated in the sea of Islam, much of the intellectual vigor surrounding this new version of Arab nationalism that emerged in the 1920s and 1930s came from Christians, primarily the Greek

---

[24] Batatu, *The Old School Classes and the Revolutionary Movements of Iraq*, p. 866. Another disturbance occurred at Kírkuk between July 14 and 17. Although this involved Commumists, Nasserites, and democrats, it also included an undercurrent of Kurdish-Turkoman violence.

Orthodox. As a minority in Islamic societies, Christians held a vested interest in separating Arab nationalism from Arab Islamic culture. In 1938, the Lebanese writer Amin al-Rihani summed up this Christian viewpoint: "The Arabs existed before Islam and before Christianity. Let the Christians realize this, and let the Muslims realize it. Arabism before and above everything."[25] From this premise sprang the Baath, the party of Saddam Hussein.

The ideology of the Baath, or Renaissance Party, originated with the Syrians Michel Aflaq, a Christian, and Salah Bitar, a Sunni Muslim. They studied together at the Sorbonne in Paris between 1928 and 1932. Returning to Damascus, they prowled among the intellectuals in the city's cafes in crumpled clothes, torn collars, and dirty fezzes. Unmarried, sometimes unemployed, and forced to live on a pittance, they planned the Arab renaissance. By 1940, a year after World War II began in Europe, Aflaq and Bitar had gathered around them a cadre of intellectuals.

Withdrawn and eccentric, Aflaq was the ideologue of Baathism. Borrowing from Marxism and nineteenth-century romantic German nationalism and superposing an Arab character on both, Aflaq poured out reams of mystical nationalist rhetoric. In his writings, he described an Arab nation stretching back through time. Within its boundaries, he included both the Fertile Crescent and North Africa as well as Celicia and Alexandretta in Turkey and Khuzistan, the Arabic region of Iran on the east side of the Shatt al Arab. In Aflaq's vision, the Arab nation could achieve deliverance from backwardness and foreign control only by breaking the shackles of religion, tradition, tribalism, and sectarianism. To Aflaq, the party he conceived was less a political organization than "an artistic creation that took the place of a novel or a poem . . . and he loved it as an artist would love his own creation."[26] Although Aflaq's ideology stressed nationalism, unity, secularism, and a vague theory of socialism, he talked of the Arab renaissance most of all. In pursuit of this renaissance, Aflaq coined phrases that ranged from the visionary party slogan "One Arab nation with an eternal mission" to the banal "Arabism is love."

---

[25] Quoted in Peter Mansfield, *The Arabs* (New York: Penguin Books, 1985), p. 225.
[26] Fouad Ajami, *The Arab Predicament: Arab Political Thought and Practice since 1967* (Cambridge: Cambridge University Press, 1981), p. 44.

Aflaq's call for an Arab revival slammed against the classical problem of how to transform an Arab society steeped in the orthodox values of Islam. Aflaq approached the dilemma by asserting that Islam comprised the most sublime expression of Arabism, for Islam originated as an Arab religion, spoke through the Koran in the Arabic language, embodied ancient Arab values, and launched the Arabs on the establishment of empire. Islam thus progressed beyond religion to become a culture that expressed what he called the Arab genius.[27] Now the Arab renaissance would unfold out of three secular realms: the elimination of the artificial boundaries imposed by World War I to release the unified Arab state, the sharing of human and material resources among all Arabs, and a commitment and strategy for the social and economic development of the whole Arab nation. With Arab nationalism perceived in terms of language, culture, and history rather than religion or ethnicity, Aflaq saw no reason, at least in theory, why non-Arabs should not fit well into the Baath national mold. Through an elaborate doctrine of rationalization, he concluded that non-Arabs such as Kurds, as inhabitants of Arab lands sharing a common history, must also share a common identity. Therefore, even though they do not speak the all-encompassing Arabic language, the Kurds were nonetheless Arab.

Aflaq's soaring rhetoric and voluminous writings stayed largely encased in the educated class, where his vision of a single independent Arab nation capable of transforming the Arab intellect and soul, its politics and society, found a following. To those drawn to the Baath, the slogan "Unity, Freedom, and Socialism" pulled the Arabs above their own unresolved conflicts and lifted from the collective psyche the burden of inferiority imposed by contact with the West. Finding in Aflaq's often quixotic writings the answer to the impotence of the Arab world, they made themselves the vanguard of a new age, rebels against all the old values. As such, they vowed to banish tribalism and other outmoded characteristics of Arab society, to make way for the future Arab state. Yet they remained a small elite.

In Iraq, Baath ideology that promised Arab identity outside Islam

---

[27] Aflaq's arguments offended both Muslims and Christians. The Muslim found unacceptable Aflaq's contention that Islam was anything other than the revelation of God. And Christians, bristling that his ideology sold out to Islam, dubbed him "Muhammad Aflaq."

created the possibility of drawing the Shia, fearful of control by the Sunnis, into the pan-Arab movement. Consequently, Baath student circles that formed in the late 1940s included both Sunnis and Shia. However, party membership remained minute until 1951 when a Shia engineering student from Nassariyah named Fuad al-Rikabi brought in members. According to Tariq Aziz, a perennial figure in Saddam Hussein's government, "Iraq was at a crossroads. There was severe pressure from the reactionary monarchy. . . . Young people had to choose. We could become right wing nationalists or Muslim Brothers or Communists or Baathists."[28] As a result, the rest of the decade witnessed the rise to prominence in the Baath Party of a generation of pan-Arab Shia drawn by the party's declared struggle against the landowning class and the urban capitalists, the perceived oppressors of the Shia. Claiming a socialist economic philosophy similar to that of the Communists, the Baath recruited Shia who refused to accept atheism as an important component of Communist ideology. The party also attracted Sunni Arab nationalists within the army who found the doctrine of a federation of Arab states preferable to Arab unity under Nasser. Many of these perceived, with a clarity missing among most Nasserites, that Arab unity under Nasser would entail Iraq's essential surrender of its sovereignty to Egypt. But as the movement crept from cell to cell, the party found it could not break the Nasserites' grip on the all-important army officer corps. Without numbers, resources, or the army, the Baath needed some dramatic act to strengthen its appeal. Thus, the decision was made to end the increasingly unpopular regime of General Qasim.

Just past six o'clock in the evening on October 7, 1959, a Baathist hit squad, including a young party tough named Saddam Hussein, hid within the bustling commerce that daily clogged the narrowest point on al-Rashid street. The moment that Qasim's tan Chevrolet station wagon, en route to a reception at the East German embassy, rolled into sight, the assassins raced from beneath the Roman-style colonnade the British had built during the mandate. They halted, unleashed a barrage of bullets, and broke toward the warren of alleyways on the opposite side of the street. All they left behind was a dead guard and the bleeding general slumped in the backseat of his

---

[28] Quoted in Joseph Kraft, "A Letter from Baghdad," *The New Yorker*, October 20, 1980), p. 158.

car. When the seriously injured Qasim finally left the hospital eight weeks later, a collection of Iraqi nationalists took to the streets shouting, "Long Live the Solidarity of the people, the Army, and the Government under the leadership of Abd al-Karim Qasim!"[29]

Despite this show of support, Qasim was a man under pressure. His postrevolution government, characterized by maladministration rather than genuine reform, had produced little for the common man except the privilege to walk on the grass in public parks. The reasonably efficient bureaucracy of the monarchy had all but collapsed when much of the civil service was hauled before a kangaroo court and charged with "supporting imperialism and subverting Arab nationalism." The anemic political parties that provided a semblance of competitive politics lay on their death beds, victims of fear and intimidation. And the initial integration of Iraq's separate communities at the beginning of the revolutionary government never challenged, much less shattered, the dominance of the Sunnis. Qasim's one notable act—the adoption of land reform—withered away. The peasants who did receive the small amounts of land that were actually distributed found ownership a disaster. Too unskilled at management to coordinate care of the irrigation works and too illiterate to understand that land reform did not mean release from labor, the peasants had put down their tools on land no longer productive, drifting instead to the burgeoning slums of cities to work as day laborers. Meanwhile, Qasim endlessly maneuvered one group against another to hold Iraq beyond the reach of Nasser and to keep himself in power. In the process, he never articulated a genuine ideology on which to construct the political and social reform vital to the health of the Iraqi state. Instead, this vain, perhaps unstable man nursed a jealous hatred of Nasser. With the support of dwindling numbers in the army, Qasim's regime degenerated into a cult of personality.

He became the "Sole Leader," the caliph of Baghdad, kept in power by a pampered segment of the army and a secret police force whose stringent security apparatus ensured his authoritarianism. Cultivating an image of devotion and martyrdom, he worked as many as twenty hours a day at the Ministry of Defense, where a giant illuminated portrait of himself hung on the front of the building. Around the clock, excerpts from his speeches burst like machine-gun fire

---

[29] Batatu, *The Old Social Classes and the Revoluionary Movements of Iraq*, p. 935.

from the government-held radio station. Like Saddam Hussein, Qasim was the self-created embodiment of the "great leader," always in uniform, towering above his people as a dictator claiming to embody the popular will. Emotionally unpredictable and lacking administrative talent, Qasim's modest accomplishments—demolition of some of Baghdad's worst slums, expanded availability of water and electricity, and increased primary education—faded as his political wounds deepened. The vultures circled. Leading the way were the pan-Arabists ready to devour Qasim and his Mesopotamian symbols of the Iraqi state. In the words of the poet al-Sayyab:

> As if ancient Babylon, surrounded by walls
> Comes back to life
> ...
> A thirsty Ishtar is dying with no flowers
> on her forehead.
> ...
> And the palm trees
> On the river bank are crying.[30]

In the spring of 1962, the Kurds added their weight to the forces gathering against Qasim. Demanding independence or at least autonomy in a federalized or decentralized Iraq, they exploded into a full-scale revolt.[31] It was one more element in the ongoing chaos in which the Communists in grudging alliance with Qasim battled from one point, pan-Arab Nasserites and Baathists fought from another, and the heavily outnumbered Iraqi nationalists opposed to Qasim struggled from a third point for control of Iraq's identity. The situation was hardly new. Qasim himself admitted that in the three and a half years since the revolution, he had personal knowledge of twenty-nine coup attempts against his government.

For several days in early 1963, battles filled the streets of Baghdad as the remnants of the army loyal to Qasim, together with the Communists, battled against the pan-Arabist elements of the army and the Baath. The army's pan-Arabist officer corps neutralized the air force before moving on to take, one by one, all the placements

---

[30] Al-Sayyab quoted in Amatzia Baram, *Culture, History and Ideology in the Formation of Ba'thist Iraq, 1968–89* (New York: St. Martin's Press, 1991), p. 88.
[31] See chapter 7.

of the government's defense. Simultaneously, the Baath militia swept the streets. Only Qasim's personal guard of fifteen hundred men and the people who had gained some little benefit from the postrevolution government—laborers, porters, and artisans from the mud huts east of the Tigris—fought for the general. By 12:30 P.M. on February 9, 1963, Qasim was a prisoner. A quick trial on charges of betrayal of the revolution condemned to death the general and the three officers who stayed at his side. Following the instant verdict, a contingent of revolutionaries including members of the Iraq Baath Party pushed Qasim and the others into the music studio of the government television station, sat them down, and shot them. Then they turned on the cameras. One body was sprawled backward on a spindly chair. Qasim lay on the floor. As if to prove the man who had tried to rule Iraq after the revolution was truly dead, a member of the execution squad grabbed the dead general's head by the hair and thrust it into the camera lens. Iraqis saw for themselves the glassy eyes and gold-capped teeth of their deposed leader. A short while later, the victors of yet another military coup appeared before a crowd of reporters gathered at a Baghdad hotel. They said simply, "We revolted against the cult of personality."[32]

THE NEW RULING TRIBUNAL, the National Council of the Revolutionary Command (NCRC), allocated power between the military and the Baath, the feeble rump of a party turned into a political force by its participation in the coup. At the time, the Baath still claimed only a thousand members. Its leadership included mostly Sunnis but also Shia and one Arabized Kurd. Its membership consisted largely of party functionaries, school teachers, and an occasional lawyer whose social class was determind by families who were peasants, workers, traders, or impoverished landlords. Lacking stature, respect, or power outside its membership in the army, the Baath accepted as president General Abd al-Salam Arif , Qasim's Nasserite counterpart in the 1958 revolution and the person to whom the deposed leader had once referred as "my son, my friend, my brother."[33] The quiet reserved army general Ahmed Hassan al-Bakr of the Baath assumed the premiership. Sixteen of the eighteen seats

---

[32] Quoted in *Time*, February 22, 1963, p. 28.
[33] *Life Magazine*, February 22, 1963.

on the NCRC and twelve of the twenty-one seats on the cabinet also belonged to the Baath. Together the Nasserites of the army and the pan-Arabists of the Baath declared the country the "Iraqi region of the Arab homeland."

In the aftermath of the coup, a cadre of some two thousand Baath sympathizers from the Azamiyah quarter of Baghdad organized to defend the new government against any possible threat of a countercoup. Assuming the name of the National Guard, they were part of the hundreds of men sent out to round up the Communists. Identified by green arm bands, they carried mimeographed lists of members of the ICP, complete with home addresses and auto tag numbers. Within a week, the regime had killed somewhere between five hundred and three thousand people whose Marxist ideology rejected pan-Arabism and whose members posed the only real challenge to the new regime. Tariq Aziz, who was in the leadership of the Baath at the time, has said, "To understand why so much blood flowed in those days you have to remember Iraq's history is not one in which political dissent has been allowed."[34]

Elimination of the Communists proved one of the few unified acts of a government with no common goal beyond the toppling of Qasim. Within weeks, the alliance between the pan-Arab army officers and the Baath within and without the army split into rival groups that reflected the ideological and to some extent sectarian differences of those who staged the coup. The pan-Arab army officers still sought union with Nasser's Egypt. The Baathists divided themselves between a "leftist" group heavily populated by Shia, which advocated a rapid transformation of Iraq into a socialist state, and the "rightists," a relatively mixed group of sectarian identities, which supported a gradual move toward socialism as well as cooperation with Iraqi nationalists within the military. A third Baathist group headed by the premier, General al-Bakr, consisted mainly of Sunni Arabs who sought little beyond their own power.

By March, the Baath had moved Abd al-Salam Arif aside over the abiding issue of Iraq's unification with Nasser's Egypt, but the maneuver did little to stabilize the political situation. The government was spiraling toward anarchy. Although every faction carried its burden of

---

[34] Quoted in Milton Viorst, "The View from the Mustansiriyah—I," *The New Yorker*, October 12, 1987, p. 104.

blame, it was the Baath's National Guard that terrorized the streets. In the wake of the coup, the Baath militia had swollen by several thousand. New recruits were no longer idealistically inclined students but were, as one Iraqi Communist leader said, "adolescents befuddled by jingoistic propaganda, declassed elements and all sorts of riffraff" who sought personal power.[35] Knocking on doors in the middle of the night, they seized suspected Baath enemies. During the day, they swaggered through the streets intimidating civilians, taking from them what they wanted. Most of all, they exercised the power of arrest. Those seized were thrown into prison or the torture chambers of the Qasr al-Nihayah, the "Palace of the End." Used for detention and interrogation since the end of the monarchy, it became the Baath's Bureau of Special Investigations, where enforcers, including a young Saddam Hussein, wielded the Baath's instruments of torture.

On June 10, 1963, the rebelling Kurds bore the brunt of a Baath government determined to establish its rule. Tanks and aircraft razed a host of Kurdish villages, killing hundreds of men, women, and children. Still, the Kurdish rebellion continued throughout the summer of 1963 while the ruling council's political differences over economic policy, the implementation of Arab nationalist ideology, and the ever-growing power of the Baath's National Guard widened. By November it was the National Guard, not the Communists or the Kurds, that the Iraqi army saw as an intolerable threat to its own historic position as the power broker of Iraqi politics.

On November 18, 1963, a collection of army officers, including some disaffected Baathists, sent tanks to secure strategic points in Baghdad. Specifically targeting the Baath organization, they fired rockets into the headquarters of the National Guard and dispatched soldiers to round up the Baath leadership. Barely qualifying as a coup, the military action purged the Baath from government. The generals, led by the deposed Arif, now ruled alone in an atmosphere in which the street power of the Communists had been tamed, the pretensions of the National Guard leveled, and the anarchy of the Baath ended. It was now Arif's turn to decide if Iraq would join the Arab world or keep itself apart.

---

[35] Quoted in Judith Miller and Laurie Mylroie, *Saddam Hussein and the Crisis in the Gulf* (New York: Times Books, 1990), p. 87.

IN HIS USUAL dark suit and tasteful tie, Abd al-Salam Arif looked more like a civilian than a solider. But almost everything about the general defied easy classification. He was a conservative Iraqi in a tumultuous time. He was an Arab nationalist. Even though the ideology of Arab nationalism struggled with Islam's power within the culture, he was a deeply religious Sunni Muslim.[36] One thing about Arif was clear. He was a military man determined to preserve the authority of the army. Declaring his Arab nationalist credentials above all else, Arif abolished the Akkadian sun and the star of Ishtar as official symbols of Iraq. Likewise, the emblems of Mesopotamia that had frequented postage stamps of the Qasim regime disappeared, replaced by images commemorating anniversaries of the Arab League and pan-Arab conferences and celebrating Arab themes connected to Sunni Arab culture. On May 3, 1964, the Arif government issued a provisional constitution declaring Iraq to be "a part of the Arab nation."

A friend and ally of Gamal Abdul Nasser, General Arif began to forge the Arab nationalists' long-awaited links between Iraq and Egypt. Acting to advance the process by bringing Iraq's economy in sync with that of Egypt, Arif nationalized all banks and insurance companies along with large industries and commercial establishments. Subsequently, the two countries signed an agreement that created what was in essence a consulting group called the Iraq–United Arab Republic Unified Political Command and alluded to some form of political union within two years. But the actual joining of the nations was anything but certain. This time, Iraqi reluctance to wed with Egypt was joined by Nasser's own hesitation to stake his country to turbulent Iraq.

Already stung by the 1961 collapse of his union with Syria, Nasser held no illusions about the feasibility of uniting Egypt and Iraq. The two countries shared no borders, and the Arif regime perched on the thinnest of foundations. In the popular phrase of the time, Arif and his supporters constituted "a minority within a minority," meaning a minority of Sunnis who totaled only one-fifth of Iraq's population. The fragility of the regime revealed itself on September 4, 1964, when the Baath attempted to regain power in another coup

---

[36] In his first meeting with the Soviet Union's Nikita Khrushchev, Arif exasperated his host by spending most of the time explaining Islam to a Marxist who regarded religion the opiate of the masses. He also sought but failed to destroy the July 14 monument because of its representation of the human figure.

while Arif's rivals in the army tried to shoot down his plane as it took off from a military base. Although both actions failed, Arif's tenure as the head of Iraq was about to end. Before he could either succeed or fail in ruling his discordant country, he died when his helicopter crashed in a sandstorm in southern Iraq on April 13, 1966.

His brother, General Abd al-Rahman Arif, took over Iraq's military government. The second Arif president devoted himself more to upholding the power of the army than to promoting Arab nationalism or union with Egypt. Despite their failure to address Iraq's internal needs, the older and younger Arif brothers did succeed in keeping the country intact and sovereign through the turmoil of threatened coups, the brutality of the Baath, the Kurdish rebellion, and the Nasserites' eternal dream of union with Egypt. One of these challenges was erased in June 1967, when the shadow that Nasser had cast over the Arab world for more than a decade disappeared.

TANGLED IN A WAR of wills since the Suez crisis of 1956, Israel and its Arab neighbors once more inched toward war. In the late spring of 1967, a swaggering Nasser trained his guns atop the heights of Sham al-Sheikh on the narrow Strait of Tiran, and boastfully declared the Gulf of Aqaba closed to ships headed for Israel's port of Elat. Rattling its own sabers, Israel angrily responded that a blockade of the Gulf of Aqaba constituted an act of war. On June 6, 1967, as dawn broke over the Moab hills, Israeli fighter planes streaked out over the calm waters of the Mediterranean, doubling back toward land to lay waste to the Egyptian Air Force, the Royal Jordanian Air Force, and Syria's fighter planes, which were sitting on the country's lone airfield north of Damascus. The Arab states, including Iraq, hastily sent their armies into battle. One by one, the Israelis destroyed them. Egypt lost the Sinai; Jordan forfeited Jerusalem and the West Bank of the Jordan River; Syria sacrificed the Golan Heights; Iraq lost nothing. Sharing no contiguous borders with Israel, Iraq's lone armored brigade and three infantry brigades sent in the name of Arab nationalism never left Jordan. On June 9, the great charismatic figure of pan-Arabism acknowledged a defeat larger in scope, more dramatic in impact than that of 1948. In the *naksa*, the Arab defeat of 1967, the logic and symbols of an entire era of Arab political thought and practice vanished. Nasser's revolution was, like Nasser himself, exhausted and finished.

In Iraq, the demise of Nasserism left the ideology of pan-Arabism to the Baath. But the Baath of 1967 was not the Baath of 1963. For one thing, the whole complexion of the party had changed. The Iraqi Baath had originally represented a genuine partnership between Sunnis and those Shia who regarded themselves first as Arabs and second as members of Islam's dissenting sect. But by 1967, the Sunnis controlled the party, benefiting from the defection of the Shia leadership that had demanded that the party embrace Marxism. As a result, 84 percent of the top command were now Sunni Arabs; 7 percent, Kurds; 5 percent, Shia; and the remaining 4 percent, from other communal groups. More significant for the future of Iraq, "the leadership of the Baath was more practical and seasoned than in 1963. Also more ruthless, more conspiratorial, and . . . more determined to seize and hold power."[37] With tight internal organization and the command of its own militia, the Baath no longer had to depend on support from the military. Thus, five years after the debacle of 1963, the Baathists were ready to reclaim the government of Iraq.

As the public resentment over Iraq's failure to contribute sufficiently to the 1967 war between Israel and the Arabs swelled, the Baath Party beat the drum of Arabism. Railing against the cowardliness of the Abd al-Rahman Arif government, the Baath sent demonstrators into the streets. Thousands more responded emotionally to Baath rhetoric that hit the raw nerve beneath the humiliation of what was being called the Six Day War. Riddled by corruption, branded with incompetence, deaf to demands for parliamentary government, Arif and his dwindling corps of army officers huddled behind the facade of authority. Iraq, which had averaged two coups or attempted coups every year since the revolution, was about to witness another.

At three o'clock on the morning of July 17, 1968, the telephone rang in the bedroom of the sleeping Abd al-Rahman Arif. When the startled president answered, the voice of a high-ranking Baath officer in the Iraqi army tersely announced, "I am speaking from the Ministry of Defense. Tanks are now proceeding toward the palace."[38] Suddenly, five rifle shots outside the window split the air. The presi-

---

[37] Phebe Marr, *The Modern History of Iraq* (Boulder, Colo.: Westview Press, 1985), p. 206.

[38] Quoted in *Time*, July 26, 1968, p. 36.

dent meekly surrendered, drank a cup of tea with those deposing him, accepted transportation to the airport, and boarded an Iraqi airliner to join his ailing wife in London. The coup, planned and executed by the Baath, was over. Coincidence struck a haunting chord: the Baath had ended military rule almost ten years to the day after the army erased the monarchy in 1958.

In retrospect, the monarchy, despite its serious shortcomings, had governed Iraq better than any government that followed. When it fell, it took most of the educated class with it. In place of the king and the educated elite, the military stepped in as the guardians of government. Under the batons of generals, the people of Iraq found that they had traded feudalism and imperialism for authoritarianism, insecurity, and economic regression. At the end of a chaotic decade of military government in which the competing ideologies of the 1958 revolution waged battle, Iraq passed into the iron grip of the Baath Party. Over the next decade, the Baath, through political organization more than military fiat, would drive fragmented Iraq toward the dictatorship of Saddam Hussein.

6

THE TRIUMPH OF
THE BAATH

It was 1978, a little over four years after the Arab oil embargo had sent its seismic shock through the international economy. Iraq, in possession of 15 percent of the Persian Gulf's frenetic oil production, pulsated with the rhythms of sudden massive wealth. In the predominately Kurdish town of Kirkuk, pumps ran at full throttle, lifting thick crude oil out of the ground and forcing it into pipelines that fed the industrialized world's seemingly insatiable hunger. In the Shia south, the sky above the port of Basra glowed orange from the tongues of surplus gas that flared from oil refineries turning viscous black petroleum into liquid gold. Between the oil fields in the north and the refining plants in the south, Baghdad stood under a roaring waterfall of money. Deal makers from Europe, the United States, and Asia fought for rooms in the precious few hotels that could call themselves "modern," or slept on broken-down sofas in the lobbies of shabby establishments that predated the oil boom. Far into the night, international businessmen hunched over tables in the open-air fish restaurants along the Tigris, pitching contracts to Iraqi bureaucrats and entrepreneurs. On both sides of the river, international construction companies on the payroll of the government razed graceful old mud-brick buildings to make room for square glass boxes that flaunted the worst of second-rate contemporary architecture. The atmosphere was electric. Nothing like this had happened since the Italian city-states burst into full bloom on the trade of the Crusades. That combination of wealth and cultural interchange had sparked the Renaissance that altered Europe forever. The same sense of rebirth permeated Baghdad. For almost a century, Arab nationalists had sought their renaissance in a political philosophy that promised to reverse Arab backwardness through unity. Now the shackles of Ottoman repression and European colonialism were dissolving at last in the black tar that had lain beneath Iraq for thousands of years.

In this new era, the official version of Iraqi identity began to exhibit subtle elements of Mesopotamian culture with a contemporary touch. The ziggurat as the signature of the city had been replaced by public art. And the king figure resided in the inescapable portraits of Vice President Saddam Hussein that hung from buildings, bridges, and overpasses. As the public face of Baath economic policy, his image promised a future of plenty to all Iraqis. Yet in prowling through the neighborhoods or sipping tea in the homes of the prosperous, it was impossible to escape the feeling of disquiet that permeated society. Those of the new middle class created by the oil boom already sensed that stability and prosperity for Iraq had come at the price of civil liberty.

From 1958 to 1968, the short line of revolutionary regimes that had passed the chairmanship of Iraq from General Abd al-Karim Qasim to the Baath Party to the Arif brothers were differentiated largely by the degree of determination each applied to crushing its rivals in the ongoing turmoil to capture and hold the Iraqi state. In the second decade after the 1958 revolution, the new Baath government employed Draconian measures of control through a one-party state encased in a well-defined institutional structure. Through the instruments of the party, the Baathists gutted the power of the army, crushed the political opposition, quelled the Kurds in a savage war in the north, and elevated to power a political tribe of Sunni Arabs. With the revenues generated by the oil boom of 1973, the Baath launched wide-reaching programs dedicated to developing among the Iraqis the skills required by a modern state. It did it all while facing serious challenges emanating from beyond Iraq's borders—from Baath rivals in Syria, the ambitions of the shah of Iran, and the complications of the Cold War. But in the process of fending off foreign threats, containing Shia anger, subduing the Kurds, and managing the bounty of the 1973 oil boom, the Baath sacrificed its ideological message of pan-Arabism, its institutional goals of economic equality, and its very soul as a party. In 1979, all decisions concerning Iraq—its identity, its resources, its people, its nature as a state—passed into the hands of one man: Saddam Hussein.

THE MORNING Iraq woke up to the new Baath regime, most Iraqis knew little of what to expect of the Baath outside the disastrous seven months that followed its coup of 1963. Given the party's clandestine and revolutionary heritage, that seemed to be the Baath way. It still is, according to Tariq Aziz and the party's own rhetoric: "The ABSP (the Arab Baath Socialist Party) is not a conventional political organization, but is composed of cells of valiant revolutionaries. . . . They are experts in secret organization. They are organizers of demonstrations, strikes, and armed revolutions. . . . They are the knights of struggle."[1]

From the day it took the reins of government in 1968, the Baath understood that survival on the merciless sea of Iraqi politics depended on consolidating the power of a party that was nothing more than a well-organized cadre of perhaps five thousand people. Success in overthrowing the Arif regime had come only through the utilization of non-Baathist officers of the military. Thus, retaining power meant that the miniscule Baath had to seize total control of the apparatus of the state as quickly as possible. Otherwise, its tenuous hold on government would break, plunging the party into the same chasm that had swallowed the Baath government of 1963.

No sooner had the door of General Abd al-Rahman Arif's plane to London closed than the Baath began the process by which it would consolidate its power. The first step was to remove the non-Baath army officers who had led the charge on the Arif regime. Naive about the grizzled veterans of Baath politics, the largely young colonels and majors who had participated in the coup believed that the new government, like all governments since the revolution of 1958, would ultimately belong to the military. For them, partnership with the Baath represented simply an alliance of convenience in which one set of army officers replaced another as the arbitrator of authority. What they failed to grasp was that the experience of 1963 had branded on the psyche of every Baath leader the essential mark of survival—never share power. Consequently, within two weeks after the coup, Baath leader Ahmed Hassan al-Bakr, the acting president and the general that the non-Baathists of the army had followed in the coup against Arif, executed a series of maneuvers aimed at limiting the military's influence over government. Wise to the role the army had played in Iraq's chaotic political history, al-Bakr and the circle of supporters around him proceeded to accomplish what no

---

[1] Quoted in Christine Moss Helms, *Iraq: Eastern Front of the Arab World* (Washington, D.C.: Brookings Institution, 1984), p. 59.

other government had achieved since 1936—elimination of the army from politics.

Before the Baath's uniformed partners in the coup comprehended the unfolding plot, al-Bakr installed his own men at the helm of both the army and the air force. On July 30, the president invited Abd al-Razzaq al-Nayif, the non-Baathist deputy director of military intelligence and potentially the Baath's most serious rival, to lunch at the presidential palace. As the general sipped his tea, Saddam Hussein, the Baath's master of strong arm politics, stepped forward, drew a revolver, and ordered al-Nayif to raise his hands. Replaying what the British had done to King Faisal's opposition in 1921, Hussein and his captive drove to the Rashid military camp, where al-Nayif was put on a plane and sent off into permanent exile. As soon as the aircraft disappeared over the horizon, al-Bakr swept al-Nayif's civilian followers from the cabinet and added to his existing titles of general and acting president those of prime minister and commander in chief of the armed forces. With all civilian and military power now in the hands of the Baath leadership, the remaining challenge was to hold onto it.

The Baath deposited its political security in a complex network of organizations prepared to dispense systematic remorseless terror aimed at intimidating and mastering the population. This was the purview of Saddam Hussein, who subscribed totally to the 1965 Baath Party statement, "The party might be compelled, especially in the early stages of the revolution, to feign terror and coercive guidance with the object of crushing the enemies of the revolution."[2] It was Hussein who had begun to build the Baath's own security force after the collapse of 1963. Recruiting men with brawn, brain, and few scruples, he organized them into self-contained cells that answered to no one but him. Called the Jihaz Haneen, or "instrument of yearning," this small tight machine of coercion was ready in 1968 to kill and intimidate in the name of the party. Its members, like menacing messengers, began to move from individual to individual, through group after group, spreading the word that the Baath regime would tolerate no challenge to its rule.

The warnings preceded action. The government announced that

[2] Roy E. Thoman, "Iraq under Baathist Rule," *Current History* 71 (January 1972): 32.

on January 5, 1969, seventeen "spies," thirteen of them Iraqi Jews, would be hanged in Baghdad's Liberation Square. By the scheduled date, the country was intoxicated with a holiday spirit fomented by state-owned radio and television. Busloads of peasants, transported into the city at the government's expense, picnicked in the shadow of the gallows while legions of workers on paid leave milled about in the carnival-like atmosphere. Just before the condemned went to their deaths, Ahmed Hassan al-Bakr, accompanied by Saddam Hussein, arrived in an open car that drove through a phalanx of cheering Baath students and stopped in the square. There they watched the condemned drop from the gallows and dangle by their necks. Behind them, Salah Umar al-Ali, the minister of guidance, worked the crowd: "Great Iraqi people! This is only the beginning! The great and immortal squares of Iraq shall be filled up with the corpses of traitors and spies."[3]

In February 1969, the whole politburo of the Iraqi Communist Party, the old nemesis of the Baath, went to jail. Members of the armed forces received notice that membership in any political organization other than the Baath was punishable by death. In January 1970, the Iraqi government ordered the deportation of thousands of Persian Shia. Ten months later, forty-four more people, accused of another shadowy conspiracy, were executed. Then the Baath leadership turned on its own.

Assassinations and executions rolled like drumbeats. In October 1970, Hardan al-Tikriti, former deputy premier and former minister of defense, was gunned down in Kuwait; the same month, Abd al-Rahman al-Bazzaz, the Baath ideologue and former prime minister, underwent imprisonment and torture. In August 1971, Abd al-Karim Nasrat, an early Baathist and one of the militia who overthrew the Qasim regime, was stabbed to death in his bed. In November, Fuad al-Kikkahi, leader of the Baath until 1959, was murdered in prison. In July 1973, Nadhim Kzark, the Shia chief of internal security, and thirty-five others were executed in the wake of an attempted coup. Ruthless against its enemies, the regime eliminated anyone—Nasserite, pro-Syrian Baathist, Iraqi Shia, or Kurd—positioned to challenge Baath dominance. They were not alone. Ordinary

---

[3] Quoted in Samir al-Khalil, *Republic of Fear: The Inside Story of Saddam's Iraq* (New York: Pantheon Books, 1989), p. 52.

people with no standing or political affiliation suffered arrest, torture, and execution simply because someone whispered into the ear of the Mukhabarat, or Special Security Section, that a civil servant, a tradesman, or a peddler had grumbled about the government.

The Mukhabarat had come out of the Jihaz Haneen, the Baath's intelligence organization that dated to the mid-1960s. Its security tasks focused on one purpose—defending the party and its hierarchy.[4]

The party, like the Mukhabarat, became omnipresent. At the top of the institutional pyramid of the Baath sat the Revolutionary Command Council (RCC), a body of senior Baath officials that theoretically drew its authority from the party's Regional Command Council, which stands outside the formal government structure. On paper, the RCC was only the party's governing body. But when it was shifted from a party organ to a state organ in the immediate aftermath of the coup, the RCC became the dominant decision-making body in the Iraqi state, fulfilling both the executive and the legislative function. Although originally representing both Baathists and non-Baathists, the membership of the RCC quickly boiled down to Ahmed Hassan al-Bakr and a handful of Baath veterans, most of whom possessed personal ties to the leader. Essentially these same people sat on the Regional Command Council and occupied all the major chairs in the cabinet. Standing behind them, more as an equal than a subordinate, was Saddam Hussein, whose underground security services and the new paramilitary Popular Army guarded against an army coup, criticism by the media, and dissent from anyone else.

The whole incestuous system was codified by the constitution of 1970, which gave the RCC the authority to approve the budget, promulgate laws, and provide for the national defense. The chairman of the RCC, who arose out of power politics within the Baath, would automatically assume the presidency, an office that also encompassed the roles of commander in chief of the armed forces and chief executive of the state. As such, the president held the power to appoint, promote, and dismiss all members of the military, the judiciary, and the civil service charged with executing the decisions of the RCC. Only one article of the constitution acknowledged Iraqis

---

[4] The security services of the Baath, like everything else in the party structure, are multifaceted. Specialized units come and go as the political situation demands. The Mukhabarat has been the constant, and to most Iraqis its name has become the generic term for the enforcement wing of the Baath's police state.

outside the Baath—the provision for a popularly elected national assembly. That provision remained dormant.

A system dominated by a tiny minority was able to function because the Baath Party continued to operate through the compartmentalized structure and clandestine methods with which it had secured power in both 1963 and 1968. Instead of pursuing the cult of personality that characterized the Nasserites, the Baathists meticulously developed and systematized the requirements of membership to ensure that the interests of the party always exceeded the interests of an individual. Rather than recruiting a mass membership, the party carefully selected candidates to be incorporated into the party. Over a period of five to eight years, each was intensely indoctrinated in well-defined steps that moved the candidate from apprenticeship to full membership and the right to the title of Baathist.

Groups of three to seven members would band together in an organizational compartment, or *halaqh*, which connected one point of Baath power to another. Most commonly arranged by neighborhood, these tight cells met in secret to carry out the directives of their Baath superiors. In turn, the *halaqhs* combined to form the *firqah*, a collection of cells that functioned much as its lower-level counterpart. These *firqahs* again combined to create divisions claiming jurisdiction over segments of cities or provinces. And so the intricate party structure built layer upon layer until it reached the national level.

Similar parallel structures based within professions incorporated selected doctors, lawyers, engineers, and teachers into the realm of the Baath. These were replicated in factories, offices, and schools. Honeycombing the bureaucracy and, most important, the military, each unit of loyal Baathists acted as the eyes and ears of the party. Although state propaganda would continue to advertise the existence of a so-called patriotic front in which all political factions were free to participate, the stark reality was that no political group, trade union, peasants' association, cultural organization, or any other collection of individuals was allowed to exist outside the tight parameters of Baath control.

Thus, the Baath reached out to affect every aspect of Iraqi life, imposing on the whole society a rigid ideological framework in which every generation would be molded into the Baath's own image. Like potters at the wheel, party functionaries shaped teenagers through student organizations, sports groups, literary and science clubs, artistic societies, and even hobby and craft groups. The Ministry of Culture exercised control over all cultural activities—movies, live theater, the Iraqi Symphony Orchestra, the Folklore troupe, and all schools of art. In the regime's description of the Department of Plastic Arts at Baghdad University lay the purpose—"to extend artistic education to the masses, by using all available means to enhance artistic awareness among the people . . . in the light of the ideas of the Arab Baath Socialist Party."[5]

Before the decade ended, there would be for every organ and function of government a unit of the party operating alongside or in place of state authority. Still the Baath was unique to the Iraqi experience only in the complexity of its institutional network. Centralized control by an elite holding all the levers of power had characterized every Iraqi government since the inception of the state. What was truly different about the Baath was a socialist ideology meant to shake the country loose from the remnants of feudalism and communalism. In the Baath concept of socialism, the government assumed direct responsibility for social welfare, from the construction of the infrastructure to education and health care. In return for these economic benefits delivered by a munificent government, Iraqis were to shed their multifaceted communal identity and fall in line behind the leadership.

While targeting all segments of society, the regime's socialist policies promised the downtrodden rural Shia the most. The Baath knew this. In its promise of economic parity within the Iraqi state, the Baath before 1968 sought to broaden its base by coaxing the Shia into the party or at least encouraging them to lend the Baath their passive support. In pursuit of that goal, the party had elevated a number of Shia Baathists to positions of leadership. This new prominence given to a Shia presence within the Baath was designed to signal to a rising generation of Shia that they could realistically expect upward social mobility through loyalty to the party. But after 1968, when the Baath was in a position to give form to promise, the door closed on Shia-Sunni equality. No Shia held a chair on the RCC and no Shia occupied a position in the regional leadership of the

---

[5] Quoted in Phebe Marr, *The Modern History of Iraq* (Boulder, Colo.: Westview Press, 1985), p. 287.

party. For all its claims that the Baath would tear down communal barriers, the party proved to be a collection of Arab Sunnis dedicated to the dominance of their own tribe.

IN THE SOCIAL ORDER originally established in 1968, the Baath declared that there was no room for communalism. Communiqué No. 1 of the new government denounced religious sectarianism and racial differentiations as remnants of colonialism. On the same day that this communiqué was issued, an article in the government newspaper branded tribalism as the epitome of backwardness and social regression. The tribes, however, would not submit to the Baath-designed order by surrendering their primary identity. In the summer of 1969 when the tribes near Amarah rebelled against the rule of Baghdad, the Baath regime found itself confronting the same challenge to the state that Faisal I had faced. Thus, within the councils of the Baath, tribalism took its place in the pantheon of forces that might threaten Baath rule.

Unlike in Faisal's time, the tribes were no longer creatures of the countryside. In the constant migration since the 1958 revolution, tribesmen had moved into the heart of the cities, particularly the country's economic mecca of Baghdad. By their sheer numbers, they altered the whole urban environment. According to one bitter urban Sunni Arab, the rural tribesmen imposed on the cities their whole "backward culture, including ignorance, brutality, vulgarity and tribal values."[6]

In both the cities and the countryside, the Baath threw up its defenses against the largest and strongest tribes. Extensive areas of land, particularly that belonging to the Sunni tribes of Jubbur, Shammar Jarba, and the Azza, went to the central government or to other tribes. A new phase of land reform attempted to drive a wedge between the Shia peasants and their sheikhs. At the same time, the Baath sent party members into impoverished Sunni villages and urban neighborhoods with promises of roads, electricity, and water systems in return for significant enrollment in the party and the security services. This recruitment of the tribes into the structure of the Baath only increased the rate of change that was already underway in the party. The original Baath had been an organization of mid-

---

[6] Omar Abbas, interview with author, Amman, Jordan, December 4, 1999.

dle-class intellectuals. That ended with the political emasculation of the educated classes at the beginning of the second Baath regime. With the addition of members of the Sunni tribes, the Baath became a party of the lower classes with little education but strong tribal ties. And even though one of the party's central tenets had always held that tribalism stood as an obstacle to modernization, the point had become immaterial to the current Baath. For in fact, nowhere was tribalism more evident than in the Baath leadership itself.

Ahmed Hassan al-Bakr and most of the Baath power structure came from Tikrit, a decayed textile town perched on the bank of the Tigris fifty miles north of Baghdad. This town is where the legendary Saladin of the Crusades was born in the twelfth century and the Mongol hordes under Tamerlane stacked the skulls of their slaughtered victims into a triumphal pyramid at the end of the fourteenth century. In an area where malaria, bilharzia, and tapeworm were rampant, the Tikritis were known as difficult people driven by poverty into an infamous toughness. From one generation to the next, families operated as gangs, stealing from each other and feuding over scarce resources. In the 1920s, the educated and refined Mawloud Mukhlis, who was close to King Faisal, urged his fellow Tikritis to enter the new national army. Many grabbed the opportunity to escape the worst of their poverty. In the remaining years of the monarchy, Tikritis staffed the army in a larger proportion to the population than did residents from any other town in Iraq. Most of them shared a common set of attitudes—hatred of Britain and the monarchy, jealousy toward the Sunni upper classes, and hostility toward the Shia. One of these Tikritis was Ahmed Hassan al-Bakr, among the conspirators of 1958 and the leader of the 1963 Baath coup. After the Baath's ignominious fall from power, al-Bakr molded his blood kin from Tikrit into the dominant faction in the party. Believing "blood is thicker than ideology," al-Bakr admitted into his close political circle his cousin—Saddam Hussein.

SADDAM HUSSEIN was born on April 28, 1937, into a miserably poor peasant family in the village of al-Auja, near Tikrit. Before his birth, Saddam's father either had died, perhaps at the hands of bandits, or had simply disappeared. Within a few years, his mother remarried within her own social class. A rare photograph of Subha and her second husband, Ibrahim al-Hassan, captures a portly woman marked with Bedouin-style tattoos on her chin, cheeks, and forehead and draped from head to toe in a black *abayah*, or cloak-like outer garment. Ibrahim sits beside her, a sun-scorched man wearing thick glasses and garbed in the traditional *disdasha*, the long shirt-like robe, and *gutra*, or head covering, of a tribal Arab. The couple appears to be what they were—illiterate peasants, the settled descendants of Arab tribesmen. It was through them that Saddam came to identify with the wretched poor within the Sunni minority. If he could claim any nobility, it came through his tribal credentials provided by his natural father's membership in the al-Bejat clan of the Albu Nasir tribe around Tikrit.

In his official biographies, Hussein claims that his stepfather Ibrahim dragged him from bed every morning yelling, "Get up you son of a whore, and look after the sheep."[7] This was tribal society, in which the father ruled the household, like a tyrant if necessary. Yet in this tribal society, the family, no matter how fractured by internal conflict, always remained the bulwark against all forces encroaching from the outside world. Behind it, the needs of one member became the responsibility of all members.

As a child, Hussein was an *ibn aziqa*, a "son of the alleys" who sold watermelons to passengers on the train that stopped at Tikrit en route from Baghdad to Mosul. He was exceptionally intelligent. At the age of ten, he left his village home to enter the Baghdad house of his mother's brother, Khayrallah Tulfah, in a neighborhood that mixed poor Sunnis and Shia. Nonetheless, the city opened a whole new world for the unschooled village boy. He enrolled in formal education for the first time, completing intermediate school at the age of sixteen. He also received his first infusion of radical pan-Arabism in the house of his uncle, a fervent Arab nationalist who had been cashiered out of the army for supporting the Rashid Ali coup in 1941. He learned self-reliance on the streets, where he was often mocked for being fatherless. Filled with ambition, Hussein, like most Sunnis seeking social mobility, looked to a military career, but the lack of any social standing and ties to a family under the monarchy's suspicion closed the door of the Baghdad Military Academy. Thus, he was denied the military credentials that are the near universal mark of

---

[7] Judith Miller and Laurie Mylroie, *Saddam Hussein and the Crisis in the Gulf* (New York: Times Books, 1990), p. 27.

contemporary Arab leaders.[8] In 1957, at the age of twenty, the strikingly handsome Hussein took another route common to his Tikriti relatives—into the Baath Party. In October 1959, he was on al-Rashid street with the Baathist hit team that machine-gunned General Qasim's car in broad daylight. According to his official biography, *The Long Days*, the wounded Hussein bravely saved his comrades by commandeering a car at gunpoint to evade the police. Escaping Baghdad alone, he wound his way northward along the eastern bank of the Tigris. Four days later when he reached al-Dhour, opposite Tikrit, he plunged into the icy water and swam to the other side.[9] From there, he began the long trek across the desert to Damascus, digging a bullet out of his leg with a knife along the way.

Hussein ended his flight in Cairo, where he took advantage of Nasser's generous support of young Arab nationalists. He entered Qasr al Nil high school in the Dokki district and then attended law school at Cairo University. Now endowed with his famous moustache, he supplemented a stipend provided by the Egyptian government by selling cigarettes on the street and hustling passengers for taxis. Like other political exiles of the era, Hussein spent much of his time in Cairo's cafes. Thirty years later the proprietor of his favorite one, the Andiana, commented, "He was what we call a troublemaker. He would fight for any reason. . . . We wanted to bar him from coming here. But the police . . . said he was protected by Nasser."[10] In 1963, the young Baathist from Tikrit dropped out of school to return to Iraq to marry his first cousin, Sajida Tulfah, daughter of his Uncle Khayrallah, and to claim a place in the Baath after the overthrow of Qasim.

Hussein was soon the rising star in the Baath underground. Despite a stint in jail following the 1963 Baath debacle, he became the organizing force of a Baath security apparatus. Over the next few years, his courage in the trenches of political warfare created his image as a *shaqawah*, a street tough, a man to be feared. It was during this period that he developed what some claim is an obsession

---

[8] Hussein's lack of military training apparently constitutes a self-imposed blight on his honor. In 1976, he had himself appointed lieutenant general in the Iraqi army. When he became president of Iraq in 1979, he promoted himself to field marshal.

[9] This swim across the river is often re-enacted for the public by one of Saddam Hussein's many stand-ins.

[10] Quoted in *New York Times*, October 23, 1990.

with Stalin, the man whose complete control of the civilian Soviet Communist Party enabled him to dominate the army. Yet given that Iraqi politics before 1968 responded to the dictates of the military elite, the civilian Hussein's path to power could only be tread in tandem with a senior military officer. That man was Ahmed Hassan al-Bakr of the al-Bejat clan of the Albu Nasir tribe of Tikrit.

In 1968, less than ten years after he had fled for his life from Baghdad, the thirty-one-year-old Saddam Hussein hovered in the background of leadership of the second Baath regime, for it was the street-level muscle that Hussein had organized around Baath ideology and operated with thuggish fervor that helped pave the way for the Baath's return to power. Within a few months of the Baath takeover in 1968, Hussein emerged from the shadows as the strongman of the regime. As the regime matured, it was Hussein who reshaped the party, transforming it from an underground cadre into a highly organized force that reached into every corner of government and society. This instrument of power allowed the civilians of the Baath to move the military out of politics. As its custodian, the charming and ferocious Hussein behaved like a tribal leader—grateful and generous to friends, merciless and unforgiving to enemies. In spite of the glitzy wardrobe he now wore, Hussein was still a Tikriti, part of a people known for their violence in the Iraqi countryside, where everybody carried a weapon and no one bowed to anything but superior force. One of his associates of the time said, "There is no real mystery about the way we run Iraq. We run it exactly as we used to run Tikrit."[11]

While the not particularly intelligent al-Bakr played the role of president of Baath Iraq, the smart and hard-working Saddam Hussein operated as the power behind the throne. At the base of everything—government and party—was the Mukhabarat, the secret police patrolling every corner of Iraq in their white Toyota Landcruisers. Manpower for this security force came from the Sunni Arab tribes around Tikrit. Each man who joined owed his position, his lavish allowance, and his allegiance to his sheikh—Saddam Hussein. The Mukhabarat, like the leadership of the Baath, spoke the new language of power, the rural vernacular of the Tikritis. Yet strong-arm

---

[11] Quoted in Andrew Cockburn and Patrick Cockburn, *Out of the Ashes: The Resurrection of Saddam Hussein* (New York: HarperCollins, 1999), p. 76.

tactics and organizational precision could not protect the Baath regime from internal and external challenges to its rule.

IRONICALLY, THE BAATH of Baghdad had come to fear the mother party that had been conceived in the womb of Arab nationalism in 1947 in Syria's Damascus. In its infancy and on into its adolescence, the Baath had held tight to the ideology of Arab unity within the universal Arab state. But in 1964 the whole Baath concept of Arab unity began to undergo a quantum shift precipitated by a complex struggle for power between the party's intellectuals and the Baath members of the Syrian military. In February 1966, the Syrian wing of the party ruptured when the military government of Hafiz al-Assad purged the intellectuals, including the party's revered founder, Michel Aflaq.

As part of a political party founded on pan-Arab ideology, the Baathists of Baghdad could not escape the intraparty conflict in Damascus. Frightened that the Syrian military would march on Iraq in the name of Arab unity, the Iraqi wing of the party reinstated Aflaq as party leader and elected a new regional organization specifically for Iraq. Thus, the Baath, the party that promised to restore Arab greatness by uniting all peoples of the Arab-speaking world, fractured along a line from Damascus to Baghdad. As a consequence, the party created the irony of having two pan-Arab "national commands," one supporting Damascus and the other Baghdad. Locked in this feud, the Iraqi and Syrian factions husbanded their mutual distrust, each convinced that the other sought to plant a Trojan horse in its ranks at the first opportunity. When the Iraqi Baath toppled the Arif regime two years after the Baath split, this intraparty conflict transformed into an interstate rivalry between two countries fixed to a common border, sharing the water system of the Euphrates, and tied to contradictory national distinctions. Oriented in different directions—Syria toward the Mediterranean and Iraq toward the Gulf—each defended its own interests. To the Iraqi Baath, the vision of Syrian-Iraqi unity that had captivated Iraq's Arab nationalists since the 1950s suddenly converted into a foreboding danger. Union with Syria presented to the new and insecure Baath regime of Baghdad the very real possibility of being swallowed up by its larger, better-entrenched Syrian counterpart. If in fact the Syrian Baath did claim Iraq for pan-Arabism, all of the labor, the clandestine lifestyle, the jail terms, and the beatings endured by Iraq's Baath leadership would have been for nothing.

Obsessed with its own self-preservation, the leadership of the Iraqi Baath became schizophrenic. While one faction still promoted the submergence of Iraq into a pan-Arab state, the dominant segment within the party, which included Hussein, demanded that Iraq remove its own interests from the sacrificial altar of Arabism. However, the latter faction of the Iraqi Baath was no more willing than the former to relinquish pan-Arabism completely. Instead, the cause of Arab unity would simply be put in a box until the party could operate in the Arab arena from a position of strength rather than one of weakness. For the moment, the Baath followed King Faisal I and General Qasim in the effort to lead Iraqis toward a specific identity outside the bounds of pan-Arabism. Opening the rhetorical floodgates on its neighbors, the Iraqi Baath accused some rival Arab regimes (that is, Syria) of treachery and deceit and derided others (that is, Egypt, under the discredited and corrupted Nasser) as detached from the masses. Withdrawing into its national boundaries, the unstable and unpopular Baath regime drove its policies toward Iraq's specific needs. That the development of a specific Iraqi nationalism conflicted with the Baath's most sacred ideal— Arab unity— hardly fazed the top echelon of Baath politicians grasping for survival in the sea of pan-Arabism.

The Syrian military threat, wearing the uniform of Baath ideology, came from the west. To the east, Muhammad Reza Shah, the Pahlavi king of Iran, was wrapping his territorial ambitions in the cloak of Cyrus the Great. Resurrecting the imagery of the ancient Persian Empire, the modern-day Cyrus set forth to crown himself the undisputed lord of the Persian Gulf. In 1969, a year into the second Baath regime, Muhammad Reza Shah challenged Iraq's exclusive claim to the 160-mile-long Shatt al Arab, the broad marshy channel of brown water connecting the confluence of the Tigris and Euphrates to the head of the Persian Gulf. Fifty miles upstream from the Gulf's northern shore lies Abadan, Iran's southernmost port. Historically, the Iranian side of the Shatt al Arab marked the Iraq-Iran border. Consequently, access to its principal oil refinery at Abadan required Iran to secure right of passage from Iraq. Declaring the *thalweg*, or the center of the main channel, as the new boundary, the shah sent an Iranian ship, escorted by Iranian naval vessels, upriver without Iraqi permission. The act constituted a direct threat to Iraq. Basra, located at the head of the Shatt al Arab and providing Iraq's only access to the Persian Gulf, is as important to Baghdad as Abadan is to Tehran.[12] Hence in retaliation, Iraq moved troops to the river and Iran responded. The shah, alarmed that the pan-Arab ideology of the Baath would prove enticing to Iran's Arab population, conspired with elements in the Iraqi military to overthrow the government in Baghdad in 1970. But the Baath's security force proved too effective. Rapidly ferreting out the quislings, the Baath put the accused Iraqi officers and their co-conspirators on trial while Iranian troops massed on Iraq's border. War was averted by an Iraqi appeal to the United Nations, which wooed both sides away from the brink. Afraid to confront each other directly, Iraq and Iran sent their surrogates into the breach. Iraq egged on Arab separatists in Iranian Khuzistan on the Shatt's eastern side and ejected some ninety thousand Iranians from Iraq. Iran, in turn, sent encouragement to the Iraqi Kurds to revolt.

BY THE TIME Iran reached across the border to incite the Kurds against Baghdad, the long-festering question of Kurdish rights in an Arab state had passed from an issue of identity among the Kurds to an element of economic survival for the Iraqi state. Between 40 and 50 percent of Iraq's oil production in the 1960s flowed out of the gently sloping hills on the southwestern edge of the Kurdish region. Kirkuk, a heavily Kurdish town, reigned as the oil capital of Iraq. As a result, the lust for oil that had originally forced the Kurds of the Mosul region of the Ottoman Empire into Iraq now chained them to Arab Baghdad, since the income necessary to develop the rest of Iraq depended on the north's petroleum production. That dependency required controlling the Kurds, who had almost continuously challenged Baghdad's authority since the reign of Faisal I.

Deprived of the promises of Woodrow Wilson's Fourteen Points, betrayed by the Treaty of Sèvres that shoved the *vilayet* of Mosul into the borders of artificial Iraq, the Kurds never totally surrendered to their fate. As the bearers of their own language, heritage, and culture, they incessantly challenged their incorporation into Iraq. At times, Faisal I attempted to respond to their grievances within the parameters of Iraq's territorial integrity. But all efforts withered under Sunni fear of their communal rivals. Sunni leaders repeatedly

---

[12] This territorial dispute as well as others played their part in the 1980–88 Iran-Iraq War. See chapter 8.

warned that if Baghdad met the demands of the Kurds, these same demands would rise from the Shia. Thus, denied any form of autonomy, the Kurds became a profoundly dissatisfied, menacing element in the national life of Iraq.

In 1926, in an early attempt to defuse Kurdish separatism, the monarchy had ruled that civil servants in the Kurdish area be Kurds and that both Kurdish and Arabic rank as the official language of the region. Some school books were actually translated into the Kurdish dialect of Sulaimaniyah, and Kurdish teachers took up posts in Kurdish primary schools. As acknowledgment that ethnic Kurds were in fact part of the Arab Iraqi state, the political system always granted to Kurds one or two places in the rotating cabinets that characterized government under Faisal I. Still, tension between the Kurds and the monarchy persisted as Baghdad held firm to its policy of blocking Kurdish autonomy. So as the weary Faisal I neared the end of his life, he reported to his cabinet, "This government rules over a Kurdish group most of which is ignorant and which includes persons with personal ambitions who call upon this group to abandon the government because it is not of their race."[13] Among those persons were two charismatic leaders carrying religious and tribal credentials—Sheikh Mahmud and Mullah Mustafa Barzani.[14]

In the aftermath of World War I, Sheikh Mahmud, a renowned religious and tribal leader among northern Iraq's Kurds, flirted with the British colonial administration lusting after oil-rich Mosul. But as soon as a deal was made, Sheikh Mahmud changed direction by claiming Kurdish independence. Between 1919 and 1923, he sent the Kurds against the British, the Iraqi puppet monarchy, or both. When he again raised the Kurds in rebellion in 1930, government forces ambushed him, permanently removing from the scene "the man whose name rang . . . bells in Kurdistan."[15] Almost immediately the Kurds' next charismatic leader stepped onto the stage of northern Iraq. And like Sheikh Mahmud, the aura and influence of Barzani radiated from religion and tribe.

---

[13] Quoted in Edmund Ghareeb, *The Kurdish Question in Iraq* (Syracuse: Syracuse University Press, 1981), p. 1.

[14] The name Mullah came from a maternal uncle. In the case of Mullah Mustafa Barzani, it carries no religious connotation as a rank in the clerical hierarchy.

[15] Rafiq Hilmi, *Kurdistan at the Dawn of the Century*, vol. 1 (Uppsala, Sweden: Rabun Forlaq, 1998), p. 159.

The origins of Barzani's tribe are hidden in obscurity. It is generally accepted that the tribe took form in the early nineteenth century on the banks of the Great Zab River. Consigned to poverty by the rugged terrain of their mountain territory, the people survived by attacking and pillaging neighboring villages. Anarchy prevailed, and only religion in the hands of a charismatic leader could impose any social order. In the remote mountains around the town of Barzan, Taj ad-Din, "the crown of religion," was a sheikh in the mystical Naqshbandi Sufi order who presided over a kind of oddball utopian society that bound the disparate elements of the region into what essentially became a tribe. Upon his death, the authority of this beloved leader passed on to his often unlucky descendants.

In 1908, Taj ad-Din's great grandson, Sheikh Muhammad, was unwittingly killed by his followers when they threw him out of the upper window of his house to test whether he was the Mahdi and if, as such, he could fly. The Turks sent Sheikh Muhammad's eldest son to the gallows in Mosul in 1914. In 1927, the reigning sheikh, Ahmed, suddenly proclaimed himself divine and purportedly ordered his followers to eat pork, drink wine, and convert to Christianity. When the more orthodox within the Naqshbandi order declared holy war against their sheikh, Ahmed's younger brother summoned to battle what was now known as the Barzani tribe. Distinguished by their red headdress, the fierce Barzani fighters from roughly 750 families trounced the rebelling Sufis as well as the nascent Iraqi army sent in to restore order. Out of this two-sided victory over rival Kurds and central authority emerged Ahmed's brother, the legendary Mullah Mustafa Barzani who would steer the course of Kurdish nationalism for almost five decades.

Mullah Mustafa personified the tough Barzani clan. Of medium height and a powerful build, he wore his tribal turban with a double-cartridge belt slung over the Kurds' traditional baggy pants. Eating food no better than that found in the poorest village, Mullah Mustafa lived the life of his men. He was the *agha*, the tribal chief who possessed the essential ingredients of charismatic leadership.

With Mullah Mustafa filling a secular role as military leader of the tribe and Ahmed, who had returned to the fold of orthodoxy, providing the traditional religious role, the Barzanis challenged Iraq's authority over the Kurds. In 1932, they defied Baghdad by refusing to pay taxes and by rejecting the government's planned transfer of Assyrians into Kurdish territory. In response, the Iraqi army attacked, forcing the two Barzani brothers over the Turkish border. When they sneaked back into Iraq, they were arrested and exiled, first to Nassariyah in southern Iraq and then to Sulaimaniyah in the shadow of the great Zagros Mountains. It was in Sulaimaniyah, where Kurdish national identity had budded at the end of World War I, that Mullah Mustafa Barzani began to stretch beyond his tribal identity to embrace the idea of Kurdish nationalism.

With the intellectuals of Sulaimaniyah providing the ideological framework, the Kurdish sense of national identity grew during the early 1940s. Calls for the political unification of Kurdistan, "the backbone of the Middle East," rang off the northern mountains as deep-rooted emotions overran the national boundaries dividing Kurd from Kurd. The cover of a small magazine published in the Barzani stronghold of Badinan illustrated the ascending rage felt among most Kurds about their division and repression since the end of the Great War. The line drawing shows a virginal maiden chained down on a map of the idealized Kurdistan, with one hand clamped fast to Ankara, another to Tehran, and a foot tied to Baghdad.

In the confusion of the war year 1943, Mullah Mustafa Barzani escaped his exile in Sulaimaniyah and returned to his ancestral seat in Barzan. Taking off his tribal headdress, he assumed the role of leader of Kurdish aspirations. It is one of the great ironies of the Kurdish national struggle that the feudal Barzanis became the vanguard of a Kurdish nationalism conceived of by urban intellectuals who detested the tribal life that defined traditional Kurdish society, feared the tribal power that rose from it, and longed for the collapse of the feudal system. It happened only because the urban Kurds commanded no fighting force with which to press Kurdish grievances on Baghdad.

With the mystical ability to command a highly emotional loyalty in the face of impossible odds, Barzani drew tribesmen, clerks, teachers, and doctors into the rigors of mountain warfare. In the cold of January 1944, he sent his forces against twenty Iraqi police posts strung out from Rawanduz to Amadiya. From what was now Kurdish territory, as opposed to tribal territory, he demanded from Baghdad the simplest needs of his people—grain for remote Kurdish villages. Then he hurled the great challenge to the integrity of the Iraqi state by calling for an autonomous Kurdish province consisting of the districts of Kirkuk, Sulaimaniyah, Erbil, Duhok, and Khanaqin. Conceding sovereignty over the Iraqi army and police to Baghdad, the Kurds demanded political, economic, and above all, cultural control of their own region. Recognizing that Iran and Turkey would exploit Kurdish grievances to the detriment of Iraq, Nuri al-Said, the serving prime minister, counseled compliance. With few others sharing his wisdom, the opposition used the Kurdish question to force al-Said from office in June 1944.

The Kurds reloaded their rifles and resumed fighting. As they fought on into 1945, Barzani's forces took possession of a region where Mullah Mustafa's charisma and personal authority enabled him to maintain an army, intervene in intertribal disputes, and hold Baghdad at bay on every issue from the distribution of government supplies to the construction of police posts. In the summer of 1945, Barzani, acting as head of a de facto territorial and political entity, called the first congress of the Kurdish Democratic Party (KDP). As the pre-eminent Kurdish political organization, it would keep Kurdish aspirations alive through the remainder of the monarchy, through the military governments of the 1960s, and into the second regime of the Baath. But the KDP has never succeeded in overriding the factionalism among the Kurds themselves.

Spanning the sociopolitical spectrum from illiterate traditionalists to Communist intellectuals, the KDP found itself from the very beginning of its existence able to speak forcefully to only one idea—Kurdish nationalism. Dominated by traditional tribal leaders whose self-interest rejected any progressive economic or social programs, the KDP constituted a social and cultural gathering rather than a well-defined political party. Before he left office in 1944, al-Said assessed Kurdish nationalism's Achilles' heel: "The Iraqi Kurds are divided [between] . . . the tribal leaders [who] live a life closer to feudalism than to civilization. They do not have a specific political goal. Their main concern is to maintain the power and influence they have inherited over their own tribes and geographical areas . . . [and] the educated class [who] want . . . to destroy the influence of the tribal leaders."[16]

Thus, it was the educated class, joined by tribes with interests opposed to those of Barzani, who lent themselves to Baghdad for the purpose of driving Mullah Mustafa Barzani and thousands of his fol-

---

[16] Quoted in Ghareeb, *The Kurdish Question in Iraq*, p. 33.

lowers across the border into Iran in 1946. There the Kurdish leader attached himself to the Soviet-sponsored Kurdish Republic of Mahabad.[17] When Muhammad Reza Shah, with the help of the United States, crushed the renegade republic, Barzani and his men found themselves trapped in a lethal triangle formed by the army of the Shah, a hostile Turkish government besieged by its own rebellious Kurds, and Baghdad, which had sentenced Barzani to death. There was nowhere else to go but the Soviet Union. Making what the Kurds now regard as their own "Long March," Barzani and his men trudged 220 miles across the Zagros Mountains, which were covered with up to twelve feet of snow. In their epic journey, they threw away their heavy automatic rifles, devised shoes from old car tires, and wrapped themselves against the cold in clothes shredding from wear. After fifty-two days, they crossed over the southern border of the Soviet Union. Unable to lay its hands on Mullah Mustafa, the Iraqi monarchy imprisoned Sheikh Ahmed and hanged four Barzani officers. It seemed that Kurdish separation from Iraq was a dead issue. But knowing the Kurds' history, an observer predicted that in the future, the "Kurds in their distant mountains and separated valleys will at times be forgotten or ignored. Then, moved by resolve or temerity, some of the characters of 1946, and others, younger and perhaps unknown in Mahabad, will be heard of once again."[18]

During the 1950s, the Kurds, like the Shia, migrated in great numbers to the cities. Most went to Kirkuk or Sulaimaniyah. Some drifted to Baghdad, where their tribal dress and sometimes distinctive looks set them apart from the Sunni and Shia Arabs. When the revolution of 1958 came, the Kurds, with little presence in the military, played the role of onlookers. But after the collapse of the Hashemites, Mullah Mustafa Barzani telegraphed the military junta for permission to return to Iraq. Arriving in Baghdad on October 6, 1958, he walked into the welcoming arms of General Qasim, who saw the Kurds as a useful balance to the Arab nationalists.

The general moved Barzani into Nuri al-Said's former mansion, gave him a sleek black limousine, legalized the KDP, and lifted restrictions on the publication of seventeen Kurdish journals. Article

---

[17] The Mahabad republic was the creation of the Iranian Kurds who were engaged in their own revolt against the Iranian government of Muhammad Reza Shah.

[18] William Eagleton quoted in Jonathan C. Randal, *After Such Knowledge, What Forgiveness?* (Boulder, Colo.: Westview Press, 1999), p. 318.

23 of the new provisional constitution of July 27, 1958, had already declared that "the Kurds and the Arabs are partners within this nation. The Constitution guarantees their rights within the framework of the Iraqi Republic."

Enjoying a recognition they had never achieved in any state, the Kurds threw themselves into battle on March 8, 1959, when the Second Iraqi Army Division stationed in Mosul revolted against Qasim in the name of pan-Arabism. In defense of the regime, the Kurds killed rebellious soldiers and pan-Arab civilians alike. Broadening the encounter, they attacked their historic rivals, the Turkomans of Kirkuk, in the hope that a grateful Qasim would reward them with self-rule. But Qasim proved less than grateful. Increasingly suspicious of Barzani's growing influence in the north, the general began to back away from the alliance. Quickly the Kurds saw their aspiration for administrative self-rule fade as the interpretation of Article 23 narrowed to mean simply an economic, social, and cultural role for the Kurds in the Iraqi state. Trying to recoup the momentum, Barzani in July 1961 submitted a list of demands to Baghdad, the first of which was full Kurdish autonomy. In that autonomous region, Kurdish would be the official language and the Kurds would control education, health services, communications, and municipal and rural affairs. Revenues would come from a large share of the money Baghdad derived from oil in the Kurdish region. Qasim refused, fearing, like his predecessors, that acquiescence would invite the dismemberment of Iraq.

By now, it was clear that the central goals of the Kurds and of Qasim were at odds. The Kurds demanded meaningful autonomy, and Qasim sought commitment to a unified Iraqi state incorporating all of Iraq's ethnic groups. With no hope of compromise on either side, Barzani gathered as many as seven thousand armed combatants to occupy strategic points in the mountain passes and expel both the government police and small military garrisons from Kurdish-held territory. Qasim answered by bombing Barzan, the Barzanis' ancestral home, in September 1961. Indiscriminate bombing of hundreds of Kurdish villages followed. Under the barrage, Kurdish factionalism diminished as more and more men strapped on their cartridge belts and climbed the mountains to join Barzani's *pesh mergas*, "those who walk before death." By 1962, the Kurds were in full-scale revolt. Barzani's forces seized all of northeast Iraq outside

the major cities and towns, posing a dire threat to Baghdad's control
of the principal oil resources of the state. Unwilling to tolerate either
secession or grant local autonomy, General Qasim threw the Kurdish
dilemma into the pot with other elements of opposition to the government— Communism, Nasserism, Baathism, and Iraqi nationalism.
It boiled over, resulting in the Baath Party coup of February 1963.

Once in power, the Baath went to war against the Kurds under
the banner of Arabism. No longer would the demographics of Mosul
allow the Kurds to hold Iraq's petroleum resources hostage. On
orders from Baghdad, the army marched toward the oil-rich regions
around Kirkuk, Khanaqin, Kifri, and Erbil. Watching raw military
power grind across the plains below the mountains, the poet
Mahmoud Darwish penned a Kurdish plea:

> In the land of Kurdistan,
> Where terror and fire keep vigil,
> Where now you say,
> "Long live Arabism!"
> Pass by the land of Kurdistan.
> Pass by, Oh Arabism.[19]

Baath repression of the Kurds lasted the short duration of its
1963 government. When General Abd al-Salam Arif and the army
reclaimed the government, the new provisional constitution of the
devoutly pan-Arab regime read, "The Iraqi people are a part of the
Arab people, whose aim is total Arab unity." In these simple words,
notice was served that there was no room in Iraq for Kurdish nationalism or Kurdish autonomy. Thus, in May 1966 the generals took up
where the Baath left off. Aircraft loaded with bombs flew protective
cover above sixty-five thousand armed combat troops that snaked
north to subdue the Kurds. But they failed to dislodge the Kurdish
guerrillas on the slopes of Mount Hindarin, northeast of Rawanduz.
Month after month, Barzani and his *pesh mergas* successfully fought
air power and heavy artillery in a classic guerrilla war. Where survival equated victory, no fixed position was defended, not even Barzan.
This is how the now fabled *pesh mergas* fought to a standstill a central government weakened and destabilized by its own internal wars.

---

[19] Mahmoud Darwish quoted in Kanan Makiya, *Cruelty and Silence: War, Tyranny,
Uprising, and the Arab World* (New York: W. W. Norton, 1993), p. 311.

By the beginning of 1968, the Kurds had established de facto autonomy over some thirty-five thousand square kilometers of northern
Iraq containing almost half of the population of Iraqi Kurdistan.
Around its perimeter, some twenty-thousand *pesh mergas*, armed
with antiaircraft guns, antitank weapons, and field artillery, stood
guard at every mountain pass as if in testimony to the Kurdish
proverb "The male is born to be slaughtered." Yet the Kurds again
faced another, equally dangerous enemy—their own factionalism.

By the late 1960s, intracommunal conflict had once again erupted
among the Kurds, a conflict that still debilitates every aspect of
Kurdish political life. During Mullah Mustafa Barzani's exile in the
Soviet Union, the KDP had fallen to Jalal Talabani and his brother
Ahmed.[20] More than a change of leadership from the Barzanis to the
Talabanis, the stewardship of the KDP had passed over the great contemporary divide of Kurdish society, between the rural tribes defending the interests of the *aghas* and the urban intellectuals demanding
social change. Although Barzani, as the premier *agha*, had succeeded
in establishing himself as the Kurdish national leader in the 1930s by
igniting the linguistic and cultural touchstones of Kurdish identity,
he had proposed no social agenda and issued no call for societal
reform that would undercut the interests of the tribes' traditional
leaders. As a result, the urbanized, more educated Kurds had found
their political home in the Iraqi Communist Party and other leftist
groups. Even though they proved effective in recruiting Kurds in the
urban centers of Sulaimaniyah and Mosul, these leftist parties never
broke the ties that bound the villager to his traditional *agha*. When
the 1958 revolution seemed to readmit the Kurds to the political
process, an intense struggle developed within the KDP between
Mullah Mustafa Barzani, the man of the tribes, and Jalal Talabani, the
town-bred intellectual. That conflict remains. In essence, the
"Kurdish nationalist struggle has been one not only between Kurds
and non-Kurdish rulers, but also between the concept of tribal rule
and modern government, the [mountainous] lands of insolence
against the [plains] lands of docility."[21]

As the Kurds battled against the Arif regime in the mid to late

---

[20] Exceeding Ahmed in rhetoric and authority, Jalal Talabani became the more visible figure in Kurdish politics.

[21] David McDowall, *The Kurds: A Nation Denied* (London: Paul and Company
Publishing Consortium, 1992), p. 20.

1960s, the Kurds also warred against each other. Speaking to his urban audiences, Talabani branded Barzani "tribal," "feudal," "reactionary." Whispering among the tribes, Barzani pasted on Talabani the labels of "urban effete" and "atheist" enslaved to Communist ideology. To defend himself against both Baghdad and his Kurdish rivals, the battle-seasoned Barzani solicited arms and funds from the shah of Iran, who feared Talabani as both a Kurd and a leftist. This was the situation in northern Iraq in July of 1968 when the Baath retook Baghdad.

FOR THE FIRST TWO YEARS of the new Baath regime, Baghdad exploited Kurdish factionalism until Mullah Mustafa Barzani utilized his Iranian-supplied arms to secure control of the KDP. Acutely aware that inability to solve the Kurdish problem had contributed to the fall of several Iraqi regimes including the Baath government of 1963, Saddam Hussein journeyed north in early March 1970 to give Barzani assurances of the Baath's good intentions toward the Kurds. Surrounded by battle-hardened *pesh mergas*, a slim Hussein, dressed in a gray suit and black tie, awkwardly stood for pictures with Barzani, resplendent in a turban and tribal dress complete with a curved dagger stuck in the cummerbund at his waist. Focused on its own survival, the Baath meant to succeed where others had failed. Therefore on March 11, 1970, the government unfurled the Manifesto on Kurdish Autonomy. Its true intent was to buy time until the Baath had gathered enough strength to crush the Kurds.

Employing the word *autonomy* for the first time in official relations between Baghdad and the Kurds, the 1970 manifesto guaranteed proportional representation of the Kurds within a national legislative body, appointment of a Kurdish vice president, expenditure of an equitable amount of oil revenues in the autonomous region, and recognition of both Kurdish and Arabic as official languages in Kurdish areas. It was, in the words of Hussein, "a completely substantial political and constitutional settlement ensuring brotherhood for all time between Kurds and Arabs."[22] Although Baghdad deliberately delayed implementation for four years, the agreement allowed both sides to claim a measure of victory. The de facto recognition of Barzani and the KDP as the sole administrative authority in the Kurdish area gave the Kurds a genuine taste of

---

[22] Quoted in *New York Times*, December 21, 1970.

autonomy, and the long postponement of the final application granted the Baath a reprieve from Kurdish defiance while it eliminated its enemies on other fronts.

By September 1971, the Baath was ready to once again subdue the Kurds. Plucking a provision out of the 1970 manifesto that read, "Necessary steps shall be taken . . . to unify the governorates and administrative units populated by a Kurdish majority," the Baath set about altering Iraq's demographics. Arab settlers were already moving into Kirkuk when the Baath expelled from Iraq some forty thousand Faili Kurds who had lived for generations in Baghdad or south of Khanaqin. The official justification read that since these Kurds were non-Arab Shia Muslims, they were actually Iranians.[23]

Biting away at the manifesto piece by piece, the Baath claimed that "the factors endangering the process of the reconstruction of peace . . . [and] constituting a danger to the security of the state and to our future cooperation" lay entirely with Barzani's Kurds and by extension, with Iran.[24] According to Baghdad, Tehran's insults to Baghdad included the flow of Iranian arms into northern Iraq, the training of *pesh mergas* in Iran, the coordination of Kurdish guerrillas and Iranian armed forces along the frontier, and the attempt to destroy the value of Iraqi currency by circulating counterfeit bills printed by Iran. What was originally a communal conflict between the Kurds and the Sunni Arab government engraved with the emblem of the Baath Party had evolved into a contest with international dimensions involving, in different degrees, Iran, the Arab states, Israel, the Soviet Union, and the United States.

As 1971 turned into 1972, the threat of Kurdish separatism forced Iraq to keep a large part of its army reserved for the north. In an attempt to tip the strategic scale weighted by Iranian arms going to the Kurds, Baghdad concluded the Iraqi-Soviet Friendship Treaty. Besides providing arms to Iraq, the pact between Baghdad and Moscow meant that any Iranian attack on Iraq translated into a potential confrontation with the Soviet Union. Suddenly the Kurdish question became part of the Cold War. The United States, anxious about military hardware passing from the Soviet Union into the

---

[23] The same month, Baath assassination squads attempted to murder Mullah Mustafa Barzani and his son.

[24] Quoted in Michael M. Gunter, *The Kurds of Iraq: Tragedy and Hope* (New York: St. Martin's Press, 1992), p. 17.

arsenal of Iraq, succumbed to the seduction of Muhammed Reza Shah's three-year, $16 million arms program for Barzani's forces. Transfused with this new armory, the Kurds repeatedly struck against the authority of Baghdad, exposing the fragility of the Iraqi state. These sporadic clashes followed by fruitless negotiations paused only for the 1973 October War between the Arab states and Israel. Then in March 1974, Saddam Hussein demanded that the Kurds accept the government's highly proscribed rights concerning their autonomy. Rejecting Baghdad's proposals as hollow rhetoric, Barzani, speaking for the Kurds, refused. With nothing left to negotiate, four divisions of the Iraqi army equipped with tanks, bombers, and French-made helicopters once more moved north. As the massive force approached, the Kurds dug in to face the full fury of the Baathist state.

Iraqi artillery acquired from the Soviet Union slammed shells into the mountain towns of Zakho and Qalat Diza, reducing them to rubble. Below on the plains, the tanks, helicopters, and artillery supporting eighty thousand troops swung into place. But the Kurds held fast to the hills. Moving from ambush point to ambush point on foot or on surefooted donkeys, wiry guerrillas picked at the Iraqi army with small arms, World War II cannons, and advanced weapons delivered via Iran. Unable to penetrate the mountains with ground forces, the Iraqi military sent in its bombers. Fire rained down on 250,000 terrified fleeing Kurds strung along the Old Hamilton Road that ran toward safety in Iran. Those who stayed behind huddled in the deep mountain caves where the fear of snakes and scorpions inside competed with the fear of airplanes outside. The rebellion continued to survive only because the shah of Iran, intent on winning Iraqi territorial concessions on the Shatt al Arab, pumped in money for food and ammunition and kept Iran's borders open to refugees and guerrilla bands. The Kurds knew they could not win against the might of Baghdad, but as long as outside help persisted, they could force on the Iraqi government a costly war within its own borders.

In a surrogate war in which each pursued its own agenda, Iran, the United States, and the Baathists of Syria fed heavy artillery and surface-to-air missiles to the *pesh mergas* while Israel quietly slipped in its own aid to the rebelling Kurds. In January 1975, Iran sent two of its own regiments over the border into Kurdish Iraq. It was another component in the mix that presented the Baath of Baghdad with the gravest challenge to its survival since its return to power in 1968. The Shia foot solider, bearing the brunt of the fight against the Kurds, was already growing ever more resentful of the Baghdad regime. Far more important, the Soviet arms supply line clogged up for reasons known only to the Kremlin. Consequently, the Sunni Arab officers of the Iraqi army could do nothing but watch as their stocks of arms and ammunition disappeared. Later, none other than Saddam Hussein confessed that on the darkest day of March 1975, "there were only three heavy missiles left in the air force and very few artillery shells."[25] Yet Baghdad prevailed, imposing on the exhausted Kurds an end to armed conflict.

Just as the war had never belonged entirely to the Kurds, neither did the peace. Confronting the presence of another party to their conflict, both Iraq and Iran realized that the Kurdish uprising had become dynamite under the original border issue on the Shatt al Arab. As the fuse burned, it seemed inevitable that the oil industries of both countries would become the primary targets of the Kurdish war. Other conclusions followed, not the least of which was that the conflict posed the possibility of drawing Iraq's Soviet patron and Iran's American ally into the Persian Gulf, threatening the region with Armageddon. Yet for Iraq, the premier issue focused not on global war but on the internal interests of the Baath. The Kurdish war of 1974–75 had financially drained the country and politically distracted the Baath. The longer it lasted, the longer the Baath government was forced to delay its program of domestic economic and social development that it saw as the linchpin of Iraq's long-term stability. It was time for peace with Iran.

In March 1975, Muhammad Reza Shah, the King of Kings, and Saddam Hussein, muscle of the Baath Party, met in Algiers at the summit of the Organization of Petroleum Exporting Countries (OPEC). Masking their bitter enmity, king and party functionary embraced, signaling an end to the dispute over the Shatt al Arab and with it Iranian support for the Kurdish rebellion. Iran recognized the

---

[25] Foreign Broadcast Information Service, Daily Report: MEA, December 29, 1980, p. E2.

1913–14 frontier of the waterway, Iraq renounced all claims to the Arabic-speaking province of Iranian Khuzistan, and Iran closed its borders to Iraqi Kurds.

With the Kurds deprived of weapons and sanctuary, the wrath of Baghdad descended on the rebels. Under the cover of darkness, army convoys rolled into Kurdish villages where uniformed soldiers jumped out of trucks to drag whole families from their beds. Loading frightened men, women, and children on the waiting vehicles, they drove them south into Arab areas. With little provided to the depor- tees beyond tents, between 50,000 and 300,000 Kurds were dumped into designated areas called "victory villages" and warned to stay there. In a grand scheme to Arabize Kurdistan, the government moved Arabs north into some of the deserted Kurdish areas and promised any Arab who took a Kurdish spouse the equivalent of $1,500. Thus in blood, transfer, and intermarriage, Baghdad strung the ropes with which to strangle the Kurds' cultural distinctiveness and political identity. Perhaps the final word on the Kurdish rebel- lion was left to a Kurdish woman of the mountains draped in a scar- let scarf trimmed with small gold coins: "Every time when a new government came to power in Baghdad, they promised to do some- thing for the Kurds, and then after, when they became strong . . . , they rejected the Kurds."[26]

In defeat, Mullah Mustafa Barzani, the living legend of Kurdish nationalism, fled again into exile, first to Karaj, a suburb of Tehran, and then to Alexandria, Virginia. There he poured out letters on behalf of the Kurdish cause to American newspapers and American officials including President Jimmy Carter. On March 1, 1979, he died of lung cancer. Denied burial in Iraq, his body went into the ground of Ushnavia in the Kurdish region of Iran. Born a traditional *agha* and dying a folk hero, Barzani remains the great Kurdish patriot, but he left behind a Kurdish national movement split over leadership, ideology, and personal interest.

Jalal Talabani pulled the urbanized, often leftist Kurds out of the KDP and deposited them in a rival political group called the Patriotic Union of Kurdistan (PUK). Two of Barzani's sons, Idris and Massoud, held the tribes within the rump KDP. From these two camps, the

---

[26] Quoted in Teresa Thornhill, *Sweet Tea with Cardamon: A Journey through Iraqi Kurdistan* (London: Pandora, 1997), p. 161.

Kurds of Iraq hurled accusations at each other, competed for territory, and schemed with foreign powers, one against the other. It was
a poisonous rivalry that would help ensure the survival of Saddam
Hussein following the disastrous Gulf War of 1991.

BEFORE THE BAATH had gone to war in 1974 to bend the Kurds to the
authority of the Iraqi state, another momentous event erupted
between Israel and the Arabs. The Arabs already had fought the
Zionist state in three wars: the 1948 war that lost Palestine; the 1956
Suez War that elevated Gamal Abdul Nasser to an Arab icon; and the
Six Day War of 1967 that stripped from Egypt, Jordan, and Syria both
honor and prime real estate. The 1967 war also snatched from Nasser
the crown of Arab nationalism. Politically debilitated and physically
ill, the Arabs' mythical Saladin suddenly died of a heart attack on
September 28, 1970.

Anwar Sadat, the obscure vice president of the United Arab
Republic, stepped into Nasser's shoes. Derided by Nasser's inner circle for his dark skin and purportedly featherweight intelligence,
Sadat kept his own counsel as he contemplated the future of his
country. Egypt, the most populous of the Arab states, the vessel of
Nasser's personal ambitions, had borne the burden and the cost of
the Arab-Israeli stalemate for a quarter of a century. In Sadat's mind,
it was time for a new era in which Egyptian interests superceded
Arab emotions. It was in pursuit of a forced peace that Sadat drew
the plans for a surprise assault on Israel's forces dug into the Sinai
Peninsula six years after the shame of 1967.

But the real battle of 1973 had been charted the previous year in
the royal salons of Saudi Arabia. Conservative, monarchial Saudi
Arabia, which had assiduously stayed out of the previous wars
between the Arabs and Israel, now wanted the large Soviet presence
that Nasser had allowed in Egypt out of the Middle East. The House
of Saud also sought cover from attacks by radical Arab nationalists
for the kingdom's failure to confront Israel. Sadat, too, wanted to
shed the "Arab cause." Together the tall, distinguished Faisal ibn Abdul
Aziz al Saud and the short, bespectacled Anwar Sadat laid plans for
an Arab war against Israel. In return for expelling the Russians from
Egypt in July 1972, Faisal delivered to Sadat close to $500 million for
Egyptian arms purchases and another $400 to $500 million to ease
the Egyptian trade deficit. In the summer of 1973, Faisal traveled to

Cairo to promise Sadat what the Arabs had so desperately wanted in 1967—an oil embargo against the supporters of Israel.

When the Egyptian attack on the Sinai came on October 6, 1973, King Faisal issued dire warnings to the United States that if American military aid flowed to Israel, the Arab oil producers would turn off the pipelines. The Nixon administration, convinced that Saudi Arabia's most basic defense and economic interests would never allow the kingdom to confront the United States, refused to listen. During the war's second week, American transport planes on the runway at al-Arish, the Sinai town directly behind the front, disgorged tanks and sophisticated weapons to replace the devastating losses Israel incurred when the Egyptians stormed across the Suez Canal. As the Arab armies continued their advance on October 19, Richard Nixon, looking at the war only in terms of the U.S.-Soviet rivalry, asked Congress for $2.2 billion in military assistance to Israel. The next day King Faisal unsheathed the oil weapon, shutting off oil exports to any country providing military support to Israel. Immediately, lines of cars wound like giant snakes around gas pumps throughout the United States. And economies dependent on imported petroleum stood at the abyss. Grabbing the golden moment to increase oil prices, the Organization of Petroleum Exporting Countries, over the remaining two months of 1973, drove oil prices from $3.10 per barrel to $5.12 to $11.65.[27] Undreamed of wealth descended on the oil-rich, sparsely populated states around the Persian Gulf. One of them was Iraq.

By sheer luck of timing, the Baath had positioned Iraq to reap the windfall. On June 1, 1972, less than a year and a half before the oil embargo sent prices soaring, the Iraqi government had nationalized the Iraq Petroleum Company.[28] It was a development important to all Iraqis, but no one welcomed the revenues of the oil boom as much as the Baath.

When it seized power in 1968, the Baath had committed itself to building a nation to its own specifications. Saddam Hussein's security services would provide the stick of compliance, and oil revenues, the carrot of Baath-style socialism. With income from petroleum

---

[27] Not all members of OPEC joined Saudi Arabia in the oil embargo.
[28] Two subsidiaries, the Mosul Petroleum Company and the Basra Petroleum Company, were not affected until later.

expanding between 1973 and 1978 from $1.8 to $23.6 billion, the Baath transformed agricultural Iraq into a rapidly developing industrialized country. No longer dependent on taxes or foreign subsidies, government allocations for industry increased twelve times in those five years, transportation eleven times, housing nine times. Networks of highways connected town to town, and electrical lines stretched through the landscape to reach almost every village. Promising to spin a "silk thread" between the government and the common man, the Baath declared *jihad* against poor health and illiteracy. Free heath care grew quickly available to a population accustomed to neglect. And schools and literacy programs proclaiming the slogan "Knowledge is Light, Ignorance is Darkness" opened everywhere from Baghdad to the most humble village on the edge of the southern marshes. Refusing to stop with basics, the government used its oil income to subsidize consumption items, putting refrigerators and television sets into almost every house, apartment, and mud hut. In this affluence, the Baath at last defined Arab socialism. According to Christine Moss Helms, the Baath formula could have read, "Whoever does more, eats more, but there will never be a hungry person."[29]

Casting off the last traces of languor, Baghdad projected the same image of frenzied construction activity and tone of supreme confidence as did Riyadh and Kuwait City. On the streets, double-decker buses imported from London traversed al-Rashid street; hawkers sold black-velvet paintings of Elvis Presley in a white sequined suit; and women from the villages, clutching plastic pocketbooks stuffed with dinars, pushed their way into the crowded gold souks. Dusty, picturesque "old" Baghdad—defined by sectarian neighborhoods, mud-brick houses fronting narrow alleys, and medieval souks—disappeared under wheezing bulldozers that operated twenty-four hours a day, six days a week. The sterile chain hotels on the banks of the Tigris and the towering palms recently planted along Palace Road attempted to give Baghdad a grandeur it had not known since the tenth century. But even the presidential palace complex, created from the confiscated embassies of several countries and the rambling English garden of the American ambassador's residence, failed to meet the challenge. Sadly, new Baghdad would never capture the thin romance of the old city. Only the name

---

[29] Helms, *Iraq*, p. 123.

evoked the fabled magic of the Arabian Nights. Baghdad was now a city with great age but little soul.

Yet Baghdad was also a city of great new wealth, creating for the Baath an ideological dilemma. The party had come to power in 1968 pledging boundless sacrifices in the service of the Arab nation, even at the expense of Iraq's own vital interests. The call to the Iraqis to conduct an arduous struggle against their own Iraqi identity hit its first detour when Baghdad confronted pan-Arabism promoted by the rival wing of the Baath in Damascus. After 1973, pan-Arabism in Iraq slammed into the ideology of Arab nationalism, which claimed that the resources of all Arabs belonged to the greater Arab nation. In the face of calls from Arabs of the nonoil states to share in the revenues of the oil states, the Baath began to move toward an Iraqi identity outside Arabism. They found help among the Iraqis themselves. After more than a half-century of statehood, most Iraqis, with the exception of the Kurds, no longer saw their state as an illegitimate creature born in sinful copulation between the foreign imperialist and the false monarchy. Seizing a most fragile sense of nationhood, the Baath once more picked up the theme of Mesopotamia, hoping to escape from the notion that the resources of one area of the Arab nation belonged to all Arabs.

The Baath sent archeologists marching into the neglected ruins of Mesopotamia to give the Iraqi people a new sense of their country's ancient history. They were followed by intellectuals who sought to validate Iraq's unique character by connecting Iraq's contemporary folklore to the cultures of Mesopotamia. Gathering it all together, the Baath ushered into the political and cultural life of modern Iraq the ceremonies, names, and symbols of pre-Islamic Mesopotamia. Iraq, the beloved homeland, was no longer a font of Arabism but "the cradle of many civilizations and cultures . . . where many nations . . . and religions lived from the time of the Sumerian and Akkadian civilizations."[30] Public education no longer drilled Iraqi schoolchildren only with Arabism but rather fed into receptive young minds the idea that Iraq possessed a distinct civilization that was at least eight thousand years old. As in the years of the Qasim regime, postage stamps again portrayed the themes of Mesopotamia. Yet in

---

[30] Amatzia Baram, *Culture, History and Ideology in the Formation of Ba'thist Iraq, 1968–89* (New York: St. Martin's Press, 1991), pp. 97–98.

suggesting ancient antiquity as the core of a common identity for Iraq's Arabs and non-Arabs, the Baath roused the wrath of Iraq's hard-line pan-Arabists. None other than Michel Aflaq, the founding father of Baathism, pointedly reminded the Baath government that modern-day Arab nationalism had never surrendered to factors within the local environment of any region of the Arab nation. Sati al-Husri, the pan-Arabist who shaped Iraqi education under Faisal I, dismissed the elevation of Iraq's ancient civilization as nothing more than "an attempt to revive . . . that which is dead and mummified."[31] The most searing denunciation came from within the Baath leadership. Scornfully, Abd al-Rahman al-Bazzaz charged that when an Arab Iraqi pointed with pride to the grandeur of Mesopotamia, he "must not forget that [he] is not of the seed of the Babylonians, nor of the Assyrians; he is an Arab, in every sense of Arabism."[32]

Despite the criticism, the Baath leadership, portraying itself as the keeper of the nation, commissioned "The March of the Baath," a monument to be placed in Baghdad's Mathaf square. When it was completed, it showed a group of figures clustered together in what appears to be the bow of a boat. On its sides, bronze bas-reliefs depict such Mesopotamian images as a stylized sheaf of grain and a facsimile of the Lion of Babylon standing above a half-naked figure of Ishtar. At the dedication, the landmark was described by the official government newspaper *al-Thawra* as "the voyaging ship which carries within it the experiences of the nation and its yearnings for the future."[33] In the hands of another government, this vision of ancient heterogeneous Iraq might have once more warped the loom of a unique and specific Iraqi identity. But the nation, like everything else in Iraq, was hostage to the survival of the Baath regime and the ambitions of Saddam Hussein.

BY 1978, the Baath Party and the Iraqi state had become virtually synonymous. At the same time, the leadership of both the party and the state was about to change in what amounted to an internal coup. Ahmed Hassan al-Bakr, the chairman of the Baath's Revolutionary Command Council and the president of Iraq, had all but disappeared

---

[31] Quoted in ibid., p. 26.
[32] Quoted in ibid., pp. 27–28.
[33] *al-Thawra*, April 23, 1987.

from the public eye. In failing health and burdened by the deaths of his wife and his eldest son, he functioned solely as a ceremonial head of state. For a decade, ever since the Baath coup of 1968, power and decision making had passed bit by bit into the hands of the vice president, Saddam Hussein. It was his portrait, often in the uniform of a general of the People's Army, that blanketed every public space in the country.[34] It was to him that the party's vast intelligence mechanism as well as the ministers of state reported. And it was to him that the Regional Command Council, the controlling body of both the Baath Party and the Iraqi state, deferred their decisions.

Saddam Hussein's carefully structured power base rested on a complex network of kinship. At its core resided the family relationships that had originally brought Hussein into Ahmed Hassan al-Bakr's circle of power. Those strands of family in turn pulled near and distant kin into positions of influence, stretching further out to draw the sons of Tikrit into key military and security posts in percentages far in excess of their numbers in the population. This was tribal politics. Although the party continued to tout "the new Iraq," spouted socialist ideology, and financed the industrialization of the Iraqi economy, the Baath of Saddam Hussein had reverted to the basic units of Iraqi society—family and clan. Having used the party to control the army, and then having merged the party with the family, Hussein sat like the godfather who eliminated his rivals and rewarded his lieutenants.

Extraordinarily popular in the Sunni triangle and tolerably so in other regions, Hussein in his flashy white suits and black ties symbolized the stability and the bounty delivered by the Baath. But behind his broad smile and erect bearing were the bones, guts, and nerves of the Baath police state. Even though oil revenues in the late 1970s had bought the regime a level of popular acceptance, Hussein continued to crank the vise of internal security ever tighter. In 1978, arrest and torture drove most of the remaining leadership of the Iraqi Communist Party out of the country. Liberal opposition, always weak in Iraq, had long since died. The Kurds had been crushed in 1975. And the Shia were kept under the microscope of the Mukhabarat. Hussein, ever vigilant to signs of discontent, moved rapidly and ruth-

---

[34] The People's Army (Al Jaysh ash Shaabi) is also cited as the Popular Army or People's Militia.

lessly against any perceived threat within the country. But in his own perception, the real danger to his personal power lay beyond Iraq's western border—in Damascus, with his Baath rival Hafiz al-Assad.

In 1979 the history of the Baath seemed to be repeating a twenty-year-plus cycle. In 1966, the proposed union of Syria and Iraq had splintered the pan-Arab Baath into two national parties. Now elements within the Iraqi Baath joined with the Syrian Baath to attempt reconciliation and with it the long-dreamed union of Syria and Iraq. In the dark shadows of Baath politics, two forces seemed to be at work. From the Syrian side was the desire of Hafiz al-Assad to achieve union with Iraq in order to strengthen Syria in its confrontation with Israel, and from the Iraqi side was the desperate hope among opponents of Saddam Hussein that unification with Syria would provide the means to check the vice president's near total hold on power. But Hussein would not be outmaneuvered.

When al-Assad arrived in Baghdad on June 16, 1979, to explore the proposed union of the two Baath wings and the two countries of Syria and Iraq, Hussein refused to go to the airport to meet him. From the viewpoint of Iraq's national interests, there were valid reasons why the Iraqi vice president would reject union with Syria: the western border of a unified Syria-Iraq would thrust Iraq geographically forward to become a confrontation state against Israel, and the petroleum of oil-rich Iraq would have to be shared with oil-poor Syria. Neither of these points mattered as much as Hussein's own personal ambitions. After years of conspiracy and brutality that had crushed the liberals and the Communists, contained the Shia, and defeated the Kurds, Saddam Hussein stood on the threshold of absolute personal power. It was power he refused to share with anyone, particularly his old Syrian nemesis Hafiz al-Assad.

On July 28, the Iraqi vice president made an ominous announcement: a plot to seize the Iraqi government had been discovered among some of the vice president's closest colleagues, in collusion with Syria.[35] Chills ran through the Baath. Eleven days later, on the evening of August 8, 1979, Hussein watched as twenty-one members of the RCC were dragged to their feet, accused of treason to the party, and executed. They included the deputy prime minister; the

---

[35] There has never been any clear evidence of just who was involved in the plot, or if there was a plot at all.

minister of Kurdish affairs; the ministers of education, industry, planning, and health; and the chief of Hussein's own office. When the "night of the long knives" ended, Saddam Hussein strode through the rivulets of blood creeping across the floor. Stepping on the balcony of the presidential palace, he raised his arms in salute. Below, fifty thousand demonstrators roared their approval and chanted, "Death to the traitors!" As he looked down, Hussein resembled the Assyrian king Sargon II depicted in the 2,500-year-old reliefs from the throne room of Dur-Sharrukin. Saluted by his victorious army, Sargon stands tall in his chariot while his soldiers pile his enemies' heads in tribute to their triumphant leader.

A weary looking President al-Bakr, Hussein's cousin, mentor, and partner in power for the last decade, resigned for "health reasons." Hussein assumed the presidency and the positions of premier, chairman of the RCC, and leader of the Baath Party. His relatives and longtime associates made up the new cabinet and lay claim to all the key posts in the military and security services. The new order was in place. Iraq, which in the previous twenty years had suffered at least ten coups and attempted coups, two armed rebellions, and a full-scale civil war, fell into the iron grip of Saddam Hussein. In forcing his will on his fractious country, Hussein had made himself the state. But the full extent of what his absolute rule would actually mean to Iraq lay in the future. In 1979, Iraq stood at the very pinnacle of the oil boom. Money flowed to every segment of society, creating a bounty no one believed would ever end. It did end a little more than a year later, when Hussein invaded the Shia-inspired Islamic Republic of Iran.

7

THE WAR OF IDENTITY

ater the color of chocolate milk was creeping slowly through the dense stands of reeds that choke the Shatt al Arab. On this early summer afternoon of 1998, at the midpoint between Basra and the Persian Gulf—part of the Iran-Iraq border—it felt like hell on earth. In the hot, still air, a sense of death hovered. For eight long brutal years in the 1980s, Arab secular Iraq and Persian theocratic Iran bled each other in these marshes. Rather than a great ideological battle, the Iran-Iraq war of 1980–88 was in its simplest terms a test of wills between two commanding authority figures—Saddam Hussein and Ayatollah Ruhollah Khomeini. Hussein, in the name of the Iraqi state, and Khomeini, in his singular vision of Islam, pursued with savage fervor the hearts, minds, and allegiance of the Arab Shia of southern Iraq. In this vicious confrontation between autocrats and cultures, every element in both societies paid a terrible price. A decade after a cease-fire was born from a stalemate, the physical, economic, and human destruction of a seemingly senseless war still littered the landscape on both sides of the border. Yet at the northern end of the Shatt al Arab, "the river of the Arabs," the carnage is celebrated in bronze and stone. Along the cornice of Basra that fronts the waterway, a line of lifelike statues immortalizes eighty Iraqi military officers killed in the Iran-Iraq War. Defiantly pointing their bronze fingers toward the frontier of Persia, they silently declare that they died in the glorious effort to prove that Iraq is Arab before it is Shia.

The Iran-Iraq War ranks as the longest conventional war of the twentieth century. Often called the First Gulf War, it killed at least a million people, wounded another 2 million, engaged almost 40 percent of the adult male population of both countries, and cost roughly $1,190 billion in economic terms. The societal costs remain incalculable, as both belligerents—one employing chemical weapons, the other child soldiers—cast aside humanity in the name of war.

For the revolutionaries of Iran, the war was waged for Islam and the protection of the soil of Iran. For Iraq, it was a war fought to protect the rule of Saddam Hussein and the territorial integrity of the fragile Iraqi state. In an uneven contest of competing identities, Khomeini carried into battle 2,500 years of Iranian cultural continuity. Hussein threw into the conflict a country void of any clear sense of itself, claiming a history of only half a century. Iran, emotionally and militarily crippled by the tumult of the Iranian revolution of 1979, survived against Iraq's far superior war machine precisely because the Iranians were called to defend the hallowed territory of their historic homeland. Iraq survived because five decades of nation building using the bricks of education, economics, and culture had persuaded the majority of the Arab Shia that their identity resided more with Arab Iraq than with Shia Iran.

But within this unpredictable unity of identity among Iraq's Arabs lurked the tragedy of the Kurds. Before the cease-fire with Iran in 1988, Hussein, by committing genocide against the Kurds, had sacrificed over a decade of attempting to gather all ethnicities into the rickety house of Iraqi nationalism. Thus, at the end of eight years of bloodshed and suffering, Iraq emerged from the indescribable horrors of the war as an Arab state but not a multiethnic nation.

IN THE "night of the long knives" in July 1979, Saddam Hussein had clenched fast in his hands the presidency, the military, the Baath Party, and the lives of roughly 13 million Iraqis. What little opposition remained was expunged over the next year when three thousand members of the Iraqi Communist Party went into exile and twenty-one former Baath officials and government ministers accused of collusion with Syria went before the firing squad. There was nothing left to challenge the Tikriti elite at the head of the Baath. The al-Bejat nobility forked into two branches of Hussein's family. The first contained his al-Majid cousins—nephews of his father Hussein al-Majid. They assumed the role of supervising the army and repressing the Kurds and Shia. The second branch incorporated the Ibrahims—Hussein's three half-brothers, Barzan, Watban, and Sabawi, sons of his mother Subha and her second husband Ibrahim al-Hassan. They took control of the intelligence and security services. Khayrallah Tulfah, the uncle who had supervised Hussein's political education and provided his wife, became mayor of Baghdad. As members of the president's extended family, they governed Iraq. In this new order, the Sunni urban elite and the Sunni intelligentsia that had exercised central authority since Ottoman times were gone, replaced by Sunnis out of the rural lower classes.[1] It had not happened overnight.

The Baath had spent a decade dismantling the old upper class of landed wealth and entrepreneurial privilege. In place of the former elite, a modern urban middle class accounting for 58 percent of the population had risen as a result of increased oil revenues and Baath economic policies. This new prosperous middle class insulated central authority, at least momentarily, from the currents that constantly flowed through the political spectrum. But the middle class was not the only beneficiary of the welfare state. The great wealth delivered by the 1973 oil embargo also flowed to the Shia peasants, leading one delighted Marsh Arab to exclaim, "We own our own land now, and since 1971 there has been no land tax, no taxes at all."[2] Individual Kurds did not fare as well, but even in the mountainous north an infusion of infrastructure projects created a marginally better life. In Baghdad, still the stronghold of the Sunnis, affluent suburbs sprang up to house the newly wealthy. In the trendy Mansur district, a cup of coffee and an order of toast in one of the upscale hotel coffee shops could cost twelve U.S. dollars. At the time, this did not seem excessive in a country whose earnings from oil exports climbed toward $25 billion a year.

Yet the regime of Hussein concerned itself with more than economics. On the level of practical politics, the new president gave circumscribed life to the National Assembly promised by the constitution that followed the 1968 revolution. In the first election since the monarchy, people went to the polls on June 20, 1980, to choose from a list of candidates carefully vetted by the Baath. None of the 250 members who were to convene in the new "Hammurabi Building" posed any real opposition to the Baath regime. By requiring

---

[1] After assuming total control of Iraq, Hussein banished the use of last names in order to obscure the number of Tikritis holding positions of authority. Thus, Saddam Hussein al-Tikriti became simply Saddam Hussein.

[2] Quoted in Gavin Maxwell, "Water Dwellers in Desert World," *National Geographic* 149 (April 1976): 519.

all candidates to be "believers in the principles of the July Revolution," anyone affiliated with an opposition group not recognized by the Baath was effectively banned. Ethnic Persians were also barred by the requirement that any candidate for the assembly must be the offspring of an Iraqi father and an Arab mother.[3]

Operating out of the presidential palace like a ward healer, Hussein published his personal telephone number and urged ordinary citizens to call him with their problems. Resurrecting the ghost of Harun al-Rashid, the president on occasion donned a disguise and went into the streets to sound out public opinion. Afloat on the stability and prosperity that the Baath had initiated a decade before, the new president enjoyed a certain level of popular acceptance. According to one resident in Iraq at the time, "Saddam Hussein was not that bad when he came in. Anyone could survive if you didn't interfere in politics."[4]

The photographs of Hussein resplendent in dazzling white suits and black silk ties that had hung conspicuously during the tenure of Hassan al-Bakr were now ubiquitous. By the end of 1979, the Ministry of Information functioned as a personal media center for the president. Any visitor to Baghdad at the time had only to step through the door before eager civil servants manning the reception desk presented "the materials." The prodigious propaganda organs of every Middle East political entity from the House of Saud to the Palestine Liberation Organization (PLO) paled by comparison. In room after room, books, pamphlets, brochures, and newspapers sat on shelves, spilled out of boxes, lay in piles on the floor. They were written in Arabic, French, English, Japanese, Chinese, and a spate of African dialects. By style and content, the publications ranged from smudged mimeographs of Hussein's speeches to a polished coffee-table book entitled *Mesopotamia Today* to a mass-produced paperback of Hussein's dubiously authentic biography, *The Long Days*. Outside Iraq, an advertising section in the *New York Times* trumpeted Iraq and its president in purple prose: "Iraq was more than once the springboard for a new civilization in the Middle East and the question is now pertinently asked, with a leader like this man,

---

[3] Of those elected to the 250-member legislature, 60 percent were Sunni, 40 percent were Shia, and 12 percent were Kurd.

[4] Mahmood Essaid, interview with author, New York City, November 16, 1999.

the wealth of oil resources and a forceful people like the Iraqis, will she repeat her former glories and the name of Saddam Hussein link up with that of Hammurabi, Ashurbanipal, al-Mansur and Huran al-Rashid?"[5] Through it all, Hussein maneuvered to broaden his base of support.

Ideologically, Hussein tended the lamps burning around the resurrected Mesopotamian myth. The reasons were the same as they had been for the Baath since the oil boom—creation of a popular history to encompass Sunnis, Shia, and Kurds; provision of a secular base of national identity; and re-enforcement of the idea that Iraq is unique, distinct, and separate within the larger Arab world. For Hussein's personal interests, the Mesopotamian myth gave the president a veneer of historical legitimacy by portraying him as part of a continuous line of Iraqi rulers stretching back to antiquity. Thus, the art, literature, and poetry that poured out of lavishly financed Iraqi cultural centers promoted an image of Saddam Hussein as the embodiment of inspired leadership that, according to Mesopotamian mythology, had sustained the land and people of Iraq over the millennia. Special attention focused on Babylon. The restoration of the ruins had already been announced in 1971 as "the revival of the enormous civilizational heritage of our country [and] . . . its far-reaching importance to human civilization."[6] In February 1978, a large drainage project began to draw off the salty groundwater that had inundated the ruins for centuries. The Lion of Babylon, presented as the protector of the Iraqi peoples, joined Sargon, the first ruler to unite the northern and southern divisions of the Tigris-Euphrates basin, as a symbol intended to transcend the schisms of Iraqi society. Even the Kurds were ethnically linked to Arab Iraqis by virtue of common historical ties that purportedly dated back to the Assyrians and Babylonians. Hussein himself stated the premise in 1979 when he said, "There was no contradiction between the 'Kurdishness of the Kurd' and his being a part of the Arab nation."[7]

Yet beneath all the wealth from oil and all the imagery promoted

---

[5] *New York Times* advertisement section, July 1, 1980.
[6] Department of Antiquities quoted in Amatzia Baram, *Culture, History and Ideology in the Formation of Ba'thist Iraq, 1968–89* (New York: St. Martin's Press, 1989), p. 45.
[7] W. Thom Workman, *The Social Origins of the Iran-Iraq War* (Boulder, Colo.: Lynne Rienner Publishers, 1994), p. 73.

by Hussein, Iraq was steeped in turmoil. Over the tenure of the second Baath regime, a great cleavage that had developed in Iraqi life separated the social sphere from the political sphere. For five decades, Iraq had been engaged in the difficult process of nation building. In the sixth decade, the oil boom delivered its economic benefits to the Iraqi population. Together the tenuous sense of Iraqi nationality and massive national wealth generated new social forces and pushed new political agendas that the original ideology of the Baath and its Tikriti elite could not accommodate. But since the Baath Party and its leadership claimed ownership of not only politics but also history, sociology, art, literature, and identity, all channels through which these emerging social forces could find political expression had closed. By 1979, the Baath no longer engaged in either political thought or societal debate. Unlike in its ideologically heavy past, real political education no longer traveled through the interconnected cells and layers of the Baath Party. There was, in fact, no real party. There was only Saddam Hussein presiding over a country in search of itself, tangled in the bonds of authoritarian rule. In September 1980, the president, his party, and his country would test the limits of survival when Hussein sent the army of Iraq over the border of Iran.

THE ROOTS OF CONFLICT between Iraq and Iran run deep. They germinated in the Persian conquest of Mesopotamia in the fourth century B.C. and took root in the competition for control of Mesopotamia between the Sunni Ottoman Empire and the Shia dynasties of Persia. They grew through centuries of endless disputes over borders, land, navigation rights, and sovereignty. And they became entangled in the issues of ethnicity, religion, and culture that pitted Semitic Arab against Aryan Persian, Sunni against Shia. In 1969, a new phase of conflict erupted when Iran's Muhammad Reza Shah launched his own version of the Persian Empire by challenging Iraq's exclusive claim to the Shatt al Arab. Less than two years later, on March 1, 1971, when Britain began its much-heralded withdrawal of its naval forces from "east of Suez," the Iranian king jumped into the resulting vacuum of power. Intent on snatching hegemony in the Persian Gulf away from all would-be rivals, he granted diplomatic recognition to the government of the island state of Bahrain with its majority Shia population and revived Iran's claim to the forlorn but strategic islands of Abu Musa and Greater and Lesser Tunbs. Desolate spots of land, they are located at the mouth of the Strait of Hormuz, Iraq's sole outlet from the Persian Gulf to the Indian Ocean. Charging Iran with denying Iraq access to the open seas, Baghdad severed diplomatic relations with Iran. But protest did little to quell the shah's expansionist appetite. For reasons of geography, ethnicity, and economics, Muhammad Reza's ambitions posed a direct threat to Iraq's increasingly important oil industry. In the northern Kurdish region, which produced nearly 65 percent of Iraq's crude oil the year the Baath resumed power, Iran's position along the common border enabled Tehran to weaken Baghdad by goading Kurdish unrest almost at will. Feeding the Kurdish insurrection of 1971–75, Iran, in essence, conducted a surrogate war against Iraq that ended with the Algiers Agreement of 1975. Over the next four years, each side scrupulously upheld its side of the diplomatic bargain. But with the 1979 Iranian revolution that ended the reign of Muhammad Reza Shah, all previous problems between Arab Iraq and Persian Iran were revived. Added to the bitter mix was Iranian incitement of religious revolution among the Shia of Iraq against the secular Baath government sitting in Baghdad. To Saddam Hussein, this was the poisonous seed that produced the Iran-Iraq War.

IN A SENSE, the war between Iraq and Iran began with two Persians: Muhammad Reza Shah and Ayatollah Ruhollah Khomeini. Their contest to determine whether Iran lived as a secular state under the rule of a king, or a theocracy in which the most renowned *mujtahid* acted as the final arbiter of political power, unfolded largely outside the purview of Iraq. As in the plot line of a grand drama, Khomeini became a mullah in 1926, the same year the Pahlavi dynasty mounted the throne of Iran. For the next three decades, the stern Shia cleric built a reputation as a teacher and Islamic scholar. By the 1950s, he had achieved recognition among the Shia as an exceptional legal talent. In 1963, Ayatollah Khomeini's religious influence crossed into the realm of politics. When Muhammad Reza Shah announced his White Revolution, a program of reforms that included the distribution of clerical lands to the peasants and the emancipation of women, Khomeini sternly warned the Muslim community of the imminent dangers the shah posed to the Koran. From the religious center of Qom in that year of 1963, Khomeini pointed his finger at the Peacock Throne and spoke the prophetic words, "Oh Allah, I have performed my first duty and if you allow me to live longer and permit me, I shall shoulder other tasks in the future."[8]

Moral authority waged with words met secular authority enforced with armed might when the soldiers of Muhammad Reza Shah attempted to silence dissent by storming the revered Faiziyeh Theological School in Qom where Khomeini taught. In the collision, two students died armed with nothing but their Korans. Forty days later, Khomeini led thousands in the traditional Shia mourning ceremonies for the dead. One symbolic act followed another until days of rioting during June 1963 engulfed Mashhad, Isfahan, Shiraz, and Qom. In 1964 when Khomeini again sent his followers into the streets—this time to denounce a military agreement between Iran and the United States—the shah dispatched the ayatollah into exile. Turning expulsion into allegory, Khomeini left for Turkey in November, cloaked in the imagery of the Prophet driven from Mecca by the Quraysh. Nearly a year later, he arrived in Najaf, the great theological center of Shia Islam in Iraq. He stayed for the next fourteen years, watching with great interest events in Iran as well as Iraq's own contest with Muhammad Reza Shah.

Ignited by the popular demonstrations of 1963, the forces demanding political reform of the monarchy and protection of Iranian nationalism from the influences of the United States gathered against Muhammad Reza Shah. By the mid-1970s when the shah was vigorously pursuing his empire in the Persian Gulf, much of the opposition to the Pahlavi king had gathered around Khomeini. Already sixty-three years old, Khomeini lived in a simple house located in a narrow alleyway behind Imam Ali's shrine in Najaf. Like the Prophet, he ate a meager diet, slept on an ordinary rug spread on the floor, and spent his days engaged in prayer and study. Through this asceticism and regimentation, he labored to hold himself aloof from any hint of corruption bred of materialism and worldly power. In the context of the Shia psyche, Khomeini reigned as the symbol of righteousness holding Islam's sword above an unjust ruler.

From Iraq, Khomeini preached rebellion against "the corrupt" Muhammad Reza Shah. In Iran, his network of clerics and theolog-

---

[8] Quoted in Robin Wright, *In the Name of God: The Khomeini Decade* (New York: Simon and Schuster, 1989), p. 50.

ical students received the ayatollah's words, mimeographed them on cheap paper, and covertly distributed them through the shrines, mosques, bazaars, and lower-class urban neighborhoods. Bit by bit, Khomeini and his followers built support for revolution. Seeking to still the voice of rebellion, Muhammad Reza Shah in October 1978 exerted pressure on his old nemesis Saddam Hussein to force Khomeini out of Najaf. Fearful of the cleric's presence in the midst of his own Shia population, Hussein complied. That left an angry Khomeini to pack his family and his entourage for sanctuary in France. Still, opposition to the shah mounted. By the end of 1978, the streets of Pahlavi Iran had become conduits for massive protests, which the sympathetic soldiers of the lower ranks of the army refused to put down. In the rising anarchy, a tearful Muhammad Reza Shah arrived at Tehran's Mehrabad airport on the morning of January 16, 1979, to fly into exile. Fifteen days later, on February 1, the black turbaned Ayatollah Ruhollah Khomeini crept down the steps of a charted Air France jetliner to lay claim to the revolution for Islam.

By March 1979, Khomeini's message of Islamic revolution was reaching beyond the borders of Iran. Carrying the weight of the ayatollah's religious and political credentials, it implied that all governments considered "corrupt" by Khomeini and his foot soldiers of God would be overthrown by Islamic subversives among their own people. In Baghdad, Saddam Hussein and the secular Baath shuddered when Hassan Ahmed al-Bakr's cable to Khomeini expressing hopes of regional peace was answered by the terse phrase, "Peace is with those who follow the righteous path."[9] The men of Baghdad knew that the theology and ideology of the Iranian revolution called to the downtrodden Shia of Iraq. Nonetheless, the imagery of revolution in the name of Islam surpassed the reality, for religion had never burrowed as deeply in Iraqi society as it did in Iranian society. Furthermore, Iraq lacked the socioeconomic infrastructure that had empowered an Islamic revolution in Iran. Still, the regime in Baghdad recognized all too well that the Iranian revolution provided a powerful catalyst for the Iraqi Shias' long smoldering resentment against Baghdad. Even more, the revolution in Iran drove home to the Baath

---

[9] Quoted in Said K. Aburish, *Saddam Hussein: The Politics of Revenge* (New York: Bloomsbury, 2000), p. 166.

of Iraq the ugly truth that any repressive political order could unravel if enough people defiantly pulled at the strings of authority.

As Tehran radio broadcast its Islamic rhetoric to southern Iraq, the Shia listened to the powerful theological theme of the just society, which resonated for a community already mounting a clandestine challenge to the Baath from the ramparts of religion. Not the same breed of organized Shia politics born of Iranian culture, the Shia opposition in Iraq emerged out of sweeping changes of the twentieth century that had created two distinct and highly disaffected Shia groups: the impoverished masses disconnected from traditional society by urbanization, and the endangered clerical class whose influence under government repression hovered on the edge of extinction.

The process of urbanization that accelerated with such force during the oil boom had knocked age-old social structures of family, tribe, and religion askew on their foundations. Although the new urbanites who had flooded into the cities from the countryside gradually developed substitute loyalties anchored in occupation and social class, these never achieved the strength or certainty provided by traditional society. Nowhere was this more true than in Baghdad's al-Thawra, the housing area General Abd al-Karim Qasim had built in the early 1960s in an attempt to accommodate the crushing needs of rural migrants from the south. By the late 1970s, al-Thawra was home to a quarter of Baghdad's inhabitants, almost all of whom were Shia. For reasons that were endemic to the Iraqi state and intrinsic to the Baath Party, the Shia of al-Thawra as well as the Shia population in general searched for genuine political power. Once, the urban Shia had gravitated toward the Communists, but after the Baath essentially destroyed the Communist Party, they were stripped of any organized means of protest except religion. The rural masses, never drawn to atheistic Communism, remained where they had always been—politically homeless.

The Shia clergy inhabited the other end of the Shia social/ideological spectrum from the urban and rural masses. Although possessing means and status, the turbaned men of religion of the shrine cities had seen their social position steadily decline through most of the twentieth century as the forces of modernization, secularization, and economic growth had provided various Iraqi governments with the means to crush the institutions of Shia Islam. In 1918, more than six thousand students were studying in the theological seminaries in Najaf. By the twilight of the monarchy, that number had dropped to perhaps two thousand, a number per capita much smaller than that found in Shia Iran, where religious and secular power had yet to collide. Under the Baath, students of Shia Islam in Iraq almost evaporated. With the ranks of the clergy reduced to a thin veneer on the institutions of Shiism and the *ulama* (the collection of clerical authority figures) drained of much of its prestige, the tithes, taxes, and fees that believers delivered to their religious leaders declined to levels dangerous to the whole clerical tradition. Used for theological education, propagation of the faith, and works of charity, it was money that underwrote clerical authority. As a result, Shia clerics who decade by decade had watched their followers desert religion for secularism felt "a growing sense that the old faith was receding, that skepticism and even disdain for traditional rites were rife among the educated Shia, that the belief of even the urban Shia masses was not as firm, and their conformism to ancient usages not as punctual or as reverent as in past time, and that the ulama were losing ground and declining in prestige and material influence."[10] Before they became totally irrelevant, the *ulama* began to organize.

At the end of the monarchy, the immediate threat to religion had resided in atheistic Communism. Yet in the decade of instability following the 1958 revolution, the clerics succeeded in stealing numbers of Shia out of the camp of Marxism. Already disillusioned by the meager fruits of the revolution, these recruits of religion came with the bitter taste of Communism's failure to secure a new order capable of redistributing economic and political power. With the ascension of the Baath in 1968, the Shia religious establishment once more went on the offensive against a threat to the faith. This time it was against a political party wed to a secularism that aggressively suppressed all competing groups and ideologies. In response, the Baath in the summer of 1968 attacked the anemic institutions of Shiism that had survived the repeated bleedings of previous governments. Locks closed the gates of the theological college in Najaf, strict censorship descended on religious publications, and imprisonment and deportation further reduced the already depleted ranks of the *ulama* and

---

[10] Hanna Batatu, "Iraq's Underground Shi'a Movements: Characteristics, Causes and Prospects," *Middle East Journal* 35 (1981): 586.

religious students. As if to pour salt into the wounds, the Baath authorized for the first time in Iraqi history the sale of alcohol in the Shia shrine cities. Propelling everything was the Baath's determination to impose secularism on Iraq.

Ideologically the Baath had always held Islam responsible for the perceived backwardness of the Arabs. But more important to the Iraqi Baath's attitude toward religion was the raw politics of power. Baath secularism invited the Shia Arabs to belong to the Iraqi state while at the same time depriving the Shia of the potent political weapon of religion that they had always exercised in Shia Iran. This is what drove the Baath's Mesopotamian theme of Iraqi culture. But the Shia clerics would not be seduced by contrived cultural identity. Instead, they damned the government's glorification of Mesopotamia's ancient pre-Islamic cultures as paganism, ignorance, and barbarism. And they called their people back to Islam, for it was through the faith that the clerics would recover their exalted position and the deprived Shia masses would find the just society of Shia theology. Both clerics and laymen discovered a voice for their yearnings in the charismatic Arab Shia cleric Muhammad Baqir al-Sadr.

Born in the early 1930s in Najaf to an Arab family of Lebanese origin, al-Sadr, like Iran's Khomeini, gained fame as a brilliant theological mind. Perhaps best known for his works *Falsafatuna* (Our Philosophy, 1959) and *al-Bank al-Labribawi fi al-Islam* (The Nonusurious Bank in Islam, 1973), he was a prolific writer who jolted traditional Muslim beliefs with the current of contemporary relevance. In Iraq where the Shia masses had always lived at the bottom of the social order, he taught his followers that God is the source of all power and the sole owner of all the earth's resources. It is to God alone that man owes homage; thus, every form of exploitation of man by man is prohibited in God's holy order. In essence, al-Sadr beckoned social revolution against what he termed "injustice" and "exploitation." Out of this revolution would come an Islamic state in which the values of Islam would direct every sphere of public life. Similar to Khomeini's concept of Islamic government, al-Sadr's model would install the most respected *mujtahid* to reign over all aspects of society until the return of the Hidden Imam, the Shia's messiah figure. This Islamic government would equalize or narrow differences in standards of living to provide to all a reasonable minimum of material comfort; it would prohibit usury, prevent the concentration of capital in the hands of the few, and devote one-fifth of the country's oil revenues to social welfare. Touching the very core of Shia needs and yearnings, al-Sadr inspired the devotion of the Arab Shia of Iraq who were so often laboring to make sense of the modern world. It was Shiism's antigovernment motif, its emphasis on oppression, its grief over injustice acted out in the passion play of Hussein's death at Karbala that so perfectly dovetailed with the instincts and sufferings of tribesmen turned into peasants and urban laborers. To them, al-Sadr was not only a Shia cleric of impeccable credentials but also an Arab within a religious hierarchy dominated by ethnic Persians. But al-Sadr, holding firm to the Shia teaching that politics profanes the pious, refused to become the "Khomeini of Iraq." That left those seeking political and economic redemption through religion to turn toward al-Dawah.

Al-Dawah al-Islamiyah, the Islamic Call, was founded in Najaf sometime in the early 1960s by a collection of clerics within the Shia *ulama*. A clandestine organization for most of the decade, it escaped notice even in the shrine city. But with the decline of the Iraqi Communist Party under the Baath, al-Dawah moved out of the shadows to direct the march of the disenfranchised toward social change. Spreading what was in essence politicized Islam through the mosques of Karbala, Najaf, and Kadhimain, al-Dawah attracted young and lower-class Iraqis, particularly the Shia. More than a specifically sectarian movement, al-Dawah sought to unite all Muslims of Iraq—Shia and Sunni, Arab and Kurd—against the Baath's secular government, which it described as "contaminated by evil."

The first tests of will between militant Islam and the secular Baath came in 1969 and 1974 when the annual Ashura procession commemorating the martyrdom of Hussein erupted into angry political protests. In 1977, religion and the state again collided when police scattered another Ashura procession winding its way from Najaf to Karbala. Screaming their outrage, the militants stormed a police station at nearby al-Haidariyah while the surrounding crowd of thousands rhythmically chanted, "Saddam remove your hand! The people of Iraq do not want you!"[11] But it was the triumph of the Islamic government in the Iranian revolution that crystallized al-Dawah's potential as a political force and precipitated the birth of

---

[11] Batatu, "Iraq's Underground Shi'a Movement," p. 194.

other militant Islamic groups, including al-Mujahedin, the Muslim Warriors.

While al-Dawah's genesis came from clerics trained in traditional religion, al-Mujahedin was created by pious graduates of modern education who carried a different attitude toward an Islamic state than did al-Dawah. Al-Dawah called for an Islamic regime governing an independent Iraq. Al-Mujahedin pledged itself to the obliteration of Iraq's national boundaries in order to create a universal Islamic state under the religious authority of Iran's Ayatollah Ruhollah Khomeini. Overriding internal competition over the ultimate objective of political Islam, guerrilla bands out of al-Dawah, al-Mujahedin, and several other Islamic groups that organized around the idea of religious revolution staged sporadic attacks against the Baath regime. Over the course of 1979, they cut telephone lines, blew up ammunition dumps, and attacked police posts and offices of the Baath party. In the sprawling Baghdad slum of al-Thawra, militant Islam's "stronghold of heroes," the Shia raised their voices to demand an end to the "infidel Baath regime."

Holding fast to Baath secularism as the prerequisite for achieving national unity among sectarian groups, an alarmed Saddam Hussein recognized in politicized religion the further fragmentation of the Iraqi state. To Christians and Muslims, Sunni and Shia, a new category of difference added its weight to the existing strains within the Iraqi state—believers and nonbelievers. But most of all, Hussein and the Baath elite perceived in militant Islam a dire threat to a secular government controlled by a tribe of Sunnis. Once more the velvet glove hid an iron fist as Hussein practiced *tawhib* and *targhib*—reward and terror.

During 1979, the government lavished as much as 24.4 million Iraqi dinars ($80.5 million) on mosques, shrines, pilgrimages, and other affairs of religion. Paying particular attention to the Shia, Hussein declared the birthday of Ali, the fourth imam, a national holiday; prayed at Shia shrines under the full blaze of television lights; and appropriated the language of Shiism by promising "to fight injustice with the swords of the Imams." [12] In the grandest gesture of con-

---

[12] Hanna Batatu, "Shi'i Organizations in Iraq: al-Da'wah al-Islamiyah and al-Mujahidin." In *Shi'ism and Social Protest*, ed. Juan R. I. Cole and Nikki Keddie (New Haven: Yale University Press, 1986), p. 196.

stituency politics, the secular president of Baath Iraq unfurled a contrived family tree tracing his direct descent from Ali and, by extension, the Prophet himself.

But as always in Saddam Hussein's Iraq, accommodation was
simply a front for coercion. When the deadly feud between the secularists of Baghdad and the *mujtahids* of the shrine cities reached
full boil in the first days of 1980, Hussein expelled over fifteen thousand Iranian nationals descended from families that had lived in Iraq
for many generations. The charge was that they were not the children of "our twin rivers." In response to this assault on the Shia's
identity as Iraqis, Muhammad Baqir al-Sadr deserted Sunni-Shia unity
against secularism to mount a head-on attack against the Sunnization
of the governing elite of Iraq. Political Islam had reached full flower.

On April 1, 1980, an Islamic militant believed to be attached to
al-Dawah lurked at the entrance of the old Mustansiriyah school in the
heart of Baghdad. When Tariq Aziz, deputy prime minister and member of the Revolutionary Command Council, arrived to open a student
conference, the messenger of political Islam rushed forward and
hurled a grenade. Although Aziz escaped death, the attempted assassination of one of the pillars of the Baath regime gave Saddam Hussein
the pretext to stomp the life out of the Shia political movement.

The white four-wheel-drive Toyotas of the security services
rolled forth to collect thousands of Shia out of their strongholds. In
Najaf, uniformed deputies of the Baath regime rousted al-Sadr and
his sister Amina Bint al-Huda from their house. They were thrown
into the dungeons of the Baath's security system where, the Shia
believe, the guardians of the regime sexually assaulted and then
killed Bint al-Huda, the "daughter of righteousness," in the presence
of her brother. Then the masters of torture turned on al-Sadr, the
unwilling symbol of Shia resistance. After setting fire to the cleric's
beard, they eliminated him from the scene of political protest by driving nails through his head. Man by man, death took the leadership of
al-Dawah and other militant Islamic groups. Every Iraqi tainted by
even the remotest connection with Iran—by birth, marriage, or
name—faced the threat of expulsion. Since the ranks of Shia clerics
were already so thin, there were no reserves ready to move into the
trenches of Shia politics cleared by Hussein. That left the Shia without leaders other than the clerics appointed by Baghdad, a group
characterized by their detractors as the *ulama al-hafiz*, service

ulama. Thus, under persecution and co-option, the organized power of militant Islam died. All that was left was the warning voice of Ayatollah Ruhollah Khomeini speaking to the Iraqi military from the Islamic Republic of Iran: "I have given up hope on the upper echelons of the Iraqi law enforcement forces. But I have not given up hope in the officers, NCO's and soldiers and I expect them to rise heroically and to destroy the foundations of oppression . . . so that they will not bear the shame of the Ba'th Party."[13] He might as well have quoted the Koranic injunction "O believers, fight the unbelievers who are near to you, and let them find hardness in you."[14]

Suddenly the historical conflict between Iraq and Iran that for centuries had encompassed ethnicity, culture, religion, and territory focused on Hussein and Khomeini. One was a secular Arab, the other a religious Persian. One stood for the nation-state of Iraq encased within the Arab world; the other represented the idea of an Islamic empire incorporating all Muslims under the leadership of the paramount *mujtahid.* Hussein and Khomeini faced off in a cataclysmic battle of words waged with the symbols of ethnicity, piety, and identity.

In a speech at Nineveh on April 15, 1980, Saddam Hussein drew the sword of Arabism against the offending Iranian clerics: "Iraq is once again to assume its leading Arab role. Iraq is once again to serve the Arab nation and defend its honor, dignity and sovereignty. Iraq is destined once again to face the concerted machinations of the forces of darkness."[15] Khomeini roared back, vowing to consign the nefarious Saddam to "the trash heap of history."[16] Khomeini's deputy, Hussein Ali Muntazari, took up his leader's message, charging that the regime of "butcher Saddam Hussein" was opposed to Islam: "I am confident that the noble blood of the martyrs of Islam will boil in the Islamic Iraqi people. . . . This blood will continue to boil until Saddam Hussein's regime is completely overthrown."[17]

As the venom flowed, Hussein calculated the strength of Iran.

---

[13] Foreign Broadcast Information Service, *Daily Report: South Asia,* April 23, 1980, pp. 115–116.

[14] Sura 9:125.

[15] Quoted in Shahram Chubin and Charles Tripp, *Iran and Iraq at War* (Boulder, Colo.: Westview Press, 1988), foreword.

[16] Quoted in Workman, *The Social Origins of the Iran-Iraq War,* p. 88.

[17] Quoted in Christine Moss Helms, *Iraq: Eastern Front of the Arab World* (Washington, D.C.: Brookings Institution, 1984), p. 162.

Peering across the border, he saw a country in the throes of not one but two revolutions: the uprising against Muhammad Reza Shah and the subsequent contest between the clerics and the secularists for the right to claim the revolution. In the tumult, it looked as if every street corner in Iran from north to south, east to west, hosted a rival government. He also saw the shah's formidable military force stripped to its bones by foot soldiers turned revolutionaries and officers hanged by ropes as a precaution against a coup. Finally he saw, with accuracy, revolutionary Iran as a pariah state isolated from the international community. In the political upheaval, military disintegration, and diplomatic quarantine of his stronger neighbor, Hussein's ambitions exploded. The Iraqi president coveted complete control of the Shatt al Arab, which he equated with power in the Persian Gulf. And domination of the Gulf would give substance to Hussein's aspiration to transform Iraq into a force within the mythical Arab nation. But above everything else, Hussein gazed on the opportunity to insulate Iraq's Shia from the contagion of the Iranian revolution by eliminating the threat at its source.

On September 17, 1980, Saddam Hussein sat down before the cameras of Iraqi television. He picked up the 1975 Algiers Agreement in which Iraq surrendered to Iran sovereignty over the Shatt al Arab and tore it to bits. Triumphantly he declared to his countrymen, "This Shatt shall again be, as it has been throughout history, Iraqi and Arab in name and reality, with all rights of full sovereignty over it."[18] Five days later, at dawn on September 22, fifty thousand Iraqi troops hit four strategic junctions along the 730-mile-long Iran-Iraq border. While the infantry thrust forward into Iranian territory from the bleak mountain ranges of northern Kurdistan to the swamplands of oil-rich Khuzistan, Iraqi planes pounded Iran's airfields and military installations. In the Persian Gulf, the supertankers hauling black crude oil from the producers to the consumers dropped anchor to wait out what everyone assumed would be a short war between two predominately Shia countries—one Arab and one Persian. They were wrong. The Iran-Iraq War would prove to be a long, incredibly costly conflict of eight years fought in four bloody stages: the Iraqi advances of 1980–81; the Iranian counterattacks of 1982–84; the entrenchment of 1985; and the grand offensives of 1986–87, fought

---

[18] Quoted in Workman, *The Social Origins of the Iran-Iraq War*, p. 89.

to end a war in which neither side could win and neither side was willing to surrender.

WITHIN DAYS of the invasion, Iraq had advanced deep into Iran, taking the port of Khorramshahr and encircling the vital oil complex of Abadan. The victories seemed to confirm the expectation of Hussein that the war would end in an Iraqi victory by the Eid al-Adha on October 20. To Hussein's surprise and consternation, the Iranian army proved less chaotic and demoralized by the revolution than he had assumed. As the war quickly bogged down in stalemate, Baghdad faced the challenge of managing three competing ideologies: the Mesopotamian myth, Arab nationalism, and Islamic revolution.

The Baath initially leaned heavily on the cultural motifs and mythologies it had cultivated over the last decade in the ongoing quest to forge a common Iraqi identity. Popular art churned out by government schools depicted the Arabs and Kurds standing together in defense of the homeland; Iraqi soldiers, women, and children surrounded by decorative themes drawn from the Iraqi landscape; and Hussein, the self-chosen representative of all Iraqi people, centered in a whole range of Iraqi historical settings. In one, he accepts a palm tree from a Babylonian figure that resembles Shamash, the sun god. In another, he stands by the Stele of Hammurabi. In still another, he mixes the symbols of Mesopotamia and Arabism by parading before a background of cuneiform dressed as an Arab warrior, mounted on a white Arab stallion, leading columns of Iraqi soldiers through Babylon's Ishtar Gate. Government rhetoric followed, telling the people, "You are the sons of the Tigris and Euphrates. You are the sons of Adam's tree and Noah's ark. . . . You are the sons of the civilization of Mesopotamia, which illuminated the world when the rest of mankind was living in darkness."[19] In all these images and words, Iraqis received the potent message that they were engaged in the heroic struggle to protect the land between the rivers from the exploitation of foreigners. Those foreigners were the Persians, intent on dismembering Iraqi territory and destroying Iraqi character.

Physically and emotionally, the first two years of the war proved relatively painless for Iraq, especially Baghdad. The men who gathered in the neighborhood coffeehouses to smoke and play dominoes

---

[19] Foreign Broadcast Information Service, Daily Report, October 20, 1980, p. 24.

could shut their minds to the war that raged along the Shatt al Arab because this was the will of Saddam Hussein. Consumer goods, except for cigarettes and butane gas, crowded the shops, delivered by a government intent on ensuring plenty. That same government addressed personal tragedy by bestowing on the families of soldiers lost at the front enough money to buy a piece of land, a new house, and a car. This was a period in which Hussein traveled the country, stopping at random in Mosul, Basra, tribal areas of the Sunni triangle, and the Shia marshes. He visited Christian churches, nodded to the Yazidi devil worshipers, and prayed in mosques maintained by Sunnis and Shia. Constantly on the move, he visited schools, pinned badges on graduating firemen, and inaugurated water mains in obscure villages. Like the star that he was, he dressed the part, once turning up at a farm in a peasant's sheepskin vest and carrying a shepherd's staff. At Baghdad University, he was a young graduate in a cap and gown; at the race track, a desert horseman; in the oil fields, the chief engineer in a specially designed construction hat. Unique in the memory of most Iraqis, Hussein's campaign of public relations followed a preordained plot line: cultural diversity was acceptable; the central government was committed to the development of all its people regardless of religion or ethnicity; and every person in Iraq was first and foremost a citizen of the unified Iraqi state.

But there was another side of the war. Soldiers in prodigious numbers were bleeding and dying on the southern front. Most of them were Shia, the enrolled and conscripted foot soldiers of the army. So it was that day after day, processions of battered taxis sped along the roads from the battlefield bearing flag-draped coffins on their roofs for delivery to the families of the fallen. Unspoken blame fell on Saddam Hussein. Then on July 11, 1982, the president entered a building in a mixed Sunni-Shia town forty miles north of Baghdad. Without warning, a group of armed men laid a barrage of gunfire on the structure, pinning Hussein inside. Two hours elapsed before heavily armed re-enforcements from the army were able to rescue him. It was the second assassination attempt in four months. Amid escalating reports of unrest and attempted coups, Hussein retreated into the presidential palace. He has rarely been seen in public since.

Meanwhile the war went into its second phase. Iran's "Army of Twenty Million," recruited from the streets and villages of revolutionary Iran, sent boys twelve, thirteen, and fourteen years old walking across minefields to clear the way for assaults against Iraqi lines. No such dedication to the war expressed itself on the Iraqi side of the border, where the Shia foot soldiers and Sunni draftees possessed neither the morale nor the motivation of their Iranian counterparts. It made a difference to the entire Iraqi war effort. With his forces driven out of Iranian territory, and unable to push back east, Hussein reduced his conditions for peace to a cease-fire and a return to the status quo ante bellum. Khomeini refused. Speaking directly to Iraq's Shia, he told them, "We are related by race, traditions, and religion. . . . No other government or nation in the world except Iran has the right to be concerned about Iraq's future."[20] In Tehran, the cloaked and turbaned Muhammad Bakr al-Hakim, an Iraqi *hojjat ol-Islam* of Persian origin who had fled to Iran in 1980, created a government in exile dedicated to establishing in Iraq an Iranian-style Islamic republic. Briefly pulling together his own followers and recruits from other militant Islamic groups, al-Hakim put together a rebel army that included Shia deserters from the Iraqi army. In sabotage operations inside Iraq, this army of Islam carried the message of the brooding Ayatollah Khomeini: the war would end only when Saddam Hussein stepped down as president of Iraq and his country agreed to pay stiff reparations to Iran. Rooted in his own political miscalculation, the Iran-Iraq War had become Hussein's war, his personal quest for survival. That survival depended on convincing Iraq's Shia Arabs that they were Arabs and Iraqis more than Shia. Thus, the official rendition of Iraqi identity shifted away from the culture of Mesopotamia to the culture of the Arabs.

Clues to this deviation in Iraqi identity began to appear even at the outset of hostilities between Semitic Iraq and Persian Iran. Only three days after Iraq had crossed the border of Iran, Baghdad domestic radio broadcast "O descendants of al-Muthanna, Sa'd Ibn Abi Waqqas, Al'Qa'aq, and Khalid Ibn al Walid. It is the banner of al-Qadisiyah and the honor of the mission once again which Iraq and the Arabs have placed in your hands and upon yours shoulders." [21] Deserting the motifs of Mesopotamia, wartime stamps touted such symbols as an Arab warrior carrying a shield etched with "Allahu Akbar" and the Dhu al-Fiqar, the two-pointed sword the Prophet acquired at the Battle of Badr. Suddenly the secular Baath regime

---

[20] Quoted in Helms, *Iraq*, p. 190.
[21] Quoted in Workman, *The Social Origins of the Iran-Iraq War*, p. 149.

held aloft its credentials as defender of the Islamic faith, which it claimed was the preserve of the Arab nation by way of the sacred Arabic language. By the end of September 1980, Iraqi soldiers had become the descendants of the heroes of the first Qadisiyah. The Iran-Iraq War was now the second Qadisiyah, in which the Arabs would once more smite the Persians.

In the early years of the war, rhetoric was converted into visual imagery at Ctesiphon, the site where the army of Islam had defeated Sassanian Persians in 637. In a sleek building of contemporary design, a 350-foot circular panorama, embellished by furious sound and flashing light, dramatizes the clash of warriors, arms, and horses as the victorious Arabs best the Persians in the first battle of the war between Arabs and Persians that Baath propaganda claims has never ended. According to official declamation, the Qadisiyah monument is "a work achieved by the Iraqis in the days of national liberation of hero Saddam Hussein, in order to restore for all Arabs the glory of their past."[22]

Other monuments followed. On July 30, 1983, the Baath regime unveiled in Baghdad the artistically magnificent Shaheed, or Martyr's Monument, commemorating the Iraqi dead of the still-ongoing Iran-Iraq War. Built on the east bank of the Tigris near the Shia slum of al-Thawra, the monument consists of two halves of a blue-tiled dome; in the center is a twisted metal sculpture depicting the Iraqi flag.[23] In its symmetry and simplicity, the monument speaks powerfully of sacrifice and martyrdom. The combination of the dome shape—so symbolic of Islam—and the unmistakable emblem of the state evokes both faith and nation, each rooted in Arab culture.

In the three years since the war had begun, Saddam Hussein had rewritten the Baath's official version of ancient Mesopotamia. In the words of the regime's historians, the history of the Arab nation did not start with Islam. Rather, it stretches back into ages of remote antiquity. Artists, poets, and writers in the service of the state likewise blurred the distinctions between the ancient Mesopotamians and contemporary Arabs. In their hands, the Sumerians, Babylonians, and Assyrians of official propaganda acquired the language and characteristics of the Arabs. Consequently, the people

---

[22] *Iraq: A Tourist Guide* (Baghdad: State Organization for Tourism, 1982), p. 53.
[23] Al-Thawra, the sprawling area that houses so many of Baghdad's Shia poor, is now known as "Saddam City."

from whom all Iraqis were purported to have sprung were no longer the sons of the twin rivers but the fathers of Arab culture. And the Mesopotamian myth that had served the Baath as the unifying message for Iraqis of any ethnicity was now the well from which Arabism sprang. In this new mythology, the genes of the Mesopotamians comprised, in a single, unbroken line, the genes of the Arabs. In the languages of the Sumerians, Babylonians, and Assyrians lay the roots of Arabic. Thus, in Baath rhetoric and Baath art, Sunni and Shia were one, submerged in a common ethnicity celebrated by the Arabic language and protected in the folds of the Arab Iraqi state. This ideological revision rang out in the words of the new national anthem: "Blessed is the Land of the Two Rivers . . . You will always be to the Arabs, O Iraq, The sun that turns night into morning." But this revision of history and identity could not end the war.

By 1984, the conflict with Iran ate at Iraq like a cancer. In the south, Basra, which once nestled "in a belt of gardens under palm trees soft and woolley as green velvet," was bombed and burned.[24] Sand bags stacked ten high failed to conceal the scars of the seesaw battles that had marred with bullets and shrapnel almost every wall in the center of the city. On the perimeter, houses stood deserted; on every street corner, young men swathed in bandages leaned on their crutches. To the north at Karbala, more and more caskets entered the main gate of Hussein's shrine. They were followed by grim processions of black-clad women shrieking with grief while solemn men in the time-honored rituals of death slapped themselves on the cheeks as they chanted dirges of mourning. Yet the bulk of the Shia, the sinew of Hussein's war machine, remained in the trenches to fight and to die for Iraq.

Although the Shia carried the brunt of battle, all Iraqis suffered the economic effects of the war. Before the invasion, Iraq had exported 3.3 million barrels of oil a day. But with the Persian Gulf mined by Iranian revolutionaries operating out of little more than inflated rafts and the pipeline through Syria shut off by Hafiz al-Assad, Iraq now struggled to put 700,000 to 800,000 barrels a day on the market. Most of the $35 billion in foreign reserves that were on hand when the war started were gone. So were the gold reserves. In four years, Iraq had been transformed from a capital surplus

---

[24] Freya Stark, *Baghdad Sketches* (Evanston, Ill.: Marlboro Press, 1996), p. 108.

nation to a debtor nation living on transfusions of money from two major donors—Kuwait and Saudi Arabia—both of whom harbored their own fears of the Iranian revolution. To cope, the government cut the generous payments to the families of those killed on the battlefield and banned the import of luxury goods, including cars, watches, television sets, and some clothing. Government edict collected gold wedding jewelry. And raging inflation crippled the middle class that had been so carefully nurtured by Baath economic policies. As the value of the dinar slid from \$3.30 toward \$.90, an Iraqi could no longer boast, "We have been spoiled with the good life, a lot of money and no poverty."[25] In place of prosperity, Hussein spun his cult of personality even larger.

In a culture that puts little emphasis on birthdays, the anniversary of Hussein's birth became a national holiday on which all Iraqis were called to hail the father of the nation. Poster-sized pictures of the president in military dress adorned cafes, bus windows, utility poles, the courtyards of mosques, and the huts of the marsh. His face decorated wristwatch dials, gold-trimmed cake plates, school notebooks, and calendars. In original art, a series of portraits painted in the artist's own blood celebrated the "Great Saddam." In government-sponsored poetry, he was "the perfume of Iraq, its dates, its estuary of the two rivers, its coast and waters, its sword, its shield, the eagle whose grandeur dazzles the heavens. Since there was an Iraq, you were the awaited and promised one."[26]

Still the war dragged on. The two armies, one Arab and one Persian, grappled in the marshes of the Shatt al Arab while artillery rained on the oil production facilities of both and missiles slammed into urban populations on both sides of the border. But neither seemed close to defeat and neither would accept the wisdom of surrender. In the stalemate, Saddam Hussein continued to sell the war against the Persians to the Arab Iraqis. In one radio broadcast after another, he characterized Iraq as "an impregnable dam protecting the entire eastern flank of the Arab homeland."[27]

In July 1986, the war entered its fourth phase as military action dramatically shifted from land to sea. Attempting to strangle the

[25] Quoted in *US News and World Report*, November 17, 1980, p. 20.

[26] Quoted in Elaine Sciolino, "The Big Brother: Iraq under Saddam Hussein," *New York Times Magazine*, February 3, 1985, p. 16.

[27] Quoted in Workman, *The Social Origins of the Iran-Iraq War*, p. 149.

Islamic Republic economically by shutting its oil exports off from Iran's main oil terminal at Kharg island, Iraq sent its superior planes and missiles out over the Persian Gulf. Since Iraqi shipping in the Gulf had already been shut off in 1984, Iran retaliated by hitting the ships of Iraq's Arab allies. Suddenly Hussein's war touched the Gulf states. Saudi Arabia hunkered down, but Kuwait screamed for help. The United States, reacting both to the imperative to keep oil flowing out of the Gulf and to bottle up an Iranian government bent on driving the West from the Islamic world, put a flotilla in the Gulf to keep navigation open.[28] Tensions and insurance rates skyrocketed. But the "tanker war" failed to break Iran. From Tehran, Khomeini vowed to fight as long as Hussein ruled Iraq. Denied victory, the embattled Iraqi president wrapped himself in his contrived history of Arab Iraq.

In the seventh year of the war, Babylon had become Saddam Hussein's Disneyland in a country trapped in deprivation and death. Located in the region of the Shia, Babylon served as the stage set on which to play out the historical unity of Iraq's Sunnis and Shia now engaged in the long terrible conflict with Iran. After a feverish program of excavation and restoration that had proceeded throughout the war years, a legion of foreign archeologists, artists, musicologists, art historians, and diplomats gathered in the southern palace of Nebuchadnezzar on September 22, 1987, for an international music festival entitled "From Nebuchadnezzar to Saddam Hussein."[29] As the last notes of the evening faded in the roofless concert hall, lasers shot into the night sky, beaming overlapped profiles of Nebuchadnezzar and Saddam Hussein. What lingered was the question of why the regime had spent so much money on an extravagant festival during a war that was bankrupting the country. The government archeologist provided one explanation: "[T]his is not just a military war. It is also a cultural war. The enemy . . . is trying to destroy our culture—Arab culture. . . . If we retreat on this question, it will end Iraq's national life."[30]

From its beginning, the Iran-Iraq War had constituted a war of

---

[28] See chapter 11.

[29] The director of the festival, seeking a performance of "indigenous" American music, asked the U.S. State Department to send Madonna. Rather than the blonde superstar, he got Joe Lee Wilson and the Joy of Jazz.

[30] Milton Viorst, "The View from the Mustansiriyah—II," *The New Yorker*, October 19, 1987, pp. 82–83.

cultures and of identity. But its main battlefield lay within southern Iraq. There the Arab Shia and the Arab Sunnis from all parts of Iraq huddled together in the trenches of a seemingly endless war trying to survive the carnage and to escape capture by the Iranians. For all its horror, the war somehow fostered a wispy spirit of Iraqi identity among most of Iraq's Arabs. Hovering above the lines of sectarianism, it blurred the distinction between Sunni and Shia and eased Shia hostility toward the Arab Baath government of Baghdad. But at this feast of Arabism, the chair of the Kurds—the largest non-Arab group in Iraq—stood empty.

THE REPRESSION of the Kurds that followed the Algiers Agreement of 1975 had choked Kurdish aspirations but failed to extinguish the Kurds' will to resist the Iraqi state. When bitter words began to fly in 1979 between Hussein and Khomeini, the Kurds pulled out their weapons to once again challenge Baghdad. Seeing an opportunity to overthrow the Baath government and achieve some form of Kurdish autonomy, the Kurdish Democratic Party (KDP) of the Barzanis and the rival Patriotic Union of Kurdistan (PUK) of the Talabanis struck an alliance. With the KDP in the lead, the Iraqi Kurds expanded their existing military bases in Iran. Into them the political clerics of revolutionary Iran funneled weapons aimed at Baghdad.[31] Kurdish guerrillas carrying Iranian guns rang the alarms of Kurdish separatism, compounding the Shia factor in Hussein's decision to invade Iran. When the war began in September 1980, the hungry Iraqi army pulled soldiers out of its garrisons in the north to send them to the front in the south. The *pesh mergas* moved into the resulting vacuum. Establishing themselves across the countryside, the guerrillas bestowed on the Kurds residing outside the cities and larger towns a level of autonomy at a time when Hussein was fighting for his very existence along the southern front. Re-enforced by thousands of Kurdish draft dodgers and deserters from the Iraqi army, the *pesh mergas* protected families and sometimes whole villages who had taken advantage of the disruptions of war to trek back north from their exile in the south. Nonetheless, the eye of Baghdad never strayed far from Iraqi Kurdistan. During periods in

---

[31] Because of the political rivalry between Baghdad and Damascus, Syria also provided arms to the Kurds.

which fighting in the south eased, the army returned to sweep the Kurds out of government-declared security zones along the borders with Iran and Turkey. During periods when the war was going badly, Hussein reverted to the same tactic employed by every Iraqi government facing Kurdish unrest: he exploited the Kurds' own internal conflicts. Although the strife among the Kurds always boiled down to personal and tribal interests, the immediate issue in 1983 between the KDP and the PUK focused on whether to continue the armed struggle against Baghdad using Iranian support or to negotiate a deal for Kurdish rights with a weakened Hussein. The KDP kept up the fight while the PUK bargained. In July 1983, after the KDP helped Iran capture the border post of Hajj Omran, the Iraqi army inflicted its punishment on the Barzani tribe. Invading the KDP's security zones, Baghdad's soldiers rounded up between five and eight thousand Barzani males and drove them south. They were never seen again. To incessant inquiries about their whereabouts, Baghdad only replied that they had been "severely punished and went to hell." This example of Iraq's ability to wreak its vengeance, plus a KDP-Iranian offensive that forced the PUK guerrillas out of Iran, led the PUK's Jalal Talabani to agree to a cease-fire with Baghdad in December 1983.

But in July 1987 during the Tanker War in the Persian Gulf, the Kurds again found unity. Putting aside their differences, the rival KDP and PUK forged another alliance known as the Iraqi Kurdistan Front that declared its intention to overthrow the Baath regime of Saddam Hussein. At the same time, Iran, attempting to open a northern front that would relieve the stress on the southern front, again encroached on Iraqi territory with the aid of the Kurds. If central government authority weakened further in the north, Baghdad feared that Turkey might attempt to occupy what Atatürk had relinquished six decades ago: Mosul province and with it as much as 80 percent of Iraq's wartime oil production. No more able than it had ever been to entice the Kurds into the thin frame of Iraqi nationalism or to seduce them with Arabism, Baghdad unleashed a new campaign of coercion.

On February 28, 1987, Hussein appointed his cousin, Ali Hassan al-Majid, to the post of secretary-general of the Northern Bureau of the Baath Party. His mandate was to "take care" of the Kurds. Al-Majid accepted in crude Tikriti slang, "Taking care of [the Kurds] means burying them with bulldozers. That's what taking care of them means."[32] Needing to kill the Kurds before he could bury them, al-Majid called for the "special ammunition" that was serving Iraq with such terrifying efficiency on the southern front.

In mid-April, as the afternoon light began to fade in the village of Sheikh Wisan, sixteen Sukhoi bombers made three low, lazy passes over the mud and thatch houses that sheltered a hundred or so families. One by one, each plane dropped its load of metal canisters and disappeared. Within seconds, the deadly gas released from the canisters began to take effect; before the sun rose again, 238 people in Sheikh Wisan had been killed.

In June, Baghdad placed two new decrees in the hands of al-Majid, now known among the Kurds as "Ali Chemical." Areas under *pesh merga* control were to be swept clean "using artillery, helicopters and aircraft at all times of the day or night in order to kill the largest number of persons."[33] Setting about his task, al-Majid commenced execution of a campaign designed to cleanse the Kurdish element from the Iran-Iraq War. Moving from the southeast to the northwest of Iraqi Kurdistan, military and security forces subjected one area after another to the same pattern. Army units arrived in a village in the dead of night, rousted people from their beds, and collected them into terrified groups that separated boys and men between twelve and fifty years old from women, children, and the elderly. Herded into different trucks whose beds were covered by military green canvas, the men disappeared down the mountain roads. Those unlikely to provide manpower for the *pesh mergas* went south to camps or dismal new villages constructed of concrete block and surrounded by barbed wire. Forced to live in appalling conditions, many of the young and the old died of starvation, disease, and abuse. The men simply vanished. Common knowledge has it that they were taken to southern Iraq and lined up before firing squads that catapulted them into mass graves.

Despite Baghdad's brutal efforts to subdue the north, perhaps as many as sixty thousand armed Kurds still operated as a guerilla army at the beginning of 1988. In control of a region encompassing 3,800

---

[32] Michael Gunter, *The Kurds of Iraq: Tragedy and Hope* (New York: St. Martin's Press, 1992), p. 88.

[33] Decree 160 of the government of Iraq quoted in Jonathan C. Randal, *After Such Knowledge, What Forgiveness?* (Boulder, Colo.: Westview Press, 1999), p. 228.

square miles, the Kurds underscored their defiance of Baghdad by demolishing installations of the Baath Party, including a summer palace belonging to Hussein, which was burned to the ground. In response, Baghdad once more ratcheted up its repression of the Kurds in the now-infamous campaign code-named al-Anfal. Derived from the eighth Sura of the Koran in which Muhammad defined the distribution of the spoils of war in a *jihad*, al-Anfal, in the lexicon of Saddam Hussein, meant a bureaucratically organized pogrom designed to remove the Kurds and others from designated security areas along Iraq's eastern and northern borders.[34]

Nowhere did the shadow of al-Anfal descend more darkly than on Halabjah, a Kurdish town of seventy thousand situated approximately 150 miles northeast of Baghdad and 15 miles from the border with Iran. Halabjah had just watched the *pesh mergas*, accompanied by elements of the Iranian army, sweep the Iraqi army out of an area near the strategic dam at Darbandikan. Days later as the clock approached 2:00 P.M. on a March afternoon of 1988, a single Iraqi warplane approached from the west, dropped low, and released several silver canisters. They hit the ground and broke open, releasing yellow, white, and pink clouds that wafted through the town and over the surrounding orchards. When the international press arrived the next day via Iran, hundreds of twisted bodies lay in puddles of water along the dirt street that marked the town's center. But it was a scene on the perimeter of the fields that captured the horror of what had happened. A mother frozen in death kneeled over her baby whose vacant eyes starred upward from beneath a hand-knitted cap. Virtually no family escaped unscathed. Five thousand members of the village died and uncounted others suffered convulsions, skin-shredding blisters, painfully swollen breasts and testicles, bleeding kidneys, and scorched lungs caused by mustard gas, nerve gas, and possibly hydrogen cyanide. It was the most notorious poison gas attack since World War I. Guptapa, Balisan, Bota, Garmyan, Yakhsamar, Karadagh, and Sargoloo joined the list of at least sixty-seven towns and villages subjected to chemical weapons during the notorious al-Anfal. But it was Halabjah that so dramatically had

---

[34] The Assyrians were also affected by operations in these security areas. Although Assyrians were less likely than the Kurds to simply disappear, thirty-one Assyrian villages, including twenty-five Assyrian monasteries and churches, were destroyed between the spring of 1987 and February of 1988.

signaled the Kurdish component in the two-pronged Iraqi offensive aimed at ending the war with Iran.

ON FEBRUARY 29, 1988, the month al-Anfal began in earnest, Baghdad initiated the second prong by sending seventeen Soviet Scud missiles crashing into Tehran. For the next four and a half months, one attack after another tore at Iranian morale as bombs hit the revered Friday Mosque in Isfahan and the shrine city of Qom. Chemical weapons recaptured the vital Fao Peninsula, location of the oil-exporting facility on the Shatt al Arab whose conquest in 1982 had marked Iran's greatest victory on Iraqi soil. In the onslaught, the mullahs of Tehran concluded that the Islamic Republic possessed neither the time nor the resources to defeat Hussein, his Arab backers, and Western suppliers. Concluding that the interests of his nation exceeded the goal of exporting Islamic revolution, Khomeini made a decision "more deadly than drinking hemlock."[35] He accepted UN Security Council Resolution 598. In what was simply a cease-fire, the resolution ended Khomeini's vendetta against Iraq's Baath and ensured Hussein's survival in the face of militant Islam. After eight long years, the guns stilled in the Shia south. But the end of the war with Iran brought no peace to the Kurds.

Poison gas, the most cost-effective method of crushing the Kurds without risking Iraqi causalities at the end of the long, punishing war with Iran had proved effective in the end. Massoud Barzani issued an order as devastating to the Kurdish cause as his father's surrender thirteen years earlier: "Everything has ended; the rebellion is over. We cannot fight chemical weapons with bare hands."[36] And so, as the journalist Alan Crowell wrote, "by the emerald rush of Habur River, on the Turkish frontier, the Iraqi armies of Saddam Hussein raised their banners . . . to signal their victory over the Kurds."[37] All that was left to the rebellion were the haunting dirges written by Sivan Perwer remembering the thousands of Kurds who died at Halabjah.

In the dying embers of Kurdish defiance, sixty thousand Iraqi troops, supported by tanks, fighter-bombers, and helicopters,

---

[35] Ayatollah Ruhollah Khomeini quoted in Foreign Broadcast Information Service, Daily Report: Near East and South Asia, July 21, 1988, p. 1.

[36] Quoted in Randal, *After Such Knowledge, What Forgiveness?*, p. 37.

[37] Alan Cowell, "Iraq's Dark Victory," *New York Times Magazine*, September 25, 1988, p. 34.

launched a six-week offensive to reimpose Baghdad's hand on Iraqi Kurdistan. To deprive the *pesh mergas* of bases and havens of refuge, they demolished village after village: its houses and barns were systematically flattened by explosives and bulldozers; animals were slaughtered; fields and orchards were rendered sterile by chemical defoliants. In Beduh, a community of five hundred people, not even a remnant of a wall was left standing along lanes that quickly overgrew with grass and wild wheat. This village, which had once defended itself against Alexander the Great, had collapsed under the force of Saddam Hussein.

By Kurdish accounts, 1,276 villages were destroyed during al-Anfal and its aftermath.[38] Those displaced moved to new settlements that in reality were concentration camps. Constructed on dusty plains away from the border, these were soulless places built close to roads and military installations where government surveillance was omnipresent. There women often pulled their hair and wiped their hands on their faces in ritualized anguish over the "lost ones of al-Anfal"—their husbands and sons, fathers and brothers.

In the eyes of the Kurds, Hussein had essentially committed cultural genocide through the inexorable destruction of traditional Kurdish society in Iraq. In doing so, he informed the Kurds that they, along with the petroleum below their lands, belonged to Arab Iraq. This the Kurds understood. Yet the Kurds would never forget al-Anfal, nor should Iraq's Arabs escape the memory of a term that has come to mean the officially sanctioned mass murder of noncombatant Kurds. Instead Iraq's Arabs came out of the Iran-Iraq War bearing a resentment bordering on hatred of the Kurds, whom they charged with betrayal of the Iraqi state to its Persian foe. Thus, the Iran-Iraq War, accompanied by al-Anfal, constructed even greater barriers between Iraq's Arabs and Kurds, making the integration of these non-Arabs into the Iraqi state more difficult than ever.

FOR IRAQ'S ARABS, a fragile sense of nationalism, nurtured by the successive governments of Iraq from the monarchy through the Baath, crawled out of the bloody battlefield of the Iran-Iraq War. The

---

[38] Some estimates go as high as four thousand villages. The U.S. State Department estimates that 250,000 to 300,000 Kurds were forcibly relocated in 1988, raising the number of Kurds uprooted since 1987 to an estimated 500,000.

Sunnis, largely protected from the carnage, never considered surrender to the Persian foe. The Shia, whose allegiance to the Iraqi state Hussein had questioned in 1980, had proved, in the end, unwilling to sacrifice their frail nation to their sectarian brothers in Iran. The reasons were ethereal—language, Arab tribal identity, and cultural affinity—and they were tangible—a half-century of national education, the largess of the oil economy, the deportation and assassination of the Shia clerical leadership, and the abiding fear of Hussein's police state. All combined to bring the Sunnis and Shia out of eight grueling years of brutal warfare with a renewed sense of Arabism and a refined vision of the Iraqi state. Each group along the sectarian divide acknowledged the nation-state of Iraq within its existing boundaries. In doing so, the Sunnis rejected once and for all the old call of Arab nationalism to dissolve Iraq in the melting pot of a pan-Arab state, and the Shia accepted membership in a solitary state in which the Sunnis remained dominant. Capitalizing on this unprecedented understanding between the Arab Sunnis and the Arab Shia, the Baath regime acted to consolidate the sentiments of the moment. Gathering up all the existing symbols of nationalism, the party dragged the monarchy out of disgrace to bask in the light of official approval. A replica of the bronze equestrian statute of Faisal I, erected in 1930 and destroyed in 1958, was placed on the original site, a square in central Baghdad now called Gamal Abdul Nasser. The royal cemetery where Faisal I and Ghazi had been put to rest underwent a $3.2 million renovation. And a collection of academic studies dedicated to the monarchy bestowed the benefits of historical revision on all the figures of the monarchy, including Nuri al-Said. But it was the Victory Arch, unveiled on the first anniversary of the end of the Iran-Iraq War, that celebrated the new: the Arab Iraqi state and the reign of Saddam Hussein.

Dominating an enormous flat parade ground in the core of Baghdad, the monument is composed of a pair of gateways that incorporate vital elements from the architecture of both ancient Mesopotamia and Islam. In each gateway, two tremendous metal forearms weighing twenty tons each grasp steel swords, replicas of the blade carried by Saad ibn-abi-Waqas, the commander of the Muslim army of 637 that defeated the Persians. Both arms and sabers are anchored in heavy concrete bases over which drapes steel netting holding 2,500 actual Iranian helmets taken from the enemy on the battlefields of the Iran-Iraq War. In the descriptive rhetoric of the Baath regime, "The ground bursts open and from it springs the arm that represents power and determination, carrying the sword of Qaddissiyah."[39]

In the hot, full sun of August 8, 1989, Saddam Hussein, mounted on a white Arabian stallion and dressed in the same ceremonial attire that King Faisal I wore during official state ceremonies, led elements of the Iraqi army beneath the monument's powerful arms (which, rumor claims, are modelled on those of the Iraqi president). It was Arab Iraq's moment. With the Sunni triangle and the Shia south bound together in the aura of Arabism, Hussein envisioned what revised Baath ideology envisioned: a proud independent state of Iraq that would stand tall over the Arab world. That dream would die in another war resulting from the ambitions, needs, and fears of Hussein.

---

[39] Official invitation to the inaugural ceremonies quoted in Samir al-Khalil, *The Monument: Art, Vulgarity, and Responsibility in Iraq* (Berkeley: University of California Press, 1991), p. 2.

8

AGGRESSION AND
REBELLION

A decade after the bombs of the 1991 Gulf War rained down on Iraq, the outer skin of Saddam Hussein's kingdom remains intact. Except in Basra, where it is difficult to differentiate the debris of the first Gulf War from that of the second Gulf War, there is almost no physical evidence to attest to the magnitude of the defeat Iraq suffered between the middle of January and the end of March 1991. In Baghdad, the twisted refuse of bridges, power grids, communication towers, and factories destroyed by the most technologically advanced weapons in the history of warfare are piled in a long recess in the earth that runs along the railway tracks that parallel the road leading in the direction of the Ziggurat of Agargouf. There are no public monuments celebrating courage under siege. There is no commemoration of the many who died in the trenches along the Iraq-Kuwait border. The only visible memorial to the war is one ruined building, the target of a tragic error. The Amariyah shelter that stands in a lower, middle-class Baghdad neighborhood is a boxlike building of beige stucco that from the outside resembles a warehouse. On February 14, 1991, over four hundred people had taken shelter in what the United States believed was a military command center. As part of the ongoing air war, an American jet streaked in, sent a "smart" bomb down the ventilation shaft, and videotaped the explosion. Today a woman named Umm Gada somberly leads visitors thorough the scorched interior where nine children from her extended family died. But in addition to the war Hussein fought to preserve his invasion of Kuwait, there was another war that winter and early spring of 1991—an internal war to suppress the Shia and Kurds rebelling against the rule of Baghdad.

In the Shia south, the majestic palms that had been part of the landscape since the age of ancient Mesopotamia have vanished from what is now a gray desolate landscape around Karbala. Within the shrine city itself, new storefronts of yellow brick face a recon-structed promenade connecting the hallowed shrines of Hussein and Abbas. But behind the facade of commerce, piles of rubble testify to the anger and savagery of Saddam Hussein's armed might that slammed down on the people and symbols of Shia culture in Iraq. To the north, the physical evidence of the Kurdish rebellion against Baghdad is less dramatic, as so many of the leveled villages date back to al-Anfal. Here, the signs of the Kurds' uprising against Hussein are scraps of tenting caught in trees on steep mountain slopes. Otherwise, persecution by Baghdad is heard in stories of flight from people who have felt more than once the wrath of Baghdad.

Hussein, the central perpetrator of the destruction and suffering of the Gulf War and its aftermath, has never accepted any responsi-bility for the ruin that fell on his country or acknowledged his humil-iating defeat. Neither have his people. The Sunnis remain silent, some from shame, all from fear of reprisals by the regime. When the Shia and Kurds whisper furtively about the Gulf War, it is of memo-ries of the Iraqi spring when they believed for a moment delivered by rebellion that they had escaped the despotism of Saddam Hussein.

In 1988, Hussein should have come out of the Iran-Iraq War as a chastened cautious man. Instead, the encounter with political mor-tality, not only for himself but also for his country, appeared to leave Hussein more ambitious than ever. Yet when the hero-president made his triumphant parade under the Victory Arch, his outward behavior masked Iraq's enormous problems—some obvious, some obscure; some old, some new. Like every Iraqi leader before him, Hussein desperately needed to consolidate his fractious population and broaden his claim to legitimacy. That required money to finance his regime's socialist agenda, his only instrument of broad popular appeal. With his economy in shambles, the self-proclaimed protec-tor of the Arabs against Iran's Islamic revolution demanded cancel-lation of Iraq's enormous war debts owed to the monarchies of the Arabian Peninsula. When Kuwait refused, the Iraqi dictator sent his million-man army southward toward disaster. A little over five months after the Iraqis crossed the border of Kuwait, war descended again on Iraq. Crushing defeat and the simultaneous uprising of the Shia and the Kurds that followed cut to the very heart of Iraqi society and the Iraqi polity. Through it all, the Butcher of Baghdad survived.

Although part of the reason lies with the coalition that fought the Gulf War, as well as the decades of fear instilled in the Iraqis by the Baath regime, the failure to end the tyranny of Hussein is shared as well by the Sunnis, the Shia, and the Kurds.

AT THE END of the Iran-Iraq War, Saddam Hussein had crawled off the battlefield swathed in a victory fabricated from what was actually a stalemate ended by a cease-fire. In important respects, image imitated reality. Politically, Hussein succeeded in minimizing Iraq's endemic internal divisions by mobilizing the Arab identity of the Shia in the service of the state. Militarily, he had brought Iraq out of eight years of punishing warfare in possession of a million-man army, the largest in the Persian Gulf. Its manpower was backed by an intimidating arsenal of weapons that included four thousand tanks, missiles endowed with the names of Mesopotamian deities that were capable of reaching Tehran and Tel Aviv, and a spectrum of chemical weapons that Baghdad had both the experience and the guts to use. Lord over it all was Hussein, the Arab who had halted Iran's Islamic revolution at the eastern gate of the Arab world. This was the central message of the war that the Iraqi president sent to his Arab neighbors and his own people. Switching from his field marshal's uniform, Hussein donned Arab dress to present himself as the legitimate leader of the Arab world.

Yet behind the carefully constructed imagery of promise and prowess, Iraq had paid a terrible price for the war with Iran. The human casualties and the mobilization of all available labor for the war effort disrupted society, increasing the social and political strains that had always plagued the country. The physical destruction of much of Iraq's industry around Basra, the crippling of Iraq's oil exports, the need for massive imports to keep the population fed, and the sheer cost of the war's military operations drained money away from the economic development program that was the hallmark of the Baath. In the economic dislocation, the soldiers who came home needed jobs in an economy too weak to absorb them back into civilian life. The middle class faced a wall of national debt that shut off the economic and social mobility they had come to expect in the years between 1973 and 1980. Backed up behind them was a restless population demanding material benefits they deemed their reward for eight years of grueling warfare. Hussein could not deliver. In pursuit of his own political survival, he looked south to his bankers of the war against Iran: the United Arab Emirates, Saudi Arabia, and Kuwait.

BEFORE SADDAM HUSSEIN went to war against Iran, Iraq had largely stayed aloof from international politics. In 1921, when London patched the country together, it was imperial Britain that determined Iraq's relations with the outside world. And it was Britain's interests that directed foreign policy. Nascent Iraq's own particular conflicts with its neighbors were largely holdovers of centuries of competition between the Ottomans and Persians for control of Mesopotamia. The only real threat to the Iraqi state came from Abdul Aziz ibn Saud, who from the northern Arabian Peninsula competed with Baghdad for possession of the Arab tribes of southern Iraq.

In 1811, the al-Saud predecessors of Abdul Aziz had led the zealous, theologically austere Wahhabis out of central Arabia to knock at the gates of Baghdad.[1] There on the Tigris the religious fervor of a Bedouin army met the military might of the Ottoman Empire. The Ottomans won. After executing the first Abdul Aziz, they sent the Wahhabis back to their capital of Diriyah, outside the present city of Riyadh. Around the time Faisal I mounted the throne of Iraq, the Wahhabis returned to southern Mesopotamia under the second Abdul Aziz to again challenge Baghdad for the loyalties of the tribes. This time they encountered the crude military technology of the British. Terrified by bombs thrown out of biplanes and machine guns mounted on Model T Fords, the Wahhabis turned their camels around and fled south.[2] But London, ever mindful of the economic burden of keeping the peace in Mesopotamia, initiated the search for a deal that would keep the tribes allied with Abdul Aziz inside the undefined boundaries of the Arabian Peninsula.

In November 1922, Sir Percy Cox, the architect of Faisal's throne and the British high commissioner for Iraq, dangled before Abdul Aziz the promise of British money. It was enough to woo into border

---

[1] As noted in chapter 4, in the West, Abdul Aziz ibn Saud is often incorrectly called Ibn Saud.

[2] Later the Ikhwan, fanatical Wahhabis that called themselves the Muslim Brotherhood, once more invaded southern Mesopotamia in defiance of Abdul Aziz's interest in keeping the frontier between Saudi Arabia and Iraq quiet. They were driven out in 1929 by a composite British unit of aircraft and armored cars dispatched by Sir John Bagot Glubb, the legendary Pasha Glubb.

negotiations the miserably poor Bedouin chief, who carried his treasury in a chest slung across the back of a camel. Mutual agreement set the meeting place at Uqair, an inlet on the eastern coast of the Arabian Peninsula near the island of Bahrain. The slender Sir Percy arrived first, wading ashore in a dark suit, slightly crooked bow tie, and trilby hat. Abdul Aziz, a massive man scarred by years of desert warfare, came by land. Sitting atop a towering camel and wearing the faded robes of a sheikh, he was followed by his sandal-clad Bedouin army and stable of slaves. In a camp where Cox sat on chairs and slept in a camp bed while Abdul Aziz reclined on a camel saddle and slumbered on a rug, the Englishman and the Bedouin engaged in high-stakes bargaining that would set the lines dividing Iraq, Saudi Arabia, and Kuwait. Understanding that boundaries in the desert ultimately reside only in the heart of the Bedouin, Cox devised an ingenious solution to protect Iraq from the problem of border raids coming across the northern frontier of the Arabian Peninsula. Drawing a flat, elongated diamond on yet another map belonging to the British, he created a "neutral zone" at the corner where the territory of Abdul Aziz met that of Kuwait and Iraq. Within it, the Bedouin and their animals retained the freedom to wander in and out, making use of wells and pasture while the governing authorities shared sovereignty and resources. Although the lines drawn by the Uqair Protocols stayed in place until Saddam Hussein invaded Kuwait in 1990, the border tensions remained. They concentrated on Iraq's one consistent theme in foreign policy—some claim on Kuwait.

In contrast to the long history of the Mesopotamian plain, the tiny territory of Kuwait possessed no form or identity until around 1710, when severe drought on the Arabian Peninsula drove a group of Bedouin toward the flat barren coast of the Persian Gulf. Ignoring the control nominally imposed by the Ottoman Empire on the sparsely populated Arabian coast, the tribesmen lived in lawless confusion. In the late nineteenth century, the Sabah family, in the tradition of the tribes rather than under an edict from Istanbul, ascended out of the chaos to impose a fragile order. Basically without resources or defenses beyond mercurial tribal allegiances, the Sabahs took advantage of the decaying Ottoman Empire to sign on with the British. As another protectorate in the string of territories along the Arabian coast of the Persian Gulf, they agreed to serve British interests in return for military protection and monetary stipends.

At the turn of the twentieth century, impoverished Kuwait lived on the trade of smuggled goods, low-grade pearls gathered from the waters of the Gulf, and slaves trafficked from Africa under the hooded eyes of the British. It all moved in single-sail, high-bowed dhows that rode the winds from the Arabian Peninsula east to India, south to Africa, and back north to the Persian Gulf. But in 1913, the old order signed its eventual death warrant when the Sabahs granted to Britain concessions to develop any petroleum that might lie beneath the sands of the sheikhdom. In 1930, as the vast potential of Persian Gulf oil grew ever brighter, the acting British high commissioner in Baghdad reminded London that Iraq and Kuwait as part of the Ottoman *vilayet* of Basra shared a vague but common history. He followed with the suggestion that Britain encourage the gradual absorption of Kuwait into Iraq. Like other imperialists of the period, he was operating on the assumption "that Kuwait was a small and expendable state which could be sacrificed without too much concern if the power struggles of the period demanded it."[3]

Nonetheless, it was King Ghazi who made Iraq's first serious claim to Kuwait. For two months in 1939, Ghazi sat before the microphone of his royal radio station disparaging the British-protected sheikh of Kuwait. Charging the Sabah family with feudalism, he called the Kuwaitis to the new enlightened leadership in Baghdad. In an era when the full extent of Kuwaiti oil resources still constituted as much hope as reality, the shallow nationalistic Ghazi seemed more interested in irritating Britannia than in actually acquiring the territory for Iraq. To his boyish delight, he succeeded in yanking the tail of the old imperialist lion. On instructions from London, the British ambassador officially protested to the king. The broadcasts ceased briefly, and then began again. Feeding off his own adrenaline rush, Ghazi ordered Iraqi troops to Zubair, near the Kuwaiti frontier. In the dead of night, the Iraqi police with a military accompaniment stole across the desert border to pull up boundary markers—so carefully set by Percy Cox almost two decades before—and move them southward toward Kuwait Bay. As defenders of Iraq's new territory, the gendarmes from Baghdad cruised inside what was, in legal terms, Kuwait's territory to shoot at startled parties hunting in the desert with their trained falcons.

---

[3] H. V. F. Winstone and Zahra Freeth, *Kuwait, Prospect and Reality* (London: George Allen and Unwin, 1972), p. 111.

Despite the hijinks, Iraq's claim to its southern neighbor was more than just rhetoric. Embedded in the frequent boasts of sovereignty were what the Iraqi power structure considered deep and genuine references to the historic and geographic continuity of Iraq/Kuwait territory. In this sense, the issue of Kuwait advanced the Iraqi nationalism that the monarchy so desperately wanted to nurture among its disparate communities. Ever since independence, Iraqi schools had drilled into every student that Kuwait had been stolen by imperialism from the territory of Mesopotamia. Thus, despite the maps drawn by the Europeans, the tiny territory remained an integral part of the Iraqi homeland by way of Baghdad's adamant claim to be the de jure heir to the Ottoman's Mesopotamian territory. Although the Iraqi declaration of possession rested more on ideological than legal foundations, it was no less real to the nationalists of the monarchy. In February 1958, even Nuri al-Said attempted to form a type of union with Kuwait by wooing it into the newly born Arab Federal Union of Iraq and Jordan. Although Kuwait refused, its British protector construed al-Said's overture as a move meant to deprive London of a vital strategic and commercial center at the head of the Persian Gulf. To some, this British concern over Kuwait may be why London stood by and watched Arab nationalists destroy the monarchy.[4]

After the 1958 revolution, General Abd al-Karim Qasim picked up Iraq's disputed deed to Kuwait. In June 1961, he retread the path of King Ghazi by ordering a buildup of troops on the Kuwaiti border at the time the sheikhdom prepared to sign a new defense agreement with Britain. On June 19, six days after Britain and Kuwait affixed their signatures to the deal, Qasim denounced the pact as a "dangerous blow" against the integrity and independence of Iraq. In the face of Kuwaiti and British vows to defend the territory, Baghdad issued a memorandum asserting that "[t]here is no doubt that Kuwait is part of Iraq. This fact is attested by history and no good purpose is served by imperialism denying or distorting it."[5] In response, Britain ordered warships from Hong Kong and Singapore to steam eastward toward the Persian Gulf. On July 4, HMS *Bulwark* put Royal Marines on

---

[4] Majid Khadduri, "Nuri al-Said's Disenchantment with Britain in His Last Years," *Middle East Journal* 54 (Winter 2000): 96.

[5] Quoted in Geoff Simons, *Iraq: From Sumer to Saddam* (London: Macmillan Press, 1994), p. 225.

Kuwait's shore under the terms of the Anglo-Kuwait agreement that originally had sparked the crisis. By July 7, a total of six thousand British troops were on the ground ready to defend Britannia's small rich protectorate of Kuwait. Outgunned and outmaneuvered, Iraq buckled under condemnation of the UN Security Council. A week later, Britain's superior force, having accomplished its mission, sailed away, leaving Qasim to bluster, "If Iraq had chosen to use force, she could have taken Kuwait long ago."[6]

More interested in its own political survival than in Iraq's territorial claims, the short-lived Baath government of 1963 acknowledged Kuwait's sovereignty. That left the Arif brothers to pursue another of Iraq's issues with Kuwait: possession of the islands of Warbah and Bubiyan. These two small spots of land at the mouth of the estuary leading to Iraq's southern port of Umm Qasr seem the very definition of the word "desolate." Yet for Iraq, a country with only twenty-six miles of coastline, the addition of Warbah and Bubiyan could increase Iraq's shoreline enough to turn Umm Qasr into a deep-water port. Kuwait refused to let go, in no small part because of a reluctance to gamble away possible offshore oil deposits.

The squabbling between Iraq and Kuwait over two forlorn islands appeared but a blip on the radar screen of a Middle East alight with the ongoing Arab-Israeli struggle. Before 1968, Iraq, geographically removed from the front lines of conflict and consumed with its own internal turmoil, performed as a bit player in the grand dramas of the 1948, 1956, and 1967 wars between Israel and its Arab neighbors. While others waged the battle over Palestine, Iraq did little beyond protecting its place in the Arab political constellation by engaging in verbal combat with the Jewish state. When stability descended on Iraq with the second Baath government of 1968, Saddam Hussein, operating from his position within the hierarchy of the Baath Party, continued to avoid territorial entanglement in the blood feud between the Arabs and Israelis. Instead, he moved to establish Iraq as a power in the Persian Gulf. There his ambitions ran into Muhammad Reza Shah, whose own aspirations had moved Iran into the vacuum of power left by the British in 1971. Checked to the east by the superior size, population, and armed force of Iran, Hussein sought allies among the Arab states of the Arabian Peninsula.

---

[6] Ibid.

As major oil producers, Iraq and the Arab Gulf states found themselves in a situation that all would have preferred to avoid since they
had little in common. Iraq was a socialist republic with major arms
agreements with the atheist Soviet Union; Saudi Arabia and the
sheikhdoms of the peninsula were conservative monarchies legitimized, in varying degrees, by their commitment to Islam and quietly
protected by the United States. Thus, rather than acting in concert
as partners in oil and Arabism, Baathist Iraq and the peninsula's
monarchies tended their different agendas. Baghdad largely avoided
the 1973 October War launched by Egypt's Anwar Sadat. And when
Saudi Arabia's King Faisal called for an oil embargo against nations
supporting Israel, the Iraqi Baath declined to participate, choosing
money over the Arab cause. After oil prices skyrocketed and the 1973
war between Israel and the Arabs ceased, Iraq thrust itself forward
as a regional power by bullying its weaker southern neighbors.

In Saudi Arabia, any threatening language coming out of
Baghdad was silenced by the strict censorship imposed on the gov-
ernment-controlled media. According to the official Saudi line, Iraq
either simply did not exist or was an Arab brother engaged in the
valiant struggle against Zionism and Iranian dominance of the
Persian Gulf. Yet most residents of the Arabian Peninsula could feel
the tension. Still, Iraq never violated the existing borders except for
a brief occupation in March 1973 of a frontier post in northeastern
Kuwait that ended under pressure from the Arab League. Baghdad's
restraint resulted from the hard reality that Kuwait, Saudi Arabia,
and the other Arab oil producers of the Gulf claimed too many powerful friends ready and willing to intervene in their defense.[7] Thus,
Iraq, the most populous state of the region, confined itself to resisting Iranian hegemony in the name of all Arab states on the western
side of the Persian Gulf and, at the same time, intimidating the Gulf
monarchies for the purpose of advancing Iraq's position in its own
front yard.

Periodically, Baathist Iraq expanded its horizons by thrusting
itself westward into the Arab arena. But Baathist Iraq, considered
hotheaded and politically unstable, attracted few Arab followers
until Egypt's Anwar Sadat deserted the Arab fold in search of a sep-

---

[7] Yemen, located on the southern tip of the peninsula, was the only government at
the time that openly allied itself with Iraq.

arate agreement with Israel. Suddenly, with the collapse of the Egypt-Syria alliance against Israel, the Arabs were in need of a new power configuration.

Egypt's president had barely finished his speech to the Israeli Knesset in Jerusalem in November 1977 when Saddam Hussein moved to fill the void left in Arab leadership. The most powerful man in the Iraqi Baath adroitly engaged his old rival, Hafiz al-Assad of Syria, in negotiations designed to bring unity between two of the Arabs' historic capitals and two rival Baathist regimes. This apparent rapprochement shook Saudi Arabia, which, in its own weakness, had always benefited from the antagonisms between Damascus and Baghdad. Nevertheless, at two high-profile meetings in Baghdad in November 1978 and March 1979 that followed the Camp David Accords, the Saudis, the Syrians, the PLO, the Libyans, and practically everybody else in the Arab world lined up behind Iraq to impose sanctions against Egypt for making peace with Israel. They did so for one reason: the defection of Cairo removed the Arab world's western flank, requiring fortification of its eastern flank. The Iraqi Baath, dusting off its stanchion of pan-Arabism, reveled in the limelight. In a communiqué of the Revolutionary Command Council issued at the time of the agreement at Camp David, Baghdad proclaimed, "It is clear that the Arab arena is waiting for a veteran knight, capable of confronting the challenges . . . of scattering the darkness and . . . frustration. . . . It [is] imperative that your party . . . and revolution should step forward to [under]take all the historical responsibility [and carry] the weight of Iraqi history, ancient and modern, in defending the dignity of the [Arab] nation."[8] Touching on the Arabized theme of Mesopotamia, the Iraqi Baath bragged, "From here Nebuchadnezzar set forth and arrested the elements that tried to degrade the land of the Arabs . . . and brought them chained to Babylon."[9]

Yet instead of championing the ideology of pan-Arabism, which the Baath at that time no longer considered to be in Iraq's best interests, Hussein aimed to establish Iraqi hegemony over the Arab world by gathering the Arab states into a bloc labeled "nonalignment." Syria, however, refused to join, as relations between the two Baathist

---

[8] Quoted in Amatzia Baram, *Culture, History and Ideology in the Formation of Ba'thist Iraq, 1968–89* (New York: St. Martin's Press, 1991), p. 107.
   [9] Ibid., p. 108.

states once more fell into their familiar pattern of intrigue and subversion. With al-Assad admitting that "the road to union between us is not carpeted with flowers," Hussein went ahead without Damascus.[10] On February 8, 1980, the president of Iraq laid before the Arab states the Eight-Point Pan-Arab National Charter. In words that would come back to haunt its author, he called all Arab states to a common defense of any member threatened by invasion. Thinking in terms of Jewish Israel and Persian Iran, a dozen countries, including Saudi Arabia, Jordan, Algeria, North Yemen, and Morocco, voiced approval. But without the muscle of Egypt and Syria and the symbolic flag of pan-Arabism carried by the absent PLO, Hussein was left at the head of a nebulous group of states gathered around the sputtering flame of Arab unity.[11] By then it mattered little to Iraq, for Hussein's attention had already shifted away from leadership of the Arab world back to dominance over the Persian Gulf.

ANWAR SADAT, the president of Egypt, and Menachem Begin, the prime minister of Israel, had met on the lawn of the White House on March 26, 1979, to sign the historic peace agreement between Egypt and Israel only nine weeks after Muhammad Reza Shah surrendered to the Iranian revolution. With Iran distracted by internal politics, the opportunity for Iraq to reign as the dominant power in the Gulf materialized before the hungry eyes of the Iraqi president. According to the calculations of ambition, dominance in the Gulf meant increased leverage in the Arab world where Iraq sought to move forward its agenda for higher oil prices and an adjustment of the Iraq-Kuwait border. That adjustment would win for Baghdad expansion of Iraq's miniscule coastline as well as a greater share of the Rumailla oil field that straddled the Neutral Zone. Thus, in September 1980, foreign policy considerations joined domestic concerns roused by the Islamic Revolution to thrust Iraq across the border with Iran, entangling the whole Persian Gulf in a war driven more by Saddam Hussein's fears than his ambitions.

Although Baghdad had come out of the Iran-Iraq War strutting a confidence bred in survival, the war had imposed on Iraq a debt of

---

[10] Quoted in Patrick Seale, *Asad: The Struggle for the Middle East* (Berkeley: University of California Press, 1988), p. 313.

[11] In the minefield of inter-Arab politics, Yassir Arafat in the matter of the Pan-Arab National Charter chose Syria over Iraq.

$70 to $80 billion. In 1989, the first year of peace, the country's oil revenues promised only an estimated $15 billion. From this, Iraq would have to service its debt, finance imports of food, and maintain Hussein's huge military machine. As the country's economy teetered on the edge of crisis, Hussein desperately searched for massive foreign credits to rebuild the socialist state that constituted the only noncoercive element of his regime, but there were no sources of financing. The Japanese government, looking at $3 billion in unpaid debt, cut off Iraq's credit. The Soviet Union pressed for payment on a $9 billion weapons bill. Even Lufthansa and Swissair, due over $150 million for maintenance of the national airline, refused to pay the government tax on tickets booked in Iraq. Yet what Iraq owed others paled in comparison to the approximately $35 billion Hussein's government had borrowed from Kuwait and Saudi Arabia to finance the war.

In February 1990, eighteen months after the cease-fire with Iran, Hussein admitted that Iraq faced economic collapse. Refusing to consider an austerity program that would require severe pruning of the welfare system, the father of the Iran-Iraq War announced that he needed not only debt forgiveness but $30 billion in new money to jump-start the Iraqi economy. At the end of June, an audacious Hussein demanded $10 billion in aid from each Arab member of OPEC. Portraying himself as the gendarme for the Arab states against the Iranian revolution, he considered it money due for services rendered. After all, Iraq had sacrificed more men in the Iran-Iraq War than all the Arab states together had lost in their wars with Israel. When his demand was rebuffed, Hussein charged Kuwait with stealing Iraqi oil from the Rumailla field and demanded compensation of $2.4 billion. Thus, the issues of money and obligation launched Hussein on a collision course not only with his neighbors but also with the norms of inter-Arab behavior. Failing to recognize just how desperate he was to save his regime and perhaps his fractured country, both Egypt's Hosni Mubarak and the House of Saud largely ignored the pleas and threats of the Iraqi president.

On July 21, amid an avalanche of rumors about triggers for nuclear devices headed for Iraq that had been confiscated at the ports of origin and evidence of a mysterious "super gun" that would render Iraq capable of delivering giant shells of poison gas, thirty thousand Iraqi troops moved southward toward the border of

Kuwait. Simultaneously Hussein lashed out again at the rich Arab oil producers, this time over petroleum prices and production quotas. In venomous words, he charged that every dollar Kuwait and the United Arab Emirates shaved off the price of a barrel of oil by exceeding the OPEC-set production quotas took from Iraq $1 billion a year in lost revenues. On July 17, Hussein used the anniversary of the Baath's assumption of power in 1968 to once more lash out at the offending Kuwaitis: "We have warned them. It is a conspiracy to make us live in famine."[12] Nine days later Kuwait gave in to the verbal barrage and agreed to lower production in order to force prices up to $18 per barrel. But the next day, the Kuwaitis announced that their oil production would be restricted only until the fall. Hussein countered by moving another thirty thousand troops toward Kuwait.

Although Hussein had positioned 100,000 men and three hundred tanks just across the border of Kuwait, the Arab world refused to believe that he intended anything beyond a grand bluff. The opinion was shared by the Americans and Soviets whose ambassadors had already left the summer heat of Baghdad to vacation in cooler climates. On July 31, Kuwaiti and Iraqi officials again met in Jeddah under the auspices of the increasingly nervous Saudis. After two hours of inconclusive talks, they adjourned. The Kuwaitis fully expected another round of meetings. After all, they held as sacred truth that Hussein would never act against the country that had kept so much of his war effort afloat. Nor did they believe in their wildest dreams that the self-proclaimed hero who vanquished the Persians would sacrifice his new role as Arab savior to threaten his Arab neighbor. Only random individuals in the American intelligence community seemed convinced by August 1 that Iraq might do the unthinkable—invade Kuwait. Despite their alarm, Hosni Mubarak in Cairo, King Hussein in Amman, and King Fahd in Riyadh tenaciously clung to the creed of Arab unity and its cardinal tenet that no Arab country blatantly attacks another. In doing so, they ignored the reality that Iraq was a country ruled by a man who had come to believe that he lived in a world shorn of all restraints and scruples.

Thus at 2:00 A.M. on August 2, 1990, 100,000 armed Iraqis rolled across the northern border of Kuwait. They arrived in tanks, per-

[12] Quoted in Said K. Aburish, *Saddam Hussein: The Politics of Revenge* (New York: Bloomsburg, 2000), p. 270.

sonnel carriers, and ordinary buses. They came from the elite
Republican Guards, the People's Army, the militia of the Baath, and
the dreaded Mukhabarat, the secret police. Within five hours, soldiers and torturers had conquered Kuwait's 7,450 square miles. In
what he called the "revolution of August 2," Hussein trumpeted that
he had righted the old imperialist wrongs against Iraq, erased boundaries that denied Iraq access to the sea, and redressed Iraqi grievances against the Gulf Arabs who had lived in luxury throughout the
Iran-Iraq War while the Iraqis had bled and died to protect them.

With the Iraqi occupation of Kuwait violating the hallowed dog-
mas of Arab nationalism, the Arab world convulsed. Left without
their bearings, the Arabs attempted to act collectively by convening
the Arab League for an emergency session. But the League could not
extract a consensus. Instead, Egypt, Syria, Saudi Arabia, Kuwait,
United Arab Emirates, Bahrain, Qatar, and Lebanon took their position against Iraq, while, for reasons particular to each, Jordan,
Yemen, and the PLO stood with Hussein.

As others took sides, Iraq plundered Kuwait in grand style. Under
the edict of the head of the secret police, Ali Hassan al-Majid, the
infamous "Ali Chemical" of al-Anfal, Kuwaiti men disappeared.
Kuwaiti women and girls were subjected to the humiliation of rape
by Iraqi soldiers. Every public building was burned or plundered. The
finest art of the Islamic Empire, painstakingly collected with
Kuwait's copious oil revenues, was trucked to Baghdad. Private
homes gave up their fine carpets, and stores surrendered their inventories. Turning a profit from official greed, a taxi service operating
out of the southern Iraqi town of Samawa abandoned its passengers,
choosing instead to carry booty from the occupied "19th province of
Iraq" to Baghdad. In the Iraqi capital, Baath propaganda blared the
official phrase of the occupation: "the Kuwaiti branch has returned
to the Iraqi tree."

Whatever the invasion of Kuwait meant in terms of Iraqi history
and interests, it fundamentally altered the Persian Gulf. In a region
crucial to the economic well-being of the industrialized world,
Hussein's army, the fourth largest in the world in terms of manpower,
sat on the world's third largest proven oil reserves, looking across
the border at Saudi Arabia with the world's second largest reserves.
If left unchecked, the tyrant would lay claim to Kuwait's financial
assets, providing him not only escape from his bankrupt economy

but also the resources that would enable the Iraqi military to threaten the whole western side of the Persian Gulf. With vital American interests at stake, the United States quickly decided that the Iraqi invasion must not be allowed to stand.

On August 6, the day the UN Security Council imposed economic sanctions on Iraq, the United States officially warned Hussein of the consequences if he refused to evacuate Kuwait. Instead of buckling under the pressure of the world's only superpower, the Iraqi president defiantly claimed that Kuwait was now an appendage of Iraq. His words were brief: "Convey to President Bush that he should regard the Kuwaiti Emir and Crown Prince as history. . . . We know you are a superpower who can do great damage to us, but we will never capitulate."[13] The encounter confirmed the opinion of Lawrence Eagleberger, deputy secretary of state: "Saddam is a tough son of a bitch."[14]

The following day, timid Saudi Arabia, reversing years of the calculated hypocrisy that had kept its American protector out of sight, invited U.S. ground troops into the kingdom. Thus, the battle lines formed. Ground and air forces from Egypt and Syria joined Saudi Arabia and the U.S.-led Western guarantors of its security, including Britain, France, and Italy. As a massive military machine opposed to Hussein's invasion of Kuwait gathered on the sands of Saudi Arabia, Hussein threatened to force thousands of Westerners working in Iraq to become human shields for his weapons facilities. To neutralize Iran and his worrisome eastern front, he relinquished the Shatt al Arab. The only gain of eight years of torturous war with Iran disappeared.

For six months, the elements of war coalesced. Egypt, Syria, Saudi Arabia, and a constellation of Arab states stayed with the American-led coalition while Hussein dropped all remnants of Iraq's contrived Mesopotamian identity to play to the Arabs' hostility to the West. Voicing the resentments of centuries, he again told the Arabs' tale of betrayal at the hands of the West and once more portrayed himself as the leader who would restore the Arabs to their rightful place in the world. In image and rhetoric, the Butcher of

---

[13] Quoted in George Bush and Brent Scowcroft, *A World Transformed* (New York: Alfred A. Knopf, 1998), p. 324.
[14] Ibid.

Baghdad transformed himself into a Robin Hood who valiantly proclaimed that justice was served by invading rich arrogant Kuwait in the name of the Arab masses. It all played well in the Arab street. In Amman, an album of recorded songs called "Saddam of the Arabs" outsold Madonna's albums by fifty to one. After all, these were the emotions that Gamal Abdul Nasser of Egypt had raised three decades before. But Nasser was the beneficiary of the Cold War. Hussein, on the other hand, had triggered the first crisis of the new world order, in which the United States and Russia had agreed to play on the same side.

One resolution after another went through the United Nations—demanding Iraqi withdrawal from Kuwait, imposing economic sanctions, setting a deadline for Iraqi compliance. Nonetheless Saddam Hussein, garbed in battle fatigues or the dress uniform of a field marshal, held firm in Kuwait. But behind this facade of a fearless leader cast in the mold of the legendary kings of Mesopotamia, Hussein was paralyzed in the headlights of approaching war. Insulated so long within his country, his family, and his sycophants, he had failed to anticipate the breadth and depth of the political boycott that Washington had succeeded in imposing. Even old friends and bankers like the French and Germans refused to talk to Iraqi emissaries. Left with no option but withdrawal from Kuwait, Iraq's leader ratcheted up his rhetoric and intimidation. Over state-run television, the president wove the magic words of Arab nationalism over his Arab subjects: "Our nation has a message. That is why it can never be an average nation. Throughout history, our nation has either soared to the heights or fallen into the abyss through the envy, conspiracy, and enmity of others."[15] Mindful of the dangers posed by the non-Arabs in the Iraqi population, Saddam Hussein dispatched his deputy, Izzat Ibrahim Duri, to warn the Kurds: "If you have forgotten Halabjah, I would like to remind you that we are ready to repeat the operation."[16]

In the last days of peace, the government canceled a Baghdad conference of Assyriologists organized around the theme "war and peace." On the southern border, the rank-and-file Shia and Kurdish

---

[15] Quoted in *Newsweek*, January 7, 1991, p. 15.
[16] Quoted in Jonathan C. Randal, *After Such Knowledge, What Forgiveness?* (Boulder, Colo.: Westview Press, 1999), p. 39.

soldiers, drafted into another of Hussein's foreign disasters, huddled in their trenches to wait for the "Mother of all Battles." Civilians in the streets of the Shia south, the Kurdish north, and the Sunni heartland sullenly awaited the inevitability of defeat.

At 2:30 A.M. ON JANUARY 17, 1991, the armed might of President George H. W. Bush's coalition hit Iraq. Hour after hour, day after day, high-tech weapons rained a whole new generation of firepower on Iraq's military installations and infrastructure. Once more, coffin-bearing taxis headed from the southern front toward the Shia burial sites at Karbala and Najaf. As he had in the war of the previous decade, Hussein spoke to the Arabs among his people: "O glorious Iraqis, O holy warrior Iraqis, O Arabs, O believers wherever you are, we and our steadfastness are holding."[17] And once more, Iraqi radio reminded all Iraqis, "Saddam Hussein, you are the smile on the lips of the young and old. You are the moon over Mesopotamia."[18]

Blankets of bombs continued to fall on the junction of aged cities and modern military bases. Acutely conscious of the political dictate to fight a "clean war," American military commanders who compiled the target lists drew heavy marks through the historical sites of Mesopotamia as well as the shrine cities of Najaf and Karbala. That may have been the only thing Hussein understood about strategic thinking in the West. These same sites had long shielded Hussein's weapons facilities. The nuclear plant at Nassariyah was located near Ur. Conventional-weapons factories and suspected chemical facilities ringed the ruins of the Assyrian palaces of Khorsabad and Nimrud. Perhaps in the mind of Hussein, the location of much of the might of Iraq was as much a psychological tactic as a defensive one. When he spoke of unleashing rivers of American blood and raising up mountains of skulls of fallen GIs, Hussein was reaching far back into the pre-Islamic past to present his foes with the might of the Assyrians. But it was Arabism defined in Iraqi terms in whose name Saddam Hussein called his Arab population to war: "When the message of the Iraqi soldiers reaches the farthest corner of the world, the unjust will die and the 'God is Great' banner will flutter with great victory in the mother of all battles. Then the skies of the Arab home-

---

[17] Quoted in *New York Times*, January 21, 1991.
[18] Quoted in *New York Times*, January 28, 1991.

land will appear in a new color and a sun of new hope will shine over them and over our nation and on all the good men whose bright lights will not be overcome by the darkness in the hearts of the infidels, the Zionists, and the treacherous, shameful rulers [of Kuwait and Saudi Arabia]."[19]

For over a month, Hussein absorbed the air war, believing that his chance, and Iraq's chance, lay with the coming ground war. It finally arrived at 4:00 A.M. on February 24, when Saudi troops followed by U.S. Marines swarmed into Kuwait behind phalanxes of hard-charging tanks. Ignoring his exhortation to "Fight them, brave Iraqis," Hussein's Iraqi army of occupation, composed largely of Shia and Kurdish conscripts, instead fled toward the border. Those who chose to fight their way out of Kuwait were the Sunni officers pulled out of headquarters finely furnished with silver, fine glassware, oriental rugs, and the obligatory, life-size portrait of Saddam Hussein. With few men behind them, they could do little beyond executing civilians and detonating explosives planted at Kuwaiti oil wells as blackmail against an invasion of Iraq.

The U.S. XVIII Corps that had moved out of Saudi Arabia's King Khalid Military City the day before continued its giant sweep north and west. As a tidal wave of assault weapons rolled into the desolate wastelands of southwestern Iraq, the largely Shia troops that Hussein had installed on his southern front poured out of their defensive trenches to surrender. Part of Iraq's highly touted million-man army, they were nothing more than young boys and old men. An amazed young U.S. first lieutenant marveled at the nature of Hussein's military organization: "Their leaders had cut their Achilles' tendons so they couldn't run away and then left them. . . . They were hungry, cold, and scared. . . . These people had no business being on a battlefield."[20] Essentially cannon fodder, they had been put there to blunt the initial allied attack while the elite Republican Guards, predominately manned by Sunnis, escaped the noose of General Norman Schwarzkopf's carefully drawn battle plan.

With all Iraqi forces in retreat, the way to Baghdad stood open. But on the forty-second day of the Gulf War, the allied advance

---

[19] Quoted in *New York Times*, January 21, 1991.
[20] 1st Lt. Greg Downey quoted in Seymour M. Hersh, "Overwhelming Force," *The New Yorker*, May 22, 2000, p. 54.

halted. The Americans, British, French, Saudis, Syrians, Egyptians, and others in the coalition declined to go on to Baghdad or to annihilate the Iraqi army. Although each held its own particular interests, the allies paused to enable Iraq's Sunni officer corps to accomplish the twin objectives of deposing Saddam Hussein and keeping Iraq intact. Right or wrong, an uneasy consensus existed among the allies that removing Hussein in the absence of a political force capable of taking his place was tantamount to opening Pandora's box to release Iraq's endemic ethnic and sectarian rivalries. Once loosened from the grip of the tyrant, Iraq might fragment, creating a large, unpredictable region that threatened the precarious stability of the entire Gulf.[21] Consequently, on March 3, General Schwarzkopf met Iraqi military commanders at Safwan, just inside Iraqi territory. In a field tent ringed by U.S. tanks and armored vehicles, the Iraqis received the terms of the cease-fire: the occupation of Kuwait was ended, military operations by both sides were suspended, all Iraqi fixed-wing aircraft were grounded. Each item was clear and simple. Yet in retrospect, the terms of the cease-fire delivered to Hussein his means of political survival—retention of his military units within Iraq and permission to fly helicopters inside the boundaries of his country. What the allied command had failed to comprehend in the euphoria of the moment was that Hussein had fought the Gulf War like a Bedouin. In traditional desert warfare, a sheikh took his tribesmen into battle only if victory was ensured. Otherwise, he withdrew in anticipation of the next encounter with his enemy. As the sheikh of Iraq, Saddam Hussein had never sent his best troops into Kuwait. Instead, he held important units of the well-armed, lavishly paid, and fiercely loyal Republican Guards in reserve to ensure his personal protection in what he perceived would be his devastated and demoralized land. Thus, the Sunni men and the equipment of the Guard were ready when the Shia and the Kurds exploded in revolt.

IN THE IMMEDIATE AFTERMATH of Hussein's humiliation at the hands of the allied coalition, the Shia of the Iraqi south and the Kurds of the Iraqi north would each stand up to hurl their historic grievances and hatreds against Baghdad and the Baath regime. But each held a different view of the Iraq they envisioned coming out of simultane-

---

[21] See chapter 10 for American foreign policy vis-à-vis Iraq.

ous but uncoordinated revolutions expressing sectarianism, ethnicity, and identity. Whereas the Kurds followed the well-defined lines of
their own nationalism that sought Kurdish autonomy or independence, the Shia acted to gain political and economic equality within
the Iraqi state. Only some among the Shia who revolted did so in the
name of an Islamic republic they saw as the solution to their political
and economic problems in Iraq. Yet neither the Kurds nor the Shia
would find redress of their grievances in rebellion.

The reasons why Shia rage exploded at the end of the Gulf War
were laid out by the writer Hasan al-Alawi in a 1989 book, *The Shia
and the Nation State in Iraq*.[22] Al-Alawi damned the British-Sunni
collusion at the dawn of the state that established the hierarchy of
power. He went on to charge that as the political elite protective of
its prerogatives, the Sunnis during the monarchy and beyond
accused the Shia of neither feeling nor demonstrating loyalty to Iraq.
In the Sunni mind, that justified the myriad of discriminations
imposed on the Shia that effectively deprived them of any real representation in the centers of power. This Shia exclusion only
increased through the repression of Saddam Hussein after 1968.
Refusing to allow his own community to escape its share of the
blame for the Shia condition, al-Alawi accused the Shia majority of
never demanding, after the revolts of the 1930s, equitable representation within the territorial boundaries of the Iraqi state. That
changed in March 1991.

Signs of the rebellion that was to explode in the sunset of the
Gulf War appeared while the bombs of the allied air campaign still
fell. On February 10, three weeks into the air war, a seething crowd
in the predominately Shia town of Diwaniyah murdered ten officials
of the Baath Party in protest over Hussein's refusal to end the bombing by relinquishing Kuwait. Four days later, mourners at the funeral
of the Shia religious leader Yusuf al-Hakim chanted the treasonous
slogan, "There is no God but God and Saddam is His enemy."

In another two weeks, Basra erupted at the same hour that
Washington halted hostilities in the Gulf War. At 5:00 A.M. on
February 28, a column of tanks retreating from the Kuwaiti front
rumbled into the deadly quiet town. Without warning, the lead vehi-

---

[22] Hasan al-Alawi was a Shia journalist who had served the Baath government from
1968 to 1981.

cle ground to a halt in front of a giant, one-dimensional portrait of the Iraqi president. The officer in command opened the hatch, climbed onto the roof of his dusty machine, looked directly at the smiling Iraqi president, raised a defiant fist, and shouted, "What has befallen us of defeat, shame and humiliation, Saddam, is the result of your follies, and your miscalculations, and your irresponsible actions."[23] He climbed back into the tank, swung its gun turret forward, and blasted the image to shreds. At that moment, southern Iraq exploded in the rage of the Shia. Suddenly Hussein faced his great terror of the Iran-Iraq War—Shia desertion of Baghdad.

Over the next hours and days, spontaneous rebellion spread from Basra to a string of other predominantly Shia towns in the south. In the onrush of anger, the streets of the revered Shia holy city of Najaf filled with rebels from every social class. With submachine guns and eighty-two-millimeter mortars, they hit the stucco and stone walls of the Baath Party headquarters, grabbed luckless party officials, and threw them to the surging mob that hacked them to death in seconds. Then they moved on to the next target and the next and the next. The same scenes repeated themselves in Karbala, Kufa, and on across the valley of the middle Euphrates. The rebels, re-enforced by defectors from the Iraqi army, exhibited neither leadership nor strategy. All they possessed was a name for their anger—the *intifadah*, an Arabic word that loosely translates as "uprising." In stark contrast to the organized revolt in 1920 in which the Shia *mujtahids* had directed rebellion against the British, there were few clerics even visible in the charge of 1991. Baghdad's efforts over the decades to drain the influence of institutional Shiism had worked. Still, what leadership did emerge in those fiery days of early March came largely out of the thin ranks of Shia clerics resident in Iraq or those exiled in Iran. Tragically for the uprising, these leaders depicted the Shia protest in terms of theocracy.

On March 3, the day General Schwarzkopf and the Iraqi commanders met at Safwan, fifteen to twenty men calling themselves *mujahedin*, or holy warriors, marched out of the main mosque of Najaf shouting, "No East, No West, we want an Islamic republic." As

---

[23] Quoted from a report by the al-Khoei Foundation of London in Kanan Makiya, *Cruelty and Silence: War, Tyranny, Uprising, and the Arab World* (New York: W. W. Norton, 1993), p. 59.

this signature slogan of Iran's Islamic revolution reverberated off the walls of Ali's shrine in the Shia heart of Iraq, somewhere between five and ten thousand Iraqi Shia prisoners of the Iran-Iraq War, along with ethnic Persians expelled by the Baath during the late 1970s and early 1980s, were creeping back across the Iranian border that runs through the marshlands around Basra. Units of the Badr Brigade, they had been organized by the Supreme Islamic Council headed by Muhammad Bakr al-Hakim, a cleric who had rallied to the Iranian side in the Iran-Iraq War. Trained and armed by Iran, the Badr Brigade injected the ideology of the Iranian revolution into what most Shia saw as a political uprising expressing historic grievances against Baghdad. On reaching Basra, al-Hakim's followers shouted "Death to Saddam the Apostate!" as they stormed the Sheraton Hotel and burned the bars and casinos of the city. Then in contradiction to the nature of the larger Shia rebellion, they proclaimed the establishment of a Shia Islamic Republic. Soon, pictures of al-Hakim and the late Ayatollah Khomeini covered the walls not only of Basra but also of Amarah and other towns of the south. From across the border in Iran, al-Hakim claimed full authority over the rebellion. In instructions to his followers in Iraq, he ordered, "No action outside the context [of an Islamic revolution] is allowed; no party is allowed to recruit volunteers; no ideas except the rightful Islamic ones should be disseminated."[24]

On the third day of the uprising when it appeared that the main-line rebels were consolidating their control of Najaf, the grand *mujtahid* Abu al-Qasim al-Khoei gathered the thousands who looked to him as their spiritual guide into the courtyard of Ali's tomb to receive a *fatwa*, or religious ruling. But rather than repeating al-Hakim's call to Islamic government, al-Khoei sought to stabilize public order. Speaking in terms of Islamic law, not Islamic politics, al-Khoei instructed his followers, "You are obligated to protect people's property, money, and honor, likewise all public institutions, for they are the property of all. . . . I also urge you to bury all the corpses in the streets, according to *sharia* rites, to refrain from maiming anybody, for these are foreign to our Islamic morals; and to not be hasty in taking individual decisions that have not been thought out and that

---

[24] Quoted in Andrew Cockburn and Patrick Cockburn, *Out of the Ashes: The Resurrection of Saddam Hussein* (New York: HarperCollins, 1999), p. 21.

go against the *sharia* and the public interest."[25] Although al-Khoei implicitly sanctioned some form of a Shia governing body, no sound evidence has ever emerged that he envisioned for Iraq an Islamic government based on the Khomeini model in Iran. In retrospect, al-Khoei's real intention hardly mattered. Among the large numbers of Shia who were secularists, the clerics had further injected into the *intifadah* the perception of a Persian theocracy. For the Sunni who made up the officer corps of the Iraqi army, even the hint of a Shia-bred religious government was enough to stampede them to the side of Hussein.

Thus, on March 4 when the Kurds added their own revolt to that of the Shia, Hussein was able to summon to his defense the Republican Guards held back from the Kuwait front as well as elements of the bruised Iraqi army. Essentially ignoring the north, Saddam's army zeroed in on the south, for it was there among the Shia that resided a series of factors that could prove fatal to the Baath regime. These factors included the proximity of the rebelling Shia to Baghdad; the presence within the capital of a large Shia population potentially capable of engulfing the government; the subversion of the Islamic Republic of Iran coming across Iraq's southeastern border; and the possibility that American forces camped within sight of the uprising might intervene on the side of the Shia. Thus, the order went out from the presidential palace to secure the southern flatlands as quickly as possible before Baghdad turned north to confront the Kurds. In Baghdad's decision to concentrate on the southern uprising, the Shia would fall subject to a level of ruthlessness previously applied only to the Kurds.

By March 7, a little over a week after the rebellion had exploded, Basra, Najaf, and Karbala as well as other Shia towns in the south were prime to become killing fields. The special forces charged with saving Hussein's regime came largely from the geographic spine of the Baath: Ramadi, Hit, Samarra, and Tikrit. Almost universally Sunni, they dedicated themselves to avenging the Shia affront to the existing order. But the army and the rebels did not duel alone. Each side benefited from the actions or inactions of at least one element of foreign power. In support of the rebels and the interests of Iran in

---

[25] Quoted in Yitzhak Naksah, *The Shi'is of Iraq* (Princeton: Princeton University Press, 1994), p. 276.

southern Iraq, Iranian President Hashemi Rafsanjani urged an end to the Baath regime while sending in just enough material support to keep the rebels fighting while keeping Iran outside the conflict. The Saudis dithered, caught between the dual threats of Saddam Hussein and a potential Islamic government sympathetic to Iran. The United States, terrified about Iranian involvement in the uprising, refused to provide the rebellion cover by standing between the army and the rebels. With the United States and its allies on the sidelines, the Iraqi Shia internally divided between secularists and theocrats. With the Sunni special armed forces secure, Hussein was ready to destroy everything that gave the Shia a separate identity within the Iraqi state.

Directing his wrath at the shrine cities, Hussein sent helicopters over Najaf to drop leaflets engraved with the threat to kill every Shia. In the city where Ayatollah Muhammad al-Sadr wrote a political theology that spoke to the political injustices borne by the Shia, anyone suspected of affiliation with al-Dawah or other groups advocating Islamic revolution faced retribution. Shia clerics were hung by their necks from sacred rafters of Ali's shrine or simply vanished. In the absence of any clerical authority, agents of the regime tore through the shrine's libraries and vaults to seize ancient treasures of jewels, gold, and manuscripts gifted by the faithful. Not even the dead escaped. Tanks rolled over old family tombs, and bulldozers ripped open mile after mile of graves that had lain one against the other for centuries. It was as if Baghdad had decreed an end to the fourteen hundred years of scholarship and learning in Najaf that had begun with Ali. When the carnage finally ended, a huge new portrait of Saddam Hussein overshadowed any remaining image of the first imam. Dressed in tweeds, the hero president paused over a mountain flower. Except for the swollen, rotting corpses that lay around the portrait, it was an image straight out of *The Sound of Music*.

If such untempered violence can be measured, Karbala suffered in the onslaught even more than did Najaf. In every neighborhood, homes collapsed under the destructive force of tank shells, and people died from automatic weapons fire unleashed against suspected supporters of the revolt. And just as in Najaf, the most sacred sites of Shia Islam became the scenes of the most hideous destruction. Artillery fire splintered the heavy wooden doors that led into the haram of the shrine of Abbas. A hundred yards away, the hallowed

dome of Hussein's shrine lost the gold leaf applied during the
Iran-Iraq War as Hussein's costly offering to the Shia. It was only the
beginning of the destruction of one of the jewels of Shia architecture. Intricate mirrored tiles on the high ceilings shattered, and tall
marble pillars in the inner sanctum chipped in sprays of machine-gun
fire that also splintered the corner of the wooden sarcophagus holding the body of Shiism's great martyr. Between the memorials to
Abbas and Hussein, bulldozers leveled the tightly packed shops of
the souk, or market. Behind them, the handsome old houses with
their overhanging *shanashils*, granite facings, and colorful mosaic
tiles fell into rubble.

As the Republican Guards squeezed the life out of the rebellious
cities of the south, thousands of terrified civilians streamed out along
the roads. Some followed the centuries-old escape routes into the
marshes to find protection among the Marsh Arabs. Others pushed
east into the Islamic Republic of Iran. The rest ran toward small villages and isolated desert communities in Iraqi territory occupied by
the U.S. Army.

Except for what the American military saw, all of the butchery
in the south unfolded in private. With all foreign journalists expelled
from the country just before the crackdown began, the chronicle of
what actually happened was left to the Baath-controlled media.
Portraying the Shia as traitors, the government's television cameras
turned on hollow-eyed Shia rebels confessing to sedition. The print
media, *al-Thawra* in particular, pumped out one article after another
that labeled Iraq's rebelling Shia as Iranians. Official doctrine aimed
at the Sunnis followed: it was this Iranian influence over southern
Iraq that had eaten away at the foundations of the Iraqi state for
decades; as a result, the Iraqi Shia had lost the deep intrinsic understanding of Islam that is characteristic of the true Arab. Dropping its
official line of the Iran-Iraq war that extolled the Shia as loyal Arabs
within Arab Iraq, Baath rhetoric bound the Iraqi Shia in "a dirty, foreign conspiracy" alien to Iraqi nationalism and identity. Yet in the
roaring flames of their rebellion, the Iraqi Shia rebels had declared
time and again that they were revolting against the inequities of the
regime of Saddam Hussein, not against the territorial integrity of the
Iraqi state. And time and again, the Shia claimed they only wanted
what they had always wanted—power and representation in secular
Iraq in proportion to their numbers within the population.

Conversely, when the Kurds rebelled, it was for autonomy within Iraq—or dismemberment of the Iraqi state itself.

STILL EXHAUSTED and demoralized by al-Anfal, the Kurds in August 1990 had pledged their loyalty to Iraq and its leader in the aftermath of the invasion of Kuwait. But as the magnitude of force assembling on the sands of Saudi Arabia foretold Hussein's inevitable defeat, the Kurds grabbed for the opportunity to free themselves from Baghdad. Demonstrating a remarkable degree of unity among its contentious factions, the Kurdish leadership prepared for revolt. As the inevitability of war became clear during the final months of 1990, Kurdish guerrillas left their sanctuaries in Iran to cross over the northern reaches of the Tigris River. Within Iraqi Kurdistan, agents dispatched by the KDP's Massoud Barzani and the PUK's Jalal Talabani quietly infiltrated the *jash*, the Kurds employed by Baghdad whom other Kurds derisively called "donkeys." As the air war raged and the ground war approached ever closer, the joint Kurdish leadership announced, "Several thousand Kurdish *peshmerga* . . . are poised to take control of the biggest population centers of northern Iraq in the event of Saddam Hussein's government collapsing in the face of the allied offensive."[26]

The Kurdish uprising broke on March 4 in the town of Rania, east of Erbil. Memories of Halabjah and al-Anfal drove an enraged and vengeful mob to deface and sack the palatial home of Ali Hassan al-Majid while the Kurdish leadership put its preconceived battle plan into operation. As calculated, the *jash* militia defected to fight alongside the *pesh merga* and their civilian cohorts. Sixty thousand Kurd and non-Kurd armed soldiers defecting from the Iraqi army joined them. Together they took most of the major cities in Iraqi Kurdistan: Erbil, Sulaimaniyah, Jalula, Duhok, and Zakho. With the liberation of Kirkuk on March 20, the Kurds held the whole of northern Iraq.

For almost a month while Hussein ravaged the south, the Kurds lived their dream of Kurdistan. Less than twenty miles north of Erbil, Massoud Barzani granted confident interviews from his luxurious new headquarters, the majestic villa of Saddam Hussein located in

---

[26] Quoted in Michael Gunter, *The Kurds of Iraq: Tragedy and Hope* (New York: St. Martin's Press, 1992), p. 50.

the hill town of Salahuddin. Echoing off the mountains, Kurdistan radio invited foreign journalists to come and visit what it called "liberated Kurdistan" to see "the most splendid victory in the contemporary history of the Kurds."[27]

But the Kurds' defeat would prove as swift as their victory. A week after the rebelling Kurds added oil-rich Kirkuk to their territory, Hussein pulled the Revolutionary Guards out of the spent south and sent it north. Soon the rumble of gunfire echoed across the emerald hills and helicopter gunships, which the cease-fire agreement of the Gulf War allowed Iraq to fly, attacked Kurdish positions near Mosul. The Kurds fought back with medieval ferocity. The tough *pesh mergas* aimed their shoulder-held rockets at the threat from the air and fired their AK-47's against the threat on the ground. The result amounted to little more than mosquitoes attacking a rogue elephant. That left Jalal Talabani, who had so recently ridden triumphantly into Zakho, to plead with the United States and its allies to sustain the uprising and Massoud Barzani to ask the outside world the obvious question: "How can boys and old men stand up to the Republican Guard?"[28]

It was impossible. When warnings of "helicopters" swept over Kirkuk, people who knew the reality of chemical weapons fled in panic. That left perhaps 150,000 soldiers from Hussein's elite units manning the heaviest weaponry in Baghdad's arsenal to retake Kirkuk in hours rather than days. Under intermittent gunfire, a Western reporter saw a man swept up off the street by the Mukhabarat. Inside the terrible prison of the security services, his voice joined the faint but terrible cries of others: "They were the screams not of fear or sharp pain but of . . . long agony."[29]

Across Iraqi Kurdistan, mothers grabbed their children, men rushed from their jobs, and store owners locked their doors in a mad rush to reach the safety of the mountains. At the entrance to the main hospital at Kirkuk, Kurdish doctors stacked the *pesh merga* dead like cordwood and fled as Arab nurses ululated in joy at the prospect of restoration of Baghdad's control. By April 15, as many as two million people were on the move in northern Iraq toward the Iranian and

[27] Ibid.
[28] Quoted in *Time*, April 15, 1991, p. 22.
[29] Quoted in *Economist*, May 4, 1991.

Turkish borders. The pathetic human caravan of refugees filled the roads out of Erbil, Mosul, Duhok, and hundreds of villages. The well-to-do rode in cars, pickup trucks, even donkey, carts piled high with belongings. Other families piled themselves on anything that might carry them into the mountains—overloaded trailers dragged by groaning tractors, wheezing buses formerly employed to transport tourists, even a bulldozer in which a family packed itself into the scoop. Thousands of the poor traveled the only way they could—on foot with their few possessions wrapped in plastic sacks strapped on their backs or tied in blankets precariously balanced on their heads. As the scores of Kurds trekked up into the barren mountains, they passed the cruel reminders of their brutalized past: the stone forts and cement pill boxes built by Hussein to police the Kurds, the stumps and stems of methodically destroyed orchards and vineyards, foundation stones and rusting pipes—the skeletal remains of traditional villages. As the tide of refugees surged, one among the Kurds lamented, "The Iraqis are continuing to herd us to these rocky cemeteries in order to rid themselves of the Kurdish problem once and for all."[30]

ALTHOUGH THE REFUGEE DRAMA continued to play itself out in the high mountains, both the civil war between the Shia Arabs and the Sunni government of Saddam Hussein and the Kurds' war of independence were already over. Encircled by a double ring of enemies, Hussein had pulled together his battered resources from the external war to win the internal war. This was the great and unsavory reality delivered to the surprised coalition that had fought the Gulf War. In declining to become involved in the simultaneous rebellions of the Shia and the Kurds, the United States and every other government that had so decisively executed the swift victory in Kuwait had assumed that Hussein would fail in defeating his internal rivals as badly as he had failed in combating his foreign enemies. But Hussein, whose defiant hopeless stand against international condemnation confirmed his limited intelligence in dealing with the outside world, proved to be the master strategist within the hatred, mass murder, and wanton desecration of the internal war. By this sole measure of political success, gaining and holding power in a domestic environment, Saddam Hussein had proved himself to be a daunting leader

---

[30] Quoted in *Time*, April 15, 1991, p. 23.

in one of the world's most difficult political arenas. Still, the great question lingers as to why simultaneous revolts in the south and north that involved a potential 80 percent of the Iraqi population failed to topple a despised regime that had just suffered the most humiliating defeat in modern warfare. The answer lies in the divisions and complexities of Iraqi society.

The sufferance of the Sunnis more than anything else allowed Hussein to survive the spring of 1991. When the Shia majority broke into full-scale revolt, all the latent fears of the Sunnis within the geographic triangle at the center of the country consumed the collective consciousness. Seeing themselves as the beleaguered minority, the Sunnis knew that if the Shia rebellion reached Baghdad, Sunni blood would flow. Therefore, the decision of whether or not to stand with Hussein shifted from the political issue of preserving Sunni privilege to the gut issue of physical survival. Concern for the survival of the state—the protector of Sunni life and rights—followed. With the Kurdish uprising added to that of the Shia, most individual Sunni Arabs quickly reached the unhappy conclusion that abandonment of Hussein without a realistic alternative government would simply provoke a fierce struggle for power among the competing groups in the Iraqi state. In that struggle, there was no guarantee of the outcome. Iraq's territorial integrity could fray if the Kurds spun off into independence. Iran might enter the chaos to claim southern Iraq, reversing the one success for which Iraqis had sacrificed so much during the terrible war of the preceding decade. The country might splinter into multiple pieces that no one person or group could control. So the Sunnis refused to add any more fuel to the fire encircling Saddam Hussein and his regime. In so doing, they stated their preference for an Iraq intact under the iron fist of Hussein to an Iraq dismembered. This was the same conclusion reached by the United States and its wartime partners who chose to stand and watch while the Shia and Kurdish rebellions were born and died.

Yet while the tacit support of civilian Sunnis proved a great boon, it was the army that guaranteed Hussein's political survival. In those first crucial days in the south, the perception that the Shia revolt held as its goal the creation of an Islamic government stemmed the flow of Shia defections out of the lower echelons of the army that were feeding the rebel forces. When the solidified army of Shia conscripts and Sunni officers linked arms with the Republican Guards, Hussein won salvation. Seeing itself more as the symbol of the nation than the defender of the Baath, the army of Iraq proved far more committed and efficient in crushing internal insurrection than in fighting to preserve Hussein's annexation of Kuwait. After all, defense of the homeland had been the army's mission since its inception under the monarchy. Perhaps to the surprise of the army itself, Baghdad's decades of nation building, the shifting, sometimes absurd, efforts to create a national identity, and the long war with Iran had aroused within the army a genuine desire to hold together the fragile country the British had so poorly conceived. Thus, while many in uniform detested their brutal reckless leader, they refused to consent to the shattering of the nation.

If the Sunnis found some consensus within imperfect criteria, the Shia did not. In spite of the valid question of whether the failure of the United States to intervene sealed the fate of the rebellion in the south, the collapse of the uprising also came from the weaknesses within the Iraqi Shia community. Behind the energy that gave it momentum, the Shia rebellion lacked the tensile strength critical to success. As outsiders in the political process, the Shia proved helpless in sustaining what turned out to be little more than a spontaneous chaotic outburst of rage. Armed largely with emotion, the Shia rebels commanded no organization capable of either mobilizing the masses or directing events. Instead they fragmented between town and tribe. Even though some sheikhs came to the rebellion demanding to march on Baghdad to redress Iraq's historic injustices toward the Shia, the majority of Shia Arab tribesmen probably never joined the uprising. The reasons were as varied as the tribes themselves. In successfully pinning the rebels with the dubious label of Persians belonging to the shrine cities, Hussein's regime succeeded in tapping the tribesmen's Arab identity. Linked to this ethnic rivalry was the fear that if the uprising succeeded, Iran would reach its hand across the border to claim land in southern Iraq belonging to the sheikhs. Other reasons for Shia nonparticipation came out of tribal culture. By tradition, the tribes never became part of the political, intellectual, and theological trends embraced by the Shia in the cities. Therefore, they were simply less ideological and certainly, as compared to the residents of the shrine cities, less religious. No less important, some tribes' sheikhs had been bought by Baghdad for years and remained collaborators with the regime. It was also in the very nature of the tribesmen to remain quiescent even while the south burned. True to their Bedouin heritage, the tribesmen chose not to fight until they were certain which side would win. And finally it was March, the harvest season, when nothing as nebulous as rebellion in the name of political equality could draw the peasants from the fields.

Although the Kurds were far more organized and politically conscious than the Shia, they suffered from their own maladies. There was fear instilled by years of repression by Baghdad. There was ideology, tradition, and politics that divided town from country, tribe from tribe. There was the imperative of survival that kept a percentage of the *jash* tied to Baghdad. And there was self-interest. One wealthy landowner, a tribal chief involved in business dealings all over Iraq, spoke for the category of Kurds who had materially benefited from the economic development policies of the Baath: "Yes, in 1975, when the Kurds were repressed, I stood by. In 1988, when chemical weapons were used against the Kurds, I stood by. In 1991, when the Kurds were driven to the mountains and many thousands died, I stood by. How could I do these things? . . . I have about seven thousand donums of land behind the mountains over there."[31] Finally the Kurds and non-Kurds of northern Iraq who shared the mass flight of 1991 could not turn common suffering into a common destiny. In the cold and miserable refugee camps, a Turkoman who was representative of his people said, "We are not Kurds. We don't want to be ruled by Kurds."[32] And the Assyrian Christians who hung on the side of the mountains with the Kurds nonetheless accused them of denying the non-Kurds their fair share of the relief supplies and of persecuting them on religious grounds.

The tragedy of the Shia and the Kurds in that reckless, heroic spring of 1991 is also the tragedy of Iraq. The rebellions were popular, broad-based movements that engaged people across ethnic and geographic lines. In this sense, they were a unifying event that if successful in toppling Hussein could have, and may yet, provide the foundation on which to build the post-Hussein Iraq. But the rebellions were also divisive in that they reflected the existing fractures in Iraqi society. In the refusal of the Sunni community to join the Shia,

---

[31] Quoted in Makiya, *Cruelty and Silence*, p. 85.
[32] Quoted in *New York Times*, June 6, 1991.

the Arab mystique created during the Iran–Iraq War dissolved in sectarianism. The Kurds remained a suspect and detested element within the Iraqi state. Christians stood apart from Muslims. Town, tribe, and family pursued their own interests at the expense of the common good. Thus, ethnicity and sect, combined with Hussein's military prowess and the failure of the United States and its coalition partners to support the revolts, sentenced the Iraqis to another decade of suffering under the edicts of their malicious leader. The pain that decade would bring upon the land between the two rivers came from both inside and outside tortured Iraq.

9

BROKEN BABYLON

At the turn of the new millennium, winter rains blanketed Baghdad, causing pools of raw sewage to bubble up through pipes broken by war and wear. Even in sunshine, the city was dismal. At its historic center, the archeological museum established by Gertrude Bell in 1923 remained closed, its collection of Mesopotamian artifacts hidden in deep storage to protect it from American air strikes that had hit periodically since the end of the Gulf War. The Mustansiriyah, renowned school of Abbasid Baghdad, encircled a forlorn courtyard where the fountain no longer flowed and flowers no longer grew. The Sunni mosques so carefully tended by the Ottomans needed not only repairs but also the return of missing chandeliers and carpets pilfered by thieves. Along al-Rashid street, stores whose windows displayed the finest of luxury goods during the great oil boom of the 1970s were now crumbling. Everywhere in the city, it was as if the 1991 Gulf War and a decade of postwar economic sanctions had dropped a dark cloak over the capital of Iraq.

On an asphalt rectangle not far from the Mustansiriyah, members of what had once been a prosperous and productive middle class picked through piles of used clothing, while near the slums of al-Thawra, now Saddam City, the lower classes poked through acres of garbage, searching for scraps of food to supplement the monthly rations provided by the United Nations under a program called Oil for Food. As for everyone in this city of four million, daily life had become a quest for survival. Caught between the pincers of a vice— Saddam Hussein and the economic sanctions imposed by the United Nations—Iraqis were struggling for life and hope. A people who in reality and perception trace their heritage to Mesopotamia's urban centers of Ur, Babylon, and Nineveh and to the glittering Baghdad of the Abbasid caliphate, a people whose art and learning flowed out of the salons of the monarchy and who once sat at the feast thrown by the oil boom, were now living in a rural tribal society governed by a tyrant.

No matter how little Saddam Hussein has understood the world beyond his rigidly patrolled borders, he has proved the master strategist in his own domain. From the ruins of war and rebellion in 1991, he rebuilt his imperiled regime by playing Sunni against Shia, Arab against Kurd. And within each of these groups he manipulated tribe against tribe. Today Hussein, dressed in his signature white silk suit, sitting on an ornate Louis XV chair, is the unchallenged leader of a hollow country stripped of civil society. This is his legacy. When he finally loses his grip on power either politically or physically, he will leave Iraq much as it was when the British created it—torn by tribalism and uncertain of its identity. It is this Iraq that threatens to inflict its communal grievances, its decades of noncooperation, and its festering suspicions and entrenched hatreds on the Persian Gulf, the lifeline of the global economy.

IRAQ IN THE SPRING of 1991 lay prostrate, bleeding from the wounds of the Gulf War and exhausted by the convulsions of the Shia and Kurdish uprisings. Baghdad, as the capital and the most technologically developed city in the country, bore the heaviest scars of Hussein's humiliating defeat. The Jumhuriya bridge that spanned the Tigris near Jewad Salim's Freedom Monument to the 1958 revolution was trisected by bombs. Twisted sections of steel and concrete hung from every other bridge that had formerly connected the east and west sides of the river. The central post office looked as if its three remaining walls had been erected only to hide the maze of blackened girders, chunks of cement, and piles of burned letters within. Symbols of authority like the Ministry of Justice had been reduced to empty shells of Baath power. It seemed that only the Victory Arch, Saddam Hussein's monument to the false victory of the Iran-Iraq War, remained unscathed. Baghdad, deprived of its infrastructure, was a city with its bones broken and its tendons cut.

Peace brought no relief. Since the first artillery fire and exploding bombs lit the night sky over Baghdad on January 17, the Baghdadis had lived in silence and darkness, imposed by the destruction of communication towers and electrical grids. With no electricity, 15 million gallons of untreated sewage bypassed sanitation pumps and flowed into the Tigris each day. Doctors trained by some of the best medical institutions in the West performed surgery by flashlight in dark hospitals. On the streets, peddlers sold oil lamps to those in need of light just as the Mesopotamians had done three thousand years ago.

In the hour of its greatest need, the Baath regime's hollow gut was exposed. The bonds of party that in the 1970s had tied member to member, cell to cell, command council to command council had long since unraveled in Hussein's police state. Whatever effective organization and discipline remained in the party disappeared when the rebels of the south and the north declared that the very label "Baathist," whether it was attached to a Sunni, a Shia, or a Kurd, was grounds for assassination. The Baathists who went into the breach in the spring of 1991 to save the regime came out of Hussein's extended tribe or represented die-hard opportunists who feared their loss of position even more than they feared the mob bent on their destruction. They were all that Hussein had to call upon, for he could no longer rally Arab nationalism, socialism, or any other ideology to draw people into the defense of his regime. The only thing left was the figure of the Iraqi president, the feared symbol of the nation. Thus, behind the slogan "Saddam Hussein is Iraq and Iraq is Saddam Hussein," the embattled leader collected the rhetoric of Baathism, deserted what remained of the once tight-knit party organization, and pulled around him all those with a stake in his survival. Then he began his resurrection.

A LITTLE OVER A WEEK after the collapse of the Shia rebellion on March 15, 1991, Hussein reshuffled his cabinet. Forsaking all subtleties, he appointed the Shia Saddoun Hammadi to the position of prime minister and left in place Taha Muhiaddin, the Kurdish vice president.[1] He removed the head of the air force, the army chief of staff, and the commander of each army corps amid rumors that eighteen army officers had been executed in the purge of the military. In a move to rid himself of civilian dissenters, the president ordered the quick processing of exit visas for anyone who wanted to leave Iraq. By the end of April, the situation had stabilized enough to allow sixty

---

[1] Saddoun Hammadi was removed a few months later, a reflection of Hussein's sense of confidence in his political survival.

thousand people of the Tikrit clan to celebrate their leader's fifty-fourth birthday by cheering an immense papier-mâché image of the president's head driven around Tikrit on a flat-bed truck. For the country at large, a television camera positioned in some undisclosed location beamed to the nation pictures of a smiling Saddam Hussein, the self-declared national symbol.

By July, even the most cynical Iraqis were expressing some degree of admiration for the rapid reconstruction of power plants, critical bridges, and essential buildings destroyed by allied bombing during the Gulf War. Electricity flowed, constantly or partially, to most areas and some phone lines once more crackled with sound. The government sponsored concerts, plays, art exhibitions, and fashion shows. On the bank of the Tigris, reconstruction began on Hussein's main palace, the massive "Home of the People." South of Baghdad, at the entrance to Babylon, new signs proclaimed "From Nebuchadnezzar to Saddam Hussein, Babylon rises again."

In August, a year after the invasion of Kuwait, Hussein pinned several pounds of medals, hung multiple sashes, and awarded honorary swords to his top lieutenants from the "Mother of all Battles." In October, he told a nationwide television audience that in the Gulf War, Iraq had been like the woman who had chosen to be killed rather than submit to rape. It was all part of a long-term survival strategy against the economic sanctions imposed on Iraq by the UN Security Council at the end of the Gulf War.

An element of the sanctions regimen was a ban on all air traffic in and out of Iraq. Consequently, anyone headed to Baghdad, except officials of the United Nations, climbed into a taxi in Jordan's Amman to make an arduous twelve-hour trip across the desert. In the nineteenth century, when overland was the only way to go, rhythmically swaying camels, tinkling bells, and star-lit nights bestowed a touch of romance to the long trip. Now there were only gas fumes and rutted roads.

For a short while the full impact of the economic blockade was hidden among the goods looted from Kuwait and in the printing-press money pumped into the economy. Despite astronomical prices, buyers patronized select food shops that sold German beer, Swiss chocolate, and French pâté. But month by month, a population once fattened on oil revenues began to feel the pain of a total economic embargo. By the fall of 1991, a sack of rice that before the war cost 12 dinars now demanded 750; a box of eggs once purchased for 2 dinars sold for 14; a single can of infant formula costing 1 dinar in July 1990 now required 16.

For people outside the regime, there was no way to keep up with inflation. The Iraqi government, as in the days of the oil boom, remained the major employer, but the generous salaries paid to civil servants, doctors, and university professors who once had filled the ranks of a proud middle class shrunk to a pittance in the rampant inflation. To supplement what little money trickled into their hands, the former stars of the Baath's economic development policies began to sell anything unnecessary for survival. Used wristwatches flooded the pawnshops, and jewelry, often wedding jewelry, passed to dealers. When those were gone, families stripped their homes of carpets, furniture, paintings, silverware, bric-a-brac—anything that would produce money for food. Some would say these were the trinkets of materialism. But there was more. Along a yellow-brick passageway in Baghdad's Souk al-Sarrai, Iraqi intellectuals squatted beside their precious books, some of which were selling for what amounted to fifteen cents apiece. In this sad sidewalk market, the final decline of Baghdad as an old and distinguished intellectual center had begun.

Given the increasing hardship suffered by the Iraqi population, the United Nations dispatched a mission in July 1991 to assess the country's humanitarian needs. Another team from Harvard University issued its own report in August, concluding that in the months since the sanctions had been imposed, the child mortality rate had doubled while the death rate among children under five had tripled. In the face of such human suffering, the UN Security Council authorized Iraq to sell up to $1.6 billion in oil every three months. Proceeds went into a special UN fund to buy food and medicine. Ready to sacrifice his own people to his goal of throwing off the sanctions without bending to the dictates of the United Nations, Hussein refused the offer on the grounds of encroachment on Iraq's sovereignty. In doing so, the Iraqi president denied the Iraqi population what was at the time 65 percent of its food needs and 80 percent of its medicine. Massive starvation was held at bay only by government rationing financed in mysterious ways. Reviving a system used during the Iran-Iraq War, the government authorized fifty thousand private shops, acting as agents for the state, to sell to a family—at subsidized prices on a monthly basis—seventeen pounds of wheat flour, three pounds of rice, half a pound of cooking oil, three pounds of sugar, a little over three pounds of baby milk, and two ounces of tea. But even subsidized prices were out of reach for many in a period of hyperinflation. Widespread hunger sent women to walk over harvested fields to glean the stray grains of wheat and barley left behind. It was as if the clock had been turned back to the time of ancient Mesopotamia.

The aim of the sanctions laid on Iraq was not to punish the Iraqi people but to deny Saddam Hussein another arsenal, especially one that included weapons of mass destruction. The reasoning of the Security Council followed the logic that an economic embargo against the sale of Iraqi oil would force such hardship on the country that Hussein would find himself with no choice but to surrender what remained of his missiles and unconventional weapons. This was the quid pro quo: surrender of weapons lifts the sanctions. But as with so much related to the Iraqi dictator, those who wrote the formula failed to understand Hussein's determination to protect his arsenal. From Hussein's perspective, just the threat that he might someday unleash biological and chemical weaponry on his neighbors guaranteed that he remained a world figure, not just another tyrant presiding over what was in danger of becoming a starving Third World country. And weapons of terror provided his ultimate hold over his own people. Thus, Hussein began his tactical war of "cheat and retreat" with UN arms inspectors. The pattern had been set for the next seven years.[2] In the meantime, once wealthy Iraq sank further and further toward the old Iraqi phrase *amara al-hijara*, a poor principality of stones.

By 1995, the value of the dinar, which had been worth $3.00 in 1979, the year Saddam Hussein assumed the presidency, had fallen to 2,500 to the dollar. In April of that year, the UN Security Council, in recognition of the level of human suffering in Iraq, adopted Resolution 986. In essence, it expanded the terms of the earlier one, Resolution 687, which permitted Iraq to sell oil in order to buy food and medicine. Once more, Hussein refused the offer. Yet on October 15, 1995, when eight million Iraqis went to the polls to cast a vote on the question "Do you agree that Saddam Hussein should be president of Iraq?" an overwhelming 99.96 percent consented. In celebration

<hr />

[2] See chapter 10.

of the result, Ali Hassan al-Majid wrote of the ordained president, "O lofty mountain! O glory of Iraq! By God we have always found you in the most difficult conditions a roaring lion and courageous horseman, one of the few true men."[3] In reality, the electoral exercise had confirmed that the Iraqis' fear of Hussein overrode the severe hardships resulting from their leader's sacrificial offering of them to the sanctions. Iraqi motivation was understandable. On any night in Baghdad and every other city in Iraq, a white Toyota with tinted windows idled at every major street corner. Inside, green-bereted members of the security services totally committed to protecting Hussein's regime at any cost stared out at everyone who passed. A taxi driver who whispered through the darkness of Sadoun street spoke for perhaps all ordinary Iraqis: "Believe me, ma'am, I am very afraid."[4] Huddled in their seemingly endless impoverishment, the Iraqis are still afraid. Yet in the end, it is the bitter rivalries and the endemic divisions between and within groups that form Iraqi society that have done so much to enable Saddam Hussein to survive war, rebellion, and sanctions.

THE MASSES OF KURDISH REFUGEES of 1991 were still clinging to the mountains of northern Iraq when Hussein invited Jalal Talabani of the Patriotic Union of Kurdistan (PUK) to Baghdad to discuss Kurdish rights as stated in the March 1970 manifesto. In full view of television cameras and foreign reporters, Talabani, in his customary beige polyester leisure suit, embraced and kissed Hussein on each cheek as if al-Anfal and the Kurdish rebellion had never happened. On that April 24, 1991, he was not alone. Nashirwan Barzani, nephew of Massoud Barzani of the Kurdistan Democratic Party (KDP), was there, too.[5] But it was Talabani who triumphantly announced the substance of the talks. Hussein had agreed to Kurdish autonomy, an end to the Arabization of Iraqi Kurdistan, and the safe passage home for the refugees of the Kurdish rebellion. For their part, the Kurds had agreed to an Iraqi military presence in the Kurdish area. According to Talabani, even that played to Kurdish demands: "We cannot remove

---

[3] Quoted in Andrew Cockburn and Patrick Cockburn, *Out of the Ashes: The Resurrection of Saddam Hussein* (New York: HarperCollins, 1999), p. 202.

[4] Quoted in *Economist*, July 20, 1991.

[5] The Kurdistan Workers Party and the Kurdistan Socialist Party were also represented.

all of the army from Kurdistan. This is Iraq."[6] Ignoring the lessons of
the past, all that the Kurds saw at this moment was a new security
derived from internal cohesion forged in rebellion. In the euphoria
of the moment, most of Iraq's Kurds believed that the glue of Kurdish
identity would, in Talabani's words, "prevent any party from [again]
sabotaging [Kurdish] unity."[7]

By May 30, most Kurdish refugees, reassured by their leaders and
protected by an American-British air umbrella over northern Iraq,
had trekked back down the mountains and into their homes. That
left only eight thousand refugees still camped on the Turkish border.
On June 7, the American military that had delivered relief to the
Kurds in Operation Provide Comfort passed those who remained
into the care of the UN High Commissioner for Refugees.[8] It was then
that Talabani once more spoke for the Kurds: "Saddam tried to crush
us and failed. We tried and failed to bring down his government. Now
we are both looking for a political and peaceful solution. A new page
will be turned in relations between the Baath Party and the Kurdish
front."[9]

But by late June, negotiations between Baghdad and the Kurds
frayed when Hussein demanded that the Kurds sign a six-point document called "The Kurdistan Front's Commitments toward the
Homeland." Each of its articles drained the essentially autonomous
region not only of its military muscle but also of its emotional link
to Kurdish nationalism. The price of peace between Baghdad and the
Kurds required that all militias belonging to the Kurdistan Front surrender their arms to the central authority of the state and then dis-
band; transfer to Baghdad all radio stations owned by the Kurdish
Front; and cease Kurdish cooperation with all states inside and outside the region. The Kurdistan Front was also to commit itself to
"developing the masses' awareness with regard to love for the homeland and readiness to defend it until martyrdom."[10] This encompassed cooperation with Baghdad in the implementation of a

---

[6] Quoted in *New York Times*, May 9, 1991.

[7] Jalal Talabani quoted in ibid.

[8] See chapter 10 for the U.S. response to the Kurdish refugee crisis at the end of the
Gulf War.

[9] Quoted in Milton Viorst, "Report from Baghdad," *The New Yorker*, June 24, 1991, 71.

[10] Cited in Michael M. Gunter, *The Kurds of Iraq: Tragedy and Hope* (New York: St.
Martin's Press, 1992), p. 71.

national program designed to spread "correct national awareness" in order to create commitment to and respect for the Iraqi state.

In the stalemate that followed the dictate, neither side moved to upset the delicate balance of power between Hussein, in control of the lowlands, and the Kurds, burrowed in the hills. Rather, each flexed its muscle against the other. On August 4, the KDP and PUK tacitly approved the incursion of Turkey into Iraq for the purpose of attacking the camps of the Kurdistan Workers Party (KPP), a faction of Turkish Kurds that Istanbul considered the mortal enemy of a unified Turkey. Baghdad was neither asked permission for, nor informed of, a military action that took place within the American-enforced no-fly zone above the thirty-sixth parallel. But below the thirty-sixth parallel, the Kurds outside the no-fly zone, guarded solely by lightly armed *pesh mergas* positioned behind dirt embankments, continued to maintain their autonomy only at the sufferance of the Iraqi president. In November, Hussein, angry about the distance the Kurds were putting between themselves and Baghdad, sent them a message of his displeasure. Laying his own edict on top of the UN sanctions already in force, Hussein banned Kurdish trade with Baghdad. The embargo included the transport of humanitarian supplies provided to the Kurds by international relief agencies. As supplies of food and fuel grew short, the Iraqi army moved steadily northward to occupy a ridge line above the Erbil hills. Shut off from the lowlands and dependent on supply lines through Turkey, the Kurds' stocks of food shrank, vehicles and machinery broke down, medicine disappeared, and prices spiraled. Suddenly refugee camps in the high mountains of northern Iraq that had been nearly empty in May overflowed with perhaps 400,000 new arrivals.

The Kurdish civil authority fought off paralysis. But the Kurds themselves, who had held such hope that the spring uprising had delivered the idealized Kurdistan, watched helplessly as thieves among them stole precious food and vehicles. Corrupt officials within the provisional government looted literally anything, including the entire inventory of a warehouse filled with cigarette filters, and moved the goods across the border to markets in Iran. Outside the cities, local militia commanders seized control of whole areas of the autonomous region and turned them into personal fiefdoms. Meanwhile, each member of the Kurdish Front, the unified command that led the uprising and now administered the Kurdish enclave, held the right of veto over every issue demanding action by the civil authority.

In the anarchy, Massoud Barzani proposed an election for both a legislative council and a supreme Kurdish leader. To run for office, a candidate was required to be a resident of Kurdistan, at least thirty years old, literate, sane, free from conviction for murder, and innocent of any crimes committed under the auspices of Baghdad. On May 19, 1992, the Kurds went to the polls. The result, however, was tarnished by a flawed electoral process that included everything from multiple votes—cast by individuals who used acid from old car batteries to wipe off the ink applied to a voter's hand—to the regulation that stated a party must win at least 7 percent of the vote to qualify for a seat in parliament. This 7 percent requirement shut out every party except the KDP and PUK. And the multiple voting left in doubt who had won the contest for leader: the KDP's Massoud Barzani with 44.6 percent of the vote, or the PUK's Jalal Talabani with 44.3 percent. This confusion guaranteed continuing deadlock within the infant political system of the Kurdish enclave. Even so, the historic election, as seen within the larger picture of Kurdish autonomy, was regarded by many Iraqi Kurds as a firm step toward independence. As a result, the new government with Barzani as its leader forged ahead despite an economy devastated by sanctions and territory seeded with land mines.

From the capital of Erbil, the Kurdish administration launched an educational system grounded in the Kurdish language; appointed a police force; and established a bureaucracy responsible for levying taxes, collecting garbage, and delivering mail. Even before the election, the Kurdish Front had created a source of income for itself by trucking oil across the border with Turkey. The twenty to twenty-five thousand barrels a day delivered to the Turkish market brought foodstuffs and other necessities back the other way. In the growing confidence, portraits of a half-dozen Kurds prominent in a century of nationalist struggle went up on Sulaimaniyah's main traffic circle, and signs planted along the boundaries of the Kurdish enclave read, "Welcome to liberated Kurdistan." Even though the new Kurdish government carefully flew the Iraqi flag and outfitted its police in Iraqi uniforms to fend off Turkish and Iranian fears of an independent Kurdistan, statehood by stealth seemed a reality.

Attempting to strengthen Kurdish unity, Massoud Barzani, as the

Kurdish leader, took over the best hotel in the mountain resort of Shaqlawa for a daylong meeting with a hundred or so tribal leaders who had staffed the *jash*, the Kurds who had collaborated with Baghdad. Their past sins were buried, their recent actions applauded, and their future cooperation in defending oil-rich Kirkuk beseeched as they were welcomed into the fold of the Kurdish authority. Henceforth, these "little donkeys" who had served as the eyes and ears of the Iraqi military, who had tracked down and eliminated the *pesh mergas*, would be called "armed revolutionaries."

Yet despite the outward signs of unity, all the fault lines that ran through Kurdish politics soon began to reopen. The most obvious appeared in the question of leadership. Although both were interested in moving the fragile statelet forward, Barzani and Talabani refused to trot in a double harness. In the intense rivalry, each of the two leaders devoted himself to besting the other and his party. Consequently, each jockeyed for support from powers on the borders of Kurdish territory—Talabani from Iran, Barzani from Turkey. Both pursued the United States, whose aircraft flew over northern Iraq guarding against any incursion by Saddam Hussein, and tended lines of communication with their common enemy in Baghdad.

By July of 1993, the Kurdistan Democratic Party and Patriotic Union of Kurdistan were gridlocked. To maintain a semblance of cooperation, a KDP minister automatically required a PUK deputy and a PUK minister, a KDP assistant. The system operated all the way down to the tea servers who worked in every government office. Still the dream of Kurdistan survived in both symbolism and reality. In the fall of 1993, the body of Mullah Mustafa Barzani was raised from its grave in Iran, flown by helicopter to the border of Iraq, transferred to a van, and escorted across the mountains to his ancestral village of Barzan, first by Barzani's former disciple Jalal Talabani and then by his son Massoud. Fourteen years after his death, the body of the most famous of all Kurdish patriots was lowered into the ground of what his descendants now regarded as Kurdistan.

The symbolism was not enough to contain the escalating power struggle between the PUK and KDP. By early 1994, they confronted each other along the great tracks of geography, linguistics, and sociology. As the representatives of the Kurds' urban branch, the PUK controlled the cities of Erbil and Sulaimaniyah in the Sorani-speaking areas east of the Greater Zab River. The KDP ruled along the Turkish border in Kurmanji-speaking, largely rural territory to the north and west of the Greater Zab. With tensions exacerbated by the UN embargo on Iraq, Hussein's boycott against the Kurdish region, and the failure of the West to extend adequate money to finance the enclave's operations and pay its civil servants, the Kurdish factions began shooting at each other in May 1994. Whether in tandem with or independent of the PUK and KDP, almost every militia of every tribe contributed to the mounting turmoil.

In June 1994, the human rights organization Amnesty International implored Kurdish leaders to cease killing and mutilating prisoners in their custody as well as abducting, killing, and torturing civilians on the basis of their political ties. In the melee, parliamentary sessions ceased, international aid agencies questioned their mission, and disgusted Kurds on both sides of the divide charged that the Kurdish authority was committing political suicide. Although a cease-fire went into effect at the end of August, it failed to end the contest between the two main Kurdish factions for outright control of the Kurdish enclave.

Combat in what had become a civil war erupted again in December. The immediate issue was the border point of Khabur, the one significant asset in the whole administrative territory. Every tanker truck filled with Iraqi diesel fuel and headed for the Turkish market lined up to pay tolls amounting to hundreds of millions of dollars a year. The problem was that Khabur lay in territory controlled by Barzani. While the dual system of KDP and PUK officials in every government job ensured that at least a portion of the money derived from the illicit oil trade went into the coffers of the Kurdish authority, most of it went into the treasury of the Barzani clan. For his part in what was a duel of grievances, Talabani refused to share power in Erbil, the administrative capital of the Kurdish enclave and home to one-fifth of its population. In the standoff, Amnesty International once more spoke out: "It is an outrage that the Kurds— having suffered gross human rights violations for so long at the hands of the Iraqi forces—should once again have to endure such abuses, only this time at the hands of their own political leaders."[11]

---

[11] Amnesty International USA, "Iraq Human Rights Abuses in Iraqi Kurdistan Since 1991," New York, February 1995.

The appeal fell on deaf ears as a multitude of smaller but significant power centers among the tribes and urban Kurds, each in pursuit of its own interests, added its weight to the fray. As for the principals, the PUK and KDP, the autonomous Kurdish region they had won by rebellion and cunning no longer mattered as much as each faction's ambition for dominance.

In early 1996, the KDP and the PUK were running a guerrilla war against each other across great swaths of the same territory. Talabani's PUK held the edge because of weapons and logistical support from Iran, earned by patrolling the Islamic republic's own troublesome Kurds. But neither the PUK nor the KDP commanded the hearts and minds of the majority of Kurds. In the internecine combat, people who had lined up by the thousands in 1992 to donate blood for victims of an Iraqi-planted car bomb now turned a deaf ear to televised appeals for blood to aid militiamen wounded by other militiamen. Disgusted with the regional government's infighting, stampeded by high prices, taxed at rival checkpoints, and harassed by one militia or another, hundreds of desperately needed doctors, engineers, professors, and other professionals of every political persuasion sold off their belongings and went abroad. The intertribal war went on without them.

On August 17, the PUK militarily attacked the KDP in its own territory on the fiftieth anniversary of its founding. The hard-pressed KDP denounced Iran for providing artillery and helicopter support to the PUK and warned that Baghdad was poised to reassert its control of the north in the name of opposing Iran. In retrospect, it was a way of saying that Massoud Barzani and his party had struck a deal with the devil to fend off their rival. Blanking out memories of the murder of three of his brothers, more than eight thousand of his clansmen, and tens of thousands of ordinary Iraqi Kurds, Barzani summoned Hussein to drive Talabani and the PUK out of Erbil.

On August 31 between four and five o'clock in the morning, three hundred artillery pieces belonging to Baghdad fired upon Erbil from the east, west, and south. Half an hour later, 350 Iraqi tanks began to advance, followed by thirty to forty thousand Iraqi troops, principally the Republican Guards. Directly in their path was Qushtapa, where Hussein had sent the Barzani women and children after the massacre in 1983. It was also the headquarters of the Iraqi National Congress and its support team from the U. S. Central Intelligence Agency (CIA).[12] Under covering fire provided by Baghdad, *pesh mergas* belonging to the KDP routed the lightly armed PUK forces while Hussein's secret police swept up opponents of the Barzani tribe and members of the CIA-financed Iraqi opposition. Using information provided by the KDP, Baghdad's secret police, sometimes dressed as Kurds, systematically hunted down their prey. With Talabani's forces falling back in disarray toward the Iranian border and Barzani in control of Erbil, Hussein pulled his military forces back. In the settling dust, the KDP ripped down the green banner of the PUK and raised its own yellow flag over buildings housing the Kurdish authority. At the end of a successful collaboration, neither Massoud Barzani nor senior KDP officials seemed ashamed of their betrayal of the Kurdish cause. All that mattered was that their tribe had survived the challenge to its interests and authority.

But despite Barzani's declaration of sole leadership of the Kurdish enclave, Talabani refused to relinquish his own claim. From the security of valleys hidden along the Iranian border, the PUK regrouped, replenished its weapons, and prepared to re-establish itself in the command structure of northern Iraq. On October 13, six weeks after being driven out of Erbil, the PUK with its arsenal of Iranian weapons swept down on Sulaimaniyah, a hundred miles to the southeast. The KDP retreated westward until Saddam Hussein sent word that he would dispatch his tanks if the PUK advanced beyond the bridge at Degla.

After Talabani's collusion with Iran and Barzani's perfidy with Hussein caused the loss of hundreds of Kurdish fighters and civilians, united Kurdistan all but evaporated. What remained were two regions: one held by the Iran-supported PUK, the other by the Baghdad-protected KDP. After one more round of fighting that confirmed Hussein's ability to enter any part of Kurdish territory at will, the Kurds borrowed the old Bedouin saying, "Kiss your enemy if you cannot kill him." Thus, Talabani joined Barzani in dispatching emissaries to Baghdad. As if to reinforce the message that the Kurds remained part of the Iraqi state, they were received by Ali Hassan al-Majid, "Ali Chemical" of al-Anfal.

Today access to any part of landlocked Iraqi Kurdistan is con-

---

[12] See chapter 12.

trolled by Turkey, Iran, Syria, or Baghdad. Movement between the eastern and western parts of the Kurdish enclave depends on jealous warlords who run territories essentially autonomous from each other. Benefiting from the protection provided by American and British air cover, the Kurds operate two relatively autonomous governments, each of which possesses its own institutions and its own education system structured on its own particular dialect. Although each government has succeeded in living just outside the grip of the Iraqi state, each has also drained away any Kurdish unity. Like their ancestors in the Kurdish national cause, the KDP and PUK have defeated the effort to win their own nation. In this most recent round of intercommunal rivalry, they have surrendered to Baghdad and to Arab Iraq the Kurdish rebellion of 1991, which now stands next to the Shia uprising in Saddam Hussein's trophy case.

IN THE SPRING OF 1991, Hussein had turned back the Shia onslaught against his regime, first by blocking the spread of the Shia insurrection into the slums of Baghdad and then by crushing the revolting Shia farther south. Next he acted to consolidate his hold on the majority of Iraq's population. Here his moves proved more subtle than the hammer blows on the Kurds. But ultimately for the life of the regime, they were more important. Although the potential loss of rich, oil-producing Kurdish areas around Kirkuk posed an ominous economic threat to Baghdad, it was the possibility that the Shia might spin out of the orbit of the central government, taking with them the bulk of the population as well as Iraq's only outlet to the sea, that foretold disaster. Consequently, Hussein had to secure the south not only for the sake of his own regime but also for the survival of the Iraqi state.

In July, three months after crushing the southern rebellion, the Iraqi president, flanked by prominent Shia leaders, repeatedly appeared on television to explain away the humiliation of the Gulf War. Comparing himself to Imam Hussein who had died at Karbala at the hands of his Sunni foes, the president said that he had not lost the Gulf War but rather had martyred himself to superior force. In private meetings with tribal sheikhs, Saddam Hussein sought his salvation through three simultaneous strategies: destruction of the environment of the Marsh Arabs, division of the Shia in the shrine cities from the Shia of the countryside, and revival of the power of the tribes.

The vast marshes, covering regions of southeastern Iraq, had plagued governments since the time of ancient Mesopotamia. In the sixth century B.C., the Chaldeans escaped the Assyrians by fleeing into the thick reeds of the swamps near Babylon. From those same reeds, the marshmen defied the Romans and Sassanians. Living on islands of flotsam, they ignored the Arab armies. It was later, by choice, not coercion, that the marshmen became Muslims and adopted the Arabic language. But that was as far as they would go in accommodating the forces outside their own universe. Refusing to bend to the will of the Ottomans, the British, and the Iraqi state, the Madan, or Marsh Arabs, continued their centuries-old tradition of harboring renegades and expediting smuggling through the maze of passageways through the reeds. Although challenged by the swamps' negative aspects, the monarchy, during its latter years, came to see the marshes as an important component in the development of a richer agricultural sector for the Iraqi economy. Success depended on capturing the waters of the Tigris and Euphrates that fed the marshes and diverting it to irrigation. With this goal, the 1951 Haigh Report, drafted by British engineers in the employ of the Iraqi government, proposed the first scheme to drain the marshlands. It envisioned collecting the waters of the Tigris by digging a large, high-banked channel through the main Amarah marsh. Construction of this channel actually began in 1953, with another phase initiated by republican Iraq in the 1960s. During the oil boom, the Baath considered further drainage as part of its own grand economic development schemes. But during the Iran-Iraq War, the denial of water to the swamps passed out of the realm of economics to the realm of defense. If the wetlands were drained, the transportation routes used by Islamic revolutionaries stealing into Iraq from Iran would disappear. Since the draining could not be accomplished during the heat of war, the marshes were still there to shield the Shia rebels during the *intifadah*. In the aftermath of the Shia rebellion of 1991, the Haigh plan found new life. This time the purpose was to obliterate the life and culture of the Marsh Arabs in order to bend them to the will of Baghdad.

By 1993, the Iraqi government was depriving roughly two-thirds of the marshlands the waters of the Tigris and Euphrates that supported their ecosystems.[13] Without the flushing effects of constantly

---

[13] Dam projects in Turkey at the source of the rivers has also contributed to shrinking the marshes.

flowing water, salt collected on soggy soil and the reeds died, leaving the abundant wildlife without cover or food. In what had become a wasteland, the Madan dragged their boats, animals, and produce through hip-deep mud. Unable to survive economically, they left the marshes to settle as refugees across the border in Iran or migrated into the towns along the disappearing swamps. Others simply died. More than anything, death seemed Baghdad's primary purpose in building the highly touted Saddam River Irrigation Project described by the United Nations as "the environmental crime of the century." In January 1995, the European Parliament passed a resolution characterizing the Marsh Arabs as a persecuted minority whose very survival was threatened by the Iraqi government. This conclusion was confirmed by an official Iraqi document found by anti-Hussein resistance forces in the remaining marshes along the Iranian border. It contained instructions to the Iraqi army operating in the area to "withdraw all foodstuffs, ban the sale of fish, poison the water and burn the villages."[14]

In transforming the unique way of life of the Marsh Arabs, Saddam Hussein has perpetrated the equivalent of his al-Anfal against the Kurds. By drying up the marshes, Baghdad has committed physical and cultural genocide against a whole segment of Iraq's population. It has succeeded to the extent that a refugee poet from the marshes must now lament the fate of his people from the damp cold of London. Rashid al-Khayyum says, "The Madan are now forced to live on the land with people with whom they share little. When they can, they return to the little islands left in the shrunken marsh to feel again their ancient past."[15]

As he destroyed the environment of the Marsh Arabs, Hussein assaulted the shrine cities of Najaf and Karbala, vowing to eradicate the last vestiges of authentic clerical influence among the Shia. After the *intifadah*, Muhammad Bakr al-Hakim, the proponent of Islamic government, continued to operate from across the border in Iran. But the regime regarded his Supreme Council for the Islamic Revolution in Iraq as more of a nuisance than a real threat. Al-Hakim was Persian, his organization stood for a theocracy in Iraq, and the leader and his followers were tainted by support for Iran during the

[14] U.S. State Department Dispatch, March 1995.
[15] Interview with author, London, October 5, 1999.

Iran-Iraq War and as beneficiaries of financial and military aid from the Islamic republic over the years since that war.

Baghdad was far more interested in containing Grand Ayatollah Abu al-Qasim al-Khoei, the cleric who had attempted to restore order in Najaf during the 1991 *intifadah*. At the time, al-Khoei, the most respected cleric of Shia Iraq, was ninety-one years old. A traditional cleric rather than a political ayatollah who followed the theology of the late Ruhollah Khomeini that merged religion and politics, al-Khoei had always preached that involvement in politics corrupted the faithful. Nevertheless, Hussein demanded al-Khoei's presence as the Iraqi president began his resurrection following the Shia rebellion. As soon as Najaf fell to Hussein's forces, members of internal security ushered the grand ayatollah and his son into a car that whisked them to Baghdad. There the cleric was placed before television cameras to denounce the Shia rebellion. Haltingly, al-Khoei "thanked God for enabling His Excellency the President to quell the sedition [and] prayed that God would exalt President Saddam in this world and the hereafter."[16] Eventually al-Khoei was sent to a heavily guarded house in Kufa where the frail old man who lay on a divan received a parade of foreign visitors brought by the government. On command, he said essentially the same thing to everyone: "What happened in Najaf and other cities is not allowed and is against God. Nobody visits me, so I don't know what is happening." On occasion he added, "I have trouble with my breathing."[17] It was not long before al-Khoei succumbed to the ravages of age.

On August 9, 1992, the day of the ayatollah's funeral, Iraqi authorities cut the telephone lines to the holy city of Najaf. A curfew followed, curtailing the movement of the thousands of mourners expected to gather in Najaf to pay their respects to the deceased ayatollah. Although the authorities announced three days of official mourning in grudging acknowledgment of al-Khoei's stature, the funeral itself was restricted to a brief private family ceremony. Afterward, Baghdad continued its repression of the Shia clergy.

In 1998, Special UN Investigator Max van der Stoel asserted that the regime was engaged in the murder of Shia clerics in order to silence dissent. The following year, Baghdad's victims included the Grand Ayatollah Muhammad Sadeq al-Sadr and his two sons, who

---

[16] *New York Times*, March 22, 1991.
[17] Quoted in Cockburn and Cockburn, *Out of the Ashes*, p. 27.

were shot to death in Najaf. The country's leading Shia cleric by
appointment of Baghdad, al-Sadr had been seen as closely aligned
with the Iraqi government. But the relationship soured when the
cleric issued a *fatwa* in which he instructed his followers to attend
Friday prayers in the mosques instead of watching state-run television. Suspecting that the ayatollah was attempting to establish an
independent base of power, the regime eliminated the most public
face of Shia Islam in Iraq. Today in Najaf and Karbala as well as in
Baghdad's Kadhimain shrine, clerics are virtually absent. In their
place are mosque administrators and portraits of Hussein in which
the Iraqi president is leading the prayers. Yet despite crushing the
Shia clergy, the real key to Saddam Hussein's survival in the south is
the well-orchestrated resuscitation of tribalism.

TRIBALISM HAS PLAYED a major role in the politics of Mesopotamia
ever since the time of the Ottomans. Over four centuries of Turkish
rule, the tribe functioned as a ministate in possession of its own
ruler, military force, and code of laws. When Faisal I arrived in
Mesopotamia to mount the throne of Iraq, he confronted great
tribal confederations resistant to control by a central government.
With their rifles and tribal flags, they signaled to Baghdad that
much of the energy of the new Iraqi state would be devoted to tam-
ing the tribes.

The monarchy created a national army that conscripted the
tribesmen. And it drew the sheikhs into the power structure with
gifts of land, money, and prestige. In consequence, tribalism began
to wane as the values of modernization undercut the values of the
tribes. After the monarchy fell, the chaotic decade of 1958–68 saw
the sheikhs increasingly identify themselves by social class at the
expense of their sectarian and tribal identities. But with the Baath
coup of 1968, a new tribalism began to take form as the Tikritis
around Hassan al-Bakr and Saddam Hussein replaced party ideo-
logues and non-Baathist military officers with their own kin. Other
Sunnis of the countryside entered the circle of the Baath through the
government-ordained Committee of the Tribes. During the 1970s, traditional tribalism, from which the challenges to Baghdad had always
come, underwent a subtle assault as the Baath attempted to sell the
Mesopotamian myth to the Iraqi people. In the flush of the oil boom,
the regime branded *taqalid*, tribal traditions, as primitive, anachro-

nistic, and at odds with Iraqi nationalism. That policy reversed during the war with Iran when Arabism returned as the official doctrine of identity, bestowing new life on tribalism.

In the dislocations of war, Iraqis from every region and class retreated into the walls of family. Families in turn renewed their ties to their larger kinship group that through history had provided individuals their only dependable form of security. In this natural revival of tribalism, Saddam Hussein sought to strengthen his own security through the tribes of the Sunni triangle. In addition to the Tikritis, who already dominated all areas of government essential to the political survival of the president, Hussein invited the tribes around Tikrit to send their sons into the Republican Guards and the even more elite Special Guards. These two organizations provided the regime with a crucial shield against the officer corps of the army, which was mired in the stalemated war with Iran. When manpower needs reached critical levels in the latter stages of the war, less geographically favored tribes took over the countryside from the People's Army, the Baath militia, that had been sent to the war front. In expediency and need, tribalism came back in vogue. When Hussein toured the trenches in 1987–88 during the last stages of the Iran-Iraq War, he routinely asked soldiers to name their tribal affiliation. On the home front, tribal sheikhs who publicly pledged allegiance to Iraq's leader won recognition and perks for themselves and their tribes. Re-enforcing this tribal renaissance, the state-controlled media extolled the tribal values of prowess, courage, valor, honor, and revenge. Thus, the pieces were in place in the spring of 1991 when Hussein reached out to tribalism, previously the bane of the Iraqi state, to save himself and his regime.

At the edge of the abyss created by Shia rage, Hussein quickly moved to co-opt any Shia tribal sheikh who shared with the Iraqi president the same cultural values. It was not difficult to find such sheikhs. After all, Saddam Hussein was himself the product of a tribal family, and he had long used traditional tribal values "to build loyalty to himself as the republican sheikh, the father of his people, the essential Iraqi."[18] Now he would utilize the tribes to rule in the manner of a wise tribal grandfather who dispenses justice, wealth, and punishment.

[18] Judith Yaphe, "Tribalism in Iraq, the Old and the New," *Middle East Policy* 7, no. 3 (June 2000): 53.

On March 17, 1991, only two days after the Republican Guards retook Karbala, Hussein invited to the presidential palace in Baghdad certain Shia tribal sheikhs whom he touted as prominent individuals in the "masses of the great Iraqi people."[19] When the rebellion died, the president personally received a delegation of major sheikhs who lowered their *aghals* to the leader of Iraq. The *aghal*, the looped black cord that holds the *gutra*, or headcloth, in place, is highly symbolic in tribal culture. Its forcible removal constitutes dishonor, necessitating the shedding of blood to remove personal shame. Its voluntary surrender implies personal humiliation, again requiring bloodshed to restore honor. Yet in the presence of Hussein, each man removed his *aghal*, essentially surrendering his honor to the president, the sheikh *mashayikh*, the chief of chiefs.

In a sense, the celebration of tribalism represented Saddam Hussein's newest cultural device intended to bridge the Sunni-Shia divide. Suddenly urban party functionaries who had so recently deplored the sheikhs as venal products of the ignorant countryside began to turn up at important tribal funerals. In selected locations in the south, the regime established its own tribal gathering place, the "Guest House of the Lord of the President." Within each, Hussein's representatives conducted a tribalized version of bureaucracy by engaging in daylong conversations with tribal leaders. At the same time, the president himself began to incorporate tribal expressions into his speeches in order to stress his own tribal roots. Inside the presidential palace, he instructed invited tribal chiefs to perform the *hosa*, the signature dance of the tribes. They responded by strapping on their rifles, hoisting their tribal flags, and circling to the chant of poetry composed for the occasion.

Even official Baath ideology took up the theme of tribalism when, in October 1992, Hussein elevated tribal values within the Baath construct of Iraqi national culture. This latest rendition of Iraqi identity was voiced in the oath taken by 586 tribal chiefs before the president at al-Hillah, near Babylon: "In the name of God . . .We, men of the monotheistic religion and chiefs of tribes . . . the sons of the District of Babylon, Babylon of history and invention and strug-

---

[19] In its most precise meaning, the term *sheikh* denotes religious leadership as well as leadership of a kinship group. I have chosen to use the term in its broader definition—the chief of a clan or tribe.

gle, Babylon of Nebuchadnezzar . . . Babylon of Saddam Hussein, we swear by God . . . and by His prophet . . . our readiness to sacrifice . . . til martrydom."[20]

For this professed loyalty to Saddam Hussein, the sheikhs gathered their rewards. Saluting them as symbols of Iraqi identity and patriotism, the state-controlled media rehabilitated clan leaders from years of abuse at the hands of urban-oriented governments that denigrated what they judged the anachronisms of Iraqi life. It was sweet victory for people imbued with the ultrasensitive honor of tribal culture. In the acclaim, a sheikh from Anbar, once part of the pre-Baath power structure, gloated, "When I visit . . . state institutions as a head of a tribe they accord me much more respect than that which I received as a member of Parliament."[21] In the realm of the tangible, tribal leaders gathered money, abrogation of the restrictions on land holdings imposed after the 1958 revolution, and land itself. Furthermore, the government in Baghdad paid inflated prices for agricultural products grown on that land, constructed hospitals and schools in tribal villages in the name of the sheikh, deferred to tribal law in criminal cases, and delivered to the doorsteps of collaborating tribal leaders shiny, new four-wheel-drive vehicles smuggled in under the sanctions. Soon it was the sheikhs in *disdashas* and *gutras* who filled Baghdad's restaurants and enjoyed the amenities of the al-Rashid Hotel. In this revolving cycle of giving and receiving, the tribes claimed a level of autonomy and Hussein secured a private army. With light arms, sometimes mortars, rocket-propelled grenade (RPG) launchers, and occasionally howitzers, the tribes relieved Hussein of the need to spread his regular troops thinly throughout the countryside.

Tribalism also increased in the cities. In many ways, tribal immigrants to Baghdad and other cities had never completely surrendered to urbanization. Tribal sheikhs and their families, who early in the history of the Iraqi state had already made peace with Baghdad, established for themselves and their progeny a continuous line of influence. By the 1990s, roughly 50 percent of the old sheikh families from the monarchy still held their social, if not their political,

---

[20] Quoted in Amatzia Baram, "Neo-Tribalism in Iraq: Saddam Hussein's Tribal Policies 1991–96," *International Journal of Middle East Studies* 29 (1997): 12.
[21] Ibid.

rank. They did so because over the years they had constituted a significant proportion of the educated and professional classes. Some of those who chose to join the Baath sat as senior government and party officials, members of parliament, and army officers. Others presided over tribal associations that positioned them beside the trade unions, student organizations, and professional societies through which the Baath had organized the urban classes. But unlike these groups based on urban needs and attitudes, most of the tribes retained their ties to the countryside, where many still identified themselves with the same geographic areas as they had under the monarchy.

Now, as purveyors of power, armed tribal units of Shia origin patrol the streets of Baghdad and hold in check the villages of the south. Their Sunni counterparts do the same. Both use their new positions of influence to exact tolls on traffic with Syria, converge on truck convoys driving the desert road from Amman, or run narcotics across the Saudi border. All of it stems from the tribes' pact with Baghdad. In the symbiosis fostered by Saddam Hussein, the state serves the favored tribes, and the favored tribes protect the state.

After three decades of gradual transformation, the Baath now functions as a tribe instead of a political party. Its attitudes are those of the countryside, not of the city. No longer does Arab nationalism and the socialist economy reside at the core of Baath ideology. Instead, the party mouths the slogans of Saddam Hussein who belongs to neither the intellectual nor the urban tradition of Iraq. Employing the old resentments between urban and rural Iraq that have plagued Mesopotamia since the Ottomans, Hussein has recruited the young of the Dulaim, Azza, and dozens of other tribes, given them money and position, and turned them into docile tools in the service of the regime. It is they who hold together the whole structure of the Baath that is now led almost entirely by the blood kin of Saddam Hussein. But like any sheikh, Hussein must manage the repeating waves of feuding within the vast clan at the center of his personal power.

FAMILY TENSIONS are rooted in the jealousies between the Majid and Ibrahim branches of the family descendants from Hussein's natural father and his stepfather, respectively. More recent are conflicts provoked by the president's second marriage to Samira Shahbandar, the blond ex-wife of the general manager of Iraqi Airways, and his third marriage to Nidal al-Hamdani, the former manager of the solar energy department of the Ministry of Industry and Military Industrialization.[22] Added to those is the sibling rivalry between Hussein's two sons by his first marriage—Uday and Qusay. Although only those who are eyewitnesses know the real truth, it is suspected that inside the walls of the presidential palaces Majid contends against Ibrahim, wife competes against wife, son schemes against son. In this deadly serious game, anyone who threatens the man to whom they all owe their position is eliminated.

A half-brother of Saddam, Bazan, went into forced exile in the mid-1980s after he protested when his son was passed over as the chosen husband of Hussein's daughter, Raghad. In 1989, Brigadier General Adnan Khayrallah, the son of Khayrallah Tulfah, the man Hussein considers his surrogate father, and the brother of Hussein's first wife, died in a helicopter crash. As minister of defense during the Iran-Iraq War, Khayrallah had gained wide popularity, leading to speculation that he might be Hussein's heir apparent. But that was before the general acquired his own following. When he died, most believed he was assassinated by contrived accident ordered by Hussein. That in turn sparked a high-stakes contest between Hussein's sons and their Majid brother-in-law for the coveted position of heir apparent.

The older son, Uday, the child whose diapers provided a hiding place for the messages that passed between the jailed Hussein and his Baath cohorts in 1963, is emotionally unstable, poorly educated, a heavy drinker, and a notorious womanizer. By some accounts, Uday's only admirable quality seems to be devotion to his mother. It was on her behalf in 1998 that he bludgeoned to death his father's trusted valet and food taster, who was accused of arranging several clandestine meetings between his father and Samira Shahbandar. Immediately after the killing, Hussein sentenced Uday to death. As stunned relatives and sycophants organized a massive campaign to beg the president to grant clemency, Uday fled to Geneva. Eventually forgiven by his father, he quietly stole back into Baghdad sometime later.

At the time, Hussein's favorite in his court seemed to be Hussein Kamel, a member of the Majid family and the husband of

---

[22] Although it has never been officially confirmed, it is widely known that Hussein wed Samira in 1986 and Nidal in 1990. He is believed to have a son by Samira.

Hussein's daughter Raghad. After the marriage, the president elevated the high-school dropout to extraordinary positions of power.
Although he had never attended military school, Kamel carried the
rank of lieutenant general as a reward for his talent at organization.
It was he who vastly expanded the Republican Guards that drove
the Iranians back into their own territory during the latter stages
of the Iran-Iraq War. He also headed up Hussein's weapons programs, demonstrating an energetic efficiency in accumulating conventional, chemical, and biological weapons as well as in recruiting
the talent and equipment for Hussein's atomic weapons program.
But the spectacular rise of the Majid son-in-law provoked jealous
rage in the Ibrahim branch of the family and envy from Hussein's
two sons.

By the time of the Kuwait invasion, Uday was pursuing his own
ambitions under the tolerant eye of his father. Between nights of
drinking and carousing, he created a voice for himself with a newspaper called *Babel* and his own radio station. Eventually he assumed
responsibility for the entire Iraqi media, took over the Ministry of
Youth Affairs, and organized "The Saddamists' Union" of high-ranking officials and army officers. In turn, the union spawned a special
fifteen-thousand-strong militia known as the Firqat Fida'iyyi Saddam,
or Saddam's Commandos, also led by Uday. Largely teenage toughs,
they drove around Baghdad in pickup trucks armed with heavy
machine guns acting as the presidential son's personal security force.
In 1994, Hussein awarded his oldest son the smuggling operations
that delivered Iraqi oil to Turkey and Iran in violation of the UN sanctions. Amounting to 150,000 barrels per day, the lucrative enterprise
gave Uday a daily income of some $2 million. It was money that had
previously been going into the pocket of Hussein Kamel, who over-
saw the oil industry.

In 1995, Uday began to zero in on Kamel's commissions derived
from purchases of army equipment, construction products, and food
imports. Around the same time, the younger brother, Qusay, took
control of the security forces that guard the president and the ruling
elite. He replaced Kamel's brother, Saddam, who was married to
Rana, another presidential daughter.[23] Day by day, Uday and Qusay

---

[23] Saddam Kamel's chief claim to fame was his starring role in the film version of
Saddam Hussein's epic biography, *The Long Days*.

circled their brothers-in-law like vultures waiting to devour the car-
casses of their rivals.

On the night of August 7, 1995, Hussein Kamel, his brother, their
wives Raghdad and Rana, their children, and fifteen relatives from
the Majid family climbed into a string of Mercedes and drove the long
flat road to the border of Jordan and into Amman. An Iraqi official, as
astonished as everyone else, speculated on the reason: "Uday and
Qusai are basically taking over the machinery of state. . . . I think he
ran for his life."[24] In Baghdad, the head of the Majid family, Ali
Hassan, "Ali Chemical," issued a terse public statement that said the
family had decided that "the traitor's blood can be shed with
impunity."[25] It was a death sentence issued under tribal law.

From the sanctuary provided by Jordan's king, Hussein Kamel
threw aside his army uniform, donned a double-breasted, gray,
pin-striped suit, and appeared before the world in the garden of one
of the king's palaces. In a statement that unleashed panic among the
leadership in Baghdad, he appealed to the army, the Republican
Guards, and the Special Republican Guards—the personal shield of
Saddam Hussein and his family—to topple the regime. In the days
that followed, Kamel established a vague opposition group named
the "Higher Council for the Salvation of Iraq" that called upon the
Sunni establishment to eliminate the reigning hierarchy.

The inner family rallied. Qusay, the brighter, more stable, and
more competent of Hussein's sons, rapidly took over important posts
vacated by Hussein Kamel. And Saddam Hussein, calling forth his
skills of manipulation and revenge, gathered his loyalists closely
around him. Assurances of forgiveness and reconciliation sent
through Kamel's father and Raghad's mother were delivered to
Amman. Saddam Hussein himself even telephoned to assure the
renegades that they could return to Iraq in safety even though Kamel
had divested himself of his secrets about Iraq's arms program. Seven
months after fleeing, the man many judged "an idiot" once more
donned his Iraqi army uniform and ordered his family into the same
Mercedes sedans that had brought them to Amman. They headed up
the desert road of eastern Jordan toward the border of Iraq. On the
other side, Uday waited. Ignoring his brothers-in-law, Uday seized

[24] Quoted in *New York Times*, August 15, 1995.
[25] Ibid.

his sisters and their children and drove toward Baghdad. On February 23, Uday's television station announced that Raghad and Rana had divorced their husbands who had "betrayed the homeland, the trust, and the lofty values of their noble family and kinfolk."[26]

Four days after their return to Iraq, Hussein and Saddam Kamel, along with their father, awaited their fate in their sister's villa in Baghdad. Armed with automatic weapons, they were ready when the representatives of their *khamsa*, the five-generation unit of males who avenges the honor of the family, arrived to extract revenge. As Uday and Qusay watched from a car parked nearby, the forces of the tribe attacked. Thirteen hours later when the gunfire ended, the two defectors, their father, their sister, and her children were all dead. It was left to the Majid clan to issue a statement of tribal justice: "We have cut off the treacherous branch of our noble family tree."[27]

Revenge struck again in December 1996 as Uday's three-car convoy of white Mercedes raced down Mansour street in west Baghdad, the enclave of the Baath elite. In the fading light of early evening, one man casually loitering on a street corner reached into the gym bag at his feet and pulled out a Kalashnikov automatic rifle, opening fire on the lead car as two men in front of a nearby restaurant and a third who came out of a side street unloaded their own weapons into the rest of the convoy. In less than two minutes, they killed the driver of the first car, seriously wounded Uday, and demobilized the rest of the party. Recalling the Qasim assassination attempt of thirty-seven years earlier, the gunmen disappeared into the streets of Baghdad.

News of the attack could not be kept secret. While the official press grudgingly supplied the details, al-Dawah, the Shia political organization crushed in 1991, claimed responsibility from the safety of Beirut. But the more likely candidate was the family of General Muhammad Mazlum of the Dalaimi.

Almost two years before, in early 1995, once fiercely loyal Sunni tribes on the upper Euphrates began to strain against the control of Baghdad. In the wind of unrest, rumors of a purported conspiracy to assassinate Saddam Hussein led to the arrest of General al-Dalaimi. In May, the government delivered his mutilated body to his relatives.

---

[26] Iraqi News Agency cited in *The Independent* of London, September 24, 1996.
[27] *Le Monde Diplomatique* quoted in Cockburn and Cockburn, *Out of the Ashes*, p. 210.

Raising the cry that blood demands blood, the family incited revolt in the Dulaim federation. It took three weeks for Hussein's elite troops to put it down. In the process, more people died and more demands for revenge accumulated. Whether or not Uday paid the price for his father's feud with an important tribe remains unknown. What is certain is that Saddam Hussein now presides over a tribal society in which one cannot exaggerate the degree to which the Iraqi state has been undermined by traditional associations of kin and clan.

IN THE THREE-PLUS DECADES in which Saddam Hussein has ruled Iraq either from inside the Baath Party or on the presidential chair, the Iraqis' frail sense of nationalism has withered. What exists today is a tribal society in which the top echelon of the state is composed of Hussein's relatives and allies. Almost universally, they are the products of villages and small provincial towns. Most of the security personnel who hold the population in bondage come out of the tribes. Although the bureaucracy is still staffed with the old educated class, the ranking officials in most government ministries are men unpolished by the urban attitudes of their predecessors. It only takes an interview with the minister of health or the minister of information to grasp the full extent to which Iraq's institutions of government are now controlled by men of little education and experience outside the bounds of tribe.

Beyond this inner circle, Saddam Hussein has put a network of tribes in place of the institutions of the state. These tribes, both traditional renditions and modern constructs of self-contained social units, take three forms. First, there is political tribalism found in the descending hierarchy of family, kin, and tribal allies that Hussein has integrated into the state in order to ensure his own status, legitimacy, and power. Then comes social tribalism, created by a government that has proved itself incapable of ruling a modern urban society. These are not classic tribes but jerryrigged "tribes," a nouveau riche mafia that includes Arab Sunnis and Shia as well as Kurds, all tied directly or indirectly to the premier tribe—the Tikritis. Collecting tribute and exercising police and judicial power, they have become an extension of the state itself. Finally, there is what might be termed military tribalism. It emerged after the uprisings of 1991 when Hussein armed both Sunni and Shia tribes in the interest of his own defense.[28] Each has added its own burden to the fragmented nature of Iraq. Together this strange mix of old communalism and new tribalism now threatens to undo the state itself.

In the cities, the tribes drive the politics of neighborhoods populated almost exclusively of kin. In these tight-knit communities, tribal leaders have replaced the urban intelligentsia, who once occasionally raised the common interest of social class above the lines of ethnicity, language, communalism, and sectarianism. In the countryside, tribe pits its power against tribe. Unlike in the days when Gertrude Bell charted the shifting balance of tribal conflict, companies of kin in the Sunni triangle, the Shia south, and the Kurdish north no longer fight with swords or even rifles. They are armed with machine guns, rocket launchers, and howitzers provided by a central government dependent on the tribes to impose the authority of Baghdad. In possession of weapons capable of inflicting high casualties, the strong engage the weak. As a result, the old mediation techniques that so successfully restored equilibrium in the past is gone. Instead, the Hussein regime, unable to flex its military muscle everywhere at the same time, allows the peripheries of the capital to live in what might be described as controlled chaos. On occasion, muted voices out of the Baath past deplore the insertion of tribalism into the pantheon of Iraqi identities. One old-line party official writing in *Babel* charged that tribalism rather than "encouraging the unity of the Iraqi people [was] sowing . . . the seeds of division . . . inciting one part of it against the other . . . providing protection . . . annulling the law and deprecating legal justice."[29]

Yet Saddam Hussein does not run a true tribal system. Instead, he presides over a rude repressive order from which no group can withdraw even if it wishes to recall its allegiance. A skilled despot, he has tamed his fractured land by turning it into a prison.

In reviving ethnic and sectarian identities, the government stokes the historic fears and suspicions of one group toward another. Even the intensified sense of Arab identity that Sunnis and Shia shared during the Iran-Iraq War has corroded. In the years since the *intifadah*, a deeper, more distinct sectarian identity of the Shia as a

---

[28] These forms of tribalism were described by Judith Yaphe in "Tribalism in Iraq, the Old and the New," *Middle East Policy* 7, no. 3 (June 2000): 51–58.

[29] Quoted in Baram, "Neo-Tribalism in Iraq," p. 17.

unique group within the Iraqi Arab population has ripened. As 60 percent of the population of Iraq, they forswear separation from the
state. Instead, they demand reform of the Iraqi political system,
reforms that would put them, as the numerical majority, in control
of the state. Furthermore, they seek a national culture that includes
Shia history, values, and identity.

At the same time, the Kurds in the enclaves of the north tend the
flame of Kurdistan. The pragmatists among them know that the
Kurds cannot achieve independence from Iraq because neither
Turkey nor Iran, both cognizant of their own Kurdish minorities, will
allow it. So the Kurds, within two administrative districts defined by
tribe and ideology, are prepared to stay physically in Iraq. But in the
emotional sense, they may no longer belong to the Iraqi state. Ten
years of autonomy in which government and education have been
conducted in Kurdish have created a population in which large numbers no longer even know Arabic.

Perhaps as many as 1.5 million Iraqis from all communal groups
now live in exile. Although some are poorly educated refugees
trapped in camps in Iran, Lebanon, and elsewhere, the vast majority
are the brightest and best among the Iraqis. Trickling out of Iraq after
the fall of the monarchy and flooding out during the years of Saddam
Hussein, they took with them their financial resources and their talents. They left behind the less able, the less educated, the less
worldly who still live in the intellectual vacuum of Hussein's Iraq.
Once the Baath nightmare ends, the exiles will be critical to the
health of the Iraqi state. But no one knows if they can be wooed back
to take the reins of government and business, or if those who stayed
behind to endure the Iran-Iraq War, the Gulf War, and the sanctions
will allow them full participation in the new order.

Like Baghdad at the end of the Gulf War, Iraq itself is a body
whose skin is intact but whose bones are broken. Instead of a nation,
it is a snarling collection of tribes who live in a society torn into
shreds by nearly a quarter of a century of Baath brutality. In this
sense, the condition of the Iraqi state is worse than it was when Faisal
I arrived in Baghdad in 1921. The shallow civil society that Faisal
labored to create has all but vanished. The spirited discourse that
engaged the minds of the Shia theologians in Najaf and Karbala has
been largely silenced in the repeated expulsions of the Shia clergy.
The merchants of the shrine towns who once traveled back and forth

between Iraq and Iran, exchanging Iraqi money and Arab ideas for Persian rugs and Persian thinking, are trapped behind walls erected by tyranny. In the place of clerics and traders, there is only the shiekh in his *mushhuf* who fingers his prayer beads while he dispenses the law of the tribe. It is he who is now the custodian of Shia minds.

The intellectualism of the Sunni urban elite of the Ottoman Empire and the monarchy is also gone. What is left is the elite of the Baath that gathers at the exclusive Hunting Club founded by Hussein, where elaborate tableaus staged by the Fashion Institute attempt to recreate with feather headdresses and silken garments the glory of Abbasid Baghdad. But the audience is not the product of the urban Abbasids, the Ottomans, or the monarchy. It is composed largely of people with peasant backgrounds and of tribal members who have pressed their ways on the culture, society, and political system of the Iraqi state. It is as if Saddam Hussein has extinguished the three thousand years of Mesopotamian urban society that began with Ur.

The old educated class that promised Iraq so much in the latter years of the monarchy and during that Iraqi spring of the 1970s—when the oil boom promised so much to so many—has been decimated. Even the material ruins of a once prosperous middle class found in the shops that line the lobby of the al-Rashid Hotel have vanished. When I returned to Iraq in 1998, the glass-fronted boutiques were still stuffed with consignments of watches, jewelry, flatware, and porcelain. Now most of that has passed into the hands of the privileged of the regime, leaving the shopkeepers with inventories of bric-a-brac from China, Iran, and Turkey that is smuggled through the increasingly porous lines of the sanctions. The used musical instruments that hung on chrome racks at intersections of the major streets are also gone, swept into the hands of foreigners paying in hard currency. The used-book market in Souk al-Sarri displays maybe fifty worn volumes, placed there more to make a statement about the sanctions than to sell. Yet the need to sell goes on. One man in a frayed suit of once fine fabric told me that the only thing he has remaining are the inside doors of his house. Those were on the market.

Although the visible poverty of the middle class is physical, the more acute poverty is spiritual. In the confines of a brutal police state, it is impossible to measure just how deep the hunger is for ideas, for conversation, for solace. It can only be guessed in snatches of candor. I experienced one powerful moment of frankness when a small, scholarly looking man forced into labor on one of the regime's minor newspapers caught me out of earshot of my government-appointed keeper. He softly and quickly said, "I am so lonely. I used to talk to people, educated people, from everywhere. Now I talk to no one." Another glimpse into the soul of an educated Iraqi came in the back pew of a Christian church in Mosul, where a distinguished-looking woman of middle age furtively whispered into my ear in perfect English, "I used to read Shakespeare, Trollope, even Hemingway. Now I read only the Bible. This I must tell you. Do not wait until there is a disaster in your nation to get right with God."

In the intellectual stagnation in which the educated are mired, ideology is as barren as the houses emptied of furniture and the minds vacant of anything beyond the will to survive. Democracy that took a few halting steps under the monarchy is no longer mentioned. Political and economic reform masquerading as Communism, which once attracted many of the educated and the downtrodden of all ethnic and sectarian groups, is nothing more than a ghost. Baath ideology originally proclaiming that Arab nationalism would bridge the political and economic chasm between all speakers of Arabic languishes in the domed tomb of Michel Aflaq, which butts against a busy Baghdad street. The Baath's socialist program, which once held some promise of pulling all Iraqis into an egalitarian economic system, is totally corrupted. And the Baath itself is only a facade before the absolute authority of Saddam Hussein.

The Baath of today is an interlocking hierarchy of people who maintain the personal power of the Iraqi tyrant. In descending order under the "hero president," there are the sycophants—the ministers and party officials; the enablers—the secret police, the Republican Guards, and the myriad of security services; the allies—the tribal sheikhs who have sold themselves into service; the entrapped—the people of the bureaucracy enslaved to the regime by the necessity of survival; and the thugs—the street-level enforcers of rural values. Together they keep the chains of bondage wrapped around the victims, the people of Iraq. The whole miserable, repressive system is centered in Tikrit, what is now the de facto capital of Iraq.

Tikrit lies just north of Samarra and east of the main highway that runs between Baghdad and Mosul. In 1937, Freya Stark wrote about the town that stands on a bluff above a bend in the Tigris: "No

one who comes upon this magnificent position can fail to realize
what an important place it must have been in the days of insecurity."[30] The same is true today. Inside Tikrit itself, whole sections of
fine homes oriented toward the river accommodate Hussein's family and closest relatives. Around the perimeter, row upon row of tall
metal towers hold high power lines that stretch across the rolling
landscape as far as the eye can see. Below them, the long noses of
tanks stick out of defensive positions dug into sandy soil. Nearby,
military installations ringed with barbed wire enclose Hussein's elite
Republican Guards. Less visible but no less present are the men and
women of the local militia, a portion of Hussein's extended tribe,
who stand ready to defend the man who has raised them out of
poverty and anonymity to a place of pride in the Iraqi state.

In an ideological wasteland policed by the Baath, there is no organized opposition capable of overthrowing the despised dictator. Instead,
the inevitability of political change is portrayed in a poorly executed
public mural. At its center is Saddam Hussein mounted on a white stallion, a rifle slung over his shoulder. He is flanked on the right and the
left by his two hawk-eyed sons. The elder, Uday, is no longer considered the heir apparent. It is Qusay, as head of all of the security services, who has apparently been chosen to don the mantle of his father.
He shares many of Saddam's characteristics—native intelligence, a
strong work ethic, skill at administration, and an unscrupulous ability
to survive in the hostile political environment of Iraq. But nothing
about the present and future leadership of Iraq is clear, tidy, or predictable. Rumors swirl that the "Great Leader" suffers from lymphoma,
a potentially fatal form of cancer. Uday seems to be challenging his
brother for the right of succession through elements of the media that
he controls—state television, the newspaper *Babel*, and the Voice of
Iraq FM, an English-language radio station that broadcasts American
rock music. The Majids and the Ibrahims circle each other in defense
of their interests. And unseen groups and individuals plot their own
rise to power. Even so, the totalitarian system built by Saddam
Hussein commands a certain stability anchored in negatives.

In the shadow of Tikriti political control, Sunnis beyond the Baath
refuse to rise against their oppressor because of their dread of the
Shia. The Shia are too fragmented into competing tribes co-opted by

---

[30] Freya Stark, *Baghdad Sketches* (Evanston, Ill.: Marlboro Press, 1996), p. 163.

the regime to mobilize their numbers against a rotten order in which they are the principle victims. While one configuration of Kurds detests the regime, the other leans on Baghdad to protect itself from its own Kurdish rivals. And everyone is terrified of the unknown future of a society that has been broken by tyranny into smaller and smaller units of identity labeled by language, religion, sect, family, and tribe.

Outside Iraq, the exiles command neither the organization nor a force on the ground capable of mounting a serious challenge to the military and security forces commanded by Hussein. This leaves just the army, "the final arbiter of political power, the 'independent variable' in modern Iraqi history, determining which regimes remain and which regimes fall," and the question of whether it can or will remove the tyrant of Baghdad, his detested sons, and the Baath regime.[31] Despite the Baath's tense history with the military, the president and the generals appear wrapped in another of those symbiotic relationships that Hussein seems to craft so cannily. The army has allowed, or served, two Baath coups. It has prosecuted two wars instigated by the Iraqi president. And it has put down two rebellions that seriously threatened to topple the whole Baath structure. Nonetheless the army, once the revered national savior, the tattered hero of the 1958 revolution, remains the only institution capable of ridding Iraq of its long nightmare.

In the absence of a deliberate move by the army, the universe created by Saddam Hussein may simply perish through circumstance. A brittle regime dependent on one man is vulnerable on several fronts: the death of the principle villain, infighting within his family, desertion by the tribes, military coup by happenstance. Or it might simply collapse under its own awful weight. When change does come, it is likely to be unpredictable and sudden, for as Gertrude Bell put it, the ultimate source of power in Iraq, "as in the whole course of Arab history, is the personality of the commander. Through him, whether he be an Abbasid Khalif or an Amir of Nejd, the political entity holds, and with his disappearance, it breaks."[32]

---

[31] Andrew Parasiliti and Sinan Antoon, "Friends in Need, Foes to Heed: The Iraqi Military in Politics," *Middle East Policy* 7, no. 4 (October 2000): 130.

[32] Quoted in Janet Wallach, *Dessert Queen: The Extraordinary Life of Gertrude Bell: Adventurer, Adviser to Kings, Ally of Lawrence of Arabia* (New York: Anchor Books, 1999), p. 187.

Yet once Hussein no longer reigns as the central force in Iraq, his legacy will remain. Over a very long time, all Iraqis will march metaphorically beneath the pointed swords of the Victory Arch, the monument to the Iran-Iraq War. The cadence will be drummed by the army, the tribes, the Kurds, the Sunnis, and the Shia. Others—the Assyrians, Turkomans, the shrunken body of Persians, and the religious minorities—will add their own muffled beat. But they will not march together. A society with so few common bonds and traumatized by more than two decades of tyranny is ill-equipped to pull itself together to smoothly traverse into the post-Hussein era. There are just too many memories of past injustices, too many wounds inflicted on those out of power by those in power, too many recriminations waiting to be delivered, and too many claims to the title of ultimate sufferer under the tyranny of Saddam Hussein.

Since no one can predict the future accurately, the Iraqis may surprise themselves and everyone else by drawing unity from the vision of Iraq promoted by successive governments. In mixed amounts, the monarchy, the military regimes of the republic, and the Baath all tended the concept of the Iraqi state. The Iraqis have now had eighty years of statehood to absorb the idea. Maybe the best of human instincts will rise to the tolerant view that every Iraqi, in one way or another, has paid a terrible price for the reign of Hussein. Or perhaps twenty years of war and siege under sanctions has left the population simply too exhausted to extract revenge, one against the other. Although there is hope that the Iraqis can quietly move into the daylight of a post-Hussein era, there are also the stark realities of both the past and the present that are found in the depth of communalism and the strength of tribalism. Tragically, they could combine to produce a bloodbath let loose by the fall of the Baath regime.

In a milieu in which all institutions beyond kinship have ceased to function, Sunni tribal elites in control of the military and security forces could well become warlords commanding tribal armies. Like all tribes, they would reach out for allies, pulling expanded numbers into the conflict. Rival tribes on the other side of the Sunni-Shia sectarian divide could recruit their own allies, turning tribal rivalries into civil war. In the grimmest of scenarios, groups would wreak revenge against each other in an attempt to expunge their own feelings of victimization. The Kurds will remember the repressed rebellion of 1970–75, al-Anfal of 1988, and the uprising of 1991. The Sunnis will brandish their fear as a minority to defend themselves against political or physical annihilation. The Shia will hold their seething anger of past repression against the open wound of the *intifadah* as they vie for their rightful place in Iraq. In the melee, any government that might somehow emerge out of the anarchy will not be the last as the country spins through the interests of the military, the tribes, the cities, the Sunnis, the Shia, the Kurds, the Turkomans, the Christians, the dictators, the democrats, and the theocrats, all battling to control or destroy the state. At least in the short term, they will be no more willing than their predecessors to cooperate in building an integrated government responsible to all. Nor will they be willing to think in terms of nation rather than state. It is sad to consider the thought that if nations emerge from a natural fusion of culture and commonality, then Iraq as a nation was cursed from the moment it was put together from component parts drawn from the geography of Mesopotamia. That leads to the question of whether Iraq the state is doomed.

The answer depends on at least two factors that dwell at the very core of conflicted Iraqi society: the acquiescence of individual Iraqis to shared or invented symbols of identity that cross at least part of the spectrum of Iraq's communal groups, and the willingness of communal groups to engage in the human interchange that creates pluralistic societies. But even this may not be enough to transform Hussein's legacy into a force of healing rather than the hammer of retribution. The poison produced by Kurdish bitterness against Arabs and Shia resentment of the Sunnis that has always sapped Iraqi nationalism is stronger today than ever before. It may now be too potent to be neutralized in a society that has never experienced an extended period of authentic political development or benefited from a government more interested in the whole of the state than in one or more of its component parts. Such animosity could fell even the most tolerant of individuals and communities. Even if violence is somehow avoided, the state may die anyway, picked to death by communalism. Its bones may then lay in heaps for the three major groups—the Shia, the Sunnis, and the Kurds—to claim their own pieces of the remains. Or they may be borne away by others on the borders of the Iraqi state. Either way, Iraq may become like fallen Babylon where "[u]pon its ruins wolves are forever howling."[33]

Yet Iraq may not be allowed to perish in spite of the Iraqis. The pools of oil under Mesopotamia are crucial to a world ravenous for energy. And Mesopotamia's location on the Persian Gulf and at the edge of the pipeline routes from the emerging energy fields of Central Asia cannot be allowed to sink into chaos. Ever since Saddam Hussein's invasion of Kuwait, the United States as the world's sole superpower and the protector of the Persian Gulf has struggled with the problem of Iraq. How that problem is addressed is among the great challenges of American foreign policy.

[33] Quote from Al-Bayyati's poem "The Return from Babylon," as cited by Amatzia Baram, *Culture, History and Ideology in the Formation of Ba'athist Iraq, 1968–89* (New York: St. Martin's Press, 1991), p. 90. Poem was published in *Diwan* (Beirut) 2 (1972): 103.

10

AMERICA BETWEEN
THE TWO RIVERS

A cartoon drawing of a grinning, heavily bearded Saddam Hussein, with a shooting target imposed over his bulky body, is tacked above the door of a hardware store in the mountain town of Highlands, North Carolina. Now faded and yellowed, it has hung there since the summer of 1990 when the United States began to mobilize its armed forces to turn back Iraq's invasion of Kuwait. It is a sober reminder to everyone coming and going that the villain of the Gulf War remains a central character in American foreign policy long after the stunning victory of 1991. Even more, the caricature drawn in simple black lines creates the illusion that Saddam Hussein is the only challenge the United States faces in Iraq. In the nature of cartoons, it ignores the complexity that Iraq presents to American foreign policy.

Angst rising out of Iraq is a new phenomenon for the United States. Until the invasion of Kuwait in August of 1990, the country at the eastern edge of the Arab world flickered only occasionally on the radar screen of the collective American consciousness. A review of the popular-news and general-interest magazines of the past fifty years is indicative of just how little Iraq interested the American press before the 1991 Gulf War. During the 1950s, the coronation of Faisal II took second billing to that of King Hussein of Jordan, crowned the same day. Nuri al-Said engendered some notice for his country at the time of the Baghdad Pact. But the revolution that killed both Faisal and al-Said rated, at best, a column in the international section of the more serious news magazines. In the 1960s when press attention fixed on the shah of Iran and his beautiful empress, the lifestyle of free-swinging Beirut, and the stunning Israeli victory over the Arabs in the Six Day War, Iraq captured the headlines only through a set of gruesome photographs that accompanied the army coup against General Abd al-Karim Qasim. On that occasion, *Life Magazine* devoted four full pages to a blurred picture of Qasim's bullet-ridden body, accompanied by an article entitled "His Gold-Capped Teeth Gleamed No More." Even during the oil boom of the 1970s, when one article after another described in breathless detail the incredible wealth descending on Saudi Arabia, Kuwait, and the United Arab Emirates, Iraq, claiming more oil resources than any of them except Saudi Arabia, barely merited mention. It was only when the United States saw Saddam Hussein and the Iran-Iraq War as a firewall against the Islamic Republic of Iran that articles on Iraq began to hit the pages of *Time* and *Newsweek* with any frequency. When an Iraqi pilot fired a missile into the USS *Stark*, killing thirty-seven American seamen, Iraq moved to the covers of those magazines. Then, in August 1990, when Iraq invaded Kuwait, the media turned its pages and air time over to Saddam Hussein. Ever since, it has been Hussein, not Iraq, on whom Americans and their leaders have riveted their attention. But the time is fast approaching when the United States, for a series of perilous reasons, will be forced to look beyond Hussein to Iraq itself. That is when all Americans will pay the price for what has been a long night of ignorance about the land between the rivers.

IN THE DAYS before the Gulf War, no American administration from that of John Kennedy to George H. W. Bush thought about Iraq as a fragile state possessing a unique character and burdensome problems arising out of the fragmented nature of its society. Rather, Iraq was always the adjunct of another issue unrelated to the Iraqi state. During the 1950s when American foreign policy was built exclusively on the Cold War, Iraq was simply another piece to be fitted into the global puzzle of U.S. strategic interests. These were the days when a swaggering Gamal Abdul Nasser, flirting with the Soviet Union and voicing Arab nationalism, confronted the premier U.S. interest in the Middle East—the security of the infant state of Israel. That slotted Iraq into two categories of U.S. interests: superpower rivalry and the confrontation between Israel and the Arabs. However, because of Britain's presence behind the Hashemite throne, Iraq was largely left to London. And it was London, implementing the grand American design to encircle the Soviet Union with military alliances, that lured Iraq into the Baghdad Pact. That agreement was essentially the death warrant of the Iraqi monarchy and the beginning of the turmoil of the Iraqi republic in the 1960s that tore at its people's tenuous sense of nationhood.

By the first years of the 1970s, London had passed the baton of Iraq to Washington. In the hand-off, American policy makers were forced to deal with a country over which they commanded little experience or knowledge. During the turbulent decade that followed the 1958 revolution, Washington failed to understand the competing forces of identity and governance that were at work in Iraq. In the Qasim regime, Washington saw only two things: the Iraqi Communist Party and arms deals with the Soviet Union. All it saw in the first Baath government of 1963 was a welcome force against Communism and Nasserism. In the period of the two Arifs, American policy makers recognized little but the return of pan-Arabism and arms purchases from the Soviet Union. When the Baath returned to power in 1968, Nasser, the mighty voice of Arab nationalism, already had been mortally wounded by the Six Day War of 1967, and soon the Iraqi Communist Party felt the avenging hammer of the Baath. But because of the Baath's continuing purchases of Soviet arms, Iraq remained suspect, isolated by Washington policy makers in the confines of the Cold War.

The cataclysmic 1973 Arab oil embargo moved the whole Persian Gulf region, including Iraq, toward the center of American vital interests. Out of severe shortages and skyrocketing oil prices, Washington adopted a series of broad principles that have consistently directed American foreign policy in the Persian Gulf ever since. Whether an administration is Republican or Democrat, the first and the most important of these strategic principles is to maintain the unfettered flow of oil at reasonable prices. The second is to preserve stability in the Gulf through security arrangements with regional allies that thwart the emergence of a dominant power hostile to U. S. interests. The third principle operates in the regional context of the Middle East—the insurance of the security of Israel.

From 1972 to 1979, Washington maintained what was called the "two-pillar policy." Built on the pilings of strong relations with Iran and Saudi Arabia, American influence bridged the Gulf. But the pillar on the western side was dangerously weak because the xenophobic Saudis insisted that U. S. military power remain a phantom in the kingdom. Therefore, American policy played to its strength on the Gulf's eastern shore—Muhammad Reza Shah, the king of kings of Iran.

In his palace in Tehran, the shah dreamed of a new Persian empire derived from Iranian power in the Persian Gulf. Until 1972, the United States let him dream alone. Then the pressures of manpower, equipment, and money for the Vietnam War led the Nixon administration to seek a surrogate to keep watch over the Persian Gulf. Handing Iran the keys to the most sophisticated American military hardware and training, the United States promoted the shah to sheriff of the Gulf.

The two-pillar policy collapsed in 1979 when the Iranian revolution swept Muhammad Reza Shah off the Peacock Throne. In his place, Ayatollah Ruhollah Khomeini spewed forth harsh rhetoric branding the United States as the "Great Satan" while soldiers of revolutionary Islam held fifty-two Americans hostage for 444 days. As a result, American foreign policy in the Persian Gulf gave way to a visceral hatred of Iran that fed on fear. Among the Shia populations of Lebanon, Bahrain, the United Arab Emirates, Saudi Arabia, and Lebanon, a politicized Islam sowed by disciples of Khomeini challenged American primacy in the Middle East. Adrift in the Gulf with little support beyond fragile Saudi Arabia and some of the tiny sheikhdoms along the eastern coast of the Arabian Peninsula, the United States searched for an ally to counterbalance revolutionary Iran. Iraq, shunned for years by American policy makers, suddenly began to materialize as a potential friend in February 1980, when Saddam Hussein voiced hostility toward the Soviet Union by calling the Communists "a rotten, atheistic, yellow storm which has plagued Iraq."[1] There were other factors, principally oil. With Iranian petroleum production disrupted by revolution, the vast reserves of Iraqi oil became more important in the world petroleum market. Thus, on April 14, 1980, Zbigniew Brzezinski, President Carter's national security advisor, set the new American tone concerning Iraq: "We see no fundamental incompatibility of interests between the United States and Iraq. . . . We do not feel that American-Iraqi relations need to be frozen in antagonism."[2] In the weeks following Saddam Hussein's attack on Iran in September 1980, U. S. foreign policy, which ignored the cultural factors at play in both countries, vacillated between Baghdad and Tehran.

---

[1] Quoted in Adeed I. Dawisha, "Iraq: The West's Opportunity," *Foreign Policy* 41 (Winter 1980–81): 134.

[2] Ibid., p. 149.

Ostensibly neutral in a war of no heroes, the United States clung to a cynical hope that both Iraq and Iran would shed so much blood in the Shatt al Arab that neither could upset the precarious balance of power in the Persian Gulf that shielded the weak oil states of the Arabian Peninsula. But by late 1981, Iraq was faltering in the war. By 1982, President Ronald Reagan concluded that U.S. national interests demanded strengthening Iraq in order to maintain the country as a counterweight to Iran. Other reasons were involved in the policy shift: the hope that Hussein might serve a constructive role in the ever present Arab-Israeli dispute, the realization that oil-rich Iraq represented an untapped market for U. S. industry and agriculture, and the desire to wean Baghdad away from Moscow once and for all. Thus, the quest began to improve the relationship between the United States and Hussein's Iraq. Desperate for help in the war, Saddam Hussein indicated that he was willing to play Pancho Sanchez to the American Don Quixote.

After Hussein severed ties with the Palestinian terrorist Abu Nidal in 1982, the Reagan administration erased Iraq's name from the list of nations engaged in state-sponsored terrorism and added it to the register of those countries eligible for assistance under the Department of Agriculture's Commodity Credit Corporation (CCC). Although the move was extremely popular with farm-state politicians in Congress, American policy toward Iraq originated principally out of the fear of politicized Islam wreaking its vengeance on the West. The validity of that fear was affirmed on October 23, 1983, when a shadowy force calling itself Islamic Jihad delivered two thousand pounds of explosives that killed 241 American Marines sleeping in a makeshift barracks at the Beirut airport. The high-profile attack on the United States perpetrated by Lebanese Shia followers of Ayatollah Khomeini's ideology shoved the United States closer to Iraq. And Iraq, taxed by its war with Iran, snuggled up to Washington. Thus, in November 1984, the United States and Iraq restored diplomatic ties. In this unfamiliar relationship, American diplomats lunched with Iraqi generals and accepted gifts of cocoa-dusted cookies sent from the presidential office. Nonetheless, every encounter, every gesture moved on the tide of Iraq's conflict with Iran, for American policy was never pro-Iraq, only anti-Iran.

Actual weaponry for Hussein's military came from France, Britain, the Netherlands, Germany, Italy, Japan, and Switzerland.

Brazilian expertise extended the range of Iraq's Russian-made Scud B missiles. Assistance from Egypt and Argentina helped build the long-range Condor missile. The nuclear program that began with the Osiris reactor purchased from France moved ahead with the technical support of scientists from an array of countries.[3] Official American help to Saddam Hussein's multifaceted military machine came through the back door of intelligence. Illicit aid came by way of deadly pathogens purchased from U.S. biological firms and perhaps $500 million in dual-use imports diverted by Iraq to the military sector.

During the first five years of the Iran-Iraq War, an American policy that balanced Iraq against Iran appeared to succeed in that neither side could win or lose a war fought from trenches along the Shatt al Arab. Then, in July 1986, the war dramatically shifted to the sea lanes of the Persian Gulf. In a reckless attempt to end the war by strangling the Islamic republic economically, Iraq sent its planes and missiles against Iran's main oil terminal at Kharg island. Since Iraqi shipping from Umm Qasr had already been shut off in 1984, the Islamic republic retaliated by attacking the shipping of Iraq's allies with mines dropped out of rubber dinghies. Within the first five weeks of 1987, sixteen ships flying the flags of almost as many nations suffered damage. Suddenly Hussein's war, which the United States originally judged as protection for the Arab Gulf states from revolutionary Iran, had delivered the conflict to their front door. Saudi Arabia hunkered down, but Kuwait screamed for help. The United States, hypersensitive to the uninterrupted flow of oil out of the Gulf, decades of concern about Soviet penetration into the Middle East, and an Iranian government bent on driving the West from the Islamic world, reacted by reflagging Kuwaiti-owned ships with the stars and stripes and putting an American flotilla in the Gulf to keep the sea lanes open. On May 17, 1987, the frigate USS *Stark* was prowling the waters of the Gulf when an Iraqi Exocet missile slammed into the rear starboard. Thirty-seven U.S. sailors went home in flag-draped coffins. Accepting the Iraqi claim of an accident of war, the arms-length alliance between the United States and Iraq went forward.

In the final stages of the Iran-Iraq War, Washington supplied

---

[3] The Osiris reactor was destroyed by Israeli planes in a bombing run on June 6, 1981.

Baghdad with reconnaissance photographs that proved invaluable in pinpointing missile targets in the "war of the cities" that finally broke Iran in the spring of 1988. Even though the Reagan administration did speak out when Iraq gassed the Kurds during al-Anfal, the White House never touched the issues of governance that have perpetually plagued the Iraqi state. In the American hierarchy of priorities, Iraq was little more than a counterweight to Iran.

Fulfilling American hopes, Iraq remained strong in its numbers of armed men. When the Iran-Iraq War ended at last, Iraq was the most militarily powerful country in the Persian Gulf. Even though rumors circulated about a secret nuclear program that could potentially counteract Israel's nuclear capability, the Reagan administration continued to regard Iraq only in the light of Iran. It was not alone in seeing the Iraqi regime as it wished to view it. At the time, a European diplomat told a Western journalist, "Whatever its faults, the regime is unquestionably the best that Iraq has had in centuries. There seems to be no serious democratic opposition to it. . . . It has a sense of purpose, a direction. It is honest and relatively efficient, and it is paternalistic, in that it has demonstrated concern for the poor. It has even mellowed over the years."[4]

During the first eighteen months of the George H. W. Bush administration, Iraq failed to garner much attention in a foreign policy arena cluttered by the collapse of the Soviet Union, revolutionary changes in Central and Eastern Europe, the process of German unification, the bloodshed in Tiananmen Square in China, and unrest in Central America. Iraq essentially went on the shelf of American foreign policy. Conventional wisdom of the day held that the searing experience of the Iran-Iraq War had produced the most stable and moderate government Iraq had known since the monarchy. Iraq's neighbors as well as Egypt and the Europeans shared the same view. They all encouraged the United States to reach out to Saddam Hussein in order to draw Iraq into the postwar order in the Gulf. Thus was written National Security Directive 26 of October 1989.

Entitled "U.S. Policy toward the Persian Gulf," the directive formalized the framework of a policy of limited engagement with Iraq. It began by stating that "access to Persian Gulf oil and the security of

---

[4] Quoted in Milton Viorst, "The View From the Mustansiriyah—I," *The New Yorker*, October 12, 1987, p. 108.

key friendly states in the area" remained vital to U.S. national security and concluded by saying that "normal relations between the United States and Iraq would serve our longer-term interests and promote stability in both the Gulf and the Middle East." The following January, President Bush signed a directive authorizing the Export-Import Bank to advance Iraq another $200 million in loan credits despite an ongoing investigation to determine whether Iraq had diverted CCC funds to purchase weapons materials. That decision, according to Secretary of State James A. Baker III, "turned out to be the high-water mark of [U.S.] efforts to moderate Iraqi behavior."[5]

Beginning in the spring of 1988, Iraq's regime did appear more moderate. Politically, the Baath endorsed a peaceful resolution of the Arab-Israeli conflict. Economically, trade ties with the United States strengthened. But the period in which the United States found a level of compatibility with Saddam Hussein's Iraq soon faded. In early 1989, evidence of a renewed Iraqi effort to produce chemical and biological weapons began to creep into intelligence reports. As a result, CIA agents stationed in Baghdad were expelled. A year later, Hussein executed a British journalist of Iranian origin on charges of espionage for Israel. Confirming earlier suspicions of Iraq's malevolent ambitions, material and devices for a series of dreaded weapons turned up on the shipping docks of several countries. As the alarm bells rang, Baghdad warned that if Iraq were attacked by Jerusalem, it would "eat up half of Israel with chemical weapons."[6] Then came the invasion of Kuwait and with it a flood of recriminations against the American government for a decade of tenuous engagement with Saddam Hussein.

The mistake the Bush administration made was not in inducement itself. It was in dealing with Iraq only as an adjunct of ongoing American efforts to contain revolutionary Islam advanced by Iran. By the end of the Iran-Iraq War, the United States, in pursuit of stability in the Persian Gulf, needed to adopt a two-track policy that reassessed American policy toward the Islamic Republic of Iran and approached the difficult and complex problem of nation building in Iraq. When Ayatollah Khomeini died in early June 1989, the upper

---

[5] Quoted in Kenneth I. Juster, "The United States and Iraq." In *Honey and Vinegar: Incentives, Sanctions and Foreign Policy*, ed. Richard N. Haass and Meghan L. O'Sullivan (Washington, D.C.: Brookings Institution, 2000), p. 57.

[6] Quoted in ibid., p. 58.

echelon of Iran's leadership, seared by the Islamic republic's own experience of a long brutal war, had already decided that the interests of the Iranian state exceeded the interests of Islam. Instead of pushing the Islamic revolution beyond its borders, the Islamic republic began to take the first halting steps to re-establish itself in the international community where its economic wounds could be tended. Yet, still emotionally tied to images of American hostages and dead U.S. Marines and haunted by the Iran Contra fiasco, the administration refused to read the signals coming out of Tehran. So instead of approaching the Persian Gulf as a lake on which the Arab side and the Persian side must be kept in equilibrium, the United States continued to engage the Iraqi regime of Saddam Hussein and isolate the Islamic Republic of Iran. As a consequence, American foreign policy failed to achieve the stability it so fervently sought. Instead, the Bush administration got the Iraqi invasion of Kuwait.

As soon as Saddam Hussein stepped over the border of Kuwait, the United States shifted into high gear to protect its vital interests in the crucial Persian Gulf. In the privacy of the White House Cabinet Room, Secretary of Defense Richard Cheney delivered a grim assessment: "Initially, we should sort this out from our strategic interests in Saudi Arabia and oil. [Saddam] has clearly done what he has to do to dominate OPEC, the Gulf, and the Arab world. He is forty kilometers from Saudi Arabia and its oil production is only a couple of hundred kilometers away. If he doesn't take it physically, with his new wealth he will still have an impact and will be able to acquire new weapons. The problem will get worse, not better."[7] But no matter how much Hussein's invasion of Kuwait threatened the United States, it could not be reversed unilaterally. The reason lay in the symbiotic relationship between the United States and Israel.

On May 15, 1948, one day after Britain surrendered its mandate over Palestine, the Zionist leader David Ben-Gurion had stood in the main gallery of the two-story Tel Aviv Museum of Art to "proclaim the establishment of the Jewish state in Palestine, to be called Israel." Eleven minutes later, President Harry Truman overrode the advice of his State Department to announce that the United States

---

[7] Quoted in George Bush and Brent Scowcroft, *A World Transformed* (New York: Alfred Knopf, 1998), p. 323.

would grant de facto recognition to the state of Israel. In the war for Palestine that followed, the Arabs suffered defeat at the hands of Zionist Jews, most of whom had come to Palestine from Europe.

The loss of Palestine translated into an intolerable loss of honor for the mythical Arab nation. As a near sacred symbol among Arabs—the site of victory over the European Crusaders in the twelfth century—Palestine crystallized into a tormenting symbol of Arab humiliation at the hands of what they judged the arrogant imperialistic West. To the Arabs, Israel, suckled on Western diplomatic and economic support, was the new Crusader state, the insidious surrogate of Western imperialism. And the 700,000 Palestinian refugees displaced by the 1948 war for Palestine became the emblem of Arab outrage at forces they could neither overcome nor vie with successfully. Ignoring the levels of their own complicity in the loss of Palestine and the refusal of most Arab states to accept the Palestinian refugees, the Arabs nursed their feelings of belittlement and humiliation, vowing to never forget or forgive.

By 1990, the United States had spent over four decades lavishing economic and military aid on Israel, providing political and diplomatic cover to every egregious action of the Jewish state against its Arab neighbors and the Palestinians under Jerusalem's post-1967 occupation. In spite of the fear Iraq had engendered in its region by its invasion of Kuwait, the United States could not unilaterally invade an Arab country without igniting the Arab masses and endangering the Arab regimes allied with the West. Understanding this, the Bush administration sought the cover of the United Nations in its confrontation with Saddam Hussein.

Embracing the idea of expelling Iraq from Kuwait with a multilateral force gathered under the auspices of the United Nations, George Bush worked the phones and dispatched his emissaries. Secretary of State James Baker drew on his personal relationship with Soviet Foreign Minister Eduard Shevardnadze to strike the crucial deal that opened the way for the Security Council resolutions under which the United States would go to war. Defense Secretary Cheney flew to Saudi Arabia with the aerial reconnaissance photographs that convinced timid King Fahd to invite American troops into the closed confines of the kingdom of the Sauds. Egypt, Syria, and the Gulf sheikhdoms repressed their anxieties about domestic reaction against their regimes to join a military force against an Arab state led by the

United States. Turkey reluctantly gave permission for U.S. planes to operate from its air bases. And the Europeans came on board. In a dazzling campaign of diplomacy, Bush collected over thirty nations into a grand coalition to confront Iraqi aggression under principles codified in the United Nations Charter. To the international law of conduct, the United States added its own strategic goals. Foremost among American objectives was to reduce Iraq's military capability to the point that Saddam Hussein could never again threaten his neighbors. But the defanging of Iraq came with a caveat related to the Islamic Republic of Iran. According to Bush, "The trick here was to damage his offensive capability without weakening Iraq to the point that a vacuum was created, and destroying the balance between Iraq and Iran, further destabilizing the region for years."[8] Thus, before the war began, the decision had already been made to ignore the needs of Iraq the nation in favor of the territorial integrity of Iraq the state, even at the price of Saddam Hussein's political survival.

The air campaign of the Gulf War began January 17, 1991, and the ground operations moved forward at 4:00 A.M. on February 24. Like the whole campaign to turn back the Iraqi invasion of Kuwait, the ground war contained two precisely defined objectives: the expulsion of Iraq from Kuwait and destruction of Hussein's Republican Guards. On the third day of combat, word came to the White House that Iraqi forces were evacuating Kuwait City so rapidly that men and machines had become tangled up on the roads and bridges leading toward Iraq. To the west, the U.S. VII Corps and XVIII Airborne Corps, Britain's First Armored Division, and the France's Sixth Light Armored Division advanced into the Euphrates valley of Iraq to entrap the Republican Guards in a snare thrown along the Kuwait-Iraqi border. The awful unknown at the time was that the Republican Guards had not been entrapped. The southern front in Kuwait had collapsed so fast that the Guards either had not been able to move out of Iraq to re-enforce the Iraqis' front line or Saddam Hussein, recognizing defeat, had held them back. Meanwhile the rest of Iraq's army continued to dissolve. With Kuwait no longer occupied, the coalition the United States had constructed no longer had a mandate. All that was left to do was to declare victory on February 27 and prepare the speedy withdrawal promised to America's Arab

---

[8] Ibid., pp. 383–384.

allies as their price for joining the coalition. Later, Brent Scowcroft, Bush's national security advisor, reflected, "In what was probably too cute by half, we agreed to end hostilities at midnight, Washington time, for a ground war of exactly 100 hours."[9]

The terms of the cease-fire were laid down at Safwan in southern Iraq. Hussein was not there, nor had his presence been demanded. After seven months of effort to bring the Iraqi president into compliance with the dictates of world order, everyone knew he would not come voluntarily. To force his presence would have required the deployment of a huge number of troops and an enormous amount of equipment to occupy the sprawling city of Baghdad, three hundred miles upstream from the Kuwait theater of operations. Failure to find him in the capital meant occupation of more of Iraq with no guaranteed exit strategy. Operations Desert Shield and Desert Storm had already cost $60 billion. How much more would it cost to shackle Hussein and march him to the peace table? No one, least of all the U.S. president, was happy. The day after the cease-fire, Bush confided to his diary. "It hasn't been a clean-end—there is no battleship Missouri surrender. This is what's missing to make this akin to World War II, to separate Kuwait from Korea and Vietnam."[10] Nonetheless, the cease-fire had come and with it the perplexing questions of peace.

IT SOON BECAME CLEAR that a significant portion of the Republican Guards had survived the war. When the Bush administration considered a return to combat to eliminate Hussein's elite forces, the president and his advisors stared into a wall of negative factors. On the home front, yellow ribbons tied to front porches and wrapped around trees meant America wanted its sons and daughters home. Leaders of the Arab countries belonging to the coalition had warned at the time they joined that they would not support any plan either to occupy Iraq or to topple its ruling regime. They knew that such an attack on the sovereignty of Iraq would inflame Western xenophobia embedded in the psyche of the Arabs. Insecure in the reality of restive populations within their own borders, none of these leaders, particularly those of Saudi Arabia and Egypt, was willing to accept the label

[9] Bush and Scowcroft, *A World Transformed*, p. 486.
[10] Ibid., pp. 486–487.

"stooge of the West" applied by his own people. With little other choice, the United States accepted the position of its Arab allies.

From the beginning of the confrontation over Kuwait, the United States had hoped a member of Iraq's Sunni officer corps would dispose of Saddam Hussein. In one swift move, the regime would change, the threat Iraq posed to its neighborhood would vanish, and the domestic order within Iraq would remain intact. Focused on a coup rather than a rebellion, the United States and its coalition partners had made no contingency plans if their preferred scenario of disposing of Hussein failed to materialize. As the dominant leader of the war effort, the United States had avoided coming to grips with Iraq's complex society and its blood-splattered history. Consequently, when the Shia *intifadah* erupted, Washington was not ready to move from a military role to a political role as nursemaid to what might be an Iraqi state released from the tyranny of Saddam Hussein.

In the Shia explosion of March 1991, the rebels fought Hussein with one arm while the United States tightened the Shia's arm against the back of its own uprising. Knowing that the insurrection would collapse without outside help, the rebelling Shia clamored for arms. But when rebels in the river town of Nassariyah broke into an Iraqi army barracks to seize desperately needed guns and ammunition, the Americans in control of southern Iraq stopped them. At the same time, U.S. Army units throughout the zone of occupation in southern Iraq systematically blew up Hussein's captured weapons stores and communications equipment rather than turning them over to the Shia insurgents. With thousands of Shia civilians streaming into the allied enclave, the U.S. Army refused for days to take formal responsibility for the refugees. While declaring it would abide by the Geneva Convention, which holds an occupying power responsible for the welfare of civilians, Washington made it perfectly clear that American forces would leave southern Iraq as soon as a permanent cease-fire under the auspices of the United Nations was arranged. At Safwan where the Gulf War had ended, terrified Shia begged fresh-faced soldiers ignorant of the subtleties of international politics not to desert them. But the Shia had been deserted, left at the mercy of a vicious, wounded wolf—the army of Saddam Hussein.

The reasons were multiple. Both the American military and Baghdad had locked the international press out of southern Iraq. Yet even if all the networks with all their cameras and on-air talent had been there, it probably would have made little difference to U.S. policy. Military support to Shia rebels was a difficult sell to an American public. During the 1980's, there had been too much rhetoric from the Islamic Republic of Iran; too many suicide bombings of U.S. embassies and American military facilities; too many hostages taken in airline hijackings or snatched off the streets of Beirut. Just the word *Shia* in whatever context raised among Americans all the images of Islamic revolution and U.S. intervention in Lebanon between 1982 and 1984. For the administration, the memory of the failed Lebanon operation evoked fears of an even larger disaster. Thus, black-draped women begging for water in southern Iraq raised little sympathy in the United States among either policy makers or an American public ignorant of the culture and politics of Iraq.

Outside the United States, the European and Arab allies of the coalition warned President Bush of the bloody quagmire the Shia *intifadah* could become. Most Bush advisors agreed. If some loose combination of rebels felled the Sunni-dominated institutions that kept Iraq together—the army, the security police, and the Baath Party—the Shia majority would be left to determine the future of Iraq. That injected the powerful voice of Israel into the deliberations in Washington. According to an official in Jerusalem, "We don't want a Shiite-based regime in Iraq, which would be even more militant than Saddam against Israel."[11] Yet as much as anything, the administration that had just rid the American people of their self-imposed disgrace over Vietnam was not about to be sucked into a civil conflict with no predictable, orderly end. Ruling out intervention, Bush drew a "no-fly zone" across southern Iraq where American aircraft provided a symbolic gesture of protection for those being pulverized by Hussein. Staying out of the Kurdish rebellion proved more difficult.

LIKE THE SHIA *intifadah*, the Kurdish rebellion unfolded under the veil of Iraqi censorship. It was in the aftermath, when television cameras along the Iraq-Turkey border broadcast pictures of thousands of fleeing refugees, that the world learned of the Kurdish revolt and its consequences. Although the Bush administration wanted the Kurdish rebellion to die before it dismantled Iraq, the Kurds, girded by the power of television, raised ever more insistent demands for

---

[11] Quoted in *Newsweek*, April 15, 1991.

Western air power to take out the Iraqi helicopter gunships that were sowing terror across Kurdistan. Instead, the Bush administration pumped out a stream of public statements clearly enunciating its decision to stay clear of the battle between the Kurds and Hussein. In a moment of frankness, a State Department official told a reporter, "It probably sounds callous, but we did the best thing not to get near [the Kurdish revolt]. They're nice people, and they're cute, but they're really just bandits. They spend as much time fighting each other as central authority. They're losers."[12] A senior Middle East analyst was more diplomatic and probably more accurate in voicing American opinion: "It's autonomy today, but a separate state tomorrow. We all know that."[13]

Despite legitimate worries that American involvement in the Iraqi north could trap the United States into deciding who should govern Iraq, the pictures and sounds of thousands of Kurds crawling over snow-capped mountains kept coming over the airwaves. In the corridors of Washington and on the op-ed pages of newspapers across the country, Americans wrestled with their responsibility in the Kurdish rebellion. The debate reflected the perpetual tension in U.S. foreign policy between idealism and realpolitik. Elsewhere, some of the allies of the coalition avoided the existential debate. In Syria, Hafiz al-Assad weighed satisfaction in seeing the fall of Saddam Hussein against the 11 percent of the Syrian population who, as Kurds, might be drawn toward a Kurdish enclave in northern Iraq. But it was Turkey, the host to the northern contingent of American air power during the Gulf War, that most pressed its concerns on Washington. As much as 25 percent of the population of Turkey is Kurdish. Turkish Kurds have always strained against the Turkish state. Now further sedition threatened to accompany the Kurdish refugees fleeing from Iraq. Determined to block a tide of Iraqi Kurds from feeding into the Kurdish insurrection that had been sputtering along in southeastern Turkey for years, Ankara sealed the refugees in the mountains of Iraq

In an attempt to escape international condemnation for ignoring the desperate situation of the Iraqi Kurds, Turkey proposed "enclaves" or "safe havens" inside Iraq where the refugees would be

---

[12] Quoted in *Newsweek*, April 15, 1991.
[13] Ibid.

protected from attack by Hussein's forces. The idea proved difficult to sell to some members of the UN Security Council, particularly the Soviet Union and China, who feared that such a move would set a precedent of UN intervention in what was essentially an internal affair. Accepting that there was little chance of pushing a resolution through the Security Council, the United States, under intensifying domestic pressure, decided to act unilaterally. Backed by Britain and France, President Bush warned Hussein against the use of fixed-wing aircraft or helicopters north of the thirty-sixth parallel and the deployment of any kind of armed force that interfered with relief efforts. Keeping humanitarian action separate from political policy, the White House continued to repeat the message that the United States had no intention of establishing a Kurdish state within Iraq. At the moment, it seemed a sensible way to thwart Baghdad's objective of pushing the dissident Kurds out of northern Iraq. It might have succeeded were it not for the swelling mass of refugees.

Twenty-four-hour television feeds from the mountains of northern Iraq beamed images of thousands of Kurds huddled in the open, deprived of the basics of survival. Public pressure mounted on the president, who defensively repeated, "No one can see the pictures or hear the accounts of this human suffering—men, women and, most painfully of all, innocent children—and not be deeply moved."[14] To understand the scope of the Kurdish refugee crisis, Bush dispatched James Baker to assess the situation on the ground. The secretary of state stepped out of a helicopter at the military base in Cukurca, Turkey, hopped into a jeep, and set off on a twisting mountain road that led to Iraq. As he came around a bend, he suddenly saw the plight of fifty thousand Kurds. After lingering for only seven minutes, he returned to his aircraft and summoned his aides to tell them, "We can't let this go on. We've got to do something—and we've got to do it now."[15]

Under the circumstances, the only organization with enough muscle and know-how to provide the instant help needed was the Pentagon. Quietly the U.S. European Command, based in Stuttgart, Germany, took over the entire relief operation. In a massive effort

---

[14] Quoted in Daniel Schorr, "Ten Days That Shook the White House," *Columbia Journalism Review* 30 (August 1991): 23.

[15] Quoted in *Newsweek*, April 29, 1991.

known as Operation Provide Comfort, U.S. soldiers entered the mountains of northern Iraq to organize the sprawls of squatters into refugee camps. Employing the largest helicopters in the American arsenal, soldiers and airmen delivered tents, blankets, medical supplies, and at least one meal a day to 700,000 people in an effort that was declared humanitarian, not political.

Thus, within weeks of the cease-fire in the Gulf War, the conflicting U.S. objectives of defeating Saddam Hussein while keeping Iraq intact had produced what a close advisor to Bush frankly called a "muddle" in American foreign policy. Later National Security Advisor Brent Scowcroft admitted, "We recognized that the seemingly attractive goal of getting rid of Saddam would not solve our problems, or even necessarily serve our interests. So we pursued the kind of inelegant, messy alternative that is all too often the only one available in the real world. . . . Had we continued the war and overthrown Saddam, we might be worse off today . . . [by committing] American troops to occupation duty indefinitely."[16]

Could the results have been different? Maybe. In important respects, the ground war went too well in that the Marine advance into Kuwait moved so fast that it closed off the left hook of the battle plan that was supposed to entrap the Republican Guards. The war probably ended too soon. According to General Norman Schwarzkopf, the allied commander, "Another two days and we would have taken out everything the Iraqis had in the south."[17] Others reply that Schwarzkopf made his own mistake by granting the Iraqis permission at Safwan to fly the helicopters that killed the Shia and Kurdish rebellions. But perhaps the biggest mistake on the side of the United States was one of omission. Iraq might have been rid of Saddam Hussein without marching on Baghdad if the United States had provided cover for that part of the Iraqi army that wanted to move north to take out the Baath despot. After all this was the preferred scenario, elimination of Hussein by the Sunni officer corps of the army. These errors were largely military. The political errors came in the rebellions.

According to William Quandt, a highly respected expert on the

---

[16] Quoted in Jonathan C. Randal, *After Such Knowledge, What Forgiveness?* (Boulder, Colo.: Westview Press, 1999), p. 299.

[17] Quoted in *Newsweek*, April 29, 1991.

Middle East, "It is appalling that we stood aside in the uprisings. We let one Iraqi division go through our lines to get to Basra because the United States did not want the regime to collapse."[18] That was because the United States was still locked in the mentality that has driven American policy in the Gulf since 1979—fear of the Islamic Republic of Iran. Rather than recognizing the Shia as predominately Arabs who held genuine, long-term grievances against Baghdad, the United States failed to allow the process of reform of the Iraqi political system to begin.

Again, America was not alone in its hesitation to act. Britain and France also accepted Hussein as a useful rampart against Iran. The Saudis and the Kuwaitis, the paymasters of the Gulf War, wanted Iraq to remain intact in the hands of the Sunnis to protect their own regimes from their own Shia. The Turks dreaded the possibility that regional instability, once unleashed by the Kurds, would infect not just Iraq but also Iran, Syria, and Turkey itself. For an additional number of governments, including that of the United States, the dismemberment of Iraq would be "tantamount to opening a Pandora's box, creating a large, unstable frontier region in which the surrounding states would have conflicting claims, both to territory and to religious and ethnic groups."[19] Thus, Saddam Hussein remained in power not because the West and Iraq's neighbors wanted him to stay but because all were terrified of inheriting the Iraq he left behind. In the aftermath of the Shia and Kurdish rebellions, the United States, the Europeans, and Iraq's neighbors—all committed to achieving regional stability—sought to contain Iraq's tyrant with another series of resolutions delivered by the UN Security Council. Rather than ridding the region of Saddam Hussein, they have further undercut the Iraqi state.

---

[18] Interview with author, Charlottesville, Virginia, April 3, 2001.
[19] Christine Moss Helms, *Iraq: Eastern Front of the Arab World* (Washington, D.C.: Brookings Institution, 1984), p. 200.

11

THE WAR OF
CONTAINMENT

A decade after the end of the Gulf War, economic sanctions hung like chains around the neck of the Iraqi people. They were there because the administrations of George H. W. Bush and Bill Clinton focused American policy vis-à-vis Iraq exclusively on containment of Saddam Hussein's conventional and nonconventional weapons. In concert with the United Nations, neither president came to grips with the reality that the long-term security interests of the United States required the engagement of the Iraqi people in a vision of their future as a nation. Shirking the challenge of the Iraqi state, the United States threw the Iraqi people into the ravenous jaws of Saddam Hussein. By the time the next crisis in the Middle East came in the form of terrorism, the United States as the hard-line proponent of sanctions appeared no more concerned about the suffering of the Iraqi people than Saddam Hussein.

After the Gulf War and the failed Shia and Kurd rebellions, the Bush administration's policy toward Iraq focused on only two principles: the preservation of Iraq's territorial integrity and the implementation of UN Security Council resolutions aimed at policing Iraq's armaments. The enforcement of these resolutions relied on sanctions imposed by the United Nations Security Council that forbid Iraq to sell oil that would provide the financial resources for weapons, and also imposed on the country a total trade embargo with the outside world that often supplied those weapons. The dangled reward was the promise to lift the sanctions as soon as the newly constituted United Nations' Special Commission on Iraq (UNSCOM) certified that Iraq was rid of its long-range ballistic missiles as well as its programs dedicated to producing chemical, biological, and nuclear weapons. Although economic sanctions were a means to limit Saddam Hussein's ability to obtain revenue with which to build up his weapons programs, the common hope was that the longer the sanctions stayed in force, the less control Hussein could exercise over his country. In the ideal, he would either comply or fall from power.[1]

Almost immediately, the carefully drawn scenario went afoul. In material terms, the man who had dominated Iraq since 1979 was determined to hang on to his weapons, his only remaining source of real power. In psychological terms, he needed to protect his honor, which was so lavishly tended by his propaganda machine. Thus, the battle lines formed between Hussein, husbanding his remaining weapons, and Bush, determined to box him in with sanctions and a large American air and sea force in the Persian Gulf.

In early June 1991, the chemists, biologists, weapons experts, and diplomats belonging to UNSCOM arrived in Baghdad to begin the mandated disarmament of Iraq. The unseen obstacle in their path was Hussein's concealment team, composed of selected members of the Mukhabarat, the ultra-elite Special Republican Guards, and the Special Security Service. Each individual was absolutely loyal to Saddam Hussein; most were related to him. Between June 21 and June 28, one of their cadres at an inspection site fired live ammunition over the heads of inspectors attempting to exercise their right under Resolution 687 to "unconditional and unrestricted" access to everything associated with Iraq's weapons programs. But the UNSCOM team members refused to retreat. Camping in a parking lot in front of the building, they held their ground until they were allowed to leave with the documents they sought. By September, the inspectors were dogging the scientists in charge of Iraq's biological and chemical programs, who were derisively referred to as "Dr. Germ" and "Dr. Gas." In October, UNSCOM succeeded in forcing Iraq to admit to the existence of a nuclear program directed at producing the dreaded "bomb." The following month, the regime made the required "full and final disclosure" of its weapons. But almost immediately inspectors discovered even more weapons stores, rendering the "disclosure" just another ploy in the cat-and-mouse game between UNSCOM and Saddam Hussein.

---

[1] An additional bonus from the ban on Iraqi oil sales kept three million barrels of oil a day off the international markets. Reduced supply in turn kept a floor under world petroleum prices, thus helping financially strapped Saudi Arabia and Kuwait.

Nevertheless, the inspectors, operating out of a fenced, nondescript building on the outskirts of Baghdad, continued to descend on suspected factories, offices, research centers, or anywhere else evidence of forbidden weapons might be concealed. The information they collected was analyzed and collated with data gathered from defectors, invoices of Iraq's overseas purchases, and photographs from high-altitude surveillance aircraft and satellites circling the globe. Then, Rolf Ekeus, the Swedish diplomat who was UNSCOM's executive director, would arrive in Baghdad and take his place across the table from ranking representatives of the Iraqi government to painstakingly address all the discrepancies uncovered by his team. It became a familiar pattern of Iraqi denials, UNSCOM discovery, partial disclosure, further investigation, and more grudging disclosure.

While the Bush administration floundered in frustration, Hussein relished the repeated confrontations with UN inspectors. Having declared that UNSCOM's right to inspect suspected weapons sites constituted an issue over which it was prepared to go to war, the United States found itself bereft of any meaningful allies except Britain. That left American air power and the threat of bombing as the only tools against Hussein's intransigence. Sometimes it worked. On July 26, 1992, the imposition of a no-fly zone for any aircraft over southern Iraq was enough to unlock the Ministry of Agriculture to the arms inspectors.

Meanwhile, the American presidential election of 1992 approached. Although an economy mired in recession was the overriding issue, some Americans also expressed an opinion about what they considered the unfinished Gulf War. If these Americans failed to understand why Saddam Hussein remained in power, Hussein failed to grasp the continuity of the United States' policy toward Iraq.

WHEN BILL CLINTON took over the problem of Saddam Hussein at noon on January 20, 1993, his new administration left Iraq policy essentially unchanged. In pursuit of the single goal of containing Hussein's weapons, Clinton reaffirmed the U.S. commitment to sanctions and the maintenance of the no-fly zones over northern and southern Iraq. To this, he added something called "Dual Containment."

In essence, Clinton's foreign policy team looked at the strategy of the 1980s in which Iraq was used to balance Iran. But instead of now engaging Iran to balance Iraq, the United States announced its intention to maintain an American quarantine on both the Islamic Republic of Iran and Iraq. Ignoring the continuing moderation of the Islamic revolution and the common interest of the United States and Iran in restraining Iraq, Clinton sent another message to Saddam Hussein via air power. On evidence of Iraqi plans to assassinate former president Bush during an April visit to Kuwait, the new president, in May 1993, ordered twenty-three cruise missiles costing $1.1 million each to hit centers of Iraqi intelligence in Baghdad. To the disappointment of Washington, it changed nothing in the seek-and-conceal scenario of arms inspection.

Despite encountering countless roadblocks thrown up by the Iraqi regime, UNSCOM still made progress. Since the spring of 1991, Hussein had been forced to give up much. By 1994, Rolf Ekeus believed that UNSCOM stood on the threshold of certifying Iraqi compliance with Resolution 687, which would pave the way for lifting the sanctions. Then Hussein Kamel turned up in Jordan in August 1995 as a defector from the regime, bringing with him Iraq's weapons secrets. Subsequently, UNSCOM unlocked a chicken shed on a farm not far from Baghdad airport. Inside was box upon box of documents, photographs, microfiches, and computer disks related to Hussein's nuclear ambitions, the production of the VX nerve agent, and biological weapons loaded on the warheads of missiles. For four years, the concealment team had outfoxed the inspectors. Armed with the new information, UNSCOM marched on and the sanctions stayed in place. Yet everyone except Saddam Hussein was beginning to suffer from inspections fatigue. Ekeus resigned from UNSCOM in July 1997 to become Sweden's ambassador to Washington. He was replaced by Richard Butler, an Australian diplomat by profession, but more an enforcer than a negotiator by temperament. Butler unleashed Scott Ritter, an eager former U.S. Marine, to run the concealment scheme to the ground. The Iraqis countered by accusing UNSCOM of spying for the United States and Israel. They backed up the charge with evidence that in 1992 David Kay, an American member of UNSCOM, had submitted Iraqi documents to the United States before giving them to the United Nations and that Scott Ritter had shared U-2 reconnaissance photographs with Israel. At the end of October 1997, Baghdad ordered Americans working for UNSCOM out of Iraq. By mid-November, the United Nations, failing to convince Hussein to rescind his order, withdrew the remaining members of

UNSCOM. In his first real test of wills with Hussein, Clinton ordered the aircraft carrier *George Washington* and four other ships to the Persian Gulf. Hussein backed down, and the inspectors returned.

UNSCOM's next round with Iraq came when Butler added Hussein's presidential palaces to the list of inspection sites. When Hussein refused to open their doors, access to palaces became the new defining issue of arms inspection for the United States. In American eyes, the grandiose structures were not residences but complexes whose size could be measured in square miles within which all manner of weapons could be hidden. To Hussein, a presidential palace was a stone-and-stucco testament to his defiance of forces from the West. Thus, while Hussein stood the ground of national sovereignty, Clinton threatened military action. But the American president's voice was one with almost no backup.

The coalition built by George Bush had been shredded by fatigue and inattention. The Saudis, whose territory was crucial to any major military action against Iraq, shut their gates to U.S. warplanes making bombing runs against Iraq. Russia and France sat at the table of the Security Council poised to veto any resolution authorizing force against Baghdad over the issue of inspection of palaces. Unable to win support from the Security Council, the United States laid claim to "national interest." With an arrogance perhaps born of frustration, Secretary of State Madeleine Albright proclaimed, "If we have to use force, it is because we are America. We are the indispensable nation. We stand tall. We see further into the future."[2]

Under this prerogative, plans to launch a military strike against Iraq moved forward. At an estimated cost of $1.4 billion, 44,000 troops, 440 aircraft, and 34 ships were collected in the Persian Gulf. By late December, Clinton was ready. The Pentagon was ready. But the administration had failed to line up its allies or to consult extensively with Congress. Nor had it sold military action to the American public.

Madeleine Albright, Secretary of Defense William Cohen, and Sandy Berger, the president's national security advisor, hit the road. On February 18, 1998, at a CNN-sponsored town hall meeting at Ohio State University, the policy they came to sell faced public condem-

---

[2] Quoted in Stephen Zunis, "Confrontation with Iraq: A Bankrupt U.S. Policy," *Middle East Policy* 6 (June 1998): 95.

nation as person after person—male and female, young and old—
stood before the television cameras to challenge the idea of sending
more American forces to the Persian Gulf. Seared by vivid images of
the protests of the Vietnam era, the emissaries retreated back to
Washington. Hung out on a limb that was now being sawed off, the
Clinton foreign policy team looked for escape from its confrontation
with Iraq. A ladder arrived in the hands of Kofi Annan, secretary-general of the United Nations.

In a meeting at the secretary-general's Sutton Place home,
Albright laid out the "red lines" of what the United States demanded
of Iraq—acceptance of UNSCOM's unrestricted access to all sites
suspected of hiding forbidden weapons as well as operational control over inspection of those sites. To ensure that everyone was on
the same page, the United States wanted a written statement from
Iraq acknowledging its understanding of the "very serious consequences" of noncompliance. Carrying the agreement of the permanent members of the Security Council, Annan flew to Baghdad,
where he won the government's agreement to the new regimen. In
what would prove a temporary truce rather than a final settlement
of the bitter inspection issue, Clinton warned that if the accord collapsed, the United States was poised to strike Iraq "at a time, place
and manner of our choosing."[3] But within the privacy of the Oval
Office, Clinton passed word to his foreign policy team that for the
time being there would be no more attempts at military action to
force Iraqi cooperation with arms inspectors. Instead, the United
States would turn the problem of Iraq over to diplomats and non-
governmental organizations pursing their own agendas.

In late April 1998, I went to Iraq with almost 10,000 pounds of
medical supplies provided by Americares, a humanitarian aid organization headquartered in New Cannan, Connecticut. As the first shipment of aid to Iraq that had been officially condoned by the
American government since the invasion of Kuwait, it was a high-
profile operation that included a film crew from NBC's show *Dateline*,
news anchor John Roberts, and actor Val Kilmer. On the day we left
Amman for Baghdad, Robert C. Macauley, the founder and chairper-
son of Americares, said in a written statement, "Today is a day to
extend a hand of friendship to the people of Iraq. And now that the

---

[3] Quoted in *New York Times*, February 25, 1998.

threat of hostilities has been reduced, there is no better time to create a human bridge between individual Americans and individual
Iraqi citizens."[4] It never happened. Saddam Hussein refused to be
coaxed into engagement with the United States by a shipment of
medical supplies for his suffering people.

Thus, on August 5, the Iraqi government, in violation of the agreement reached by Kofi Annan in February, announced that it was ter-
minating all cooperation with arms inspectors, thereby ending their
searches. In October, Scott Ritter, the former American Marine who
had resigned from UNSCOM during the summer, turned himself into
a celebrity by accusing the Clinton administration of restraining
inspectors in order to avoid another flare-up with Iraq. In an interview
on NBC's *Nightly News* with Tom Brokaw, he said, "The fix is in . . .
between Saddam and Kofi Annan and the U.S. administration. . . . If
the Security Council continues down the path Iraq will emerge from
this whole effort . . . having stood up and confronted the world and
won. We'll have lost the Gulf War."[5] On the same program, Dr. Khidhir
Hamza, a top scientist in Iraq's nuclear weapons program who had
defected, told NBC's Andrea Mitchell, "Producing weapons of mass
destruction . . . is [Hussein's] major goal. He'll never give up on that.
This is the thing that keeps him in power now."[6]

On November 1, Hussein upped the ante again by suspending
UNSCOM's long-term monitoring program of previously inspected
sites. Events now fell into their familiar pattern. The Security Council
condemned the Iraqi action but remained divided on whether to
authorize military strikes. The Clinton administration insisted that a
legal basis already existed for bombing Iraq, empowering the United
States to act alone. This time garnering support from Egypt, Syria,
and six Arab states of the Persian Gulf, but lacking the Security
Council votes of France, Russia, and China, Clinton ordered another
show of American military force. By November 11, 27,500 U.S. troops
were in the Gulf. On the decks of the USS *Eisenhower* and the USS
Enterprise, pilots sat in the cockpits of their F-14 and F/A-18 Hornet
warplanes ready to take off to inflict damage on Saddam Hussein's

---

[4] Quoted in *Jordan Times*, April 25, 1998.

[5] Transcript available at www.msnbc.com/news/200998.asp, October 6, 1998.

[6] Transcript available at www.msnbc.com/news/201386.asp, October 6, 1998.

Iraq. Only fifteen minutes before "go time," Clinton called off the attack. Hussein had backed down.

On December 9, less than three weeks after UNSCOM had returned to Iraq, Hussein barred inspectors from the Baghdad City headquarters of the Baath Party. Richard Butler reported to the secretary-general on December 15 that Iraq had not provided its full cooperation as promised on November 14. Baghdad not only had initiated new forms of restrictions on the commission's work but also had "ensured that no progress was able to be made in either the fields of disarmament or accounting for its prohibited weapons programmes."[7] On December 16, the day the House of Representatives was scheduled to vote on the impeachment of President Bill Clinton, the United States let loose its firepower in Operation Desert Fox.[8] Once more the night skies over Baghdad lit up as television cameras from around the world broadcast the spectacle from the roof of the international press center. To the north, missiles hit Tikrit, Samarra, and Mosul. To the south, they fell on Kut, Qurnah, and Basra. The target of them all was the Republican Guards, who, according to Secretary of Defense Cohen, "are the lynchpin of Saddam's grip on power. They defend him personally. They brutally repress all dissent in Iraq, and they control and hide his chemical and biological weapons."[9]

Back in his battle fatigues, Hussein fought back with rhetoric: "Our great people and our brave armed forces resist and fight them."[10] But on the street, the people greeted the latest U.S. efforts to enforce weapons inspections on Hussein with weary resignation. With neither side considering their welfare, they remained the victims of the standoff between the United States' sole goal in Iraq—containment of Saddam Hussein—and the Iraqi president's premier interest—rebuilding his ravaged arsenal.

Twenty hours after the bombing began, Clinton ordered

---

[7] Letter dated December 15, 1998, from the executive chairman of the Special Commission established by the secretary-general pursuant to paragraph 9 (b) (i) of Security Council Resolution 687 (1991) addressed to the secretary-general.

[8] At the time, pundits charged, and many Americans believed, that Operation Desert Fox was nothing more than a diversionary tactic in the Monica Lewinsky scandal.

[9] Quoted in *New York Times*, December 21, 1998.

[10] Quoted from the Iraqi News Agency, quoted in *New York Times*, December 18, 1998.

American forces to stand down, and Hussein shut down all cooperation with UNSCOM. Seven years after the Gulf War, arms inspections were ended with Hussein still gripping a remnant of his precious weapons store of 1991 and the potential to wreak havoc in his neighborhood. A glum administration official admitted, "Nobody that I know has a strategy that they think will get rid of Saddam in the next six months or year, unless you are willing to put in a large U.S. ground force there."[11] That left Washington with expanded rules of engagement in the no-fly zones to chip away at Iraq's air defenses. Consequently, day after day through 1999, U.S. and British aircraft bombed Iraqi targets in a silent war to which American public opinion paid little attention while the UN Security Council struggled to structure some type of new arms inspection formula acceptable to Baghdad. In January 2000, the United Nations Monitoring, Verification and Inspection Commission (UNMOVIC), a watered-down "son of UNSCOM," was finally born. But Iraq refused to admit arms inspectors under its provisions.

Outside Iraq, Richard Butler, the hard-nosed chief of UNSCOM, still fought on. In a book published in the summer of 2000, he charged that Iraq has the know-how to put together an atomic bomb within twelve months if it can obtain fissionable material, which will be purchased at some point, probably on the black markets of the former Soviet Union. But Ritter, the bulldog of UNSCOM, now maintained that "Iraq no longer possesses any meaningful quantities of chemical or biological agents, if it possessed any at all. . . . The same was true of Iraq's nuclear and ballistic missile capabilities."[12] In its waning months of office, the Clinton administration, exhausted by the eight-year joust with Saddam Hussein, said nothing as it waited to pass the dilemma of Iraq onto another president.

UNABLE TO TOPPLE Saddam Hussein or bring him to heel on arms inspections, U.S. policy on Iraq under the administrations of both George H. W. Bush and Bill Clinton fell by default to sanctions. Imposed by the UN Security Council four days after the invasion of Kuwait, sanctions—explicitly linked to arms control—were sold as the mechanism by which Iraq would be disarmed. But instead of rid-

---

[11] Quoted in *New York Times*, December 23, 1998.
[12] Quoted in *New York Times*, July 3, 2000.

ding Iraq of its most noxious weapons, sanctions have been the playing field on which Saddam Hussein and the United States, attended by Britain, have spent over a decade slowly slaughtering Iraqis and their frail society.

Seizing the offensive, Saddam Hussein blocked attempts by international relief organizations to minister to hundreds of thousands of Iraqis suffering under Iraq's collapsed infrastructure. Thus, while millions of dollars worth of infant formula and high-protein food packages sat in warehouses, the Iraqi government refused to allow distribution as long as sanctions stayed in place. As a result, the special nutrition centers across the country stayed closed. And their clients, Iraqi children under five who were the most vulnerable to malnutrition and infectious disease, sickened and often died. It was also Baghdad that stifled the implementation of the UN oil-for-food program that turned innocent Iraqis into hostages to their leader's refusal to comply with the UN mandate on disarmament.

For five long years, Saddam Hussein rejected every Security Council proposal designed to supply food and medicine to the Iraqi people. From the start, he staked out two complementary reasons for the rejection of help: relief provided under the United Nations would lead to further UN intrusion into Iraq's internal affairs, and the country's humanitarian and economic development needs could be addressed only by the complete lifting of the sanctions. Meanwhile, the Iraqis sunk toward a level of poverty approaching that of Bangladesh. By 1995, the United Nations estimated that a quarter of Iraq's children were suffering from malnutrition. Furthermore, the government ration on which the survival of the masses depended was meeting only 50 percent of their nutritional needs. But food was only one factor contributing to the Iraqis' pain. There were no medicines to treat infection, no insulin for diabetics, no saline solution for children dehydrated by diarrhea caused by contaminated water, and no vaccines to fight typhoid, diphtheria, and polio.

Stalked by the hard truth that desperation has a way of fomenting revolution, Hussein in 1996 finally yielded to UN Security Council Resolution 986 known as "oil for food." Originally offered in 1991, Iraq was to be allowed to sell $1.6 billion worth of crude oil every six months. The proceeds were to go into an escrow account from which UN supervisors would buy food, medicine, and other essentials for the Iraqi people. In 1995 at the height of Iraq's humanitarian needs,

Resolution 986 increased the limit on oil sales to $1 billion every ninety days. From this, the United Nations would purchase goods to be distributed in Iraq by the Iraqi government.[13] Under this plan, the first shipment of food—a load of chickpeas and white flour from Turkey—arrived in March 1997. Month by month, food became more plentiful. However, hidden obstacles that diverted a portion of relief supplies to the regime assured that help did not always reach the Iraqis who needed it the most. Drew Hannah, back in Iraq to follow up on that high-profile aid mission that landed in Baghdad in April, told me, "Americares is furious about the amount of time the government is taking in testing the medical supplies we sent. It has been two months since the shipment arrived. The testing is yet to be done."[14]

By August 1999, Secretary-General Kofi Annan was telling the Iraqi government that it could do more to help mothers and children under the oil-for-food program. Although Iraq's revenues from oil exports had risen sharply, the government was allocating almost six and a half million dollars less on nutritionally enhanced food products needed by children and lactating women than it was in 1996. Baghdad was also ordering through the oil-for-food program smaller quantities of essential foods for the general public. As a result, the number of calories provided in monthly food rations had declined. The medicines purchased did not always get distributed, particularly in suspect areas like the south. Instead, they showed up in the markets of Lebanon, Syria, and Jordan. At the same time, Iraq's cooperation with the UN's humanitarian programs began to experience the same harassment as the arms inspectors. In 2000, Baghdad refused to admit a team of nutritionists and medical experts who were sent to assess the living conditions of Iraqis for the purpose of revising the oil-for-food program. A UN plan to spur the Iraqi economy by using some of the money from the country's oil sales to buy locally produced goods was similarly rejected. Offers by private relief organizations were turned down. As a result, milk from the Netherlands spoiled and a British "flying hospital" never landed. Not even UN humanitarian workers remained safe. In July 2000, the United

---

[13] Part of the proceeds went to Kuwait as compensation for the destruction of its oil facilities at the end of the Gulf War, and the rest was held to finance UN operations in Iraq, including arms inspections.

[14] Interview with author, New Canaan, Connecticut, June 24, 1998.

Nations pulled its employees out of southern Iraq after a gunman believed to have been dispatched by Baghdad opened fire on the UN Food and Agriculture Organization office. In all of these instances, Saddam Hussein was sending the message that he intended to take control of the money generated by Iraqi oil sales as well as the aid it purchased.

As Hussein held the Iraqis out as bait to end the sanctions, so did the United Nations, under intense pressure from the United States, lash them to arms control. With single-minded determination, disarmament took precedence over humanitarianism. In the unrelenting blockade on the economy imposed by the sanctions, a form of starvation developed that lay outside the absence of food.

Every single item legally imported by Iraq under the provisions of Resolution 986 had to be submitted for approval to the sanctions committee operating under the auspices of the Security Council. Within its membership, it was the United States more than any other country that scrutinized which items were approved and which rejected. The most seemingly inoffensive item, like a school pencil made with graphite, could be rejected on the grounds that it possessed a military as well as a civilian application. This designation of "dual use" stopped at the border of Iraq all manner of goods needed by the civilian sector—computers, car parts, tires, chlorine, fertilizer, and scientific journals. As a result, Iraq's infrastructure declined ever further as one shortage led to another. For example, rusted irrigation pipes stagnated food production, and broken equipment denied Iraq the levels of oil production allowed under Resolution 986, which led to further shortages due to reduced revenues. Even spare parts that did pass muster before the sanctions committee often got bogged down in a bureaucratic morass where it could take a year to win approval on one item.

In terms of water alone, the inability to restore old treatment plants or to build new ones reduced per capita consumption from 350 liters a day to 150. Water that was available bypassed nonfunctioning water treatment plants, or it came directly out of the rivers, dipped into skin bags, thrown over the backs of donkeys, and hauled home in the same manner as in the days of the Ottoman Empire. In this as much else, it seemed that time in Iraq had reversed. A middle-aged man carrying a kerosene lamp through a house darkened by the inadequacies of existing electrical facilities lamented, "The world has moved from oil lamps to electricity while Iraq has moved backward from electricity to oil lamps."

Even after help began to arrive under Resolution 986, the toll continued to hit children the hardest. In 1997, the office of the UN secretary-general reported chronic malnutrition in at least a quarter of Iraq's children. Among the poorest in the population, a thirteen-year-old often looked no larger than an eight-year-old. In the hospitals, ailing or dying children lay on beds with no sheets, coughed without medicine, gasped for air from antiquated inhalers, and stared at the ceiling while doctors adjusted electrodes improvised from metal buttons. Although the wards of the sick served well the regime's endless propaganda campaign against the sanctions, anyone who walked through them had to give some credence to a statement by Dr. Walid al-Tawil, the head of public health at Baghdad Medical School:. "Man does not live by bread alone. Not by weapons alone do people die."[15]

The full impact of the sanctions depended somewhat on where the victims lived. The Kurds, able to receive food and medicine ditributed directly within their northern enclave, suffered the least. The Shia of the south suffered the most. But no one outside the confines of the elite escaped. Increasingly, popular anger focused on the organization that had imposed the sanctions and now administered the purchase of food and medicine—the United Nations. Once inside the chain-link-fenced compound of the UN headquarters in Baghdad, I saw a four-wheel-drive vehicle carrying UN tags with a newly smashed windshield. The vandalism could have been part of a government-orchestrated campaign of harassment, but more likely it was a statement of popular resentment against the influx of UN officials, whom the Iraqis perceived as a new colonial class highly paid in hard currency.

The link between sanctions and arms control was made even more obvious by the fact that the UN's humanitarian staff and its arms inspectors shared the same building in Baghdad. However, they did not share the same mission. Every morning, arms inspectors left on their search-and-destroy missions and the aid workers went to survey the clinics and the food distribution centers. In Baghdad, I

---

[15] Interview with author, Baghdad, December 12, 1999.

asked Dennis Halliday, the UN humanitarian coordinator for Iraq at the time, if the dual role the United Nations was playing as policeman and altruist generated tensions within the building they shared. The bearded Irishman flashed a shy smile and said, "We do have our moments."[16] Halliday subsequently resigned in protest over the devastating effect of the sanctions on the Iraqi people, as did his successor Hans von Sponeck. But these voices of conscience failed to moderate United States policy on Iraq.

In both the Bush and Clinton administrations, the elimination of Hussein's weapons took priority over the physical condition of the Iraqis. Most Americans who paid attention to the debate on the sanctions may have agreed with the embargo, seeing it in terms of an ax chipping away at the power of Saddam Hussein. Nevertheless, a small percentage of the U.S. population refused to accept its government's argument that ending the sanctions would only increase the stores of Hussein's weapons of mass destruction.

From the day sanctions were imposed in 1991, some religious and peace groups in the United States went on the offensive against an American policy they claimed held the Iraqi people hostage to politics. The most vocal among them was Voices in the Wilderness, whose membership hurled both accurate and inflated figures of malnutrition and child mortality at the government's sanctions policy. These numbers, along with pictures of gaunt, hollow-eyed children circulated by other groups, had an effect. Year by year, the tide of domestic opposition rose. By 1998, Ramsey Clark, the grand warrior of protest, presided over a coalition of groups called the Iraq Sanctions Challenge. In May 1998, it delivered a shipment of medical supplies to Iraq in violation of American law. A combative Clark stood before a press conference in Baghdad to tell the world, "We have come in defiance of our own government. We do not feel any people can be forced to ask permission of a genocidal power."[17]

That Christmas, the American Friends Service Committee ran large ads in major newspapers carrying the names of a broad range of organizations and individuals including Thomas Gumbleton, auxiliary bishop of Detroit, and Daniel Berrigan, a once famous leader of protest against the Vietnam War. Above them, boldfaced type

---

[16] Interview with author, Baghdad, April 29, 1998.
[17] Quoted in *Atlanta Journal Constitution*, May 10, 1998.

across the top of the page read, "200 Iraqi civilians die every day from sanctions. How may Iraqi civilians will die tomorrow?" The tide of protest rose higher.

In 1999, attendees of a conference on Iraqi sanctions at the University of Michigan previewed a new film entitled "Silent Weapon: The Embargo against Iraq." Produced on behalf of the Compassion Iraq Coalition, it was targeted toward American churches of every denomination. Before the videos of the film went into circulation, speakers at the conclave claimed that the "inhuman and arbitrary policies of the American and UN overseers of the program . . . [continue to] block shipment of vital medicines and supplies [to Iraq] on the spurious grounds that they could serve a dual civilian and military purpose."[18] And Dr. Abbas al-Nasrawi, professor of economics at the University of Vermont, charged that the "aim of the United States in insisting on the maintenance of sanctions is: the destruction of Iraq as a modern industrial society and the prevention of its reemergence as a regional power in any way capable of challenging the interests of imperialism."[19]

The gathering in Ann Arbor was not an isolated incident. The issue of Iraqi sanctions was infiltrating the nation's campuses. On the tenth anniversary of the end of the Gulf War, a conference on American policy in the Persian Gulf brought protestors to camp out on the lawn of the University of Virginia. By then the sanctions were already collapsing.

MORE THAN CRIES of conscience, it was Iraq's control over 10 percent of the world's oil reserves that drove a wedge in the Security Council that presided over the sanctions regimen. Yet over the first seven years of the embargo, the impact of oil was as much negative as positive. During 1997, Iraq, under provisions of Resolution 986, pumped an additional million barrels of oil a day into the world's petroleum pipeline. Increased supply drove prices downward. In 1998, the growing gap between falling prices and the dollar amount of oil that Iraq was allowed to sell combined to double Iraqi production. Near-maximum capacity of Iraq's oil production facilities, an Asian economic

---

[18] Report on the University of Michigan Conference on Iraqi Sanctions, available at World Socialist Web Site, www.wsws.org, October 22, 1999.
[19] Ibid.

crisis, and two consecutive winters of unusually warm weather in the United States and Europe dropped oil prices under $10 a barrel. Then the always delicate balance in the oil market between demand and supply tipped the other way. Between January 1999 and September 2000, crude oil prices tripled in a market now defined by strong demand. Even though the price per barrel of benchmark crude topped $30, the world cried for oil. The Security Council had already doubled the cap that Iraq was allowed to spend for spare parts and equipment to restore its oil production facilities damaged by two wars and almost a decade of sanctions. The increased production allowed Iraq to send unauthorized shipments of oil to its neighbors—Turkey, Jordan, Syria—as well as to India and Pakistan via Iran and to Dubai by way of the Iraqi port of Umm Qasr. Even though the United Nations continued to collect revenues on legal sales, Baghdad was pocketing $25 to $40 million a month. Still, world demand continued to work at the bonds of the sanctions. In December 1999, the Security Council adopted Resolution 1284 that "[a]uthorizes States . . . to permit the import of any volume of petroleum and petroleum products originating in Iraq . . . [and] the use of additional export routes for petroleum and petroleum products."[20] Iraq was once again awash in money. As they had during the halcyon days of the oil boom, emissaries of international business flocked to Baghdad. But this time they did so by broaching the walls of the sanctions.

It seemed an opportune time for Saddam Hussein to launch another offensive to break the UN hold on his oil revenues. Under the sanctions, he could not increase production without upgrading the equipment in his oil fields. That required UN approval. But he could flex his muscle by withholding Iraqi oil from the market. A unilateral cut in Iraqi production by 1.2 million barrels per day in September 1999 caused the petroleum price to rise. Now in even tighter markets, the simple threat in December 2000 to halt completely exports of Iraqi oil sent the price of the benchmark Brent crude blend up to $32.19, the highest price commanded by a barrel of oil since August 1981. After serving notice to OPEC and everyone else that only Iraq would decide whether Iraqi oil would be on the market or off, Hussein withdrew the threat.

---

[20] United Nations Security Council Resolution 1284, December 1999, Articles 15 and 16.

Demand and prices in the international oil markets reverberated in the Security Council. France, lusting after the profits that could be realized in an Iraqi market freed from sanctions and seeking $4 billion of Iraqi debt owed to Paris, continued to raise the voice of dissent against the sanctions. Cash-starved Russia, owed $8 billion from Iraq's arms purchases in the 1960s and 1970s, joined in. China, for a variety of reasons ranging from potential Iraqi contracts to national pride, completed the trio of permanent members of the Security Council that left the United States and Britain clinging to the boat of sanctions in the rising flood of rejection.

In August 2000, Venezuelan President Hugo Chavez, the sitting chair of OPEC, arrived in Baghdad as the first foreign head of state to visit Iraq since the Gulf War. Belittling those who would demonize Hussein, he shrugged, "We're all sons of God."[21] Three months later, representatives of more than 1,500 firms from forty-five countries defied the ban on commerce with Iraq to lay out their wares at the Baghdad International Trade Fair. That same November, Baghdad sent flights to Basra and Mosul, both of which lay inside the no-fly zones patrolled by American and British warplanes. The inauguration of domestic air service followed the arrival, at the once ghostly Saddam Hussein Airport in Baghdad, of dozens of international flights from countries seeking an end to the sanctions.

Even Richard Butler, now diplomat in residence at the Council on Foreign Relations, had come to favor modifying the sanctions: "When you've got an immoral and utterly determined regime . . . sanctions might work initially. . . . However, given this immorality and ruthless determination, the longer the time sanctions are applied, the less and less effective they become, to the point where they invert in their effectiveness for two reasons. One, they get busted through a black market, and two, the leadership is able to parley this into a reason for staying in power."[22]

As the Clinton administration approached its end, it was becoming ever more apparent that the sanctions alone were never going to disarm Saddam Hussein or drive him from power. In the way that everything that touches Hussein seems to become perverted, the

---

[21] Quoted in *New York Times*, August 8, 2000.
[22] Quoted in *New York Times*, March 25, 2000.

sanctions over the years actually increased the tyrant's hold over Iraq's population. By establishing a dependency on food rations distributed through the state bureaucracy, the sanctions turned ordinary Iraqis into vassals of the government. More than ever before, they became the pliant subjects of a feared regime whose collapse threatened their very lives. Playing a major part in the destruction of the middle class, the sanctions also laid waste to the force most likely to mount a successful challenge to the regime. Reduced to penury, struggling through the daily grind of survival, or forced into exile, the body of educated Iraqis drew its last breath as a possible political opposition. In spite of the factionalism that has always plagued their state, the Iraqis found in the sanctions a certain commonality.

In a situation in which an intensely proud people had been stripped of their dignity by the mandate of others, Saddam Hussein told the Iraqis they were victorious over their foes. Whether they believed it or not, the population became hardened and embittered against the United States, the perceived emissary of their suffering. In the heat of a Baghdad summer, a formerly upper-class woman fanning herself with a straw fan once used only by peasants snarled at me, "I will teach my children to hate Americans forever."

She is far from alone in her hostility. The generation that is approaching adulthood under the sanctions is increasingly radicalized. They are collecting into loose groups independent of any institution and void of any ideology other than revenge on the United States and its allies—Kuwait, Saudi Arabia, and Israel. When Saddam Hussein is gone, they are the ones who will pick that fine thread of ultranationalism that runs in some groups through Iraq's contemporary history. They are the ones who will push Iraq's regional ambitions, which are grounded in the certitude that Iraq is the true leader of the Arab world just as it was in the days of the Abbasids. In pursuit of lost status for themselves and their country, they will push revanchism—political revenge. It will come in an Arab world linked in honor and empathy with the Iraqis.

From the time the sanctions were imposed, the agony of ordinary Iraqis resonated throughout the Arab world. Despite the great chasm that opened between Arab states at the time of the Gulf War, the mythology of Arab unity and the reality of Arab identity quickly turned the suffering of the Iraqis into a common cause. Across the Middle East, Arabs laid on the United States the lion's share of the blame for the suffering of the Iraqi people. They accepted as an article of faith that it was American power that kept the sanctions in place. The United States could not delude itself that logic could change that opinion. Madeleine Albright only added to the resentment in a 1996 television interview when she answered a question regarding the cost of sanctions in the lives of half a million Iraqi children: "We think the price is worth it."[23] In the Arab world, this became one of the famous phrases of the late twentieth century. In the souks and on the streets, both the truths and the exaggerations about the effect of the sanctions circulated constantly. The masses embraced the idea that I heard over and over in Jordan and the Gulf: "The punishment is so much worse than any wrong Iraq might have done."

In truth, the sanctions had come to isolate the United States far more than Saddam Hussein. Refusing to bend to the suspect West, the master of Iraq increased his standing throughout the region. Although the Arabs did not ignore who and what he was, Hussein's esteem was due to his refusal to bow to the mighty United States whom Arabs perceived as tending the Israeli oppression of the Palestinians. Beyond the Middle East, all who resented the world's sole superpower held their own grudging admiration for Hussein's tenacity. The Iraqi president understood this. In his mind, a certain reality took hold that the day the sanctions were lifted and Iraq was once again open for business, that "he [could] then stand up to the people who want[ed] to trade with him, who want[ed] to sell him arms, who want[ed] to buy his oil and remind them how strong he was, that he did not buckle under at the height of American pressure."[24]

No one can argue that the United States' concern over Saddam Hussein's arsenal and his real and potential weapons of mass destruction is not justified. Twice in ten years he invaded a neighbor, wreaking physical, economic, and societal destruction on both Iran and Kuwait. And no one can claim that caging the maniacal Hussein while leaving the Iraqi people untouched is simple. But Washington made the mistake of pursuing arms control through sanctions without considering their impact on the fabric of Iraqi society.

What little civil society was left intact by the brutality of Hussein

[23] Madeline Albright, CBS News, *60 Minutes*, May 12, 1996.
[24] Adeed I. Dawisha, interview on CNN, transcript available at www.cnn.com/SPECIALS/1998/iraq/saddam.profile/, December 17, 1998.

had been further eroded by the sanctions, leaving the Iraqi state a hollow shell. An international aid worker who has spent most of the years since the Gulf War in Iraq observed, "Once the sanctions are lifted, the economy can recover quickly. But the society will take at least three decades."[25]

The sanctions essentially created a whole new society in Iraq of "haves" and "have-nots." The "haves," those engaged in illegal activities surrounding "sanctions busting," drove through the streets in sleek new European cars accompanied by carefully coiffed girlfriends wearing designer clothes. They made sport of running up behind the wheezing dilapidated cars of ordinary Iraqis to honk, point, and laugh. At night, they took their high-powered speedboats out on the river to swamp the small craft in which Iraqi families outside the Baath elite attempted to catch a cool breeze. This obnoxious behavior of the young against their elders of any class was only one symptom of a collapsing society that has been anchored for centuries in the family.

Sanctions, imposed on top of the economic dislocations of the Iran-Iraq War, seriously eroded the whole family structure that is the very foundation of Iraqi society. Many men, particularly those of the middle class, were forced to go abroad in search of work. They left behind wives who tended their families as best they could in a patriarchal society. The lower classes possessed no skills that were marketable abroad, so they sent their children into the street to earn a few dinars anyway they could. They shined shoes, sold cigarettes, hung on the sides of cars begging for money, or practiced prostitution at a dollar a trick.

Decadence seeped into every level of society. It began at the top and descended through the layers of the social hierarchy. Once proud bureaucrats now accepted bribes as a necessary way of life. Those outside government often sold the only resource they possessed, a portion of their precious food ration. Others stole. Although theft once represented an intolerable humiliation for the thief's family, that humiliation no longer mattered so much in conditions where a stolen car or a small wad of money picked from a pocket could buy food or a pair of cheap shoes.

In this social dislocation, there was a lost generation that had

---

[25] Anonymous source, interview with author, Baghdad, April 29, 1998.

never experienced anything other than war against Iraq's neighbors or deprivation delivered both by their own political leader and by forces from the outside determined to deny that leader his arsenal of weapons. As far back as 1980 when the Iran-Iraq War began, most Iraqi children lost access to quality education. By 2000, two decades of sons and daughters of the bright, highly literate Iraqis of the past had worked their way through an educational system that was poor by anyone's standards, or they had been deprived of many levels of education all together. Without ambition, they were angry and filled with hatred. Like the rest of the Iraqis, they lived in isolation from any influence beyond Saddam Hussein. Consequently, there was no intellectualism, little creativity outside the visual arts, no thinking about the future of the country. An Arab who often travels to Iraq said it all: "It is like talking to people who only have five letters of the alphabet when you have 26." In this wasteland, one wondered if there was even any memory of the past before society was rent by the dual forces of the inside and the outside. What did exist was a popular poem that circulated in the streets:

> My country is wounded
> Besieged by sanctions
> Tens of children are falling victim every day
> Until when, until when, this destruction.

This is the Iraq that the Clinton administration passed on to the administration of George Bush the younger. It fell to him and many of the men who quarterbacked the Gulf War to jostle with the twin problems of Saddam Hussein and the Iraqi state, mortally wounded by tyranny and sanctions.

12

THE ROAD TO BAGHDAD

here is a certain irony in the fact that the
tenth anniversary of the beginning of the Gulf
War, fought under the leadership of George H. W. Bush, came just
before his son, George W. Bush, took the oath of office as president
of the United States. Underscoring the point in Baghdad on January
17, 2000, Saddam Hussein boasted over the Iraqi airwaves, "Iraq has
triumphed over the enemies of the nation. . . . On a day like this day
10 years ago, evil and all those who made Satan their protector lined
up in one place, facing those who represented the will to defend right
against falsehood and who had God as their protector."[1]

Thus, when George W. Bush assumed the presidency three days
later, he, like his two predecessors George H. W. Bush and Bill
Clinton, also confronted the challenge of Saddam Hussein. As he
had been at the time of the invasion of Kuwait, Hussein remained a
tangled bundle of narcissism, megalomania, ruthlessness, and irra-
tional ambitions who still sat on his throne-like presidential chair
exercising absolute control over the Iraqi state and its people. More
than ever before, he basked in the glow of a success earned through
cunning, defiance, perseverance, and steadfastness under duress.
This is why a prediction made in 1991 by R. K. Ramazani, the
esteemed authority on the Persian Gulf, was so prescient: "A strong
likelihood exists that by the year 2000 the Persian Gulf War will be
revisited so long as the prospects for political change in the Middle
East and foreign policy change in the United States continue to be
as dim as they are in the immediate aftermath of Desert Storm."[2]
Inheriting a foreign policy in which the United States had removed

---

[1] Quote from www.cnn.com/2001/WORLD/meast/01/17/iraq.hussein/index.html.
[2] R. K.Ramazani, *Future Security in the Persian Gulf: America's Role* (Washington,
D.C.: Middle East Insight, 1991), p. 7.

itself from Iraq's political needs in 1991 and then had pummeled Iraqi society with sanctions ever since, it was now the turn of George Bush the younger to chart America's response to the challenge of Saddam Hussein.

Only two days after taking office, the new Bush administration demonstrated its resolve to keep Hussein's military potential caged by publicly reacting to a report that Iraq had rebuilt a series of factories previously destroyed as suspected chemical weapons plants. Warning the Iraqi president to abide by the standing prohibitions on his arsenal, Colin Powell, the incoming secretary of state, sounded the same alarm that the United States had sounded repeatedly since the end of the Gulf War: "[Saddam's] only tool, the only thing he can scare us with are those weapons of mass destruction, and we have to hold him to account."[3]

Less than a month later, on February 16, twenty-four American and British fighter planes targeted five Iraqi air defense installations posing an increased threat to air patrols over northern and southern Iraq. Canceling the Clinton era imperative of keeping Iraq out of the news, the new president appeared before reporters to announce that the exercise had been "a routine mission to enforce the no-fly zone."[4] In essence, it was routine. During the strikes that were heard in Baghdad, Iraqi television, as it had during similar incidents in the past, switched off its regular programming to broadcast military music and messages of defiance. Saddam Hussein appeared on the airways to tell his people, "The wound which does not kill us will strengthen us."[5] And news followed that the Iraqi foreign minister had sent word to Kofi Annan that UN arms inspectors would never be allowed to return to Iraq. Then came the announcement that "His Excellency Leader President Saddam Hussein . . . has met with . . . a number of researchers and technicians from the Atomic Energy Organization. . . . Tell the enemies of the Arab nation that Iraq—as long as it exists and continues to play a pioneering role as predestined by God—will not give the enemies the opportunity to harm any part of the Arab nation with-

---

[3] Colin Powell press conference, January 22, 2001, reported in *New York Times*, January 23, 2001.

[4] Quoted from www.cnn.com/2001/WORLD/meast/02/16/iraq.airstrike.02/index.html.

[5] Republic of Iraq television, February 27, 2001, Foreign Broadcast Information Service translation from Arabic.

out expecting a reaction from Iraq in proportion with this harm. . . . [For] Iraq is the chest of the Arab nation."[6]

The veterans of the Gulf War who now held some of the top positions in the administration of George W. Bush faced a more complex problem in Iraq than they had faced at the end of the administration of George Bush senior. Containment was costing the United States around $100 million a year. The repeated tours of duty demanded by maintenance of the no-fly zones was sucking career pilots out of the air force. Sanctions, adopted to force arms control on Saddam Hussein, were sounding the clarion call of anti-Americanism for millions of people across the Middle East. And the embargo was leaking like a sieve as front companies, flush with cash from the increase in Iraqi oil revenues, smuggled into Iraq equipment, spare parts, and even weapons. Hooked on the horns of the Iraqi dilemma, the administration either had to learn to live with Saddam Hussein or had to get rid of him. Either choice carried its own risks. Living with Hussein meant an intense, and possibly fruitless, effort to rebuild the international coalition that represented the only real hope of containing the Iraqi dictator and his weapons. To remove him would set in motion all the uncertainties within the complex dynamics of Iraq's communal politics, which Washington had never comprehended and perhaps never would.

Delaying the choice between two ugly options, the new Bush administration undertook a "policy review." Behind closed doors, various appointees to a number of foreign policy teams attempted to wade out of the mire of confusion surrounding Iraq left by the Clintonians. In doing so, they confronted the essential question that has hung over American policy in the Persian Gulf since the end of the Gulf War: What is the primary objective of the United States' policy toward Iraq? Subquestions followed: Is it the containment of Saddam Hussein and his weapons of mass destruction? Is it to rid the people of Iraq of the tyrant of Baghdad? Is it, as it has been since the oil embargo of 1973, to stabilize the Persian Gulf in order to ensure that oil flows at a reasonable cost? Or is it all of these? That, in turn, led to further questions: How should these goals be prioritized? Once prioritized, how can they be accomplished? Finally, in the execution of the defined goals, what are the options?

---

[6] Republic of Iraq television, February 27, 2001, Foreign Broadcast Information Service translation from Arabic.

The defenders of living with Saddam Hussein at the helm of Iraq gathered in one camp and the proponents of eliminating the president of Iraq grouped in another. Harking back to Vietnam terminology, the "doves" were Colin Powell and his State Department advisors, while the "hawks" were Secretary of Defense Donald Rumsfeld and a cohort of civilians in the Defense Department, right-wing Republicans in Congress, and a chorus of editorial-page opinion makers decrying the evil incarnate in Baghdad. The White House was silent. In his West Wing office, Vice President Dick Cheney weighed his inclination to join the hawks against the imperative to keep Persian Gulf oil flowing.

Colin Powell made the first public move by announcing a new approach to the sanctions, termed "smart sanctions." The guru of this new policy was Richard Haass who, as a member of the National Security Council in the administration of George Bush senior, had helped strategize the Gulf War. In the intervening years, Haass had come to question the wisdom of the sanctions regimen in operation against Iraq. He, as well as his boss Powell, recognized that by brutalizing the Iraqi people, the sanctions had done much to destroy the grand coalition that had supported and fought the Gulf War and that was still needed to contain Hussein. Others, coming from their own perspective, shared the view that the sanctions were causing more harm than good. The former UN humanitarian coordinator for Iraq, Hans von Sponeck, charged that "[s]anctions have not unseated the government; not brought about a change in leadership; have not destabilized the ruling elite. [Instead] they have enhanced Saddam Hussein's political capital as they have prompted a rallying round the flag effect."[7] Fouad Ajami, the eloquent Middle East scholar from Johns Hopkins University, added his own observation: "The United States [has] shown neither purpose and resolve, nor mercy."[8] Thomas Friedman, writing in the *New York Times*, was less poetic. "If Colin Powell tries really hard, launches a real P.R. campaign against Saddam, he might be able to hold together the sanctions long enough to get them lifted in an orderly way and replaced by a U.N. ban on all military sales to Iraq."[9]

Smart sanctions took official form in the Security Council in May

---

[7] Hans von Sponeck, "Sanctions: Efficacy and Morality," *Global Dialogue* 2 (Summer 2000): 68.

[8] Ibid.

[9] *New York Times*, February 6, 2001.

2001 as a joint British and U.S. sponsored resolution, timed to correspond to the semiannual renewal of the oil-for-food program. Under its provisions, Iraq would continue to be required to readmit arms inspectors expelled in December 1999 and to be certified free of biological, chemical, and nuclear weapons as well as missiles with a range of over 150 kilometers before sanctions would be lifted completely. In the meantime, the Security Council would draw up two explicit lists of prohibited weapons and weapons-related goods—one for weapons of mass destruction and another for conventional armaments. Individual items on those lists would still require approval from the sanctions committee before crossing into Iraq. Everything else would be permitted to flow freely.

Within the context of arms control, which had always been the focus of the sanctions, the central goal of smart sanctions was to deny Saddam Hussein the financial windfall he was reaping from illicit oil sales. Under the new plan, the cross-border oil deliveries to Turkey, Syria, and Jordan would continue. But instead of smuggling operations, the transport of petroleum would be open and governed by the receiving countries, with the proceeds going into Iraq's escrow account at the United Nations that is used to buy food and medicine for Iraqi civilians. Because all these countries had fragile economies, especially Syria and Jordan, each would receive some unspecified forms of compensation in return for their efforts to stop armament shipments at the border of Iraq.

Smart sanctions made sense for the United States. They promised to keep Hussein's weapons contained while ridding Washington of the onus of cruelty to ordinary Iraqis. Furthermore, by unshackling civilian goods from review by the sanctions committee, Saddam Hussein could no longer blame Iraq's hungry people and dying children on the evil forces of Washington.

On the down side, smart sanctions required a complex multilevel, multinational approach to reigning in the terror of the Persian Gulf. This is where the complications lay. Yet despite the challenges, the United States and Britain forged ahead by submitting their plan for revised sanctions to the Security Council shortly before the June 4th date for renewal of the oil-for-food program. Russia, China, and France, pushing for even more relaxation of the sanctions, put it on hold. That satisfied the hawks in the American government to whom any moderation of the sanctions was anathema.

The hawks roosted in the upper echelons of policy planning in the Defense Department. They included, in varying degrees of passion, Defense Secretary Donald Rumsfeld; Assistant Secretary Paul D. Wolfowitz, the hard-liner of the hard-liners; and Undersecretary of Defense Policy Doug Feith, a close ally of Wolfowitz. On the issue of Iraq, the secretary and his advisors shared a single, compelling goal: to get rid of Saddam Hussein. Their motivations grew out of two major considerations: the demands placed on the U.S. military budget by the ongoing containment of Baghdad and the interests of Israel.

Rumsfeld's personal position on Iraq had been enunciated in a public letter of January 1998, when, speaking as a private citizen, he called for the elimination of Saddam Hussein as the leader of Iraq. Wolfowitz was a frequent voice of U.S. action against Iraq in the media, as was Richard Perle. Within days of the inauguration of the Bush administration, Perle, one of the president's foreign policy advisors during the campaign and now head of the Defense Policy Board of the Pentagon, stated the opinion of members of his board, which among other high-profile personalities included former Speaker of the House Newt Gingrich: "What we have in mind is making it clear to Saddam and the world that we're in favor of seeing this regime change."[10]

Support for the Defense Department hawks against the State Department doves came from the conservatives in Congress who kept up their own chant against modifying the sanctions while leaving Hussein in place. According to Senator Sam Brownback, speaking during a committee hearing on Iraq in January 2001, "If we continue on the current course, smart sanctions, we are further on the road of eroding resolve. It will not be long before Saddam is out of the gate. . . . This is a key time. There is a new administration and this is a fork in the road. I hope we would all work to decide to take a more robust approach toward Iraq."[11] Behind closed doors, the powerful conservatives of the Republican congressional delegation pressed Colin Powell: Why had he gone "soft" on Saddam Hussein? Where was the policy to overthrow him? At the White House, the vice president had already quietly put together his own group of for-

---

[10] Quoted in *New York Times*, January 23, 2001.
[11] Transcript of hearing of the Foreign Relations Subcommittee on Near Eastern and South Asian Affairs available at www.meib.org/articles/0102_ir1.htm.

eign policy experts. Predominately hawks, they represented another decisive power center in the internal debate on Iraq.

In the public arena, academics in largely conservative think tanks and the editorial writers of some of the nation's most influential newspapers and magazines on the political right cranked out position papers and columns that proposed measures to force a regime change in Baghdad, even at the cost of sending in American ground troops. Together, policy planners, congressmen, a cadre of academicians, and pundits moved the issue of Iraq into the spotlight of American foreign policy in the infant administration of George W. Bush. Short of the sudden death of Hussein or some inescapable calamity in the Middle East, the bureaucratic battle over Iraq policy was going to be protracted. Jim Hoagland, writing in the *Washington Post*, predicted, "This will be a war fought in Washington with bullets of secret position papers, historical analogies, news leaks and other bureaucratic artifice."[12] Yet in the minds of most Americans, Saddam Hussein and Iraq remained suspended somewhere between a comforting notion of a contained threat and an unsettling fear of weapons of mass destruction. The tyrant still reigned in Baghdad, but he appeared to be no more of an immediate menace to the United States than he had been at the end of the Gulf War over a decade before. The tattered sanctions were still officially in place. American military aircraft continued to patrol the skies over the no-fly zones of northern and southern Iraq. Periodic air assaults on Iraqi radar installations and the widely spaced attacks on the centers of Baath power seemed to signal that America was on guard against a resurgent Hussein. Even the Iraqi president's rhetoric in early August 2001, coming on the anniversary of the end of the Iran-Iraq War, sounded like a roar from a toothless lion: "Iraq is threatening the American aircraft of aggression which break through its air, trespassing upon its skies, the sanctity of its sovereignty, its land, its people and its wealth."[13] Ten days later, Baghdad's mouthpiece, the newspaper *al-Jumhuriyah*, issued a warning that few in the United States heard: "All of this blatant aggressiveness by the United States is being met with angry Arab positions that might go as far as martyrdom operations against the hostile US presence on the Arab

---

[12] *Washington Post*, April 8, 2001.
[13] Iraqi News Agency, August 8, 2001.

nation's land."[14] Then came September 11, 2001, when the issue of Iraq moved into the crosshairs of the American war on terrorism.

THE LOUDEST VOICES accusing Iraq of complicity in terrorism came from the cadre of Paul Wolfowitz; Richard Perle; James Woolsey, former director of the CIA; and David Wurmser, a Middle East expert at the American Enterprise Institute who long had been beating the drum for American military action to topple Saddam Hussein. The accusations were disseminated by Laurie Mylroie, publisher of a newsletter called *Iraq News*. In 2000, Mylroie wrote a book entitled *Study of Revenge: Saddam Hussein's Unfinished War against America* in which she compiled a mountain of data to reach the dubious conclusion that Saddam Hussein was behind the 1993 bombing of the World Trade Center. According to Mylroie and her supporters, the United States, in going after the terrorist network of Osama bin Laden, also had to go against the state of Iraq ruled by Saddam Hussein.

Refusing to be pulled into the conundrum of Iraq, the White House kept public attention focused on bin Laden, his Islamic militants, and the Taliban, the religious and political rulers of Afghanistan. In the weeks immediately following September 11, Colin Powell from the State Department continued to cite bin Laden, al-Qaeda, and the Taliban as the sole targets of U.S. military planning. Vice President Dick Cheney, appearing on *Meet the Press*, responded to a question about whether the U. S. government believed Hussein was part of the events of September 11 with a clear and simple "no." Even Secretary of Defense Donald Rumsfeld carefully sidestepped the issue of Iraqi culpability in the attack on America. At the time, it was enough to keep American attention focused on bin Laden's network and the mountains of Afghanistan. But hanging in the air was the question of whether the administration could, or ultimately wanted to, keep the public quiet on the issue of Saddam Hussein and writing a final end to the Gulf War by eliminating the despot of Baghdad and his weapons of mass destruction.

As military operations unfolded in Afghanistan late in 2001, the rhetoric of some within the Bush administration increasingly indicated that the war on terrorism provided a rationale for attacking the Iraq of Saddam Hussein. As the Taliban collapsed under pressure

---

[14] Quote from www.uruklink.net/jumhuriya.

from American bombing, U.S. Special Forces operations, and the Northern Alliance of Afghani opponents of the Taliban regime, the hawks of the administration sunk their talons into the doves. Riding the crest of what appeared for the moment to be a successful and largely painless military victory over medieval tribesmen and their foreign foot soldiers, Donald Rumsfeld displaced Colin Powell as the president's most authoritative adviser. Behind him, the hawkish advisors, proponents in Congress, and mouthpieces in the media became what is essentially a war party. Pointing to the experience of Afghanistan, they began selling the idea that the same operational methods could be repeated in Iraq, by conducting airstrikes and by using Special Forces to provide field training and tactical direction to Iraqi exiles and Kurdish militias. If that view prevails, the United States will walk into the quicksand of Iraq, to be sucked into the resentments of the Arab world, the hostilities of the Iraqis, and the challenge of nation building in what has become an intensely tribal society at the core of American vital interests in the oil-rich Persian Gulf. This is where wishful thinking and misplaced priorities run head on into reality.

The hawks on Iraq are focused on one thing and one thing only: the elimination of Saddam Hussein in order to eliminate the threat of his weapons. No one can argue that an end to the chemical, biological, and perhaps nuclear threat of Saddam Hussein is in the interest of world order. Nor can it be denied that a U.S. military operation against Hussein is seductive. In purely military terms, it all seems relatively easy—if such a thing could be said about war. Baghdad no longer commands an army that could thwart, or perhaps even delay, an American incursion into Iraqi territory. Nor could Saddam Hussein hide forever from a U.S. military force determined to run him into the ground, even if it required large numbers of American soldiers to wear gas masks. But no invasion of Iraq would be simple or predictable, because the risks to the United States are political more than military. Those risks come from two major sources: decades of failed American policy in the Middle East and Iraq itself.

EVEN THOUGH geographic location has subjected Iraq to the influences of Persia and Turkey, Iraq by culture is inescapably Arab. As a consequence, Iraq is part of the Arab world, considered by other Arabs as part of a brotherhood bonded by common language and culture as well as similar perceptions and attitudes. One of those atti- tudes is a profound resentment of the West. Some of that resentment is grounded in misconceptions and half-truths, some in authentic grievances. Together, perception and reality frame much of the rela- tionship that exists between Arabs and the West, profoundly impact- ing on American foreign policy between the Nile and the Persian Gulf.

Arab hostility to the Western world began in the eleventh century when the Crusaders from Europe stormed into the Levant, slaugh- tered uncounted numbers, and, through the establishment of the Christian/European Crusader States, essentially wrote the end of the Islamic Empire in the Fertile Crescent. Westerners returned as colo- nizers after the collapse of the Ottoman Empire when Britain and France carved Syria, Transjordan, Iraq, and Palestine out of Istanbul's Middle East territories. But it was Zionism in Palestine, seen by the Arabs as another form of Western imperialism, that has fed a seething Arab anger, more against the United States than the West as a whole, that began after World War II and continues until today. The issue is American policy toward Israel.

For more than half a century, American foreign policy in the Middle East has all but surrendered U.S. national interests to Israel. In 1950, two years after the war for Palestine birthed the Zionist state, the United States was the generous donor of economic, mili- tary, and diplomatic aid that would enable Israel to survive and pros- per. Through the remainder of the administration of Harry Truman and on through the administrations of Dwight Eisenhower, John Kennedy, and Lyndon Johnson, American foreign policy consistently ignored the endemic economic, political, and social problems of the young Arab states that tensions with Israel, and the presence of Palestinian refugees dispossessed in the 1948 war, only intensified. Thus, while the Arab states labored, stumbled, and fell as they emerged from centuries of occupation that largely ended after World War II, Israel sold itself as culturally superior to its neighbors. Almost universally, Americans bought into that image—not only psycholog- ically but also politically. The United States embraced Israel as the only democracy in the Middle East, the only country deserving of American respect and support in the climate of the Cold War. In pop- ular rhetoric fed by Hollywood, a largely pro-Israeli press, and ranks of politicians of both political parties looking to the next election, the Arabs were subtly and overtly derided among most of the

American population as "rag heads" and "camel jockeys." The Six
Day War of 1967, which created another set of territorial issues and
another group of Palestinian refugees, played to the American public
as the modern-day drama of David defeating Goliath.

Prior to 1973, the Nixon administration had come to regard Israel
as part of the solution to the United States' anxieties in the Middle East
rather than as a major part of the problem. In fact, the Jewish state
came to be regarded as Washington's helpful junior partner in that
supreme test of superpower wills known as the Cold War. It was only
with the shock delivered by the 1973 oil embargo that the importance
of the Arab states to American economic interests began to push its
way into public awareness. Almost overnight, Washington began to
peer at the Middle East through the prism of the needs of the United
States rather than the interests of Israel or the demands of the Cold
War. But the change of attitude was only momentary. Henry Kissinger,
secretary of state in Nixon's second term, held a formalistic view of
the international system. Diplomacy took place among states, not
between a state and a revolutionary movement. Not only did sugges-
tions of a dialogue between the Palestine Liberation Organization
(PLO) and the United States go unheeded but also Kissinger promised
Israel, in writing, that the United States would not negotiate with the
PLO until the organization recognized Israel's right to exist.

In 1977, Jimmy Carter became the first American president willing to utter the pregnant code word in the United States' diplomatic
vocabulary—Palestinian "homeland." For reasons of their own internal bickering, the Palestinians dropped the ball, so Carter moved on
to negotiate peace between Israel and Egypt. Despite the great
rejoicing that greeted Carter, Anwar Sadat, and Menachem Begin
when they came down from Camp David, the crucial and complex
issue of the Palestinians was passed over. At least Carter had tried.

During the Reagan presidency, the flawed precepts on which the
United States had based its foreign policy in the Arab world found
more ardent supporters. In the arena of domestic politics, the
pro-Israeli lobby was reinforced by the politically energized religious
right. The Christian fundamentalists, with clout derived from a covey
of high-profile religious broadcasters and intense grass-roots political organization, had helped put Ronald Reagan in the White
House. Now they flexed their muscle in foreign policy. To them, a
militarily powerful United States must stand guard against godless

Communism, and Israel must be allowed to realize its manifest destiny, for Israel is not a state exhibiting the ambitions and foibles of any nation-state—it is biblical fulfillment. Hence, any challenge to Israeli government policies, no matter how detrimental they are to the stability of the Middle East or the interests of the United States, is a challenge to God.

Over eight years, the Reagan administration never came to terms with the reality that in Arab eyes the United States and Israel are tied together. The sins of one are the sins of the other. From this perspective, the United States shared with Israel the responsibility for the plight of the Palestinians, the occupation of Arab land after 1967, the 1982 invasion of Lebanon, and the continued humiliation of the Arabs.

As in administrations before, Washington remained so dismissive of Arab public opinion that the United States sponsored no Arabic-language radio programs directed at disseminating the American perspective into Arab societies. When the rage of the Palestinians exploded in the *intifadah*—the "uprising"—in December 1987, it was Arab radio and television that day after day reported a rebellion of stones thrown at an Israeli army firing weapons often supplied and paid for by the United States. Even though accumulating imagery ate away at American vital interests, Washington put few restraints on Israel. Nor did the United States seriously engage the Palestinian question, the one constant in Arab politics and the one issue from which no Arab leader can separate himself.

Weighed down by years of unqualified support of Israel, the United States after Iraq's invasion of Kuwait found it difficult to convince Saudi Arabia to allow American troops on its soil and to bring Syria and Egypt into the alliance against Saddam Hussein. For the same reason, the United States could not win the acquiescence of its Arab allies to go to Baghdad to put an end to the Baath regime. Not since 1973 had the United States so directly felt the consequences of its decades-long arrogance toward and neglect of the Arab world.

The Oslo Accords of 1993, negotiated by Norway, promised an end game for Israel, the Palestinians, the Arab states, and the United States. Although the agreement faced the complications of the Palestinians' own internal conflicts and the assassination of Israeli prime minister Yitzhak Rabin, its death knell began to be sounded by Benjamin Netanyahu, who failed to meet a series of deadlines established in the Oslo Accords for Israeli withdrawal from occupied land.

Ignoring the obvious signs from Jerusalem that Netanyahu's Likud Party desired land over peace, the policy makers in the White House and the lawmakers in Congress never acted to reduce military and economic aid for Israel or to deny the diplomatic coverage to the Zionist state that the United States has provided for so long in the United Nations and elsewhere. Instead, they watched as a second *intifadah* that began in September 2000 all but destroyed what was left of the Oslo peace process. After the Herculean efforts of Bill Clinton to find the key to a settlement during his final year in office, the incoming George W. Bush administration seemed willing to allow the embers of peace to die in the ashes of indifference. Even after September 11, when long-standing hostility toward the United States brought war inside America's borders, the Bush administration refused to touch on the answer to the question, "Why do they hate us so much?" American condemnation fell on Palestinian suicide bombers, but little was said about what might be called state-sponsored terrorism when Israel sent F-16s and Apache helicopters against unarmed civilians, subjected much of the Palestinian population to an endless economic blockade, conducted assassinations of Palestinian leaders, and laid explosives on a road that killed children going to school.

Much of the reason why this Bush administration allowed the Palestinian issue to fester was that achieving any balance between Israel and the Palestinians would require doing battle with two powerful domestic constituencies. One has long been known as the "Jewish lobby," a juggernaut that has rolled over Congress and presidents for years. The other, more important to the political operatives in the Bush White House, is the Christian right. Thus consciously or unconsciously, American Zionists, Christian fundamentalists, and the hawks of the Bush administration seem willing to continue to put the interests of Israel above the needs of the United States. In doing so, they ignore the obvious—the Palestinian struggle for land, identity, and justice permeates every aspect of U.S. vital interests in the Middle East. It adds fuel to Arab suspicions of the West present since the Crusades. It feeds militant Islam. It provides rhetoric for terrorists. It threatens the regimes of American allies in the region. And it hamstrings American options vis-à-vis Saddam Hussein.

In the absence of extraordinary circumstances, American military intervention in Iraq without a real resolution of the Palestinian issue may unleash the pent-up anger against the United States found on the streets of the Arab world. Fed by a half-century of past grievances, this street power will target the regimes that have served American interests in the Arab world and the Persian Gulf: Egypt, Jordan, and especially Saudi Arabia. Although the governments of Egypt and Jordan are important to the United States, Saudi Arabia's House of Saud is crucial. Denying the real implications of the loss of Saudi oil to political conflict, even temporarily, some inside and outside government claim that the United States, receiving only 17 percent of its oil from Saudi Arabia, could survive the disruption with little economic damage to the American economy. They are wrong. The specific source of any country's oil supply is immaterial. It is how much oil is flowing through the international pipeline that determines supply and price. Others argue that in the case of political upheaval in Saudi Arabia, Russia, holding the world's second largest reserves, could step in to fill the void left by disruption of Saudi production and distribution. They are also wrong. While Saudi Arabia can easily produce ten million barrels a day, Russia's production capacity for the foreseeable future is under six million barrels per day. Russian petroleum has a high sulfur content; it is far more expensive to produce than Saudi oil; delivery is more difficult; and production is controlled by individuals who essentially operate as a Mafia beyond the control of Moscow. Perhaps most important, the United States, in choosing to depend on Russian oil, risks selling itself to an untested ally in control of formidable military power. That returns Saudi Arabia to the position of the indispensable nation in the equation of American economic interests.

With so much history, hostility, and hopelessness hanging on the Palestinian issue, the United States cannot send military forces into Arab Iraq with any guarantee of impunity, for no matter how the various scenarios for invading Iraq are laid out, the road to Baghdad ultimately runs through Jerusalem. It is this link between Israel and U.S. foreign policy in the Middle East that is the American dilemma concerning Saddam Hussein outside the boundaries of Iraq. The other part of that dilemma is inside those boundaries.

ALL THE DOMESTIC FORCES of disintegration that have plagued the Iraqi state since 1921—the sectarian resentments, the ethnic conflicts, the tribal rivalries—are still tearing at Iraqi society. Even before Saddam Hussein ascended to power, the Iraqis had yet to find the answer to the question of national identity or to develop any firm sense of nation. After more than two decades of rule by Hussein, the hostilities and suspicions between communities has increased, pushing the Iraqis toward the perilous slope of vengeance and disintegration. Today no vision of the Iraqi nation is strong enough to bind its people together to ensure the survival of the Iraqi state. Furthermore, the Iraqis, many of whom proclaim themselves the heirs of the high cultures of Mesopotamia and Islam, have been essentially stripped of their humanity and deprived of civil society. Although more than anyone else, the Iraquis have an interest in emerging from their long nightmare under Saddam Hussein as a stable, civilized society, the United States, consistently seeking stability in the Persian Gulf, also shares that interest. Tragically, there is no visible leadership capable of leading the Iraqis out of the wilderness of the Baath.

If arms control has constituted the major frustration of American foreign policy in Iraq since the Gulf War, the lack of any viable internal opposition to the Baath regime follows closely behind. At the time the aborted Shia and Kurdish rebellions ended the possibility of replacing Hussein through a military coup, Christine Moss Helms, a scholar at the Brookings Institution, gave the dismal assessment of the nonmilitary opposition groups in Iraq. According to Helms, these groups "had years to create a workable agenda and they've not done it. Whatever they say, if they come to power it will be a temporary alliance."[15] The same could be said about the Iraqi National Congress (INC), the group in which the hawks among U.S. policy makers would invest not only the future of the Iraqis but also the risk that an American invasion of Iraq will become a long-term occupation carrying enormous political, military, and economic costs.

The INC is the creation of Ahmed Chalabi, the son of a wealthy and powerful Shia family under the monarchy. In the wake of the failed rebellions of 1991, Chalabi began to collect representatives from a wide range of Iraqi ethnic, sectarian, and political groups and herded them into a political front dedicated to the overthrow of Saddam Hussein. They included Sunnis, Shia, Kurds, Turkomans, and Assyrians; ex-Baathists, ex-Communists, capitalists, democrats,

[15] Quoted in *Newsweek*, April 15, 1991.

monarchists, and Islamists; people from the urban intelligentsia and people of the tribes.

Tainted somewhat by conviction in an Amman court for raiding millions of dollars from a Jordanian bank he founded, the arrogant, silver-haired Chalabi began to wave his impressive credentials, a doctorate in mathematics from the University of Chicago and a command of several languages, to attract attention for himself and his group. In 1992, the George H. W. Bush administration, bereft of an acceptable alternative opposition group, allowed the CIA to sponsor a meeting in Vienna, Austria, of the neophyte political front. There the INC issued grand declarations that predicted the imminent downfall of Saddam Hussein, and floated plans to rid Iraq of its hated dictator that ranged from the vague to the impossible. Not only did the common agenda of those involved begin and end with their abhorrence of Saddam Hussein, but also these exiles mirrored the fractious nature of Iraqi society and commanded no power on the ground in Iraq. Rather than devoting the organization to the goal of building a sense of Iraqi nationhood, the INC operated as an umbrella under which its member groups most often pursued their own communal interests or promoted the self-interest of their leader.

Yet despite the INC's obvious weaknesses, the United States was willing to back its efforts to gather Iraqi dissidents into one corral as long as its political posturing carried no risk of American involvement on the ground in Iraq. Washington even provided money, largely through the CIA.

With covert American backing and protection from the no-fly zone over northern Iraq, the INC set up its headquarters in the Kurdish enclave. In command of a radio station, a television outlet, and a newspaper, the INC labored to create the image of a viable opposition to Saddam Hussein. At the same time, the Iraqi National Accord (INA), another opposition group composed of former figures of influence in the Iraqi Baath, was operating out of Amman, also under the eyes and out of the pockets of the CIA. Its mission was to coordinate with members of the military inside Iraq to bring down Saddam Hussein. In late June 1996, the Mukhabarat, acting on information provided by informers planted in the INA, swept up the whole Jordan wing. Having ruled out collaboration with Iraqi Islamist groups based in Iran, the Clinton administration was left with the INC as the only opposition game on the table.

Two months later, the INC fell victim to Kurdish infighting. On August 31, 1996, when Hussein invaded the Kurdish enclave at the invitation of Massoud Barzani, Iraqi troops crushed the INC camp at Qushtapa, east of Erbil. By the time Baghdad withdrew, hundreds of Iraqis had been executed or arrested on suspicion of affiliation with the INC.[16]

For the next two years, Ahmed Chalabi acted the role of a Moses figure leading the INC through the wilderness. The more American frustration with Hussein's moves against arms inspections grew and the closer the Republicans in Congress closed in on the beleaguered Bill Clinton, the nearer the INC inched toward the promised land of renewed U.S. aid. In October 1998, Chalabi's supporters in Congress succeeded in passing the "Iraq Liberation Act" authorizing $97 million of taxpayer money to arm and train the Iraqi opposition. The president signed the bill but sat on the money while Chalabi cultivated ties to Israel in order to increase his clout with the United States, prowled the halls of Congress gathering support, and pumped the well of American public opinion.

A glimpse inside the INC explains the reluctance of the Clinton administration to hand American money and interests over to Chalabi. In the fall of 1999, the organization called together more than three hundred Iraqi exiles from such widely divergent locations as northern Iraq, the United States, Britain, Canada, Turkey, Iran, Lebanon, Syria, Saudi Arabia, and Jordan. They shared little beyond a commitment to overthrow the only person they loathed more than each other—Saddam Hussein. But even the specter of Hussein could not quell their rivalries. In the dimly lit corridors of a Manhattan hotel, men representing the spectrum of the exiled Iraqi community wearing *gutras*, turbans, fine-tailored suits, and cheap jackets huddled to argue the interests of the particular group to which each belonged. Amid the squabbles that led to one episode of shoe throwing, a delegate sighed, "No one likes each other."[17] Yet in the end, they succeeded in electing a seven-man presidency that included repre-

---

[16] American retaliation for Qushtapa came on September 2 and 3. Because Saudi Arabia and Turkey flatly refused to allow U. S. warplanes to attack Iraq from their territory, President Clinton sent unmanned cruise missiles from U.S. ships patrolling the Persian Gulf. An announcement followed that the United States was extending the southern no-fly zone from the thirty-second to the thirty-third parallel.

[17] Janine di Giovanni, "The Enemy of Our Enemy," *New York Times Magazine*, February 20, 2000, p. 46 (p. 1 from Lexis/Nexis Print Delivery).

sentatives of all the major factions, with Ahmed Chalabi exercising an undefined role as godfather.

The INC moved on to London in July to meet under the new structure. Tensions had improved only marginally. There, according to an internal memo sent by e-mail to Chalabi's supporters,

> There was a fight [in the preceding meeting in New York] between the Independent Democrats and al-Wifaq [also known as the Iraqi National Accord] because Wifaq would not budge on giving the Democrats more than two seats. [In London], Chalabi allowed the Wifaq to usurp the seats for the Independent Democrats, the Arab Nationalists and the Tribes. . . . Chalabi gave two of the six seats that belong to the Liberals to the Independent Democrats so as not to re-ignite the fight between them and al-Wifaq over why the Wifaq took the two seats set aside for Independent Democrats for themselves. Now, al-Wifaq is trying to bargain their way back into the Central Council. . . . However, the rest of the Leadership does not want the Wifaq back, and would rather fix the problem of Turkoman and Assyrian representation by taking advantage of Wifaq's departure. Al-Wifaq, being Arab Nationalists and former Baathists, were always against increasing minority representation inside the INC Leadership, saying that two Kurds are enough. This they did, of course, when the microphones were turned off and the doors were closed."[18]

Despite the fact that the group often cannot even agree on the content to post on its Web site, for its American supporters the INC remains a viable entity, one that a number of senators believe the United States should entrust with the removal of Saddam Hussein. They include among others Senators Trent Lott of Mississippi, Joseph Lieberman of Connecticut, Jesse Helms of North Carolina, and Sam Brownback of Kansas. As chairman of the Foreign Relations Subcommittee on Near Eastern and South Asian Affairs, Brownback has become the most vocal spokesman for the INC's fantasy to use American money and American military backup to establish a beachhead in southern Iraq. From there, Ahmed Chalabi, the patrician

---

[18] E-mail received by author, July 7, 2000, 2:56 P.M.

Shia, would inspire thousands of disgruntled soldiers and millions of downtrodden Iraqis to rise up and slay the tyrant of Baghdad.

Even if by some miracle the INC did succeed in toppling Hussein, it cannot give the Iraqis the answer to the question of identity nor can it act as a shadow government capable of governing the Iraqi state. On the issue of identity, the INC has made no more progress than past Iraqi governments in defining a national identity to which most Iraqis can ascribe. Ideologically, each faction within the INC possesses its own vision of a post-Hussein government, ranging from a theocracy to a constitutional monarchy under the Hashemite heir to the defunct throne of Iraq. Politically, too many within this coalition of ethnic, sectarian, and ideological groups are wedded to the idea of decentralizing the state in order to meet the competing communal demands for political power. That robs the INC of its ability to act as a stabilizing force in post-Saddam Iraq. Furthermore, individuals from many of these same groups are already competing for positions in a new government. At the head of the list is Ahmed Chalabi, who privately, if not publicly, claims the presidency by divine right. Even the magic word *democracy*, which the INC claims is its cure all for Iraq's political ills, is no more viable than its plan to overthrow Saddam Hussein in a popular rebellion led by exiles. First, a predominately Shia organization claiming leadership of a majority Shia country means, in the shorthand of Iraqi communal politics, Shia political control. That cancels the support that an American-sponsored invasion behind the INC needs from the current Iraqi military, which is heavily populated by Sunnis. This is not the only fatal flaw in the grand scheme of the INC. Arriving in Iraq behind Western military power, the INC ignites among the Iraqi populace all the bitter memories of British colonialism. By the same token, an organization openly allied with Israel would face quick defeat by the ground forces of Saddam Hussein or a population that refuses to sign on with Jerusalem. Those who truly understand Iraq know this, even if members of Congress and such prestigious editorial writers as Jim Hoagland of the *Washington Post*, William Safire of the *New York Times*, and the editorial staff of the *Wall Street Journal* do not. It is from the ranks of the American military assigned the task of backing up any INC intrusion into southern Iraq that the most accurate assessment of the INC's operational plan has come. According to Marine Corps General Anthony Zinni, former commander of

American forces in the Middle East, the INC is "pie in the sky. They're going to lead us to a Bay of Goats, or something like that."[19]

If rebellion against Saddam Hussein comes, it will have to come from those on the inside of Iraq, not delivered by self-appointed usurpers from the outside backed by American military power. And if that rebellion is successful at anything beyond toppling Saddam Hussein, those in its leadership must guide the Iraqis toward an identity and a commitment not just to the state but also to the idea of nation. Yet even if the majority signs on to this vision of a unique, authentic Iraqi nation in which all claim some sense of identity, it will take years to make Iraq whole again. Benevolent states and international organizations can help, but the old and new fissures in Iraqi society can only be repaired by the Iraqis themselves.

The process has to begin with the Arabs. This means that among the overwhelmingly Arab population, the historic grievances of the Shia must be addressed. It also means that the Shia, as the most populous group in the country, must assume their rightful position within the power structure of any new government. At the same time, the Shia must comprehend and appreciate the Sunnis' very deep, very real fears of annihilation in both the political and the physical sense. Simply handing out political, economic, and military power by the numbers will never succeed in creating a stable Iraqi state, just as the rule of the minority over the majority so miserably failed Iraq in the past. But the Arabs are not the only residents of Iraq. Both Shia and Sunni must be cognizant of the presence of the Kurds. And they must realize that Iraq can stay whole and become healthy only if the Arabs can convince the Kurds that their future, as that of the Arabs, lies in the Iraqi state. This requires finding a definition of Iraqi identity that is broad enough to include elements of Kurdish culture as well as structuring the state in such a way as to give the Kurds some form of autonomy within which they can express their own particular identity. This same sensitivity to identity and culture also applies to Iraq's other religious and ethnic minorities.

Wrapping wounded Iraq in the blanket of civil society is where the much-maligned Iraqi opposition can serve its role. To its credit, the INC has at least attempted to forge a coalition of Shia, Sunnis, Kurds, Turkomans, and Assyrians of varying political stripes who

---

[19] Quoted in *New York Times*, July 3, 2000.

now live in exile. As imperfect as the effort has been, the INC contains within its ranks the bureaucrats, entrepreneurs, engineers, and professionals that Iraq will desperately need to begin the process of recovery and salvation for the Iraqi state.

In a perfect world, Shia, Sunni, and Kurd, followed by a company of other minorities, would walk into the post-Hussein Iraq as a liberated people united by common suffering. But as all those who plot the way of nations are so acutely aware, the world is not perfect. Those in the administration of George W. Bush and all those voices who so eagerly call for an invasion of Iraq to rid the United States and the Persian Gulf of Saddam Hussein cannot ignore the threats to American security that could come with Hussein's demise. Chaos on the Persian Gulf and between Iran and the Fertile Crescent poses for the United States risks that are different but ones that are potentially as difficult as containing Hussein's real and suspected weapons of mass destruction. Even with the best and most honest intentions for the welfare of the Iraqis, an invasion to do nothing more than change the regime in Baghdad thrusts the United States into that most imprecise and most difficult of tasks—"nation building." All those who advocate American intervention in Iraq must understand that militarily engaging Saddam Hussein is one thing: transforming a tribal society into a nation is something else.

To the Iraqis, the United States, exceeded only by Israel, carries the more suspect credentials to conduct the task of preserving the Iraqi state and building the Iraqi nation. Bitter memories of abandonment of the Shia and Kurdish uprisings of 1991 and isolation and impoverishment over more than a decade are too fresh. With American troops on the ground and no governing authority capable of taking charge, the United States faces the real possibility of a secular version of militant Islam. The motivation of those who would likely join what would be a guerrilla war against a U. S. presence in Iraq would not be avenging Islam or even demanding dignity in a global system that moves to the rules of the West. Instead, the mostly young men of this guerrilla army would be seeking revenge against the United States, rather than Saddam Hussein, for the suffering they endured under the sanctions. Thus, American military forces rotate in and out, U.S. taxpayer money finances the occupation, and Iraqi hostility to a Western presence increases. There is no exit strategy except retreat. But in retreat, Washington jeopardizes that basic tenet of American foreign policy in the Persian Gulf: stability in which oil freely flows at reasonable prices.

Despite all the high-level risks, U.S. military intervention in Iraq may have to come if Saddam Hussein disrupts the flow of oil out of the Persian Gulf or if Hussein's nuclear potential becomes a reality, thereby changing the strategic balance of his region. Or it may come if post-Hussein Iraq sinks into chaos as the furies of communalism do battle to rule or destroy the state. But the United States may not wait for any of these circumstances. An invasion of Iraq has become almost a given in the unfolding war on terrorism. If hard evidence ties Saddam Hussein directly to either the events of September 11 or biological warfare against American civilians, the United States will attack. Yet even without that evidence, terrorism provides the excuse the hawks of Iraq policy have been waiting for to accomplish what they have long regarded as the only acceptable end of the Gulf War— the annihilation of the regime of Saddam Hussein.

If the United States, by circumstance or choice, does invade Iraq, policy makers have to understand the real Iraq, not an Iraq built on some exaggerated expectation that the removal of the despot of Baghdad will solve all of Iraq's problems and all the challenges to the United States in the Persian Gulf. And every American has to understand what the United States is walking into and what the unanticipated results of that intervention might be. Already engaged in a war against terrorism in another tribal society, the United States cannot wade unaware into Iraq as it once waded into Vietnam. Granted, Iraq is not Vietnam. From one perspective, the geopolitical stakes in the Persian Gulf are indisputable. From another perspective, there is among the Iraqis no nationalism powerful enough to inspire civilians to fight for years in the cause of their nation. Nevertheless, the ghosts of Vietnam hover around Iraq. They are there because the United States is again in danger of stumbling into the internal conflicts of another people, only to become trapped in old feuds it never comprehended. In this new era of the American experience that began on September 11, 2001, the United States can no longer afford to be seduced by its own military power or by a naive faith that foreign worlds always can be simplified and mastered.

AFTERWORD

The threat of war hung like a pall over the Christmas season of 2002. Against the backdrop of sacred music and holiday ditties, the administration of George W. Bush rattled the sabers of America's awesome military power over the Iraq of Saddam Hussein. In the Persian Gulf, the implements and personnel of the U.S. war machine gathered in preparation for attack—four aircraft carriers, nine thousand Apache helicopters, hundreds of M1-A1 Abrams tanks, Bradley vehicles, armored personnel carriers, precision-guided munitions, common mortars, and sixty thousand soldiers, sailors, marines, and airmen. Daily American jets flew through the no-fly zone in southern Iraq, practicing mock bombing runs against Iraqi airfields and military bases. From his headquarters in the tiny sheikdom of Qatar, General Tommy R. Franks, head of Central Command, coordinated it all. Back in Washington, the Pentagon stood ready to mobilize as many as 265,000 reservists to protect vital installations in the United States while as many as 200,000 to 250,000 regular military forces stormed into Iraq. From the stage provided by the White House, President George W. Bush beat the drums of war but held up both the possibility that war might be avoided and the order to call up the reserves. Meanwhile, Christmas shoppers swarmed the malls in what seemed a mindless denial that war would probably come by February.

In important respects, the Bush administration's thrust toward a war against Saddam Hussein began on September 11, 2001, when the agents of al-Qaeda collapsed the twin towers of New York's World Trade Center and flew into the Pentagon in Washington. On November 13, a month after the United States began bombing Afghanistan to crush al-Qaeda and its Taliban patrons, Bush and his advisors began the debate on the second phase of the war on terrorism.

The president's attitude toward Iraq immediately after September 11 had been one of restraint. He overruled his advisors who wanted to take on Iraq along with Afghanistan because he was not convinced that Saddam Hussein's fingerprints were on the terrorist attacks in New York and Washington. But in the ensuing weeks, he received intelligence briefings on documents found by American ground forces in Afghanistan that revealed how much al-Qaeda wanted to acquire a nuclear dimension. Suddenly, Saddam Hussein materialized as a potential supplier. National security advisor Condoleeza Rice explained why: "It's not because you have some chain of evidence saying Iraq may have given a weapon to al-Qaeda. But it is because Iraq is one of those places that is both hostile to us, and frankly, irresponsible and cruel enough to make this available."[1] In early June, the president, as if confirming Rice's analysis, told the cadets at West Point, "If we wait for threats to fully materialize, we will have waited too long."[2] Thus by the end of 2001, Iraq had moved into the crosshairs of American guns.

In January 2002, when he delivered his State of the Union address to Congress, Bush highlighted the danger of terrorists acquiring weapons of mass destruction. Zeroing in on what he considered the most likely purveyors of these weapons, the president chained Iraq, Iran, and North Korea together in an "axis of evil." Among the three, Iraq was the most evil of the evil. For the administration, the question had become not whether the United States would depose Saddam Hussein but when and how.

Behind closed doors, the ongoing struggle between the doves and the hawks of the administration proved to be as much ideological as strategic. On one side stood Secretary of State Colin Powell, holding the near-sacred book of American foreign policy. According to principles established in 1941 when America entered World War II, the United States through every administration—Democrat or Republican—had practiced multilateralism. Even in the deep freeze of the Cold War and in the darkest days of Vietnam, the United States had recognized the importance of prudence in its actions and cooperation with the international community. And the cardinal rule of every president could be reduced to the simple statement that "It is better

[1]*Wall Street Journal*, June 14, 2002.
[2]Ibid.

to make friends than enemies." To Powell and the multilaterists, that concept contained even more wisdom in the age of globalization.

On the other side of the ideological divide were the unilateralists, personified by Secretary of Defense Donald Rumsfeld, who saw the United States' position of sole superpower as a golden moment to exercise American muscle and achieve American interests. Giving voice to the unilateralist view were Paul Wolfowitz and Richard Perle, who for thirty years had rallied against the constraints put on the United States by the demands of coalition diplomacy. Determined to reorder American foreign policy before the 2004 presidential election, the hawks of the Pentagon and the neoconservatives in the Republican Party seized on Saddam Hussein, a villainous character straight out of central casting in Hollywood, as the target that would turn ideology into policy. Some of the hawks went beyond the tyrant of Baghdad, arguing that the war on terrorism should be extended to Iran, Syria, Lebanon, and the Palestine Authority of Yassir Arafat. Some even favored targeting Washington's longtime ally, Saudi Arabia. According to Meyrav Wurmser, director of Middle East Policy at the Hudson Institute and an ally of Perle's, "What [the Bush administration] has in mind is a broad vision which really involves changing the character of the Middle East."[3] This point of view did not escape criticism. Anthony Cordesman, the much respected and normally cool military analyst at the Center for Strategic and International Studies, was scathing in his comments. Speaking of toppling Saddam Hussein so that democracy could flourish throughout the Middle East, he said, "It may be excusable as a fantasy of some Israelis reacting to the trauma of the second Intifadah. As American policy, however, it crosses the line between neo-conservative and neo-crazy."[4]

Ignoring the admonition, the president and his hawkish advisors had already announced earlier in September a new strategic plan that shattered the body of international law and agreements concerning offensive war. In what will someday be known as the Bush Doctrine, the administration announced that the United States would take preemptive action against any state or group that it judged a threat to American security. The rest of the world howled.

---

[3] *Asian Times*, September 28, 2002.
[4] Ibid.

Europeans charged that the United States was undermining the international coalition fighting against terrorism. And that Washington was ignoring the crisis between Israel and the Palestinians which was boiling emotions and shaking governments across the Arab world. Turning a deaf ear to America's closest allies, Rumsfeld, Wolfowitz, Perle, the Defense Policy Review Board, and the neoconservatives, along with Vice President Dick Cheney, continued to sound the cadence of an American war against Iraq. Seemingly shut out of the war council, Colin Powell and the doves roosted in the State Department, their feathers torn and bloodied by the hawks. By midsummer, rumors circulated that Powell might resign. Then in mid-August, help arrived from the foreign policy team of George Bush senior.

The first to speak out was Brent Scowcroft, the national security advisor and close personal friend of the first President Bush. The normally taciturn Scowcroft used an op-ed piece in the *Wall Street Journal* to fire a shot at the hawks. Attacking the idea that Iraq become part of the war on terrorism, Scowcroft argued, "There is scant evidence to tie Saddam Hussein to terrorist organizations, and even less to the September 11 attacks. Indeed Saddam's goals have little in common with the terrorists who threaten us, and there is little incentive for him to make common cause with them."[5] He went on to say, "The central point is that any campaign against Iraq, whatever the strategy, cost and risks, is certain to divert us for some indefinite period from our war on terrorism. Worse, there is a virtual consensus in the world against an attack on Iraq at this time. So long as that sentiment persists, it would require the U.S. to pursue a virtual go-it-alone strategy against Iraq, making any military operations correspondingly difficult and expensive. The most serious cost, however, would be the war on terrorism."[6]

Others in the upper echelon of George senior's foreign policy team lined up with Scowcroft. Lawrence Eagleberger, secretary of state in 1992, undertook a media blitz to publicly urge the president to drop his unilateral approach and pursue Saddam Hussein through the United Nations. Others including James Baker, secretary of state at the time of the 1991 Gulf War, General H. Norman Schwarzkopf,

[5]Brent Scowcroft, "Don't Attack Saddam," *Wall Street Journal*, August 15, 2002.
[6]Ibid.

U.S. military commander in that war, and General Anthony Zinni, former head of the Southern Command, made the same argument. Zinni particularly took on the hawks, noting the lack of military experience of the civilian leadership of the Pentagon: "It's pretty interesting that all the generals see it the same way and all the others who have never fired a shot and are hot to go to war see it another way."[7]

The White House apparently heard the message delivered by the veterans of the first Gulf War. On September 12, George W. Bush grudgingly went before the United Nations to call for a new Security Council resolution to disarm Saddam Hussein. Meticulously chronicling Hussein's past failures to comply with UN resolutions, the president delivered the crux of his message: "My nation will work with the UN Security Council to meet our common challenge. If Iraq's regime defies us again, the world must move deliberately, decisively to hold Iraq to account. We will work with the UN Security Council for the necessary resolutions. But the purposes of the United States should not be doubted."[8]

Bush returned to Washington to shore up domestic support. Although claiming that the congressional resolution passed at the time of the 1991 Gulf War gave the president the authority to act against Iraq, Bush was persuaded by politics to seek congressional approval for military action against Saddam Hussein. For a time, it looked as if the American people, through their representatives, would at last weigh the crucial issue of war or peace. During hearings before the Senate Foreign Relations Committee, retired General Joseph P. Hoar expressed confidence that the United States would ultimately win a war against Saddam Hussein but asked at what price. And Wesley K. Clark, former NATO military commander, while acknowledging the right of the United States to act unilaterally to defend its interests, questioned the timing. "What's the sense of urgency here, and how soon would we need to act unilaterally? So far as any of the information has been presented, there is nothing that indicates that in the immediate, next hours, next days, that there's going to be nuclear-tipped missiles put on launch pads to go against our forces or our allies in the region."[9]

---

[7]*Tampa Times*, August 24, 2002.
[8]www.whitehouse.gov/news/releases/2002/09/20020912-1.html.
[9]*New York Times*, September 24, 2002.

Scattered citizens' groups used the occasion of the congressional hearings to rally opposition to unilateral U.S. action against Iraq. Their efforts produced feeble demonstrations and full-page newspaper ads. One of those ads, sponsored by Business Leaders For Sensible Priorities, surrounded pictures of President Bush, Vice President Dick Cheney, and Defense Secretary Donald Rumsfeld with a banner that declared "They're Selling War. We're Not Buying."[10] Another ad, on the same day in the same newspaper, was dominated by a drawing of Osama bin Ladin pointing his finger at the reader. The caption read, "I Want You to Invade Iraq."[11] But in the political heat of the 2002 midterm elections, the president and his supporters successfully branded anyone opposed to an invasion of Iraq as "soft on terrorism." As the vote on the resolution drew near, the Republicans, including Senator Chuck Hagel of Nebraska, the most outspoken and knowledgeable critic of the hawks, fell in behind the president. As for the Democrats, they simply caved in. Although Senate Majority Leader Tom Dashcle called into question some of the language in the resolution, Richard Gephardt, minority leader of the House, marched to the White House to stand shoulder to shoulder with the president. On October 10, the resolution authorizing the president to go to war against Saddam Hussein passed by a vote of 296 to 133 in the House and 77 to 23 in the Senate. In the glow of victory, the administration went back to work in the United Nations Security Council.

While the White House continued to call for "regime change" in Baghdad, Colin Powell took charge of diplomatic efforts to win Security Council approval of a resolution limited to putting United Nations arms inspectors back on the ground in Iraq after a four-year absence. On November 8, he achieved what most observers had regarded as an extremely difficult, if not impossible goal—a unanimous vote on Resolution 1441. The resolution imposed strict requirements on Iraq including an accounting of all weapons, weapons programs, and production sites by December 8; unfettered access to all sites chosen by the arms inspectors, including presidential palaces; and the surrender of all weapon hardware and material as required by the United Nations in 1991. After the vote, the

---

[10] *New York Times*, October 14, 2002.
[11] Ad sponsored by TomPaine.com, *New York Times*, October 14, 2002.

world waited for Iraq's response. It came on November 13 when Saddam Hussein announced Iraq's compliance. President Bush answered with the warning, "There's no negotiation with Mr. Saddam Hussein. Those days are long gone, and so are the days of deceit and denial. [If Saddam fails to comply], we will disarm him."[12]

American weapons and manpower continued to flow into the Persian Gulf while U.S. diplomats went on the offensive in the game to build an international coalition against Saddam Hussein. Envoys fanned out across Europe, the Middle East, and southwest Asia to secure diplomatic and financial support, military forces, and basing agreements for troops and aircraft for the American invasion force. Adhering to the old adage that nations have no permanent friends, only permanent interests, the United States solicited the aid of its nemesis of the last two decades—the Islamic Republic of Iran. Washington wanted Tehran's agreement to stay on the sidelines of the U.S.-Iraq conflict, to discourage the Iraqi Shia from forming a breakaway republic after the fall of Saddam Hussein, and to allow Iran's client, the Supreme Council of the Islamic Republic of Iraq, to become part of a U.S.-led invasion of Iraq. In return, the mullahs wanted the release of billions of dollars of Iranian assets frozen in U.S. banks since 1979.

Elsewhere, Kuwait and Qatar quickly came on board. And it was assumed that behind closed doors deals also had been struck with several governments in Central Asia. But the nations of Europe, except for Britain, resisted American entreaties to back the U.S. war plan. So did others. Turkey, with several bases that would be essential to American troops and aircraft operating in northern Iraq, proved a hard sell. Indications were that Ankara would eventually comply with the American request but at a steep price. It included a multibillion-dollar aid package, economic compensation for the loss of Iraq as a trading partner, assurances that the Iraqi Kurds would not be allowed to form a separate state, and U.S. pressure on the European Union to accept Turkey into its membership.

The other critical piece in Washington's scenario was Saudi Arabia. The kingdom possessed geographical location and military facilities that would make any invasion of Iraq far less difficult. But the House of Saud was reluctant to deal. It had hosted the United

---

[12] CNN World News, November 13, 2002.

States for the 1991 Gulf War and was still living with the consequences in its own domestic environment. The senior princes, perhaps better than anyone else, were acutely aware that if the House
of Saud facilitated an American invasion of Arab Iraq, it might not
survive.

For the same reason, Jordan rejected the use of its territory for
an assault on Saddam Hussein's Iraq. Other Arab governments in the
region carefully weighed the benefits of an alliance with the United
States against the anger of their own populations. Without the
authorization of war by the United Nations, they sat on the fence,
denying U.S. military planners a set of knowns as they plotted their
strategy against Saddam Hussein.

Meanwhile, suspicions grew in the Middle East and among many
Americans that oil was an important component of Washington's war
objectives. Whether this was true or not, oil was a vital part of the
equation simply because Iraq possesses the second largest oil
reserves in the world. An American military conquest of Saddam
Hussein also meant an American conquest of Iraq's oil fields.
Consequently, conspiracy theories that always surround oil companies and consumer nations began to surface. They took several
forms. The United States by invading Iraq would secure enough
Persian Gulf oil to insure that petroleum continued to flow in case
political upheaval in Saudi Arabia disrupted production there. Repair
and modernization of Iraqi oil fields could bring, in a relatively short
time, an additional five million barrels a day to market. Higher supplies would mean lower prices, maybe as little as $12 per barrel.
Finally, control of Iraqi oil was the motivation behind the Pentagon's
incorporation of the Iraqi National Congress (INC) into its invasion
plans. This is where conspiracy theory gave way to the reality that
the Bush administration was still divided into two camps—the
hawks and the doves, the unilateralists and the multilaterists.

One proposal circulating through the Pentagon in the late fall of
2002 called for American troops to seize territory inside Iraq where
exile groups, protected by U.S. military power, would set up an
interim capital. Proponents of the plan, including its chief cheer-
leader Newt Gingrich, former Speaker of the House of Representatives, claimed that by creating an alternative government on Iraqi
soil, military commanders and government officials would be
encouraged to break with Saddam Hussein, hastening the collapse

of Baghdad. But the State Department and the CIA disagreed, arguing instead that the administration needed to encourage a homegrown leadership rather than imposing the INC on the Iraqis. One State Department official caustically asked, "[What are we going to do], parachute in our government-in-exile and say, 'Here are your new rulers'? Let's be realistic."[13] To the realists, a provisional government installed by the United States amounted to giving the INC a head start in controlling the country's vast oil wealth, causing resentment and perhaps even civil war between the INC, seen as outsiders, and those inside Iraq.

In contrast to the Pentagon's approach, the State Department favored the creation of an interim council representing Iraqis from both inside and outside the country that would be charged with guiding Iraq's reconstruction. The oil fields would pass under the administration of the United Nations backed by the U.S. military until such time as a democratic government could be created, a process that could take years. In this scenario, oil would be the prize the Iraqis would earn by holding the country together.

Perhaps neither plan would keep the post-Saddam Iraq state intact and stable. The Pentagon's vision of installing a government sounded like the British creating the monarchy. And the State Department's idea of putting Iraq's oil resources under the United Nations smacked of the mandate system. In the end, either plan was likely to inflame the Iraqis' deep distrust of colonialism.

One possibility missing from the official rhetoric was that given some time Saddam Hussein's regime might simply crumble. Over the months in which Iraq policy was debated, the emphasis was always on Hussein's strengths. Few pointed out his weaknesses. Chief of these was his dependence on tribal allies to shore up the regime. Simply getting the inspectors back into Iraq and keeping them there created among the Iraqis a sense of Hussein's vulnerability. In the code of tribal politics, a weakened patron is the signal to move on to other alliances. Evidence that the tyrant of Baghdad understood his waning powers was found in another of Hussein's versions of Iraqi identity. This time it was Islam. The Mother of All Battles mosque, which opened in Baghdad toward the end of 2002, was just one of a

---

[13] *New York Times*, October 10, 2002.

series of large, elaborate mosques that Hussein was raising across Iraq. Ignoring, or perhaps attempting to usurp the frightening power of religion to a secular ruler, Saddam Hussein declared Islam as the common denominator of Arab Sunnis and Shia and the ethnically different Kurds and Turkomans. Like all previous renditions of Iraqi identity, some groups were left out. This time it was the Christians. In all probability, Hussein would topple under external or internal forces before he or the Iraqis could know if Islam had succeeded any better than Arab nationalism, ancient Mesopotamia, or the celebration of Arabism had in giving the people of Iraq a common identity on which nationalism is based. For Iraq's future had shifted far to the west of Baghdad. In the last days of 2002, its fate lay in Washington.

There the hawks considered only the benefits from what they saw as a quick surgical war—the demise of Saddam Hussein's threat to American interests in the Persian Gulf; the establishment of unilateralism in American foreign policy; the exercise of the policy of preemption against perceived threats to American security; the protection of Israel without forcing Tel Aviv to address Palestinian rights; and access to Iraq's rich trove of oil. From their viewpoint, the doves saw grim endgame scenarios—the unleashing of chemical and biological weapons in Saddam Hussein's own version of Got Rotterdam; an Iraqi attack on Israel met by the Jewish state's nuclear warheads; a fiery explosion of the Arab world fed by Arab anger at the United States' unstinting support of Israel at the expense of the Palestinians; political chaos caused by the collapse of the government of Egypt, Jordan, or Saudi Arabia or all three; economic consequences of unilateralism in a global economy; and a wave of terrorism inflicted on Americans inside and outside the borders of the United States by people who feel powerless in the face of America's overwhelming military power.

If the administration's true believers were right, Baghdad at the moment of Hussein's fall would look something like Paris when Allied troops rolled through the Arc de Triomphe in August 1944. As then, American troops would be cheered as liberators and the democracy bestowed on Iraqis by an American occupation would spread across the Middle East, reordering the whole region. If the more prudent voices of the doves proved right, the American presence in Iraq could be long and difficult with a host of accompanying repercussions. The one certainty was that however the boot of Saddam Hussein was lifted from the neck of Iraq—by the Iraqis themselves, by the United Nations enforcing the will of the international community, or by the unilateral action of the United States—the legacy of the Butcher of Baghdad would remain. It would be present in both the conditions and attitudes that allowed Hussein to take control of Iraq and the processes and structures left by his regime.

The Iraqi state, as all states, has always embodied its own particular hierarchy. It has taken form in differentials of power and status. Because of the conditions in which the Iraqi state was born, the Arab Sunnis were always favored over all others in the disparate state. Yet the acquisition of power that protected their property, status, and position was far more complex than simply Arab Sunni dominance over Arab Shia, Kurds, Turkomans, Chaldeans, and others. In the early Iraqi state, the Sunnis managed the rivalries and antagonisms of tribe, sect, ethnic group, and class to keep themselves on top. They did so, in part, by controlling military power that held politics hostage to the vision and interests of the elite. Certainly by the 1950s, the two pillars of the Iraqi political structure—the tight circles through which power moved and the dominance of military force—had been joined by a third. It was the economic force of oil revenues. Thus elitism, military force, and oil wealth monopolized by government completed the triangle of authoritarian rule.

Saddam Hussein reinforced what had preceded him and then moved on to build a powerful security apparatus that neutralized the army and crushed all political activity not dictated by him. In the process, he excluded all except those who are tied to him by family, tribe, or alliance. With his demise, Iraqis will once more compete for the right to define the state and their place in it. They will do so in a society that has undergone decades of tyranny, war, and economic sanctions.

One of the fantasies that rose out of Washington toward the end of 2002 was that Iraq promised the United States the opportunity to revisit the post–World War II successes of reconstruction in Germany and Japan. Those who promoted this Wilsonian vision saw Iraq placed under U.S. military rule, handed a constitution, and infused with political and economic expertise that would transform Iraq into the model for all countries in the Arab world. Missing from the scenario was the reality that both Germany and, especially, Japan were homogeneous societies, and that every German and Japanese held a strong sense of identity which took form in nationalism. In fact, it could be said that in large part World War II was the result of German and Japanese nationalism gone amok. Yet after the war, that nationalism, although bloodied and bowed, provided the structure which nurtured the responsible societies that had once existed in both countries.

Those planning war against Iraq in 2002 needed to recognize that the pattern could not be repeated in Iraq. The Iraqis share no deep sense of nationalism. They possess only the tensions of tribalism, sectarianism, and ethnicity. Furthermore, the tyranny of Saddam Hussein devoured whatever commonality previous governments had achieved. In post-Saddam Iraq, the crisis of governance occurring, in all probability under foreign occupation, may prove so consuming that those Iraqis open to the idea of democracy and pluralism may retreat into the order of the past that created, if nothing else, a level of stability. In the contest to write the narrative of the Iraqi state, the legacy of Saddam Hussein, in both its domestic and foreign aspects, frames the real possibility that "existing privileges will be entrenched and Iraqis will have good reason to fear subjection once more to a regime that equates power with force and dissent with treason."[14]

On Christmas day of 2002, the American people and much of the world anxiously watched as the hawks and the doves of the administration of George W. Bush, holding their competing views of when and how to end the regime of Saddam Hussein, struggled for control of the Iraq agenda. Whose view triumphed would become clear early in the New Year. What would follow? A world eradicated of the scourge of Saddam Hussein, the world's second largest oil reserves secured, the Middle East in equilibrium and the United States exerting its will unencumbered by entangling alliances? Or the United States functioning as part of the international community, pressuring the United Nations to act against Saddam Hussein and his weapons of mass destruction but allowing the inspections regime to follow its preordained course? Each of these questions contained a subquestion. To what extent was the United States going to be pulled into the abyss of Iraq?

—December 25, 2002
Atlanta, Georgia

---

[14] Charles Tripp, *A History of Iraq*, 2nd ed. (Cambridge: Cambridge University Press, 2001), p. 297.

SELECTED BIBLIOGRAPHY

Abu-Lughod, Ibrahim, ed., *The Transformation of Palestine: Essays on the Origin and Development of the Arab-Israeli Conflict.* Evanston, Ill.: Northwestern University Press, 1987.

Aburish, Said K. *Saddam Hussein: The Politics of Revenge.* New York: Bloomsbury, 2000.

Ajami, Fouad. "Summer of Arab Discontent." *Foreign Affairs* (Winter 1990–91): 1–20.

———. *The Arab Predicament: Arab Political Thought and Practice since 1967.* Cambridge: Cambridge University Press, 1981.

Baker, Randall. *King Husain and the Kingdom of the Hejaz.* New York: Oleander Press, 1979.

Baram, Amatzia. "Neo-Tribalism in Iraq: Saddam Hussein's Tribal Policies 1991–96." *International Journal of Middle East Studies* 29 (1997): 1–31.

———. *Culture, History and Ideology in the Formation of Ba'thist Iraq, 1968–89.* New York: St. Martin's Press, 1991.

Batatu, Hanna. "The Old Social Classes Revisited." In *The Iraqi Revolution of 1958:The Old Social Classes Revisited,* ed. Robert A. Fernea and William Roger Louis. London: I.B. Tauris, 1991.

———. "Shi'i Organizations in Iraq: al-Da'wah al-Islamiyah and al-Mujahidin." In *Shi'ism and Social Protest,* ed. Juan R.I. Cole and Nikki Keddie. New Haven: Yale University Press, 1986.

———. "Iraq's Underground Shi'a Movements: Characteristics, Causes and Prospects." *Middle East Journal* 35 (Autumn 1981): 578–594.

———. *The Old Social Classes and the Revolutionary Movements of Iraq: A Study of Iraq's Old Landed and Commercial Classes and of Its Communists, Ba'thists, and Free Officers.* Princeton: Princeton University Press, 1978.

Bush, George, and Brent Scowcroft. *A World Transformed.* New York: Alfred A. Knopf, 1998.

Chalabi, Ahmad. "Iraq: The Past as Prologue." *Foreign Policy* 83 (Summer 1991): 20–29.

Chubin, Shahram, and Charles Tripp. *Iran and Iraq at War.* Boulder, Colo.: Westview Press, 1988.

Cockburn, Andrew, and Patrick Cockburn. *Out of the Ashes: The Resurrection of Saddam Hussein.* New York: HarperCollins, 1999.

Cowell, Alan. "Iraq's Dark Victory." *New York Times Magazine*, September 25, 1988, 34–36.

Dawisha, Adeed I. "Iraq: The West's Opportunity." *Foreign Policy* 41 (Winter 1980–81): 134–153.

de Gaury, Gerald. *Three Kings of Baghdad: 1921–1958*. London: Hutchinson, 1961.

di Giovanni, Janine. "The Enemy of Our Enemy." *New York Times Magazine*, February 20, 2000, 46.

Dorraj, Manocher. *From Zarathustra to Khomeini: Populism and Dissent in Iran*. Boulder, Colo.: Lynne Rienner Publishers, 1990.

Duri, A. A. *The Historical Formation of the Arab Nation: A Study in Identity and Consciousness*. London: Croom Helm, 1987.

Ellis, William S. "The New Face of Baghdad." *National Geographic* 167 (January 1985): 80–109.

Fagan, Brian M. *Return to Babylon: Travelers, Archaeologists, and Monuments in Mesopotamia*. Boston: Little, Brown, 1979.

Farouk-Sluglett, Marion, and Peter Sluglett. "The Social Classes and the Origins of the Revolution." In *The Iraqi Revolution of 1958: The Old Social Classes Revisited*, ed. Robert A. Fernea and William Roger Louis. London: I.B. Tauris, 1991.

Fernea, Elizabeth Warnock. *Guests of the Sheikh: An Ethnography of an Iraqi Village*. Garden City, N. Y.: Anchor Books, 1969.

Fernea, Robert A. "State and Tribe in Southern Iraq: The Struggle for Hegemony before the 1958 Revolution." In *The Iraq Revolution of 1958: The Old Social Classes Revisited*, ed. Robert A. Fernea and William Roger Louis. London: I.B. Tauris, 1991.

Friedman, Thomas L. *From Beirut to Jerusalem*. New York: Farrar, Straus and Giroux, 1989.

Frye, Richard N. *The Heritage of Iran*. London: Cambridge University Press 1975.

Garner, James. "One with Nineveh and Tyre." *National Review*, May 13, 1991, 52–54.

Ghareeb, Edmund. *The Kurdish Question in Iraq*. Syracuse: Syracuse University Press, 1981.

Gunter, Michael M. *The Kurds of Iraq: Tragedy and Hope*. New York: St. Martin's Press, 1992.

Helms, Christine Moss. *Iraq: Eastern Front of the Arab World*. Washington, D.C.: Brookings Institution, 1984.

Hersh, Seymour M. "Overwhelming Force." *The New Yorker*, May 22, 2000, 49–82.

Hilmi, Rafiq. *Kurdistan at the Dawn of the Twentieth Century*. Volume 1. Uppsala, Sweden: Rabun Forlag, 1998.

Hourani, Albert. *A History of the Arab Peoples*. Cambridge, Mass.: Belknap Press of Harvard University Press, 1991.

Hunt, Richard P. "Clues to Iraq's Mystery Man." *New York Times Magazine*, June 28, 1959, 34–37.

Iraq: A Tourist Guide. Baghdad: State Organization for Tourism, 1982.

Ireland, Philip. *Iraq.* London: Jonathan Cape, 1937.

Juster, Kenneth I. "The United States and Iraq." In *Honey and Vinegar: Incentives, Sanctions and Foreign Policy,* ed. Richard N. Haass and Meghan L. O'Sullivan. Washington, D.C.: Brookings Institution, 2000.

Khadduri, Majid. "Nuri al-Said's Disenchantment with Britain in His Last Years." *Middle East Journal* 54 (Winter 2000): 83– 96.

———. *Independent Iraq 1932–1958: A Study in Iraqi Politics.* London: Oxford University Press, 1960.

al-Khalil, Samir. "Iraq and Its Future." *New York Review,* April 11, 1991, 10–14.

———. *The Monument: Art, Vulgarity, and Responsibility in Iraq.* Berkeley: University of California Press, 1991.

———. *Republic of Fear: The Inside Story of Saddam's Iraq.* New York: Pantheon Books, 1989.

Kraft, Joseph. "A Letter from Baghdad." *The New Yorker,* October 20, 1980, 140–165.

Lacey, Robert. *The Kingdom.* New York: Harcourt, Brace, Jovanovich, 1981.

Lawrence, T. E. *Seven Pillars of Wisdom: A Triumph.* New York: Anchor Books, 1991.

Lopez, George A. "The Sanctions Dilemma." *Commonweal,* September 11, 1998, 10–12.

Lukitz, Liora. *Iraq: The Search for National Identity.* London: Frank Cass, 1995.

Makiya, Kanan. *Cruelty and Silence: War, Tyranny, Uprising, and the Arab World.* New York: W. W. Norton, 1993.

Mansfield, Peter. *The Arabs.* New York: Penguin Books, 1985.

Marr, Phebe. "Comments." *Middle East Policy* 7, no. 4 (October 2000): 87–91.

———. *The Modern History of Iraq.* Boulder, Colo.: Westview Press, 1985.

Maxwell, Gavin. "Water Dwellers in Desert World." *National Geographic,* 149 (April 1976): 502–523.

McDowall, David. *The Kurds: A Nation Denied.* London: Paul and Company Publishing Consortium, 1992.

Miller, Judith, and Laurie Mylroie. *Saddam Hussein and the Crisis in the Gulf.* New York: Times Books, 1990.

Morony, Michael G. *Iraq after the Muslim Conquest.* Princeton: Princeton University Press, 1984.

Mottahedeh, Roy. *The Mantle of the Prophet: Religion and Politics in Iran.* New York: Pantheon Books, 1985.

Naksah, Yitzhak. *The Shi'is of Iraq.* Princeton: Princeton University Press, 1994.

Owen, Roger. "Class and Class Politics in Iraq before 1958: The 'Colonial and Post-Colonial State'." In *The Iraqi Revolution of 1958: The Old Social Classes Revisited,* ed. Robert A. Fernea and William Roger Louis. London: I.B. Tauris, 1991.

Parasiliti, Andrew, and Sinan Antoon. "Friends in Need, Foes to Heed: The Iraqi Military in Politics. " *Middle East Policy* 7, no. 4 (October 2000): 130–140.

Petrushevsky, I. P. *Islam in Iran.* Albany: State University of New York Press, 1985.

Powers, Richard M. *The Land between Two Rivers.* New York: World Publishing, 1962.

Pryce-Jones, David. *The Closed Circle: An Interpretation of the Arabs.* New York: Harper Perennial, 1991.

Ramazani, R. K. *Future Security in the Persian Gulf: America's Role.* Washington, D.C.: Middle East Insight, 1991.

Randal, Jonathan C. *After Such Knowledge, What Forgiveness?* Boulder, Colo.: Westview Press, 1999.

Rose, Kenneth. *Superior Person: A Portrait of Curzon and His Circle of Late Victorian England.* New York: Weybright and Talley, 1969.

Sachar, Howard M. *The Emergence of the Middle East 1914–24.* London: Allen Lane, 1970.

Sachedina, Abdulaziz Abdulhussein. "Activist Shi'ism in Iran, Iraq, and Lebanon." In *Fundamentalisms Observed,* ed. Martin E. Marty and R. Scott Appleby. Chicago: University of Chicago Press, 1991.

Schorr, Daniel. "Ten Days That Shook the White House." *Columbia Journalism Review* 30 (August 1991): 21–23.

Sciolino, Elaine. "The Big Brother: Iraq under Saddam Hussein." *New York Times Magazine,* February 3, 1985, 16–21.

Seale, Patrick. *Asad: The Struggle for the Middle East.* Berkeley: University of California Press, 1988.

Shikara, Ahmad Abdul Razzaq. *Iraqi Politics 1921–1941: The Interaction between Domestic Politics and Foreign Policy.* London: LAAM, 1987.

Simon, Reeva S. *Iraq between the Two World Wars: The Creation and Implementation of a Nationalist Ideology.* New York: Columbia University Press, 1986.

Simons, Geoff. *Iraq: From Sumer to Saddam.* London: Macmillian Press, 1994.

Sluglett.—See Farouk-Sluglett.

Stark, Freya. *Baghdad Sketches.* Evanston, Ill.: Marlboro Press, 1996.

Starr, Chester G. *A History of the Ancient World.* New York: Oxford University Press, 1991.

Thesiger, Wilfred. *The Marsh Arabs.* London: Longmans Press, 1964.

Thoman, Roy E. "Iraq under Baathist Rule." *Current History* 71 (January 1972): 31–37.

Thornhill, Teresa. *Sweet Tea with Cardamon: A Journey through Iraqi Kurdistan.* London: Pandora, 1997.

Tripp, Charles. *A History of Iraq.* Cambridge: Cambridge University Press, 2000.

Troutbeck, Sir John. "The Revolution in Iraq." *Current History* 38 (February 1983): 36–85.

Vatikiotis, P. J. *The History of Egypt.* Baltimore: Johns Hopkins University Press, 1980.

Viorst, Milton. "Report from Baghdad." *The New Yorker,* June 24, 1991, 55–73.

———."The House of Hashem." *The New Yorker,* January 7, 1991, 32–52.

————."The View from the Mustansiriyah—II." *The New Yorker*, October 19, 1987, 76–96.

————. "The View from the Mustansiriyah—I." *The New Yorker*, October 12, 1987, 92–114.

von Sponeck, Hans. "Sanctions: Efficacy and Morality." *Global Dialogue* 2 (Summer 2000): 67–73.

Wallach, Janet. *Desert Queen: The Extraordinary Life of Gertrude Bell: Adventurer, Adviser to Kings, Ally of Lawrence of Arabia.* New York: Anchor Books, 1999.

Winstone, H. V. F., and Zahra Freeth. *Kuwait, Prospect and Reality.* London: George Allen and Unwin, 1972.

Woodson, LeRoy. "We Who Face Death." *National Geographic* 147 (March 1975): 364–386.

Workman, W. Thom. *The Social Origins of the Iran-Iraq War.* Boulder, Colo.: Lynne Rienner Publishers, 1994.

Wright, Robin. *In the Name of God: The Khomeini Decade.* New York: Simon and Schuster, 1989.

Yaphe, Judith. "Tribalism in Iraq, the Old and the New." *Middle East Policy* 7, no. 3 (June 2000): 51–58.

Yousif, Abdul-Salaam. "The Struggle for Cultural Hegemony during the Iraqi Revolution." In *The Iraqi Revolution of 1958: The Old Social Classes Revisited*, ed. Robert A. Fernea and William Roger Louis. London: I.B. Tauris, 1991.

Zunis, Stephen. "Confrontation with Iraq: A Bankrupt U.S. Policy." *Middle East Policy* 6, no. 3 (June 1998): 87–108.

INDEX

Page numbers in *italics* refer to maps and illustrations.